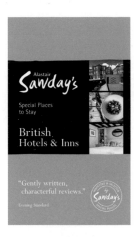

Alastair **Sawday's**

Special Places to Stay

British Hotels & Inns

"Gently written, characterful reviews."

Evening Standard

Special Places

Pubs & Inns of England & Wales

"No one can touch Sawday's for its quirky recommendations."
The Times

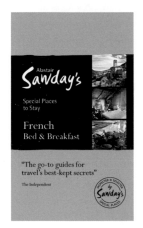

Alastair **Sawday's**

Special Places to Stay

French Bed & Breakfast

"The go-to guides for travel's best-kept secrets"

The Independent

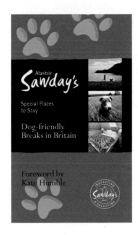

Alastair **Sawday's**

Special Places to Stay

Dog-friendly Breaks in Britain

Foreword by Kate Humble

Alastair **Sawday's**

Special Places to Stay

Twentieth edition
Copyright © 2015
Alastair Sawday Publishing Co. Ltd
Published in September 2015
ISBN-13: 978-1-906136-74-1

Alastair Sawday Publishing Co. Ltd,
Merchants House, Wapping Road,
Bristol BS1 4RW, UK
Tel: +44 (0)117 204 7801
Email: info@sawdays.co.uk
Web: www.sawdays.co.uk

The Globe Pequot Press,
P. O. Box 480, Guilford,
Connecticut 06437, USA
Tel: +1 203 458 4500
Email: info@globepequot.com
Web: www.globepequot.com

Series Editor Alastair Sawday
Editor Wendy Ogden
Assistant to Editor Lianka Varga
Senior Picture Editor Alec Studerus
Picture Editor Ben Mounsey
Production Coordinators Lianka Varga,
Sarah Frost Mellor
Writing Wendy Ogden, Jo Boissevain,
Nicola Crosse, David Ashby
Inspections Angie Collings, Aideen Reid,
Rebecca Harris, David Ashby, Alison
Skinner, Jacqui Vallis, Neil Brown, Sue
Birtwistle, Auriol Marson, Nicky
Tennent, Mandy Barnes, Margot Rawson,
Sophie Gore Browne, Scott Reeve, Sue
Brayne, Julie Franklin, Wendy Ogden,
Nicola Crosse, Heather Stephenson
*Thanks also to others who did an inspection
or write-up or two.*
Marketing & PR
0117 204 7801
marketing@sawdays.co.uk

*We have made every effort to ensure the accuracy
of the information in this book at the time
of going to press. However, we cannot accept
any responsibility for any loss, injury or
inconvenience resulting from the use of information
contained therein.*

Production: Pagebypage Co Ltd
Maps: Maidenhead Cartographic Services
Printing: Pureprint, Uckfield
UK distribution: Travel Alliance, Bath
diane@popoutmaps.com

Cover photo credits.
Front 1. Stokenham House, entry 100   2. Chipperkyle, entry 554   3. Colet Gardens, entry 279

Back: 1. Ramsden Farm, entry 257   2. Launceston Farm, entry 161   3. The Guest House, entry 188

Spine: The Old Manor House, entry 469

Alastair Sawday's

Special Places to Stay

British
Bed & Breakfast

4 Contents

Front

Guide entries

Photo: Tom Germain

Is the market for B&B almost unlimited? I begin to wonder, as the fashion for staying in the houses of other people takes hold. People are opening their houses, flats and basements to strangers all over the world, in a happy frenzy of trust, generosity and self-interest. This is marvelous news, though it is tough on hotels and other official 'places' that have to pay taxes and obey regulations. It will be interesting to see where it all ends. Will governments crack down on unregulated places to stay?

If the sheer exuberance and individuality of our newest Special Places owners is a guide, then the B&B 'scene' is indeed alive and well. This year we have a new house in Dorset whose owner sells her own cut flowers. The house is awash with flowers, the air scented, the garden a riot of colour and the house poised between heaven and earth. Another new arrival is a 1940s RAF control tower in Norfolk, imaginatively decorated with Art Deco miscellany. We have a Scottish castle of ravishing loveliness, and Gladstone's old library in a Grade I-listed building in North Wales. Here you can sink into literary dreaming, surrounded by peace and by the finest residential library in Britain. Go there to write your long-postponed novel. A farmhouse in Warwickshire has 700 acres and teeming wildlife: fallow deer, roe deer, muntjac, woodpeckers and two kinds of owl. We really can provide you with the peace and beauty you crave.

As with hotels and pubs, B&Bs are changing at hectic speed to keep up. People expect so much more now: power showers, soap untouched by human hand, fresh milk in the rooms, beds fit for emperors, the finest cotton sheets. All this is fine, but when it emerges from a sense of entitlement I do sympathise with the owners, many of who have battled to keep old houses going – or to inject personality into unusual buildings. However, I gather that Sawday visitors are a flexible bunch keen to enjoy the individuality of each Special Place. We are certain that they will.

Alastair Sawday

It's simple. There are no rules, no boxes to tick. We choose places that we like and are fiercely subjective in our choices. We also recognise that one person's idea of special is not necessarily someone else's so there is a huge variety of places, and prices, in the book. Those who are familiar with our *Special Places* series know that we look for comfort, originality, authenticity, and reject the insincere, the anonymous and the banal. The way guests are treated comes as high on our list as the setting, the architecture, the atmosphere and the food.

Inspections

We visit every place in the guide to get a feel for how both house and owner tick. We don't take a clipboard and we don't have a list of what is acceptable and what is not. Instead, we chat for an hour or so with the owner and look round. It's all very informal, but it gives us an excellent idea of who would enjoy staying there. If the visit happens to be the last of the day, we may stay the night. Once in the book properties are re-inspected every four years or so, to keep things fresh and accurate.

Feedback

In between inspections we rely on feedback from our army of readers, as well as from staff members who are encouraged to visit properties across the series. This feedback is invaluable to us and we always follow up on comments. So do tell us whether your stay has been a joy or not, if the atmosphere was great or stuffy, the owners cheery or bored. The accuracy of the book depends on what you, and our inspectors, tell us. A lot of the new entries in each edition are recommended by our readers, so keep telling us about new places you've discovered too. Please visit our site, www.sawdays.co.uk/recommend to tell us about your discoveries.

However, please do not tell us if the bedside light was broken, or the shower head was scummy. Tell the owner, immediately, and get them to do something about it. Most owners are more than happy to correct problems and

Photo: Hopton House, Shropshire, entry 374

will bend over backwards to help. Far better than bottling it up and then writing to us a week later!

Subscriptions

Owners pay to appear in this guide. Their fee goes towards the high costs of inspecting, developing our website and producing an all-colour book. We only include places that we like and find special for one reason or another, so it is not possible for anyone to buy their way onto these pages. Nor is it possible for the owner to write their own description. We will say if the bedrooms are small, or if a main road is near. We do our best to avoid misleading people.

Disclaimer

We make no claims to pure objectivity in choosing these places. They are here simply because we like them. Our opinions and tastes are ours alone and this book is a statement of them; we hope you will share them. We have done our utmost to get our facts right but apologise unreservedly for any mistakes that may have crept in.

You should know that we don't check such things as fire regulations, swimming pool security or any other laws with which owners of properties receiving paying guests should comply. This is the responsibility of the owners.

Photo above: Habton House Farm, Yorkshire, entry 531
Photo right: The Old Manor House, Warwickshire, entry 469

Finding the right place for you

All these places are special in one way or another. All have been visited and then written about honestly so that you can take what you like and leave the rest. Those of you who swear by Sawday's books trust our write-ups precisely because we don't have a blanket standard; we include places simply because we like them. But we all have different priorities, so do read the descriptions carefully and pick out the places where you will be comfortable. If something is particularly important to you then do check when you book: a simple question or two can avoid misunderstandings.

Maps

Each property is flagged with its entry number on the maps at the front. These maps are a great starting point for planning your trip, but please don't use them as anything other than a general guide – use a decent road map for real navigation. Most places will send you detailed instructions once you have booked your stay.

Symbols

Below each entry you will see some symbols, which are explained at the very back of the book. They are based on the information given to us by the owners. However, things do change: bikes may be under repair or a new pool may have been put in. Please use the symbols as a guide rather than an absolute statement of fact and double-check anything that is important to you – owners occasionally bend their own rules, so it's worth asking if you may take your child or dog even if they don't have the symbol.

Photo above: The Slate Shed at Graig Wen, Gwynedd, entry 615
Photo right: Waterlock House, Kent, entry 241

Children – The 🛝 symbol shows places which are happy to accept children of all ages. This does not mean that they will necessarily have cots, high chairs, etc. If an owner welcomes children but only those above a certain age, we have put these details at the end of their write-up. These houses do not have the child symbol, but even these folk may accept your younger child if you are the only guests. Many who say no to children do so not because they don't like them but because they may have a steep stair, an unfenced pond or they find balancing the needs of mixed age groups too challenging.

Pets – Our 🐕 symbol shows places which are happy to accept pets. Do let the owners know when booking that you'd like to bring your pet – particularly if it is not the usual dog! Be realistic about your pet – if it is nervous or excitable or doesn't like the company of other dogs, people, chickens, children, then say so.

Owners' pets – The 🐈 symbol is given when the owners have their own pet on the premises. It may not be a cat! But it is there to warn you that you may be greeted by a dog, serenaded by a parrot, or indeed sat upon by a cat.

Quick reference indices

At the back of the book you'll find a number of quick reference indices that will help you choose the place that is just right for you.

In this edition you'll find listings of properties where:
• at least one bedroom or bathroom is accessible for wheelchair users
• children of all ages are welcome. Cots, highchairs etc are not necessarily available
• credit cards are accepted
• there are vegetarian meal options (arrange in advance)
• guests' pets are welcome.

Types of places

Some houses have rooms in annexes or stables, barns or garden 'wings', some of which feel part of the house, some of which don't. If you have a strong preference for being in the throng or for being apart, check those details. Consider your surroundings when you are packing: large, ancient country houses may be cooler than you are used to; city places and working farms may be noisy at times; and that peacock or cockerel we mention may disturb you. Light sleepers should pack ear plugs, and take a dressing gown if there's a separate bathroom (though these are sometimes provided).

Some owners give you a front door key so you may come and go as you please; others like to have the house empty between, say, 10am and 4pm.

Rooms

Bedrooms – We tell you if a room is a double, twin/double (i.e. with zip and link beds), suite (with a sitting area), family or single. Most owners are flexible and can juggle beds or bedrooms; talk to them about what you need before you book. Staying in a B&B will not be like staying in a hotel; it is rare to be given your own room key and your bed will not necessarily be made during your stay, or your room cleaned. Make sure you are clear about the room that you have booked, its views, bathroom and beds, etc.

Bathrooms – Most bedrooms in this book have an en suite bath or shower room; we

only mention bathroom details when they do not. So, you may get a 'separate' bathroom (yours alone but not en suite) or a shared bathroom. Under certain entries we mention that two rooms share a bathroom and are 'let to same party only'. Please do not assume this means you must be a group of friends to apply; it simply means that if you book one of these rooms you will not be sharing a bathroom with strangers. If these things are important to you, please check when booking. Bath/shower means a bath with shower over; bath and shower means there is a separate shower unit.

Sitting rooms – Most B&B owners offer guests the family sitting room to share, or they provide a sitting room specially for guests, but do not assume that every bedroom or sitting room has a TV.

Meals

Unless we say otherwise, a full cooked breakfast is included. Some owners – particularly in London – will give you a good continental breakfast instead. Often you will feast on local sausage and bacon, eggs from resident hens, homemade breads and jams. In some you may have organic yogurts and beautifully presented fruit compotes. Some owners are fairly unbending about breakfast times, others are happy to just wait until you want it, or even bring it to you in bed.

Apart from breakfast, no meals should be expected unless you have arranged them in advance. Although we don't say so

Photo: Meall Mo Chridhe, Argyll & Bute, entry 551

If you do decide to head out for supper, you can find recommendations of our favourite pubs on our *Special Places to Eat and Drink* microsite, see: www.sawdays.co.uk/pubs. If a B&B has a pub nearby, you can see this on their page on our website, too.

Prices and minimum stays

Each entry gives a price PER ROOM for two people. We also include prices for single rooms, and let you know if there will be any extra to pay, should you choose to loll in a double bed on your own.

The price range for each B&B covers a one-night stay in the cheapest room in low season to the most expensive in high season. Some owners charge more at certain times (during regattas or festivals, for example) and some charge less for stays of more than one night. Some owners ask for a two-night minimum stay and we mention this where possible. Most of our houses could fill many times over on peak weekends and during the summer; book early, especially if you have specific needs.

Booking and cancellation

You may not receive a reply to your booking enquiry immediately; B&Bs are not hotels and the owners may be away. When you speak to the owner double-check the price you will pay for B&B and for any meals.

Requests for deposits vary; some are non-refundable, especially in our London

on each entry – the repetition a few hundred times would be tedious – all owners who provide packed lunch, lunch or dinner need ADVANCE NOTICE. And they want to get things right for you so, when booking, please discuss your diet and meal times. Meal prices are quoted per person, and dinner is often a social occasion shared with your hosts and other guests.

Do eat in if you can – this book is teeming with good cooks. And how much more relaxing after a day out to have to move no further than the dining room for an excellent dinner, and to eat and drink knowing there's only a flight of stairs between you and your bed. Very few of our houses are licensed, but most are happy for you to bring your own drink.

Photo above: The Old Store House, Powys, entry 634
Photo right: The Duck Yard, entry 483

homes, and some owners may charge you for the whole of the booked stay in advance. Some cancellation policies are more stringent than others. It is also worth noting that some owners will take the money directly from your credit/debit card without contacting you to discuss it. Ask them to explain their cancellation policy clearly before booking to avoid a nasty surprise.

Payment

Most of our owners take cash and UK cheques with a cheque card. Some take credit cards; if they do we have given them the appropriate symbol. Check that your particular credit card is acceptable.

Tipping

Owners do not expect tips. If you have been treated with extraordinary kindness, write to them, or leave a small gift. Please tell us, too – we love to hear, and we do note all feedback.

Arrivals and departures

Say roughly what time you will arrive (normally after 4pm), as most hosts like to welcome you personally. Be on time if you have booked dinner; if, despite best efforts, you are delayed, phone to give warning.

Closed

When given in months this means the whole of the month stated.

Alastair
Sawday's

'More than a bed
for the night…'

Britain
France
Ireland
Italy
Portugal
Spain

www.sawdays.co.uk

Self-Catering | B&B | Hotel | Pub | Treehouses, Cabins, Yurts & More

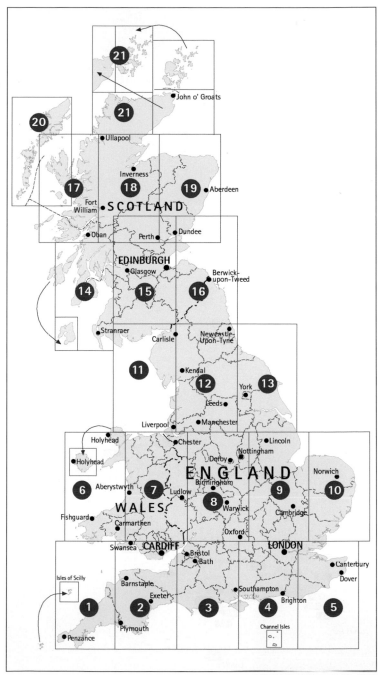

© Maidenhead Cartographic, 2015

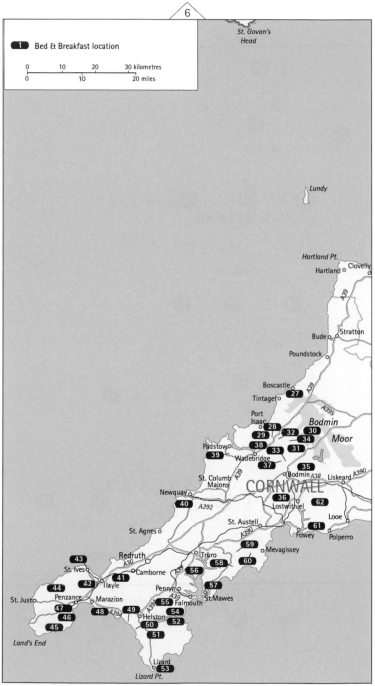

6

1 Bed & Breakfast location

0   10   20   30 kilometres
0   10   20 miles

St. Govan's
Head

Lundy

Hartland Pt.
Hartland   Clovelly
A39

Bude   Stratton
Poundstock

Boscastle
Tintagel   27   A39   A395

Port   Bodmin
Isaac   28   32   30   Moor
29   34
Padstow   38   33   31
39   Wadebridge
37   35
St. Columb   Bodmin   A38   Liskeard   A390
Majo   CORNWALL
Newquay   36   62
40   A392   Lostwithiel
Looe
St. Agnes   St. Austell   61
59   Fowey   Polperro
Redruth   Truro   Mevagissey
43   A30   58   60
St. Ives   Camborne   56
44   42   Hayle
St. Just   Penzance   Marazion   57
47   55   Falmouth
46   48   49   Helston   St. Mawes
45   50   54
51   52
Land's End

Lizard
53
Lizard Pt.

Map 2 19

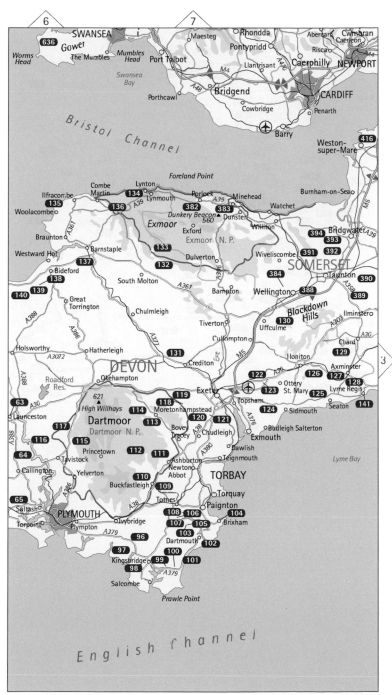

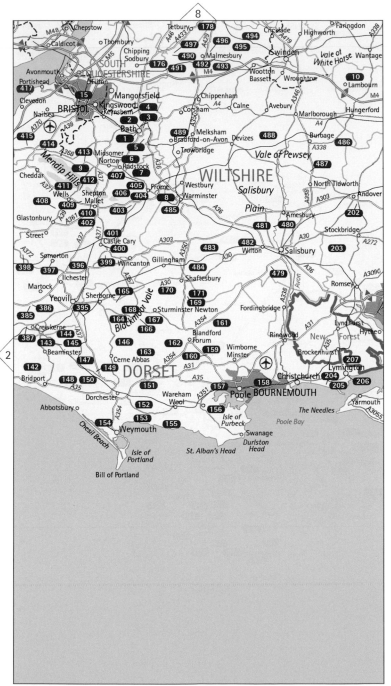

Map 4   21

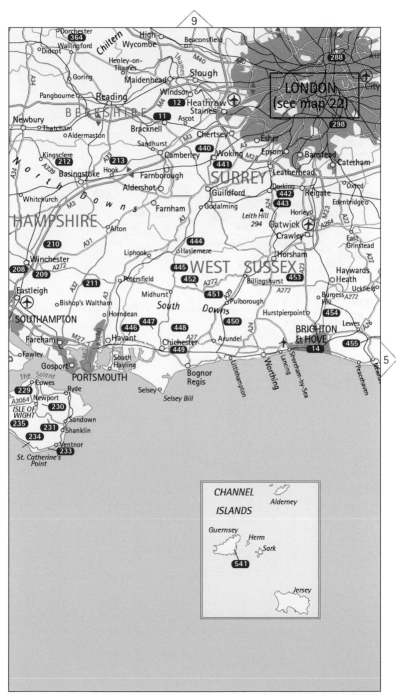

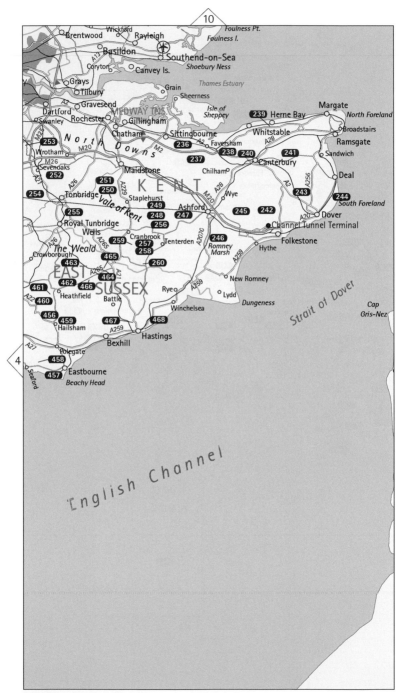

Map 6   23

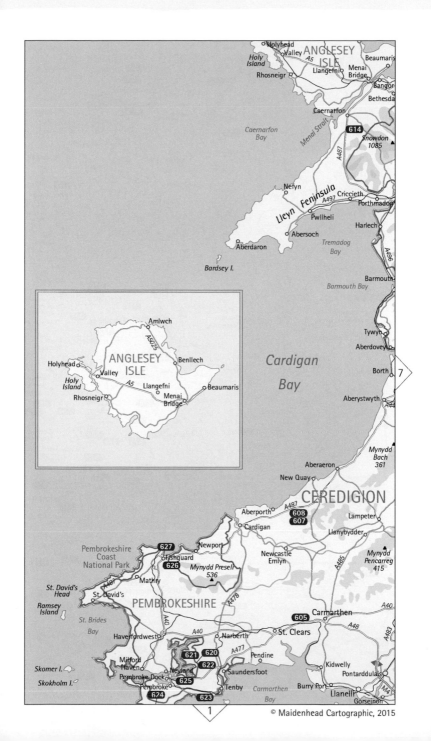

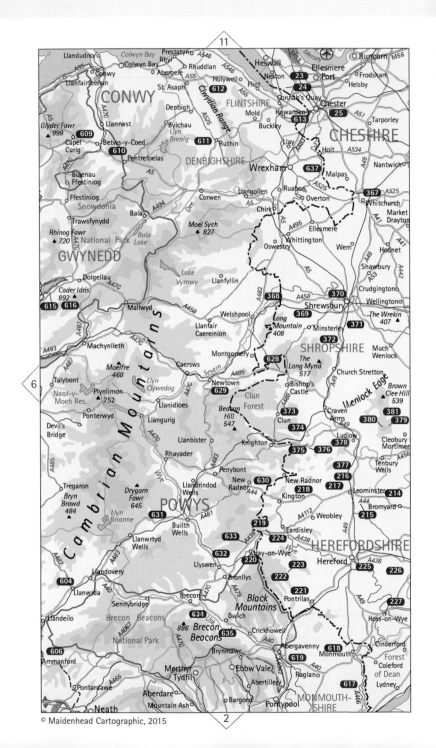

Map 8   25

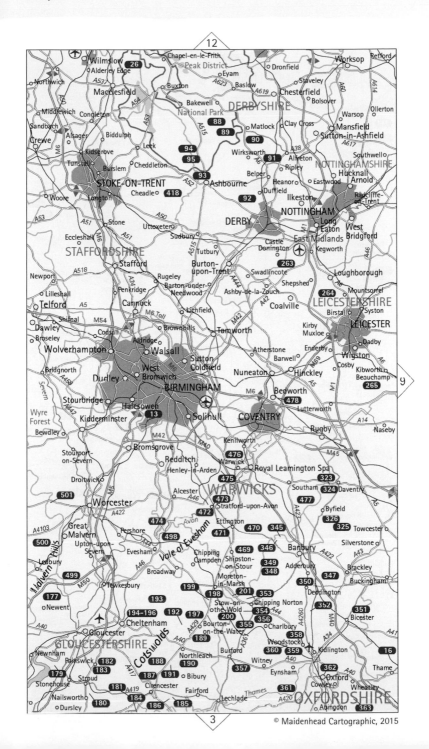

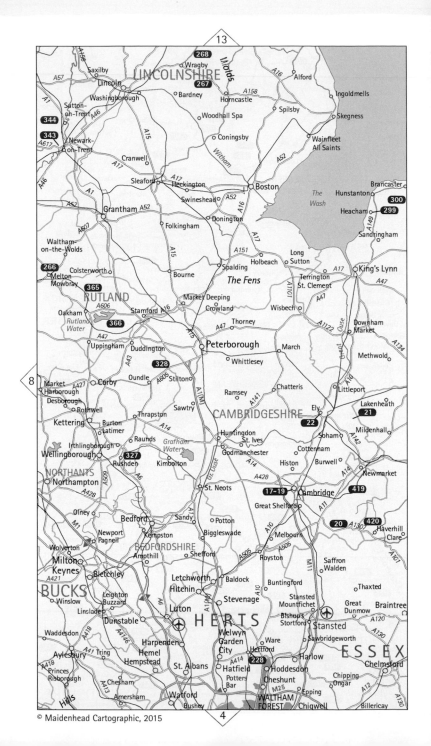

Map 10   27

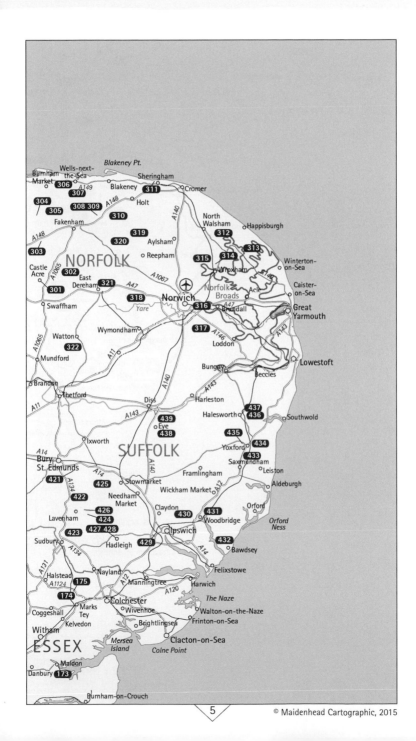

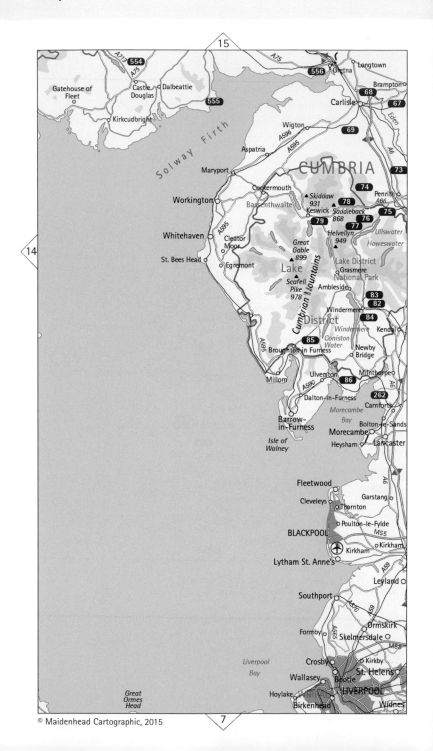

Map 12   29

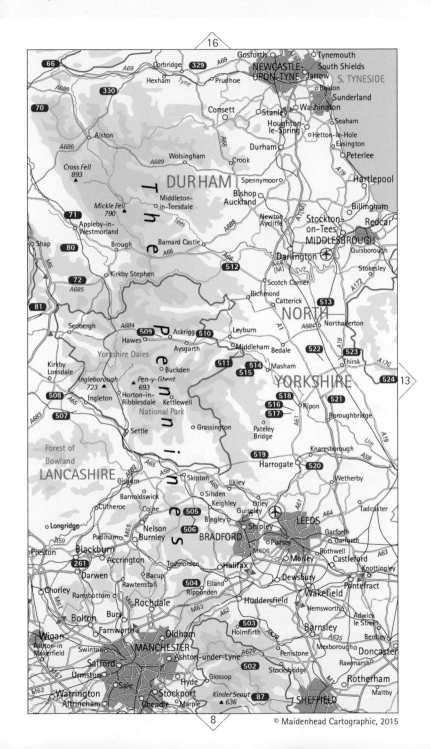

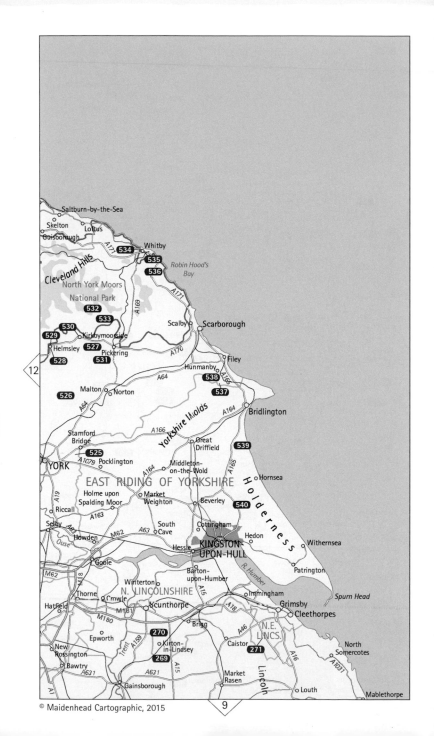

Map 14   31

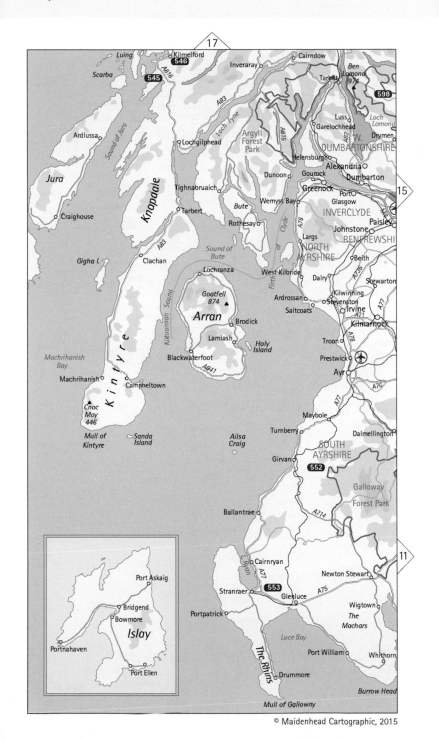

© Maidenhead Cartographic, 2015

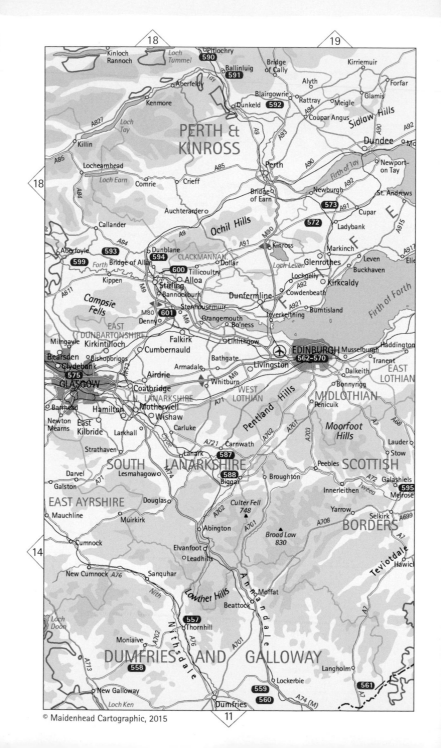

Map 16   33

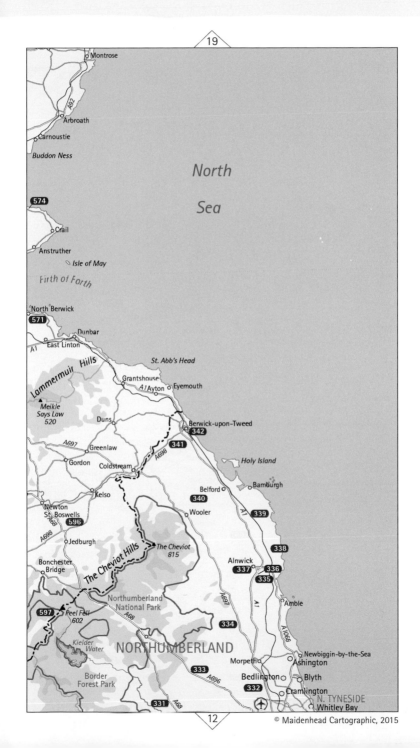

19

Montrose

A92

Arbroath

Carnoustie

Buddon Ness

North

Sea

574

Crail

Anstruther

⌒ *Isle of May*

Firth of Forth

North Berwick

571

Dunbar

A1   East Linton

Lammermuir Hills

St. Abb's Head

Grantshouse

A1 Ayton   Eyemouth

▲ Meikle
Says Law
520

Duns

Berwick-upon-Tweed

342

A697   Greenlaw

A698

341

Gordon

Coldstream

Holy Island

Belford   *Bamburgh*

Kelso

340

Newton
St. Boswells

596

Wooler

339

A698

Jedburgh

The Cheviot Hills

The Cheviot
815

338

Bonchester
Bridge

Alnwick

337   336

Northumberland
National Park

335

A697

A1

597   Peel Fell
602

A68

334

Amble

A1068

Kielder
Water

NORTHUMBERLAND

Newbiggin-by-the-Sea

333

Morpeth   Ashington

Border
Forest Park

A696   Bedlington   Blyth

332

331   A68

Cramlington

N. TYNESIDE

12   Whitley Bay

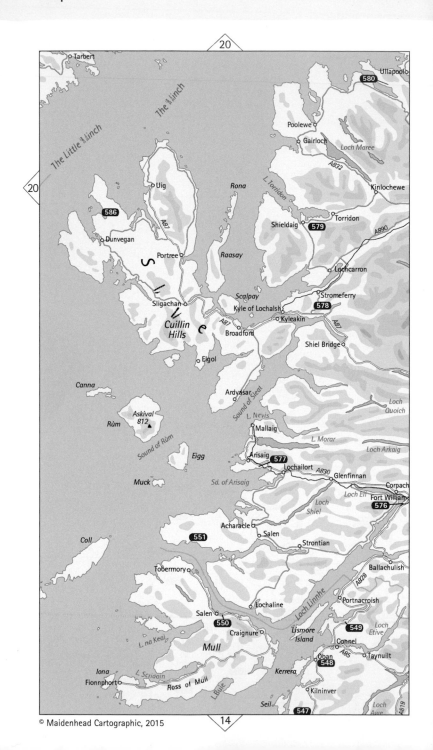

Map 18   35

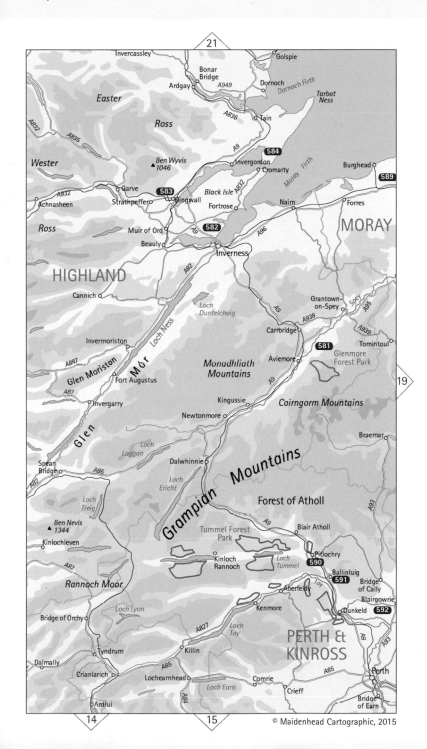

© Maidenhead Cartographic, 2015

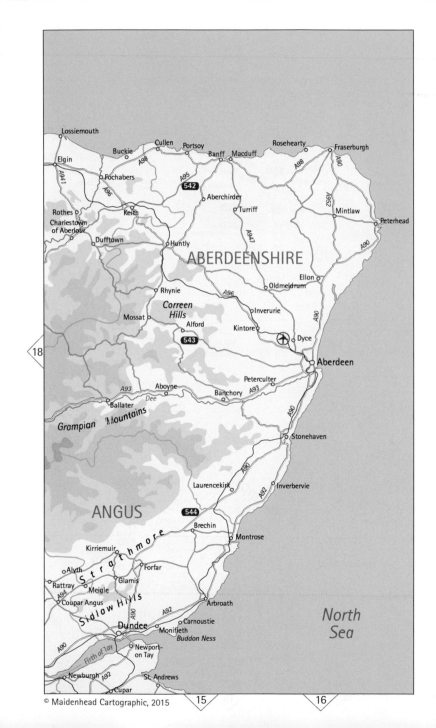

Map 20   37

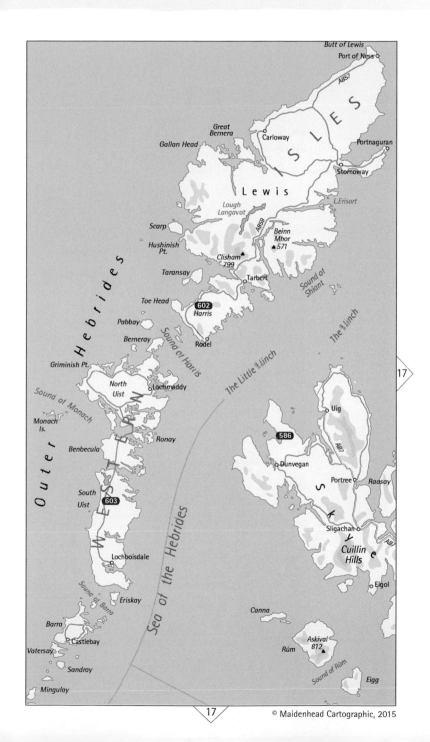

© Maidenhead Cartographic, 2015

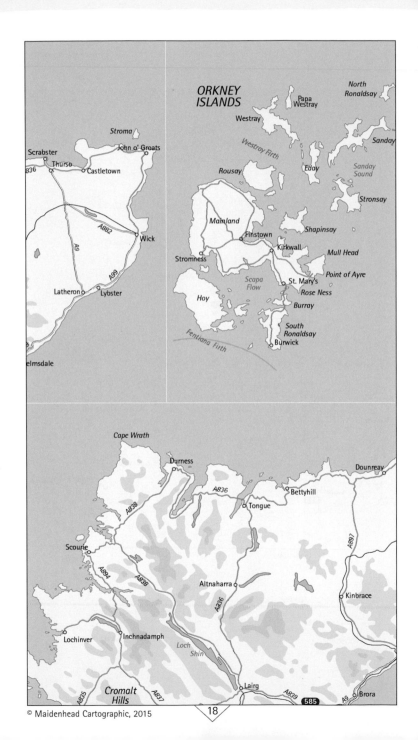

ORKNEY ISLANDS

North Ronaldsay

Papa Westray

Westray

Westray Firth

Sanday

Sanday Sound

Stroma

Scrabster
John o' Groats
Thurso
836
Castletown

Rousay

Eday

Stronsay

Mainland

Finstown

Shapinsay

A882

Wick

Kirkwall

Mull Head

Stromness

Point of Ayre

A9

St. Mary's

Scapa Flow

Rose Ness

A99

Latheron
Lybster

Hoy

Burray

South Ronaldsay

Fentland Firth

Burwick

elmsdale

Cape Wrath

Durness

Dounreay

A836

Bettyhill

A838

Tongue

A897

Scourie

A894

A838

Altnaharra

A836

Kinbrace

Lochinver
Inchnadamph

Loch Shin

A835

Cromalt Hills

A837

Lairg

A839

A9

Brora

585

© Maidenhead Cartographic, 2015

Map 22   39

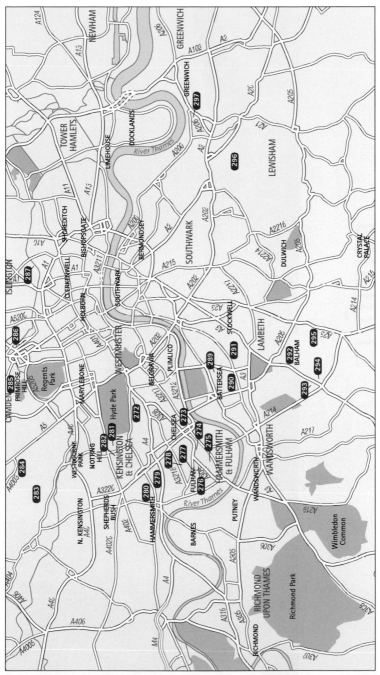

England

Bath & N.E. Somerset

Pitt House

You couldn't be closer to the centre, nor on a calmer street. This Grade I-listed, seven-storey house, once home to William Pitt the Younger, is now inhabited by a warm, creative couple with a wry sense of humour. Inside: Georgian splendour matched by 21st-century eccentricity. Find sanded floorboards, walls of pure white, dazzling marble busts, a cow hide rug, a tumble of classical and oriental styles… collectors of antiques will keel over in a state of bliss. Bedrooms (up four flights of stairs) are only marginally less exotic, and share a fabulous bathroom and sitting room. Breakfast is the finest of continental. Outstanding.

Rooms	2 doubles sharing bath/shower (separate shower): £90–£110. Singles £75–£80.
Meals	Continental breakfast. Pubs/restaurants 2-minute walk.
Closed	Rarely.

David & Sarah Bridgwater
Pitt House,
15 Johnstone Street,
Bath, BA2 4DH

Tel	+44 (0)1225 471580
Mobile	+44 (0)7710 124376
Email	david.j.bridgwater@btinternet.com

Entry 1   Map 3

Bath & N.E. Somerset

77 Great Pulteney Street

Elegant stone steps lead down past exotic ferns to a spacious garden flat in this broad street of grand Grade I-listed houses. Inside all is pale wood, modern art, bergère chairs and palms. Downstairs is a large, smart bedroom and bathroom with loads of books and its own door to a delightful small sunny garden. On fine mornings you breakfast here, or choose the gorgeous upstairs dining room: fine local bacon and sausages and fruit from the allotment. Ian is a keen cook so dinner will also be special, but there are lots of good places to eat – and shop – nearby. Henry may play the Northumbrian pipes for you if you ask nicely…

Minimum stay: 2 nights at weekends.

Rooms	1 double: £85–£110. Singles from £60.
Meals	Dinner £25. Packed lunch from £5.
Closed	Rarely.

Ian Critchley & Henry Ford
77 Great Pulteney Street,
Bath, BA2 4DL

Tel	+44 (0)1225 466659
Email	critchford@77pulteneyst.co.uk
Web	www.77pulteneyst.co.uk

Entry 2   Map 3

Bath & N.E. Somerset

Sir Walter Elliot's House

Utterly wonderful hosts at this Grade I-listed house. On one of Bath's finest Regency terraces, it has been so beautifully restored that the BBC filmed it for *Persuasion*; Jane Austen Society members often stay. Up several stairs are bedrooms flooded with light, two with views over Sydney Gardens, one with a bathroom in marquina marble, cherrywood and ebony. Have breakfast in the convivial family kitchen, or in the plant-filled conservatory. For the adventurous, Mechthild will serve an Austrian alternative – cold meats and cheeses, fresh rye breads and homemade cakes. Herrlich!

Minimum stay: 2 nights at weekends.

Rooms	3 twin/doubles: £95-£155.
	Singles £90-£115.
Meals	Pub/restaurant 300 yds.
Closed	Rarely.

Julian Self
Sir Walter Elliot's House,
95 Sydney Place, Bath, BA2 6NE
Tel +44 (0)1225 469435
Mobile +44 (0)7737 793772
Email visitus@sirwalterelliotshouse.co.uk
Web www.sirwalterelliotshouse.co.uk

Entry 3 Map 3

Bath & N.E. Somerset

The Power House

On top of Bath's highest hill lies Rikki's Bauhaus-inspired home, its glass walls making the most of a magical spot and a sensational view; on a clear day you can see the Welsh hills. In the vast open-plan living space – homely, inviting, inspiring – are treasures from a lifetime of travels: ancient Tuareg camel sacks, kitsch Art Deco pots, gorgeous Persian chests. Bedrooms in the house are airy, with doors onto a huge balcony; the snug, colourful studio room has a wood-burner and little kitchen. Rikki is an incredible chef and uses the finest ingredients from Bath's farmers' market, ten minutes away. Breakfasts are superb – good coffee too.

Self-catering available in the studio.

Rooms	1 double: £100-£120.
	1 single: £70.
	1 studio for 2 with kitchen: £100-£120.
	2 further small doubles available, sharing bathrooms.
Meals	Dinner £25.
	Pubs/restaurants 3-minute drive.
Closed	Rarely.

Rikki Howard
The Power House,
Brockham End,
Lansdown,
Bath, BA1 9BY
Tel +44 (0)1225 446308
Email rikkijacout@aol.com

Entry 4 Map 3

De Montalt Wood

Deep valley views, acres of gardens and woodland to roam, pretty places to sit and muse… all just a couple of miles from Bath. Charles and Ann's Victorian house is a smart family home with a comfortable country feel. Airy bedrooms have big beds with fine linen, a sofa, TV, and garden vistas; bathrooms are luxurious with rain showers and scented things. You breakfast in the elegant dining room: a full English, smoked salmon and scrambled eggs, fruits on the sideboard, lashings of coffee. There are lovely walks with good pubs on the way, bluebells fill the woods in spring and Bath brims with history, spa and good restaurants.

Minimum stay: 2 nights at weekends & in high season.

Rooms	1 double; 1 double with separate bath: £140–£160.
Meals	Pubs/restaurants 5-minute drive.
Closed	Christmas & New Year.

Charles & Ann Kent
De Montalt Wood,
Summer Lane, Combe Down,
Bath, BA2 7EU
Tel   +44 (0)1225 840411
Email bookings@demontaltwood.co.uk
Web www.demontaltwood.co.uk

Entry 5   Map 3

Pitfour House

Georgian gentility in a village near Bath. This is where the rector would live in an Austen novel: it's handsome, respectable, and the feel extends inside, where convivial hosts Frances (a keen cook) and Martin (keen gardener) put you at ease in their elegant home. The creamy guest sitting room gleams with period furniture, the dining room is panelled and parqueted, fresh flowers abound. The two bedrooms — one with en suite shower, one with a private bath — are compact but detailed with antiques. Take tea in the neat walled garden, admire the vegetable patch, then taste the spoils in one of Frances's fine suppers.

Minimum stay: 2 nights at weekends.

Rooms	1 twin/double; 1 twin/double with separate bath: £88–£100. Singles £70–£75.
Meals	Dinner, 2-3 courses, £28.50–£36. Restaurant 1.5 miles.
Closed	Rarely.

Frances Hardman
Pitfour House,
High Street, Timsbury,
Bath, BA2 0HT
Tel   +44 (0)1761 4/9554
Email pitfourhouse@btinternet.com
Web www.pitfourhouse.co.uk

Entry 6   Map 3

Hollytree Cottage

Meandering lanes lead to this 16th-century cottage, with roses round the door, a grandfather clock in the hall and an air of genteel tranquillity. The cottage charm has been updated with Regency mahogany and sumptuous sofas. The bedrooms have views over undulating countryside; pretty bathrooms have oils and lotions. On sunny days breakfast is in the lovely garden room looking onto a colourful ornamental patio, sloping lawns, a pond, flowering shrubs and trees. A place to come for absolute peace, birdsong and walks; the joys of elegant Bath are 20 minutes away and Julia knows the area well; let her help plan your trips.

Reeves Barn

Drive under the huge willow to find prettily converted barns and an away-from-it-all feel. Artist Barbette welcomes you with tea and cakes — or prosecco and canapés if it's early evening. The independent studio room comes with big glass doors, soft colours, limed beams, a simple wet room with scented oils (and, if you pay extra, a mini kitchen for meals). Choose an English breakfast or a breakfast hamper — wake and eat when you want! The bedroom in the main barn has its own entrance and a lovely roll top tub. Snooze in the sun by pots of roses, curl up by the wood-burner. A sweet retreat, with Bath, Wells and Babington House close by.

Rooms	1 double, 1 twin, 1 four-poster: £85-£95. Singles £60-£65.
Meals	Pub/restaurant 0.5 miles.
Closed	Rarely.

Rooms	Main barn – 1 double: £85-£115. Studio – 1 double with sitting room & kitchenette: £85-£115. Extra bed/sofabed available £10 per person per night.
Meals	Dinner, 3 courses, £35. Pub 2 miles.
Closed	Rarely.

	Julia Naismith
	Hollytree Cottage,
	Laverton, Bath, BA2 7QZ
Tel	+44 (0)1373 830786
Mobile	+44 (0)7564 196703
Email	jnaismith@toucansurf.com
Web	www.hollytreecottagebath.co.uk

	Barbette Saunders
	Reeves Barn,
	17 Whitbourne Springs, Corsley,
	Warminster, BA12 7RF
Tel	+44 (0)1373 832106
Mobile	+44 (0)7796 687806
Email	barbettesaunders@gmail.com

Bath & N.E. Somerset

The Post House

Four centuries old, this was Chewton Mendip's post office; now it's a delightful home with a sunny feel. Smiling, stylish Karen loves meeting new people – make the most of her and John's knowledge of Bath, Bristol and Wells. After a day's exploring, return to fresh, lovely bedrooms and bathrooms; the suite, limewashed, pretty and private, has oak floors and a fridge. Huge flagstones cover the oldest part downstairs, there's a big stone fireplace in the Old Bakery Cottage and the odd low beam; pale walls display charming sketches from an artist friend, much of the furniture is French country, and a Gallic-rustic mood prevails.

Rooms	1 double, 1 suite for 2 with sitting room: £80–£120. The Old Bakery Cottage – 1 double: £80–£120.
Meals	Pub 0.5 miles.
Closed	Rarely.

Karen Price
The Post House,
Bath Way, Chewton Mendip,
Wells, BA3 4NS
Tel +44 (0)1761 241704
Email info@theposthousebandb.co.uk
Web www.theposthousebandb.co.uk

Entry 9 Map 3

Berkshire

Sheepdrove Organic Farm

Sheepdrove is special. Its 2,250 acres are sustainably farmed, its ethos is ethical, its spirit is creative, and there's something green or natural at every turn. The Eco Centre soars, the Physic Garden glows, the amphitheatre is a marvel, the lake is peaceful, and the cattle, sheep, pigs and hens flourish. The farmhouse communal kitchen is big and friendly; tuck into fresh pastries from the on-site bakery and delicious produce from the farm. Bathrooms have aromatics from Neal's Yard Remedies, crisp modern bedrooms have beds topped with unbleached organic cotton linen; some rooms wrap themselves around a mosaic'd courtyard, others open to the garden.

Self-catering option available.

Rooms	7 doubles, 1 twin, 1 family room for 4 with separate bathroom: £102–£120.
Meals	Continental breakfast. Pubs/restaurants 3 miles.
Closed	Rarely.

Kerry Harris
Sheepdrove Organic Farm,
Warren Farm, Sheepdrove,
Lambourn, Hungerford, RG17 7UU
Tel +44 (0)1488 674737
Email myevents@sheepdrove.com
Web www.sheepdrove.com

Entry 10 Map 3

Berkshire

Whitehouse Farm Cottage

In the quiet village of Binfield, an idyllic find: a 17th-century farmhouse with a gorgeous garden (NGS), and two charmingly converted buildings. Garden Cottage has a beamed drawing room downstairs and an immaculate gallery bedroom. The Forge – deliciously cosy – keeps the blacksmith's fireplace and overlooks an atmospheric courtyard garden with pebble mosaics. The single is in the house with its own cosy sitting room. Fabulous locally sourced breakfasts with freshly baked bread are served in the house by delightful Keir and Louise, film prop makers by profession. Hugely popular with guests and just about perfect!

Rooms	1 single with sitting room: £75–£85. Garden Cottage – 1 double with sitting room: £85–£120. The Forge – 1 double & summerhouse: £85–£120. Singles £80–£90.
Meals	Pubs/restaurants within 1 mile.
Closed	Occasionally.

Keir & Louise Lusby
Whitehouse Farm Cottage,
Murrell Hill Lane, Binfield,
Bracknell, RG42 4BY
Tel   +44 (0)1344 423688
Mobile   +44 (0)7711 948889
Email   garden.cottages@ntlworld.com

Entry 11   Map 4

Berkshire

Gilbey's

Step up the stairs to your elegant top-floor studio; it's above a buzzy restaurant and in the heart of pretty Eton. Charming staff greet and look after you, and all is gleaming with rich autumn colours, cream carpets, immaculate linen, smart bathrooms and a rooftop view of Windsor Castle. Relax or work – there are a huge comfy sofa, flat-screen TV and desks. A generous continental breakfast is delivered to you: fresh bread and croissants, yogurts and fruit. There are interesting shops and galleries galore, you're a stroll from the college or river trips on the Thames, and Waterloo is 50 minutes by train.

Rooms	1 double: £175–£200.
Meals	Continental breakfast. Supper £18.50. Pubs/restaurants 300 yds.
Closed	Christmas.

Emma Brett
Gilbey's,
82-83 High Street, Eton,
Windsor, SL4 6AF
Tel   +44 (0)1753 854921
Email   eton@gilbeygroup.com
Web   www.gilbeygroup.com/eton

Entry 12   Map 4

Birmingham

Woodbrooke Quaker Study Centre

A pleasure to find ten tranquil acres (woodlands, lawns, lake and walled garden) so close to the centre of Birmingham – run by such special people. This impressive Georgian mansion was donated by George Cadbury to the Quakers in 1903, as a place for study and contemplation. And so it remains. There are corridors aplenty and public rooms big and small: a library, a silent room, a lovely new garden lounge, and a dining hall where organic buffet meals feature fruit and veg from the grounds. Bedrooms, spread over several buildings, are carpeted, comfortable, light and airy, and most have en suite showers. Welcoming, nurturing, historic.

Rooms	7 doubles, 7 twins: £68. 45 singles: £50. Most rooms are en suite.
Meals	Lunch & dinner £10. Pubs/restaurants 15-minute walk.
Closed	Christmas & Boxing Day.

Becky Thomas
Woodbrooke Quaker Study Centre,
1046 Bristol Road,
Selly Oak, B29 6LJ
Tel   +44 (0)121 472 5171
Email   enquiries@woodbrooke.org.uk
Web   www.woodbrooke.org.uk

Entry 13   Map 8

Brighton & Hove

The Art House Hove

Peaceful, close to the sea and in the heart of popular Hove, this Victorian villa is a friendly town treat. Bedrooms on the top floor are furnished in an eclectic style, mixing antique finds with quirky light-fittings; art books, flowers, splashes of colour and brand new marble and mosaic bathrooms complete the picture. Dexter and Liz give you a breakfast feast: muesli, fruit salad, patisseries fresh from the bakery that morning, eggs, smoked salmon, hash browns. Liz runs mosaic courses and her wonderful work decorates the house. Dozens of cafés and bistros are on the doorstep; Brighton is a 15-minute amble along the promenade.

Minimum stay: 2 nights at weekends.

Rooms	2 doubles: £95–£115. Singles £65–£75. Supplement applies in high season.
Meals	Pubs/restaurants 0.5 miles.
Closed	Rarely.

Dexter Tiranti
The Art House Hove,
27 Wilbury Road,
Hove, BN3 3PB
Tel   +44 (0)1273 775350
Email   enquiries@thearthousehove.co.uk
Web   www.thearthousehove.co.uk

Entry 14   Map 4

Bristol

9 Princes Buildings

A super city base with comfortable beds, charming owners and, without a doubt, the best views in Clifton. You're a hop from the elegant Suspension Bridge, restaurants, shops and pubs of the village and a ferry to whisk you to town or the station; yet all is quiet and the garden is large and leafy. You walk in to a big square hall; the drawing room has a peaceful feel and a veranda for the views. Bedrooms are sunny and traditional: one downstairs overlooks the garden, the top floor double is furnished more simply. Simon and Joanna give you a good, leisurely breakfast too: local sausages and bacon, homemade jams and marmalade.

Rooms	2 doubles, 1 twin/double; 1 twin/double with separate bath: £95-£105. Singles from £60.
Meals	Pub/restaurant 100 yds.
Closed	Rarely.

Simon & Joanna Fuller
9 Princes Buildings,
Clifton,
BS8 4LB
Tel +44 (0)117 973 4615
Email info@9pb.co.uk
Web www.9princesbuildings.co.uk

Entry 15   Map 3

Buckinghamshire

Long Crendon Manor

Masses of history and oodles of character at this timbered listed house with high chimneys, dating from 1187... no wonder film companies are keen to get through the arched entrance and into the courtyard! The vast dining room is a dramatic setting for breakfast: sausages from Sue's pigs, home-baked bread, plum and mulberry jam from the gardens. Windows on both sides bring light into the fire-warmed drawing room with leather sofas, gleaming furniture, family bits and bobs, pictures galore. Sleep soundly in comfortable, country-house style bedrooms (one with gorgeous yellow panelling). Peaceful.

Rooms	1 double, 1 four-poster, 1 double with extra twin in dressing room: £100-£200. Singles £80-£100.
Meals	Supper £30. Pubs/restaurants 3-minute walk.
Closed	Occasionally.

Sue Soar
Long Crendon Manor,
Frogmore Lane, Long Crendon,
Aylesbury, HP18 9DZ
Tel +44 (0)1844 201647
Email sue.soar@longcrendonmanor.co.uk
Web www.longcrendonmanor.co.uk

Entry 16   Map 8

Cambridge University

Buses, bicycles and punting on the Cam: huge fun when you're in the heart of it all. Enter the Great Gate Tower of Christ's College to be wooed by tranquil, beautiful quadrangle gardens, breakfasts beneath portraits of hallowed masters, and a serene chapel. At smaller Sidney Sussex – 1598-old with additions – you can play tennis in gorgeous gardens, picnic on perfect lawns and start the day with rare-breed sausages. Churchill has a great gym, Downing has Quentin Blake paintings on the walls, St Catharine's has a candlelit chapel. Bedrooms (some shared showers) and lounges are functional; well-informed porters are your first port of call.

Rooms spread across 13 colleges.

Rooms	60 doubles, 206 twins: £75–£128. 804 singles: £44–£79. 3 apartments for 2-3: £85–£150.
Meals	Breakfast included. Some colleges offer dinner from £7. See website for details.
Closed	Mid-January to mid-March, May/June, October/November; Christmas. A few rooms available throughout year.

	University Rooms Cambridge University, Cambridge
Web	www.universityrooms.com/ en/city/cambridge/home

Duke House

Opposite Christ's Pieces, one of the city's oldest green spaces, and right in the centre: perfect! This house has been refurbished from top to toe and all is gleaming and generous. Settle into the guest sitting room (chandelier, Regency style furniture, calm colours) and sleep soundly under Irish goose down in beautiful bedrooms all named after dukes; top-floor's Cambridge suite has a romantic balcony. The lovely breakfast room has separate tables with fabric-backed chairs overlooking a little plant-filled courtyard; Liz serves an excellent organic and homemade spread. Shops, botanical garden, restaurants… a happy stroll.

Children over 10 welcome. Minimum stay: 2 nights at weekends.

Rooms	4 doubles: £120–£150. 1 suite for 2 (extra sofabed): £160–£195. Singles £115–£160.
Meals	Pubs/restaurants 5-minute walk.
Closed	Rarely.

	Liz Cameron Duke House, 1 Victoria Street, Cambridge, CB1 1JP
Tel	+44 (0)1223 314773
Email	info@dukehousecambridge.co.uk
Web	www.dukehousecambridge.co.uk

Cambridgeshire

5 Chapel Street

Exemplary! Where: in a lovely, comfortable, refurbed Georgian house 20 minutes' walk from Cambridge centre. How: with warmth, pleasure, intelligence and local knowledge. Bedrooms have good quality mattresses, bedding and towels. Characterful pieces too – antique brass bed, freestanding bath, oriental rugs on polished floors – with flowers and garden views. The breakfasts are delicious, largely organic and local: fresh fruit salad, kedgeree with smoked Norfolk haddock, home baking (three types of bread; gluten free, no problem). If you'd like to swing a cat book the biggest room; borrow vintage bikes and thoroughly enjoy your break.

Minimum stay: 2 nights at weekends & high season usually. Over 11s welcome.

Rooms	2 doubles, 1 twin: £95-£130. Singles £85-£95.
Meals	Pubs/restaurants 5-minute walk.
Closed	Rarely.

Christine Ulyyan
5 Chapel Street,
Cambridge, CB4 1DY
Tel +44 (0)1223 514856
Email christine.ulyyan@gmail.com
Web www.5chapelstreet.com

Entry 19 Map 9

Cambridgeshire

Springfield House

The former school house hugs the bend of a river, its French windows opening to delightful rambling gardens with scented roses... and a yew garden, and a mulberry tree that provides fruit for breakfast. It's an elegant home reminiscent of another age, with fascinating history on the walls and big comfortable bedrooms for guests; one is reached by narrow stairs and has steps out to the garden. The conservatory, draped with a huge mimosa, is an exceptional spot for summer breakfasts, and the breakfasts are rather delicious. Good value and peaceful, yet close to Cambridge, of which Judith is a fund of knowledge.

Rooms	2 doubles; 1 twin/double with separate bath: £70-£85. Singles £45-£60.
Meals	Pubs 150 yds.
Closed	Rarely.

Judith Rossiter
Springfield House,
14-16 Horn Lane,
Linton, CB21 4HT
Tel +44 (0)1223 891383
Email springfieldhouselinton@gmail.com
Web www.springfieldhouselinton.com

Entry 20 Map 9

Cambridgeshire

The Old Vicarage

Tug the bell pull and step inside a 19th-century parsonage with a labyrinth of rooms. Homemade flapjack and chocolates await, peaceful bedrooms are countrified and classy with stylish bathrooms – one a lovely en suite. Original artwork peppers every wall and is mostly for sale online. Take breakfast overlooking a big mature garden and brace yourself for a wonderful full English. Cats, dogs and chickens roam freely and if you're lucky you'll spot a proud peacock or muntjac deer within the trees. Explore Cambridge, walk Wicken Fen with its Konik ponies and birdlife, then stroll to one of the locals.

Rooms	1 twin/double; 1 double with separate bath: £90–£100. Singles £55–£60.
Meals	Pubs in village.
Closed	Christmas & New Year.

Gill Pedersen
The Old Vicarage,
7 Church Street, Isleham,
Ely, CB7 5RX

Tel	+44 (0)1638 780095
Email	bookings@old-vicarage-isleham.com
Web	www.oldvicarageisleham.co.uk

Cambridgeshire

Peacocks B&B

Above their delightful riverside tearoom in the heart of Ely, George and Rachel have created two suites. Each has its own sitting room stocked with books and squashy sofas. Brewery House has a fireplace and river views; Cottage is cosy and pretty with flowery wallpaper. Both have goose down duvets and tea trays. Enjoy breakfast by the Aga: perhaps savoury crumpets, omelette or delicious Croque Madame. Browse the nearby antique centre, visit the cathedral, stroll out for dinner or explore Cambridge and the Fens; but make sure to leave time for tea – there are 70 kinds! The Peacocks are friendly and funny – lovely hosts.

Rooms	1 suite for 2; 1 suite for 2 with separate bathroom & wc: £125–£150.
Meals	Pubs/restaurants 3-minute walk. Tearoom closed Monday & Tuesday.
Closed	Rarely.

Rachel Peacock
Peacocks B&B,
65 Waterside,
Ely, CB7 4AU

Mobile	+44 (0)7900 666161
Email	peacockbookings65@gmail.com
Web	www.peacockstearoom.co.uk

Cheshire

Goss Moor

Crunch up the gravelled drive to the big white house, a beautifully run family home. Bedrooms are light, bright and decorated in creams and blues; bathrooms are spotless and warm. Be cosseted by fluffy bathrobes, biscuits or flapjack, decanters of sherry – all is comfortable and inviting. After a day's exploring the Wirral and Liverpool, historic Chester and the wilds of north Wales – a short drive all – return to a kind welcome from Sarah. Expect a generous and delicious breakfast by the sunny bay window; in the summer, you are free to enjoy the garden and pool (not always heated!).

Rooms	1 twin/double; 1 double with separate bath: £80–£85. Singles £50–£55.
Meals	Occasional dinner with wine, £25. Pub/restaurant 2 miles.
Closed	Rarely.

Chris & Sarah White
Goss Moor,
Mill Lane, Willaston,
Neston, CH64 1RG
Tel   +44 (0)151 327 4000
Mobile   +44 (0)7771 510068
Email   sarahcmwhite@aol.com
Web   www.gossmoor.co.uk

Entry 23   Map 7

Cheshire

Trustwood

Small and pretty and wrapped in beautiful country, Trustwood stands in peaceful gardens with National Trust woods at the end of the lane. Outside, sweet peas flourish to the front, while lawns run down behind to a copse where bluebells thrive in spring. Inside, warm, fresh, contemporary interiors are just the ticket: super bedrooms, fabulous bathrooms, and a wood-burner and sofas in the sitting room. Free-range hens provide eggs for delicious breakfasts, Lin accounts for the lovely scones. As for the Wirral, much more beautiful than you probably imagine; coastal walks, botanic gardens and the spectacular Dee estuary all wait.

Rooms	2 doubles: £75. Singles £50.
Meals	Restaurants 2 miles.
Closed	Occasionally.

Lin & Peter Friend
Trustwood,
Vicarage Lane, Burton,
Neston, CH64 5TJ
Tel   +44 (0)151 336 7118
Mobile   +44 (0)7550 012462
Email   lin@trustwood.freeserve.co.uk
Web   www.trustwood.freeserve.co.uk

Entry 24   Map 7

Cheshire

Cotton Farm

Only a four-mile hop from Roman Chester and its 900-year-old cathedral is this sprawling, red-brick farmhouse. Elegant chickens peck in hedges, ponies graze, lambs frisk and cats doze. The farm, run by conservationists Nigel and Clare, is under the Countryside Stewardship Scheme – there are wildflower meadows, summer swallows and 250 acres to roam. Farmhouse bedrooms are large, stylish and cosy with lovely fabrics, robes, a decanter of sherry and huge bath towels, but best of all is the relaxed family atmosphere. Breakfasts, with homemade bread, are delicious and beautifully presented.

Children over 10 welcome.

Rooms	2 doubles, 1 twin: £85. Singles £55–£60.
Meals	Pub 1.5 miles.
Closed	Rarely.

	Clare & Nigel Hill
	Cotton Farm,
	Cotton Edmunds, Chester, CH3 7PG
Tel	+44 (0)1244 336616
Mobile	+44 (0)7840 682042
Email	information@cottonfarm.co.uk
Web	www.cottonfarm.co.uk

Cheshire

Harrop Fold Farm

Artists, foodies and walkers adore this antique-filled farmhouse with soul-lifting views. On the edge of the Peak District, the oldest building on the farm dates from 1694 (Bonnie Prince Charlie visited here). The B&B part has a warm peaceful breakfast room, a stone-flagged sitting room, a spectacular studio. Fresh flowers, antique beds, fine fabrics, hot water bottles with chic covers, bathrooms with fluffy robes: you get the best. Gregarious Sue and daughter Leah hold art and cookery courses so the breakfast too is outstanding. Bedrooms have stupendous views – and flat-screen TVs and DVDs just in case the weather spoils!

Rooms	2 doubles, 1 suite for 2: £100. 1 suite for 4: £175. Singles from £75.
Meals	Wine bar, restaurant & pub 1.9 miles.
Closed	Rarely.

	Sue Stevenson
	Harrop Fold Farm,
	Rainow,
	Macclesfield, SK10 5UU
Tel	+44 (0)1625 560085
Email	stay@harropfoldfarm.co.uk
Web	www.harropfoldfarm.co.uk

Cornwall

The Old Parsonage

A spellbinding coastline, secret coves, spectacular walks. All this and a supremely comfortable Georgian rectory with pretty gardens. Morag and Margaret are relaxed and welcoming hosts. Superb pitch pine floors and original woodwork add warmth and a fresh glow, the big engaging bedrooms (one on the ground floor) have a quirky, upbeat mix of furniture and furnishings, and the bathrooms are pampering. Breakfasts are wonderful: savoury mushrooms, Cornish oak-roasted mackerel, French toast with bacon… In front of the house the land slopes away to the Atlantic, just a five-minute walk across a SSSI. A peaceful retreat.

Minimum stay: 2 nights. Over 12s welcome.

Rooms	5 twin/doubles: £95–£118. Singles from £75.
Meals	Packed lunch £5.95. Pub/restaurant 600 yds.
Closed	November–March.

Morag Reeve & Margaret Pickering
The Old Parsonage,
Forrabury, Boscastle, PL35 0DJ

Tel	+44 (0)1840 250339
Mobile	+44 (0)7890 531677
Email	morag@old-parsonage.com
Web	www.old-parsonage.com

Entry 27   Map 1

Cornwall

Tremoren

Views stretch sleepily over the Cornish countryside. You might feel inclined to do nothing more than wander the lovely garden or snooze by the pool, but the surfing beaches, Camel Trail and Eden Project are so close. The stone and slate former farmhouse is smartly done. Bedrooms come with soft colours, pretty china, crisp linen, a comfortable bathroom; the downstairs double has its own separate sitting room; upstairs has a sumptuous sofa in the room. For summer, there's a flower-filled terrace, perfect for a pre-dinner drink. Lanie, bubbly and engaging, runs her own catering company – bread from the wood-fired oven, delicious dinners!

Rooms	1 double, 1 double with sitting room: £90–£100.
Meals	Dinner, 4 courses, £26. Inns 0.5 miles.
Closed	Rarely.

Philip & Lanie Calvert
Tremoren,
St Kew,
Bodmin, PL30 3HA

Tel	+44 (0)1208 841790
Email	la.calvert@btinternet.com
Web	www.tremoren.co.uk

Entry 28   Map 1

Cornwall

The Corn Mill

This restored mill in a quiet Cornish valley is a relaxed and friendly home. Step inside and find a country cottage medley of flowers and family furniture, antique rugs and interesting market finds. Artist Suzie has her studio in a folly in the pretty garden; ducks and geese wander in the orchard. Cosy bedrooms have flowery fabrics, antique eiderdowns, warm blankets and good cotton; bathrooms are simple and fresh with fluffy towels. Breakfast well in the farmhouse kitchen on a locally sourced spread and bread fresh from the Rayburn. Exceptional coastal walking, music festivals, great beaches and Port Isaac are all nearby.

Rooms	1 double: £90–£120.
	1 family room for 4: £90–£120.
Meals	Pub/restaurant 2 miles.
Closed	Christmas & New Year.

Susan Bishop
The Corn Mill,
Port Isaac Road,
Trelill,
Bodmin, PL30 3HZ
Tel   +44 (0)1208 851079
Email jemandsuzie@icloud.com

Entry 29   Map 1

Cornwall

The Barn at The Old Stables

At the end of a long private drive with open green views… all is peaceful. You have your own entrance to the converted hay barn, and the smart contemporary interior blends well with the old building. Find a lavish bedroom with a sublime 'sink in' mattress, vast bathroom, furniture made by Judith's son and a welcoming bottle of wine. Judith lives opposite and gives you a cream tea on arrival – in your room or the garden if sunny. Her Aga-cooked breakfasts are delicious: local produce, fruit, croissants. After a day's walking or cycling the Camel Trail and Cornish coast, you can eat dinner in the candlelit dining room, the valley unfolding beyond.

Minimum stay: 2 nights at weekends.

Rooms	1 suite for 2: £85–£105.
Meals	Dinner, 3 courses, £27.50.
	Pub/restaurant 5 miles.
Closed	Christmas & New Year.

Judith Argent
The Barn at The Old Stables,
Helland, Bodmin, PL30 4QE
Tel   +44 (0)1208 75543
Mobile +44 (0)7786 558641
Email   juargent@hotmail.com
Web   www.thebarnincornwall.co.uk

Entry 30   Map 1

Cornwall

Higher Lank Farm

Families rejoice: come if you have a child under seven! Bring older siblings too. Celtic crosses in the garden and original panelling hint at the 500-year history of this friendly, busy farmhouse. Bedrooms have comfy beds, toys and large TVs; soaps are handmade; eco-friendly too with biomass energy and local real nappies. Nursery teas begin at 5pm, grown-up suppers are later and Lucy will cheerfully babysit while you slink off to the pub. Farm-themed playgrounds are safe and fun, there are piglets, lambs, goats, chicks, eggs to collect, pony and trap rides, a sand barn for little ones and cream teas in the garden. Lovely atmosphere.

Minimum stay: 3 nights, 5 nights in high season.

Rooms	3 family rooms for 4: £110–£160. Singles by arrangement.
Meals	Supper £23. Nursery tea £7. Pub 1.5 miles.
Closed	November–Easter.

Lucy Finnemore
Higher Lank Farm,
St Breward,
Bodmin, PL30 4NB
Tel   +44 (0)1208 850716
Email   lucyfin@higherlankfarm.co.uk
Web   www.higherlankfarm.co.uk

Entry 31   Map 1

Cornwall

Quies Cottage

The Cornish ensign may be fluttering as you arrive at this 17th-century former farmhouse in the centre of the village. Inside calm pervades, as it should given its name. A traditional sitting room is hung with family paintings charting their progress, a wood-burner sits in a stone fireplace and the piano is in tune if you fancy. Country fresh bedrooms are in a new extension and have glowing pine floors with upbeat rugs and views to the rear garden: bathrooms are smart and gleaming. A very civilised haven with well-travelled and engaging hosts: raise a glass with the Lawtons and settle in for some excellent stories.

Pets by arrangement.

Rooms	1 double; 1 twin/double with separate bath: £75. Singles £45.
Meals	Pubs/restaurants 100 yds.
Closed	Rarely.

Marigold Lawton
Quies Cottage,
Churchtown, St Tudy,
Bodmin, PL30 3NN
Tel   +44 (0)1208 850094
Email   quiescottage@aol.com
Web   www.quiescottage.co.uk

Entry 32   Map 1

Cornwall

Lavethan

A glorious house in the most glorious of settings: views sail down to the valley. It rambles on many levels and is part 15th-century: walls are stone, floors are flagged, stairs are oak. Bedrooms have big comfy beds and reviving decanters of sherry, giving a homely country house feel. The sunny bedroom in the house has panelled walls and a smart bathroom; bedrooms across the courtyard are very private with their own entrances and have pretty quilted bedspreads. Caroline has made the guest sitting room hugely welcoming with books, flowers and piano. Find a heated pool in the old walled garden, Celtic crosses and ancient woods.

Children over 10 welcome.

Rooms	1 double, 2 twin/doubles: £100. Singles £55.
Meals	Pub 0.25 miles.
Closed	Rarely.

Christopher & Catherine Hartley
Lavethan,
Blisland,
Bodmin, PL30 4QG
Tel   +44 (0)1208 850487
Email   chrishartley@btconnect.com
Web   www.lavethan.com

Entry 33   Map 1

Cornwall

Antonia Fraser
– Bed & Breakfast in Cornwall

A sunny courtyard with planted pots leads to the guest entrance of artist Antonia and Jamie's barn. They love their new home and have created a harmonious blend of colourful rugs, painted furniture, beautiful lamps, original art. Light streams through big French windows in the wood-burner warmed living space; breakfast comes with great coffee and stunning views; your cosy bedroom has white linen, paintings and pretty sofa. Plans are afoot for the meadow: a terrace, formal and veg gardens, a grove of native trees. Heaps to do nearby: hire a bike for the Camel Trail, explore Bodmin and north Cornwall beaches, book a Rick Stein course in Padstow.

Minimum stay: 2 nights at weekends.

Rooms	1 twin/double with separate bath: £95.
Meals	Pubs/restaurants 10-minute drive.
Closed	Rarely.

Antonia Fraser
Antonia Fraser – Bed & Breakfast in Cornwall,
Stable Barn, De Lank, St Breward,
Bodmin, PL30 4ND
Tel   +44 (0)1208 368566
Mobile   +44 (0)7788 840542
Email   afraser16@talktalk.net
Web   www.antoniafraserbandb.co.uk

Entry 34   Map 1

Cornwall

Cabilla Manor

There's a treasure round every corner and an opera house in one of the barns. Instant seduction as you enter the old manor house out on the moor, brimful of interest and colour. Rich exotic rugs and cushions, artefacts from around the world, Louella's sumptuous hand-stencilled quilts, huge beds, coir carpets, garden flowers. There's a dining room crammed floor to ceiling with books, many of them Robin's (a writer and explorer) and a lofty conservatory for friendly meals overlooking a semi-wild garden – with tennis and elegant lawns. The views are heavenly, the generous hosts wonderful and the final mile of the approach thrillingly wild.

Rooms	1 double; 1 double with separate bath & shower; 1 double, 1 twin sharing bath & shower (let to same party only): £90. Singles £45.
Meals	Dinner, 3 courses with wine, £35. Pub 4 miles. Restaurant 8-10 miles.
Closed	Christmas.

Robin & Louella Hanbury-Tenison
Cabilla Manor,
Mount,
Bodmin, PL30 4DW
Tel	+44 (0)1208 821224
Mobile	+44 (0)7770 664218
Email	louella@cabilla.co.uk
Web	www.cabilla.co.uk

Entry 35   Map 1

Cornwall

Koeschi

In the middle of ancient bluebell woods, an eco home extraordinaire! Designed by Pete and Celia's nephew it teems with great features: a green roof covered in wild flowers, timbers from their woods, solar and wood-burner heating, wool insulation. You have your own part of the house, all clean lines and comfort, with a terrace leading into the woodland – woodpeckers and tree creepers keep you company. Wake for sourdough toast, local bangers and bacon, very good coffee. Pete, a sculptor, has his studio next door (have a tour, book a course), it's a hop to the Eden Project and Fowey fishing... and the peace is blissful.

Rooms	1 suite for 2 with separate bath/shower & sitting room: £80-£100. Singles £70.
Meals	Pubs/restaurants 0.5 miles.
Closed	Rarely.

Celia Robbins
Koeschi,
Lanlivery,
Bodmin, PL30 5BX
Tel	+44 (0)1208 871029
Email	celia@petegrahamcarving.co.uk
Web	www.cornwallecohome.co.uk

Entry 36   Map 1

Cornwall

Menkee

From this handsome Georgian farmhouse there are long views towards the sea; you're 20 minutes away from the coastal path and wild surf but you may not want to budge. Gage and Liz are deliciously unstuffy and look after you well: newspapers and a weather forecast appear with a scrumptious breakfast, your gorgeously comfortable bed is turned down in the evening and walkers can be dropped off and collected. The elegant house is filled with beautiful things, gleaming furniture, fresh flowers, roaring fires and pretty fabrics – all you have to do is slacken your pace and wind down.

Minimum stay: 2 nights in high season. Two charging points for electric cars available.

Rooms	1 double, 1 twin: £80–£90.
	Singles from £40.
Meals	Pub/restaurant 3 miles.
Closed	Rarely.

Gage & Liz Williams
Menkee,
St Mabyn,
Wadebridge, PL30 3DD
Tel   +44 (0)1208 841378
Mobile   +44 (0)7999 549935
Email   gagewillms@aol.com
Web   www.cornwall-online.co.uk/menkee

Entry 37   Map 1

Cornwall

Trewornan Manor

Drive through the white gate and listed pillars to a house that began in 1211. You'll fall in love the moment you arrive, and your hosts' enthusiasm is infectious. Guests are spoiled in off-beat boutique style in one beautiful, sprawling wing: dining and lounging downstairs, and four bedrooms up. It is sumptuous and gorgeous but definitely not swanky and the attention to detail is delightful: hot water bottles, sweeties, cookies, natural toiletries, bikes and food that tastes as gorgeous as it looks. Lose yourself in 25 acres of woods, water meadows and historic gardens – or sally forth, to Padstow and Rock.

Rooms	1 double, 3 twin/doubles: £110–£170.
	Singles £100–£150.
Meals	Pubs/restaurants 1 mile.
Closed	Rarely.

Paul & Lesley Stapleton
Trewornan Manor,
St Minver,
Wadebridge, PL27 6EX
Tel   +44 (0)1208 812359
Email   enquiries@trewornanmanor.co.uk
Web   www.trewornanmanor.co.uk

Entry 38   Map 1

Cornwall

Molesworth Manor

It's a splendid old place, big enough to swallow hordes of people, peppered with art and interesting antiques. There are palms and a play area in the garden, two charming drawing rooms with an honesty bar and open fires for cosy nights, a carved staircase leading to bedrooms that vary in style and size – His Lordship's at the front, the Maid's in the eaves – and bathrooms that are lovely and pampering. The whiff of homemade muffins and a delicious breakfast lures you downstairs in the morning, Padstow and its food delights will keep you happy when you venture out. A superb bolthole run by Geoff and Jessica, youthful and fun.

Rooms	7 doubles, 1 twin/double; 1 twin with separate shower room: £85-£125. Singles by arrangement.
Meals	Pubs/restaurants 2 miles.
Closed	November-January. Open off-season by arrangement for larger parties.

Geoff French & Jessica Clarke
Molesworth Manor,
Little Petherick,
Padstow, PL27 7QT
Tel   +44 (0)1841 540292
Email   molesworthmanor@aol.com
Web   www.molesworthmanor.co.uk

Entry 39   Map 1

Cornwall

Myrtle Cottage

A proper cottage – beautifully kept, low-ceilinged and light – in a traditional Cornish village with a good foodie pub. Rooms, with distant sea views, are invitingly cosy: uneven white walls, prettily quilted beds, pale-carpeted or varnished creaking boards, flowers fresh from the garden. Sue does great breakfasts: homemade bread, muffins and preserves, local eggs and bacon, in the dining room, the sun room, or out on the patio. There are games and toys for tots and maps for walkers to borrow. You're a 15-minute stroll from the South West Coast Path so near many outstanding beaches; Porth Joke's a favourite. Lovely.

Minimum stay: 2 nights at weekends.

Rooms	1 double; 1 twin with separate bath: £75-£85. Singles £55-£65.
Meals	Dinner or light supper may be available on request. Pub/restaurants 0.5 miles.
Closed	Rarely.

Sue Stevens
Myrtle Cottage,
Trevail, Cubert,
Newquay, TR8 5HP
Tel   +44 (0)1637 830460
Mobile +44 (0)7763 101076
Email   enquiries@myrtletrevail.co.uk
Web   www.myrtletrevail.co.uk

Entry 40   Map 1

Cornwall

House at Gwinear

An island of calm, this grand old rambling house sits in bird-filled acres but is only a short drive from St Ives. The Halls are devoted to the encouragement of the arts and crafts which is reflected in their lifestyle. Find shabby chic with loads of character and no stuffiness – fresh flowers on the breakfast table, a piano in the corner, rugs on polished floors, masses of books. In a separate wing is your cosy bedroom and sitting room, with a fine view of the church from the bath. The large lawned gardens are there for bare-footed solace, and you can have breakfast in the Italianate courtyard on sunny days.

Rooms	1 twin/double with separate bath & sitting room: £80-£90.
Meals	Supper, 2 courses with wine, £25. Pub 1.5 miles.
Closed	Rarely.

Charles & Diana Hall
House at Gwinear,
Gwinear,
St Ives, TR27 5JZ
Tel +44 (0)1736 850444
Email charleshall@btinternet.com

Entry 41   Map 1

Cornwall

Penquite

A doll's house of a B&B in a constellation of Cornwall's best attractions, set in a quiet village overlooking the Hayle estuary and bird reserve. A doctor's house from 1908, it oozes Arts and Crafts with chunky stone walls, sloping roof, winding stairs and polished oak enhanced by Stephanie's ceramics. There's a snug, bay-windowed sitting room; a private suite of cute bedrooms in the eaves; a mature garden of lofty pines, palms and summer house; a generous continental spread on the terrace or light-filled dining room. Stroll to pubs and deli, or past a golf course to the coastal path and St Ives Bay views.

Rooms	1 double: £90.
	1 family room for 3: £85-£130.
	1 single (extra z-bed, let to same party only): £85-£110.
	Singles £85-£110.
Meals	Continental breakfast. Restaurant 2-minute walk.
Closed	Rarely.

Stephanie Pace
Penquite,
Vicarage Lane, Lelant,
St Ives, TR26 3EA
Tel +44 (0)1736 755002
Email stephaniepace@hotmail.com
Web www.penquite-seasidesuite-cornwall.com

Entry 42   Map 1

Cornwall

11 Sea View Terrace

In a smart row of Edwardian villas, with stunning harbour and sea views, is a delectable retreat. Sleek, softy coloured interiors are light and gentle on the eye – an Italian circular glass table here, a painted seascape there. Bedrooms are perfect with crisp linen and vistas of whirling gulls from private terraces; bathrooms are state of the art. Rejoice in softly boiled eggs with anchovy and chive-butter soldiers for breakfast – or continental in bed if you prefer. Grahame looks after you impeccably and design aficionados will be happy.

Over 12s welcome.

Rooms	3 suites for 2: £100–£135. Singles from £75.
Meals	Dinner with wine, from £25 (groups only). Packed lunch from £15. Pubs/restaurants 5-minute walk.
Closed	Rarely.

Grahame Wheelband
11 Sea View Terrace,
St Ives, TR26 2DH
Tel   +44 (0)1736 798440
Mobile   +44 (0)7973 953616
Email   info@11stives.co.uk
Web   www.11stives.co.uk

Entry 43   Map 1

Cornwall

Keigwin Farmhouse

Off the glorious coast road to St Ives, in two walled acres overlooking the sea, is a very old farmhouse lived in by Gilly. Walk to the beach at Portheras Cove, dine well at Gurnard's Head, return to little whitewash-and-pine bedrooms with views that make you want to get out your paints, and a big shared bathroom with a massive old bath, fresh with organic cotton towels. A treat: Gilly's scones on arrival, eggs from her hens, stacks of books above the stairs and an arty feel – wide floorboards, creamy colours, family pieces, sculptures, ceramics, glass. A relaxed, delightful – and musical instrument-friendly – B&B.

Rooms	2 doubles sharing bathroom (let to same party only): £75–£80. 1 single sharing bathroom (let to same party only): £40.
Meals	Pubs/restaurants 3 miles.
Closed	Rarely.

Gilly Wyatt-Smith
Keigwin Farmhouse,
Keigwin, Morvah,
Penzance, TR19 7TS
Tel   +44 (0)1736 786425
Email   sleep@keigwinfarmhouse.co.uk
Web   www.keigwinfarmhouse.co.uk

Entry 44   Map 1

Cornwall

Cove Cottage

Down a long lane to a rose-clad cottage in the most balmy part of Cornwall… peace in a private cove. Your own door leads up steps to a gorgeous suite with luxurious linen on an antique four-poster, art, sofas… and a flowery balcony with spectacular views of the sea and subtropical gardens. Settle in happily to the sound of the waves. Sue is friendly and serves a great breakfast in the garden room: home-laid eggs, homemade jams and their own honey. The Penwith peninsula hums with gardens, galleries and stunning sandy beaches; Minack Theatre and Lamorna are close. Arrive to a salad supper chosen from a small but special menu. Paradise!

Minimum stay: 3 nights in high season.

Rooms	1 suite for 2: £130–£135.
Meals	Salad suppers from £12.50. Pub/restaurant 3 miles.
Closed	Rarely.

Sue White
Cove Cottage,
St Loy, St Buryan,
Penzance, TR19 6DH
Tel   +44 (0)1736 810010
Email   thewhites@covecottagestloy.co.uk
Web   www.covecottagestloy.co.uk

Entry 45   Map 1

Cornwall

The Hideaway

A tucked away little gem in the garden. Your Hideaway is behind Julie and Howard's terraced house in the heart of this popular, pretty fishing village – it has its own gate, and a small courtyard full of sun and colourful pots. Step inside to an inviting living space with a table by the window, books, TV and a very comfy bed; the bathroom is big and sparkling. Friendly hosts bring over breakfast with homemade jams: a full English, or compote and croissants perhaps – there's a fridge and kettle for independence. Teeming with things to do: galleries and cafés in the village, Minack theatre, St Michael's Mount, arty St Ives… and a stream of stunning beaches.

Dedicated parking just up the road.

Rooms	1 suite for 2: £90.
Meals	Pubs/restaurants 2-minute walk.
Closed	Rarely.

Julie & Howard Whitt
The Hideaway,
Pengarth, Commercial Road,
Mousehole, TR19 6QG
Tel   +44 (0)1736 731252
Email   thehideawaymousehole@gmail.com
Web   www.thehideawaymousehole.com

Entry 46   Map 1

Cornwall

Venton Vean

Everything at Venton Vean is tip-top. Immensely helpful owners Philippa and David moved from London with their family and have transformed a dilapidated Victorian house into a supremely cool and elegant B&B. Moody colours, mid-century design classics and interesting reclamation finds make for a stunning and eclectic interior. Food is a passion – expect freshly ground coffee in your room and some of the most tantalising breakfasts around: Mexican, Spanish, even a good old full English will have you dashing down in the morning. Arty Penzance is a joy as is the craggy-coved beauty all around.

Minimum stay: 2 nights.

Rooms	4 doubles: £75–£95.
	1 family room for 4: £110–£140.
	Singles from £60.
Meals	Dinner, 3 courses, from £20.
	Packed lunch from £5.
	Cream tea £4.
Closed	Rarely.

	Philippa McKnight
	Venton Vean,
	Trewithen Road,
	Penzance, TR18 4LS
Tel	+44 (0)1736 351294
Email	info@ventonvean.co.uk
Web	www.ventonvean.co.uk

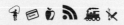

Entry 47   Map 1

Cornwall

Ednovean Farm

There's a terrace for each fabulous bedroom (one truly private) with views to the wild blue yonder and St Michael's Mount Bay, an enchanting outlook that changes with the passage of the day. Come for peace, space and the best of eclectic fabrics and colours, pretty lamps, Christine's sculptures, fluffy bathrobes and handmade soaps. The beamed open-plan sitting/dining area is an absorbing mix of exotic, rustic and elegant; have full breakfast here (last orders nine o'clock) or continental in your room. A footpath through the field leads to the village; walk to glorious Prussia Cove and Cudden Point, or head west to Marazion.

Over 17s welcome.

Rooms	2 doubles, 1 four-poster: £100–£130.
Meals	Pub 5-minute walk.
Closed	Rarely.

	Christine & Charles Taylor
	Ednovean Farm,
	Perranuthnoe,
	Penzance, TR20 9LZ
Tel	+44 (0)1736 711883
Email	info@ednoveanfarm.co.uk
Web	www.ednoveanfarm.co.uk

Entry 48   Map 1

Cornwall

Parc Mean

The 1903 house in its sylvan setting is half a mile from the sea; on stormy nights, you can hear the rollers pounding. You are surrounded by 1,200 acres of National Trust parkland, minutes from breathtaking coastal paths, magical Loe Pool, and Porthleven with its amazing choice of good places to eat – Michelin star Kota, twin restaurant Kota Kai, Rick Stein... Christine spoils you at breakfast at the pine table; country bedrooms have bags of old-fashioned comfort – sofas, dressing-tables, big beds, colourful Cornish art. All feels settled with no one to rush you, the house is filled with good cheer and you'll leave with a spring in your step.

Rooms	1 double, 1 twin/double, each with separate bath: £100.
Meals	Pubs/restaurants 1 mile.
Closed	Christmas.

Chrissie Harvey
Parc Mean,
Penrose Estate,
Porthleven,
Helston, TR13 0RB
Tel   +44 (0)1326 574290
Email   chrissie.parcmean1@gmail.com

Entry 49   Map 1

Cornwall

Nanspean Farmhouse

Head down long country lanes to arrive in this glorious setting overlooking the sea and Loe Pool – the largest natural freshwater lake in Cornwall. Simon and Sally have that happy knack of making you feel at home; Sally is a ceramicist and their whole house is full of art and interesting pieces. They give you a tucked away suite: a light, pretty bedroom, a comfy sitting room with flowers, views and lots of books; sunsets from the bedroom window are breathtaking. Simon bakes bread and the dining room is a lovely spot for breakfast: dark wood, oil family portraits, sun streaming in. Join the coastal path from the farmland... perfect!

Check availability on owners' website.

Rooms	1 suite for 2 with separate bath: £100-£120. Singles £70-£80.
Meals	Pubs/restaurant 1.5 miles.
Closed	Christmas & occasionally.

Simon & Sally Giles
Nanspean Farmhouse,
Gunwalloe,
Helston, TR12 7PX
Tel   +44 (0)1326 569525
Email   sallycgiles@yahoo.co.uk
Web   www.staywestcornwall.com

Entry 50   Map 1

Cornwall

Halzephron House

The coastal path runs through the grounds and the view is to die for – you can see St Michael's Mount on a clear day. Be greeted by homemade biscotti and organic coffee roasted in Cornwall: lovely Lucy and Roger are foodies as well as designers. The suite is contemporary, quirky and full of charm: space, art and bowls of wild flowers, velvet sofa and a big antique French bed; drift off under goose down to the sound of the waves. The drawing room leads onto a deck overlooking the garden and the sea; soak up the stunning sunsets. You can walk to three amazing beaches, a 13th-century church, a golf course and a gastropub. Heaven.

Rooms	1 suite for 2 with sitting room: £110–£130. Extra bed/sofabed available £30–£45 per person per night.
Meals	Pub 0.25 miles.
Closed	Rarely.

Lucy Thorp
Halzephron House,
Gunwalloe,
Helston, TR12 7QD
Mobile +44 (0)7899 925816
Email info@halzephronhouse.co.uk
Web www.halzephronhouse.co.uk

Entry 51   Map 1

Cornwall

The Hen House

A generous, peaceful oasis. Sandy and Gary are warmly welcoming, and have oodles of local information on places to visit, eat and walk – with OS maps on loan. Ground floor rooms, in individual barns, are spacious and colourful with bright fabrics, king-size beds and stable doors to the courtyard. Relax in the hot tub in the wildflower meadow, bask on the sun loungers, wander by the ponds and watch the ducks' antics; the central courtyard is fairy-lit at night. Scrumptious locally sourced breakfasts are served in the dining chalet surrounded by birdsong. Tai-chi in the meadow, reiki and reflexology in the Serpentine Sanctuary... bliss.

Minimum stay: 2 nights. Over 12s welcome.

Rooms	2 doubles: £80–£90. Singles £70–£80.
Meals	Pub/restaurant 1 mile.
Closed	Rarely.

Sandy & Gary Pulfrey
The Hen House,
Tregarne, Manaccan,
Helston, TR12 6EW
Tel +44 (0)1326 280236
Mobile +44 (0)7809 229958
Email henhouseuk@btinternet.com
Web www.thehenhouse-cornwall.co.uk

Entry 52   Map 1

Cornwall

Bay House

Perched on the edge of the map, high on rugged, seapink-tufted cliffs, Bay House is almost as close to the sea as you can get. Rooms are spacious (one with a bay window), the dining room defers to stunning sunsets and the attention to detail is immaculate. Expect fine original artwork and antiques, Ralph Lauren dressing gowns, designer linen, Molton Brown lotions, iPod docks and DVD players. Scramble down to secluded beaches, stroll to the famous Lizard Lighthouse or relax to the sound of the surf in the beautiful garden under rustling palms and hovering kestrels. Breakfast is outstanding – with John's homemade bread and jams.

Children over 8 welcome.

Rooms	2 twin/doubles: £150-£175.
Meals	Pubs/restaurants 5-minute walk.
Closed	Christmas.

Carla Caslin
Bay House,
Housel Bay,
The Lizard, TR12 7PG

Tel	+44 (0)1326 290235
Mobile	+44 (0)7740 168805
Email	carla.caslin@btinternet.com
Web	www.mostsoutherlypoint.co.uk

Entry 53   Map 1

Cornwall

Trerose Manor

Follow winding lanes through glorious countryside to find the prettiest, listed manor house, a warm family atmosphere and welcoming tea in the beamed kitchen. Large, light bedrooms, one with floor-to-ceiling windows, sit peacefully in your own wing and have views over the stunning garden. All are dressed in pretty colours, have comfy seats for garden gazing and smartly tiled bathrooms. A sumptuous breakfast can be taken outside in summer, there are wonderful walks over fields to river or beach and stacks of interesting places to visit. Tessa and Piers are engaging hosts, and you're looked after very well – guests love it here.

French, German & Italian spoken.

Rooms	2 doubles, 1 twin/double: £120-£130. Singles £80.
Meals	Pubs/restaurants within walking distance.
Closed	Rarely.

Tessa Phipps
Trerose Manor,
Mawnan Smith,
Falmouth, TR11 5HX

Tel	+44 (0)1326 250784
Email	info@trerosemanor.co.uk
Web	www.trerosemanor.co.uk

Entry 54   Map 1

Cornwall

Bosvathick

A huge old Cornish house that's been in Kate's family since 1760 — along with Indian rugs, heavy furniture, ornate plasterwork, pianos, portraits... even a harp. Historians will be in their element: pass three Celtic crosses dating from the 8th century before the long drive finds the imposing house (all granite gate posts and lions) and a rambling garden with grotto, lake, pasture and woodland. Bedrooms are traditional, full of books, antiques and pots of flowers; bathrooms are spick and span, one small and functional, one large. Come to experience a 'time warp' and charming Kate's good breakfasts. Close to Falmouth University, too.

French spoken. Post code has been changed from TR11 5RD; Sat Nav will find new post code if updated.

Rooms	2 twin/doubles: £90.
	2 singles: £45-£70.
Meals	Supper, from £25.
	Packed lunch £5-£10. Pubs 2 miles.
Closed	Rarely.

Kate & Stephen Tyrrell
Bosvathick,
Constantine,
Falmouth, TR11 5RZ
Tel   +44 (0)1326 340103
Email kate@bosvathickhouse.co.uk
Web   www.bosvathickhouse.co.uk

Entry 55   Map 1

Cornwall

Trevilla House

Come for the position: the sea and Fal estuary wrap around you, and the King Harry ferry gives you an easy reach into the glorious Roseland peninsula. Inside find comfortable airy bedrooms with homemade quilts on the beds — the twin with a sofa and old-fashioned charm, the double with stunning sea views. Jinty rustles up delicious locally sourced breakfasts and homemade jams, and you eat in the sunny conservatory that looks south over the sea. Trelissick Gardens, with its intriguing newly opened house, is nearby — worth visiting for the view down the Fal alone. From there you are able to take a ferry to Truro, St Mawes or Falmouth.

Rooms	1 double, 1 twin: £85-£95.
	1 single, sharing bath with double
	(let to same party only): £50-£55.
Meals	Pubs/restaurants 1-2 miles.
Closed	Christmas & New Year.

Jinty & Peter Copeland
Trevilla House,
Feock, Truro, TR3 6QG
Tel   +44 (0)1872 862369
Mobile +44 (0)7791 977621
Email jinty.copeland@gmail.com
Web   www.trevilla.com

Entry 56   Map 1

Cornwall

Pollaughan Farm

B&B with a twist. Your own converted barn next to Valerie's farmhouse where you choose your breakfast style: a generous continental left in the fridge, or a full Monty platter ordered the night before and brought over in the morning. The beamed open-plan space is charming and light with seating at one end, a luxuriously dressed bed at the other (local chocs on the pillow), books, TV and doors on to a private sunny deck. Porthcurnick beach is a 20-minute walk — return to a great value supper: Valerie's delicious crumbly pies, pork chops with Cornish cider perhaps — and an excellent fish and chip van comes round twice a week!

Minimum stay: 2 nights.

Rooms	1 double: £110–£130.
Meals	Dinner £9–£12.
	Pubs/restaurants 3.5 miles.
Closed	Rarely.

	Valerie Penny
	Pollaughan Farm,
	Portscatho,
	Truro, TR2 5EH
Tel	+44 (0)1872 580150
Email	holidays@pollaughan.co.uk
Web	www.pollaughan.co.uk

Cornwall

Hay Barton

Giant windows overlook many acres of farmland, and Jill and Blair look after you so well! Breakfasts are special with the best local produce, homemade granola, yogurt and more. Arrive for tea and lovely home-baked cake, laid out in a comfortable guest sitting room with a log fire and plenty of books and maps. Bedrooms are fresh and pretty with garden flowers, soft white linen on big beds and floral green walls. Gloriously large panelled bathrooms have long roll top baths and are painted in earthy colours. You can knock a few balls around the tennis court, and you're near to good gardens and heaps of places to eat.

Minimum stay: 2 nights in summer.

Rooms	3 twin/doubles: £85.
	Singles £65.
Meals	Pubs 1–2 miles.
Closed	Rarely.

	Jill & Blair Jobson
	Hay Barton,
	Tregony,
	Truro, TR2 5TF
Tel	+44 (0)1872 530288
Mobile	+44 (0)7813 643028
Email	jill.jobson@btinternet.com
Web	www.haybarton.com

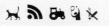

Cornwall

Ashby Villa

Lesley is friendly and outgoing and invites you for a cream tea in the kitchen of her Edwardian home. The village is lively but the Dog House, just for guests, is peacefully tucked behind, overlooking gardens and fields. Comfy bedrooms have a roll top tub or power shower, cosy rugs on tiled floors, local art, French country furniture and a shared terrace; one wood-lined studio has a wood-burner and its own patio. Zip over to the conservatory for a tasty breakfast and John's homemade bread. The Roseland Peninsula has secret coves and Truro is close. Return with fish for your own barbecue, then relax in the candlelit conservatory. Bliss.

Rooms	Dog House – 1 double: £85.
	Dog House – 1 family room for 3: £95.
	Dog House – 2 studios for 2 each
	with extra sofabed & kitchenette:
	£90–£100.
Meals	Pub 300 yds.
Closed	Rarely.

Lesley Black
Ashby Villa,
Fore Street,
Tregony,
Truro, TR2 5RW
Tel   +44 (0)1872 530189
Email   blacklesley5@aol.com
Web   www.cornwallvillagebedandbreakfast.co.uk

Entry 59   Map 1

Cornwall

Tubbs Mill House

Be sure to arrive in time for tea when Vic bakes fresh scones, which you can take in the pretty riverside garden beside this wisteria-clad Georgian house. A wonderfully calm sitting room is a good place to plan your trip, and well-stocked with entertainment. Stylish bedrooms showcase much of arty Denise's hand-painted furniture: one is up in the eaves with two bathrooms, one en suite, and a more pampering one at the bottom of the wooden stairs. Enjoy a very tasty, mostly organic breakfast in the wooden conservatory, and hear tales of time in Africa. A house full of fun and interest run by the kindest East Enders imaginable – you'll feel at home here.

Minimum stay: 2 nights at weekends. Over 12s welcome.

Rooms	1 twin/double; 1 double with
	separate bath: £100–£110.
	Dinner, B&B £67–£83 per person.
Meals	Dinner £12–£28.
	Pubs/restaurants 4 miles.
Closed	Rarely.

Denise Hall
Tubbs Mill House,
Caerhays,
Gorran,
St Austell, PL26 6NB
Tel   +44 (0)1872 531852
Email   denise@goosebarn.net

Entry 60   Map 1

Cornwall

Tredudwell Manor

Winding lanes lead to this handsomely refurbished Queen Anne style house. Surrounded by lawns and mature trees the views are south to the sea and the total peace is just the tonic. Inside is a marble bar for more reviving and the mix of sofas, mini-ottomans, parquet floors with Persian rugs and family portraits make for a genteel atmosphere. First floor bedrooms are large enough to waltz in with toile de Jouy wallpaper, antiques and views. In the roof space are more compact but delightful rooms – uncluttered and calm with low beams, shuttered windows and modern bathrooms. Breakfast is a treat with the best produce from nearby Fowey.

Rooms	6 doubles: £85-£125.
	1 family room for 4: £125-£165.
	Singles £65-£100.
Meals	Pubs/restaurants 2 miles.
Closed	Rarely.

Justin & Valérie Shakerley
Tredudwell Manor,
Lanteglos,
Fowey, PL23 1NJ
Tel   +44 (0)1726 870226
Email   justin@tredudwell.co.uk
Web   www.tredudwell.co.uk

Entry 61   Map 1

Cornwall

Botelet B&B

The farmhouse at the end of the wild-flowered lane is an inspired synthesis of stone, wood, Shaker simplicity and comfy old chairs: the chicest of shabby chic. Rustic bedrooms reached by a steep stair have planked floors, antique beds and beautiful linen; the bathroom is just along the hallway. Breakfasts – organic, home-baked, home-picked, vegetarian – are enjoyed at a scrubbed table by the Rayburn. Drink in the pure air, explore the farm, walk the wooded valley; return to a therapeutic massage in the treatment room. Botelet has been in the family since 1860 and is quirky, friendly, artistic, huge fun. The yurts are amazing.

Children over 10 welcome.

Rooms	1 double, 1 twin/double sharing bath
	(let to same party only): £70-£100.
	2 yurts for 2: £50-£90.
Meals	Continental breakfast (£15 for yurt).
	Pub 2 miles.
Closed	December to Easter.

The Tamblyn Family
Botelet B&B,
Herodsfoot,
Liskeard, PL14 4RD
Tel   +44 (0)1503 220225
Email   stay@botelet.com
Web   www.botelet.com

Entry 62   Map 1

Cornwall

Beechgrove

A striking Victorian home in this historic market town with views across to mysterious Bodmin Moor. Richard and Jane, relaxed and friendly hosts, give you dinner using local and seasonal produce, often with home-grown fruit and vegetables and served on fine china. Stoke up with a delicious traditional, or more adventurous, breakfast with plenty of choice and homemade preserves and bread. Sleep peacefully in the very private guest suite upstairs with its super-king bed and extra single, its comfy sitting room, soft robes and a smart bathroom; the feel is spacious and contemporary, the colours restful. A hidden gem.

Minimum stay: 2 nights.

Rooms	1 suite for 1-4 with sitting room & adjoining single (let to same party only, extra small bed available): £95-£105. Singles £75.
Meals	Dinner, 2-3 courses, £19.50-£25. Pubs/restaurants 10-minute walk.
Closed	Rarely.

Jane & Richard Herman
Beechgrove,
47a Dunheved Road,
Launceston, PL15 9JF
Tel   +44 (0)1566 779455
Email   enquiries@beechgrovecornwall.co.uk
Web   www.beechgrovecornwall.co.uk

Entry 63   Map 2

Cornwall

New Entry

Spring Cottage

Follow the flower-massed lanes with long views over Dartmoor to this tiny hamlet. Sally gives you complete independence at one end of her medieval hall house. Step into a beamed open-plan sitting room with huge fireplace, bright rugs and cosy sofa; at one end is a tiny spotless kitchen. Up winding stairs find a large, light bedroom with a super big wooden bed and sparkling bathroom. Sally brings over a breakfast tray, laden with fresh-baked pastries and more, in time for a brisk start or a lazy morning in bed. For special occasions she rustles up a fantastic cooked Cornish spread. The stunning Tamar Valley is at your feet. Bliss.

Pets by arrangement.

Rooms	1 double with own self-contained sitting/dining room/kitchen: £80-£92.
Meals	Dinner, 2-3 courses, £15. Pubs/restaurants 1.5 miles.
Closed	Rarely.

Sally Harvey
Spring Cottage,
Tutwell,
Callington, PL17 8LU
Tel   +44 (0)1579 370955
Email   seharvey7@gmail.com

Entry 64   Map 2

Cornwall

Lantallack Farm

You will be inspired here, in generous Nicky's heart-warming old Georgian farmhouse. Find a straw-yellow sitting room with a log fire, books to read and a grand piano; views are breathtaking across countryside, streams and wooded valley. Bedrooms have deliciously comfy beds; Polly's Bower, a romantic hideaway in the old cider barn, is a charming open-plan space with whitewash and old beams, wood-burner and freestanding tub. Breakfast in the walled garden on fine days: apple juice from the orchard and bacon and sausages from down the road. There are 40 acres to explore, a leat-side trail and a heated outdoor pool. Marvellous.

Over 16s welcome.

Rooms	1 double: £120–£135. Polly's Bower – 1 double with sitting area and kitchen: £120–£135 (3 nights from £345).
Meals	Supper on request in Polly's Bower, £25. Pubs/restaurants 1 mile.
Closed	Rarely.

Nicky Walker
Lantallack Farm,
Landrake,
Saltash, PL12 5AE

Tel	+44 (0)1752 851281
Email	enquiries@lantallack.co.uk
Web	www.lantallackgetaways.co.uk

Cumbria

Willowford Farm

Lauren and Liam are enthusiastic about their organic farm and their guests. Two single-storey stone byres have been converted environmentally with thermafleece wool in the roof and a wood-burning boiler for heated slate floors. In one byre: the bedrooms, fresh, stylish, with slate floors and lofty beams, perhaps windows looking onto the farmyard, or skylights for the stars. In the other: a cosy sitting room with views of sheep and hills, and tables for meals of home-reared lamb and beef, and tasty veggy dishes; or head off to the pub! Hadrian's Wall, forts, museums and walks are all here – and Millie the sheepdog gives a welcome to visiting dogs.

Rooms	5 twin/doubles: £80–£85. Singles £55–£60.
Meals	Packed lunch £6. Lunch & dinner £6–£16 at owners' pub 1 mile away; owners can provide transport.
Closed	Christmas.

Liam McNulty & Lauren Harrison
Willowford Farm,
Gilsland,
Brampton, CA8 7AA

Tel	+44 (0)1697 747962
Email	stay@willowford.co.uk
Web	www.willowford.co.uk

Chapelburn House

Yomp in the most dramatic scenery close to the best bits of Hadrian's Wall, then head for Chapelburn House. Matt and Katie are young, charming, unflappable, food is reared happily then cooked with more flavour than fuss. Honey is from their bees, bread is home-baked. You have a sitting room with an open fire, lots of books and squishy sofas, *and* a south-facing garden room for summer dreaming. Bedrooms are deeply comfortable and bathrooms (one definitely not for fatties!) brand spanking new. Children are more than welcome to join in. This would delight exhausted refugees from London, too.

Warwick Hall

The position here is magnificent, a slice of English heaven. The house stands resplendently in 260 acres on the banks of the river Eden, one of the best salmon beats in the country; a two-mile stroll hugs the water. Inside, the vast windows flood the place with light; there's a lived-in drawing room with sofas in front of the fire; a dining room with views of hill and river. Delightful country-house bedrooms have high ceilings, beautiful fabrics, super bathrooms; one has its own fire. Bonnie Prince Charlie once stayed, though not in the comfort you can expect. Val is friendly and the food is delicious, too.

Rooms	2 doubles: £75–£95.
Meals	Dinner, 3 courses, £25.
	Packed lunch £5–£7.50.
	Restaurant 5 miles.
Closed	Christmas & New Year.

Rooms	7 twin/doubles: £118–£146.
	2 suites for 2 with kitchenettes: £159.
	Singles £118–£124.
	Dinner, B&B £107–£116 per person.
	Extra bed/sofabed available £25 per person per night.
Meals	Dinner, 3 courses, £40.
	Restaurant 1 mile.
Closed	Rarely.

	Matthew & Katie McClure
	Chapelburn House,
	Low Row,
	Brampton, CA8 2LY
Tel	+44 (0)1697 746595
Email	stay@chapelburn.com
Web	www.chapelburn.com

	Val Marriner
	Warwick Hall,
	Warwick-on-Eden, Carlisle, CA4 8PG
Tel	+44 (0)1228 561546
Mobile	+44 (0)7818 448756
Email	info@warwickhall.co.uk
Web	www.warwickhall.org

Cumbria

Hawksdale Lodge

Spring heaven! Bowl along blissfully quiet roads while sheep bleat and daffs bob in the breeze. This is supremely comfortable B&B at any time of the year though and your hosts look after you with great charm from their stunning 1810 gentleman farmer's house with pretty garden. Home baking and local produce at breakfast, sumptuously dressed bedrooms with plenty of space and seating, warm and inviting bathrooms with proper windows. The National Park is only six miles away for strenuous walking and cycling, the northern Lakes and fells beckon, Hadrian's wall is near. Return to something homemade and delicious. Lovely.

Minimum stay: 2 nights at Easter & New Year.

Rooms	1 double; 1 double with separate bath: £95-£150. Easter £135 (min. 2 night stay) & New Year £150. Singles £70-£100.
Meals	Supper on request, 2 courses, £20. BYO. Packed lunch on request, from £5. Pubs/restaurants less than 1 mile.
Closed	Christmas.

Lorraine Russell
Hawksdale Lodge,
Dalston,
Carlisle, CA5 7BX
Mobile   +44 (0)7810 641892
Email   enquiries@hawksdalelodge.co.uk
Web   www.hawksdalelodge.co.uk

Entry 69   Map 11

Cumbria

Sirelands

Sirelands, once a gardener's cottage, stands among rhododendrons and trees on a sunny slope, a stream trickling by: a stunning spot. The Carrs have lived here for years and the house has a relaxed and homely feel. Enjoy a chatty aperitif then home-grown produce at dinner on a polished table; retire to the sitting room, delightful with log basket, honesty bar, flowers and books. Sash windows overlook the wooded garden, visited by roe deer and a wide variety of birds. Bedrooms and bathrooms are pleasant, peaceful and spotless; one loo has an amazing view! Friendly Angela loves cooking and treats you to tea and homemade cake.

Rooms	1 twin; 1 double with separate bath/shower: £100. Singles £50-£60.
Meals	Dinner, 2-3 courses, £22-£27.50. Pubs within 5 miles.
Closed	Christmas & New Year.

David & Angela Carr
Sirelands,
Heads Nook, Brampton,
Carlisle, CA8 9BT
Tel   +44 (0)1228 670389
Mobile   +44 (0)7748 101513
Email   carr_sirelands@btconnect.com

Entry 70   Map 12

Cumbria

Kirkby Thore Hall

A gorgeous, imposing village house with 14th-century beginnings, architectural treats and kind, helpful hosts. Walk straight in to a large hall/dining room with roaring fire, gleaming antiques and interesting pictures. You breakfast here on Cranstons of Penrith sausages, local farm eggs and homemade jam; a library with a desk and your own sitting room are just next door. Two bedrooms upstairs are huge with beamed ceilings (one like an up-turned boat), some exposed stone, light-filled windows, pretty fabrics; bathrooms are spotless. This valley is quiet, with gentler hills than the Lakes, and you are near the Pennines too.

Rooms	1 double, 1 twin/double: £90. Stays of 2 nights or more: £84. Extra bed available.
Meals	Restaurant 0.5 miles.
Closed	Rarely.

Christine & David Tucker
Kirkby Thore Hall,
Kirkby Thore,
Penrith, CA10 1XN

Tel	+44 (0)17683 62989
Email	manxhorizon@btinternet.com
Web	www.kirkbythorehall.co.uk

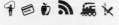

Entry 71   Map 12

Cumbria

Kelleth Old Hall

Glorious unimpeded views of fields, cows and the Howgill Fells from this fun and characterful B&B. Charlotte – chutney enthusiast, writer of three novels – has moved into an ancient manor (the fourth owner in 400 years); now it glows with paintings, antiques and books. Short steep stairs lead from 17th-century flagstones to a big canopied brass bed and yellow silk curtains at mullion windows. All is warm, charming, inviting, and that includes the roll top bath beneath a vaulted ceiling. Fuel up on a Cumbrian breakfast, return to a delicious supper of exotic flavours. Near the A685 but peaceful at night.

Rooms	1 double (extra single bed available): £80-£90. Singles £60-£65.
Meals	Dinner, 2-3 courses, £18-£22. Pub/restaurant 5 miles.
Closed	Occasionally.

Charlotte Fairbairn
Kelleth Old Hall,
Kelleth, Penrith, CA10 3UG

Tel	+44 (0)1539 623344
Mobile	+44 (0)7754 163941
Email	charlottefairbairn@hotmail.co.uk
Web	www.kelletholdhall.co.uk

Entry 72   Map 12

Cumbria

Lazonby Hall

The pinky sandstone façade rises, château-like, from bright flowers, box hedges, crunchy gravel: enchanting. Views, from sash windows and garden folly, yawn over the Eden valley to the Pennines. Step past pillars to panelled, antique-filled rooms of heavy curtains, marble fires, mahogany and oils. Formal, yet not daunting – the Quines and their dachshunds bring life, flexibility, and delicious Cumbrian breakfasts. Wake to birdsong and garden views. This sweet area of winding lanes and dry stone walls is near the north Lakes, Penrith, Carlisle, Scotland – ripe for exploration by foot, bike, canoe or train.

Rooms	2 doubles; 1 double, 1 twin sharing bath: £90–£135. Singles £80–£100.
Meals	Dinner, 3 courses, £35–£50. Pub/restaurant 2 miles.
Closed	Rarely.

Mr & Mrs Quine
Lazonby Hall,
Lazonby,
Penrith, CA10 1AZ
Tel   +44 (0)1768 870300
Email info@lazonbyhall.co.uk
Web   www.lazonbyhall.co.uk

Entry 73   Map 11

Cumbria

Johnby Hall

You are ensconced in the quieter part of the Lakes and have independence in this Elizabethan manor house – once a fortified Pele tower, now a family home. The suites are airy and each has its own sitting room with books, children's videos, squashy sofas, pretty fabrics and whitewashed walls. Beds have patchwork quilts, windows have stone mullions and all is peaceful. Henry gives you sturdy breakfasts, and good home-grown suppers by a roaring fire in the great hall; he and Anna can join you or leave you in peace. Children will have fun: hens and pigs to feed, garden and woods to roam, garden toys galore. Walks from the door are sublime.

Rooms	1 twin/double, 1 family room for 4, each with sitting room: £125. Singles £87. Extra bed/sofabed available £20 per person per night.
Meals	Supper, 2 courses, £20. Pub 1 mile.
Closed	Rarely.

Henry & Anna Howard
Johnby Hall,
Johnby,
Penrith, CA11 0UU
Tel   +44 (0)17684 83257
Email bookings@johnbyhall.co.uk
Web   www.johnbyhall.co.uk

Entry 74   Map 11

Cumbria

Cumbria

Whitrigg House

On the edge of the Lake District National
Park, a handsome 1700s house with original
features galore. Period colours blend with
contemporary pieces, eclectic finds and local
art, the red sitting room is warmly inviting,
and attractive wooden shutters frame your
view. Mike and Robbie live nearby and look
after you well; the Whitrigg breakfast
includes homemade bread, jams and muesli,
fruit with crème fraîche and a tip-top full
English. Beds are wonderfully comfy;
Scottish weaves hang from deer horn above.
Stroll to the pub for supper, or if you arrive
late tuck into a complimentary bowl of soup,
or winter mulled wine. Perfect!

*Please check owners' website for availability before
enquiring. Over 12s welcome.*

Greenah

Tucked into the hillside off a narrow lane,
this 1750s smallholding is surrounded by
fells, so is perfect for walkers. Absolute
privacy for four friends or family with your
own entrance to a beamed and stone-flagged
sitting room with wood-burning stove,
creamy walls and cheery floral curtains.
Warm bedrooms have original paintings,
good beds, hot water bottles, bathrobes and
a sparkling bathroom with a loo with a
remarkable view. Malcolm is a climber;
Marjorie is totally committed to organic food
so you get a fabulous breakfast, and good
advice about the local area. Fell walking is
not compulsory!

Children over 8 welcome.

Rooms	2 doubles: £85-£105.
	1 single: £60.
Meals	Pubs/restaurants 5-minute walk.
Closed	Rarely.

Rooms	1 double, 1 twin sharing shower
	(let to same party only): £92-£96.
	Singles £60-£65.
Meals	Pubs/restaurants 3 miles.
Closed	November-January.

	Mike Taylor
	Whitrigg House,
	Clifton,
	Penrith, CA10 2EE
Tel	+44 (0)1768 895077
Email	info@whitrigghouse.co.uk
Web	www.whitrigghouse.co.uk

	Marjorie & Malcolm Emery
	Greenah,
	Matterdale, Penrith, CA11 0SA
Tel	+44 (0)1768 483387
Mobile	+44 (0)7767 213667
Email	info@greenah.co.uk
Web	www.greenah.co.uk

Entry 75   Map 11

Entry 76   Map 11

Cumbria

Lowthwaite

Leave your worries behind as you head up the lanes to the farmhouse tucked into the fell. Jim, ex-hiking guide, and Danish Tine are charming, helpful and well-travelled. Their barn is dotted with Tanzanian furniture and your peaceful bedrooms are in the view-filled wing. Beds are made of recycled dhow wood, sparkling bathrooms sport organic soaps; the garden room has its own patio. Breakfasts with homemade granola, bread and muffins are delicious – perhaps halloumi with mushrooms, tomatoes and egg or smoked salmon with creamed spinach. Birds galore in the garden, a trickling stream... endless fells to explore too – advice is happily given.

Rooms	2 twin/doubles: £85–£90.
	2 family rooms for 4: £90–£120.
	Singles £55–£65.
Meals	Packed lunch £6. Dinner £18–£27.
	Pubs 2.5 miles.
Closed	Christmas.

Tine & Jim Boving Foster
Lowthwaite,
Matterdale,
Penrith, CA11 0LE
Tel +44 (0)1768 482343
Email info@lowthwaiteullswater.com
Web www.lowthwaiteullswater.com

Entry 77   Map 11

Cumbria

Robyns Barn

Wow, fabulous views – fells and mountains in every direction including Blencathra, the most climbed fell in the Lakes. Robyns Barn is attached to the main house, and it's all yours. Step into a large, welcoming open-plan space: limewashed walls, big oak table, beams, antique pine, toasty wood-burner and plenty of DVDs, books and games. Inviting bedrooms, upstairs, have sheepskins on wooden floors. Wake when you want – Kathryn leaves a continental breakfast with homemade bread, muesli, fruit, yogurts; there's a farm shop close by serving excellent cooked breakfasts too. The garden has a picnic area, barbecue – and those views!

Minimum stay: 2 nights. Children over 8 welcome.

Rooms	Barn – 1 double, 1 twin with
	sitting/dining room & kitchenette
	(let to same party only): £90.
Meals	Continental breakfast. Supper £20.
	Pubs/restaurants 1 mile.
Closed	Rarely.

Adrian & Kathryn Vaughan
Robyns Barn,
Lane Head Farm, Troutbeck,
Keswick, Penrith, CA11 0SY
Tel +44 (0)1768 779841
Email robynsbarn@hotmail.co.uk
Web www.robynsbarn.co.uk

Entry 78   Map 11

Cumbria

Howe Keld

Dismiss all thoughts of the chintzy Keswick guest house: David and Val have swept through with carpets made of Herdwick sheep wool, local wood and slate, bedroom furniture made by a local craftsman and contemporary wallpapers and fabrics. It's luxurious but not flashy, and there's a cosy sitting room crammed with info on the area; theatre, shops and restaurants are all within strolling distance (choose rooms at the front if you need total quiet). Fill up at breakfast on home-baked bread, freshly made smoothies or a jolly good fry-up. A friendly, supremely comfortable place.

Minimum stay: 2 nights at weekends, 3 on bank holidays.

Rooms	13 doubles: £110–£130. 1 single: £55–£95.
Meals	Pub/restaurant 300 yds.
Closed	Part of December including Christmas. Most of January excluding New Year.

David Fisher
Howe Keld,
5/7 The Heads,
Keswick, CA12 5ES
Tel   +44 (0)1768 772417
Email david@howekeld.co.uk
Web   www.howekeld.co.uk

Cumbria

Drybeck Hall

Looking south to fields, woodland and beck this Grade II*-listed, 1679 farmhouse has blue painted mullion windows and exposed beams. Expect a deeply traditional home with good furniture, an open fire and pictures of Anthony's predecessors looking down on you benignly; the family has been in the area for 800 years. Comfortable bedrooms have pretty floral fabrics and oak doors; bathrooms are simple but sparkling. Lulie is relaxed and charming and a good cook: enjoy a full English with free-range eggs in the sunny dining room, and home-grown vegetables and often game for dinner. A genuine slice of history.

Rooms	1 double, 1 twin: £100. Singles £50.
Meals	Dinner, 3 courses, £25. Pub/restaurant 4 miles.
Closed	Rarely.

Lulie & Anthony Hothfield
Drybeck Hall,
Appleby-in-Westmorland, CA16 6TF
Tel   +44 (0)1768 351487
Email lulieant@aol.com
Web   www.drybeckhall.co.uk

Cumbria

Lapwings Barn

In the back of most-beautiful-beyond, down narrow lanes, this converted barn is a gorgeous retreat for two – or four. Delightful generous Gillian and Rick give you privacy and an upstairs sitting room with log stove, sofa and a balcony with views. Bedrooms downstairs (separate entrances) are pleasingly rustic with beams and modern stone-tiled bathrooms. Breakfast is delivered: sausages and bacon from their Saddlebacks, eggs from their hens, superb homemade bread and marmalade. Stroll along lowland tracks, watch curlews and lapwings, puff to the top of Whinfell. Ambleside and Beatrix Potter's house are near. One of the best.

Rooms	Barn – 2 twin/doubles & sitting room: £66-£90. Singles £55. Extra bed/sofabed available £20 per person per night.
Meals	Packed lunch £5. Dinner £20. Pub/restaurant 3.5 miles.
Closed	Rarely.

Rick & Gillian Rodriguez
Lapwings Barn,
Whinfell, Kendal, LA8 9EQ

Tel	+44 (0)1539 824373
Mobile	+44 (0)7901 732379
Email	stay@lapwingsbarn.co.uk
Web	www.lapwingsbarn.co.uk

Cumbria

Parsonage House

The lane to this handsome Lakeland stone house is bordered by fields and fells, a beck runs through the garden and hens wander in the orchard. Step into a long hall with polished oak and Persian rugs, and be greeted as friends by Jeni and Steve. Their deeply comfortable home embraces you with log fires, books, family photographs, beautiful fabrics, excellent bedrooms and lots of art by Jeni. Morning sun streams into the dining room, and breakfast is served at separate linen-clad tables: fruits, granolas and a full cooked Cumbrian with local sausages and bacon. You can stroll to the pub for a good supper.

Minimum stay: 2 nights. Over 12s welcome.

Rooms	3 doubles: £85-£120.
Meals	Restaurants 400 yds.
Closed	Rarely.

Jeni & Steve Calvert
Parsonage House,
Kings Garth, Ings, Kendal, LA8 9PU

Mobile	+44 (0)7881 385129/ +44 (0)7881 382892
Email	parsonagehousebb@gmail.com
Web	www.parsonagehouse.co.uk

Cumbria

Fellside Studios

Off the beaten tourist track, a piece of paradise in the Troutbeck valley: seclusion, stylishness and breathtaking views. Prepare your own candlelit dinners, rise when the mood takes you, come and go as you please. The flower beds spill with heathers, hens cluck, and there's a decked terrace for continental breakfast in the sun – freshly prepared by your gently hospitable hosts who live in the attached house. In your studio apartment you get oak floors, slate shower rooms, immaculate kitchenettes with designer touches, DVD players, comfy chairs, luxurious towels. Wonderful.

Minimum stay: 2 nights.

Rooms	1 double, 1 twin/double, each with kitchenette: £80-£100. Singles £50-£60.
Meals	Continental breakfast. Pub/restaurant 0.5 miles.
Closed	Rarely.

Monica & Brian Liddell
Fellside Studios,
Troutbeck,
Windermere, LA23 1NN
Tel   +44 (0)1539 434000
Email   brian@fellsidestudios.co.uk
Web   www.fellsidestudios.co.uk

Cumbria

Gilpin Mill

Come to be seriously spoiled. Down leafy lanes is a pretty white house by a mill pond, framed by pastures and trees. Steve took a year off to build new Gilpin Mill, and Jo looks after their labs and guests – beautifully. In the country farmhouse sitting room oak beams span the ceiling and a slate lintel sits above the log fire. Bedrooms are equally inviting: beds are topped with duck down, luscious bathrooms are warm underfoot. Alongside is a lovely old barn where timber was made into bobbins; in the mill pond is a salmon and trout ladder and a dam, soon to provide power for the grid. And just six cars pass a day!

Children over 10 welcome.

Rooms	3 twin/doubles: £95-£115. Singles £63-£73.
Meals	Pub 2.5 miles.
Closed	Christmas.

Jo & Steve Ainsworth
Gilpin Mill,
Crook,
Windermere, LA8 8LN
Tel   +44 (0)1539 568405
Email   info@gilpinmill.co.uk
Web   www.gilpinmill.co.uk

Cumbria

Cockenskell Farm

The house and hill farm garden with its wild rhododendrons and damson orchard sits on the fells at the southern end of Lake Coniston. Step inside to a friendly home with beamed rooms, art and antique pine; comfortable bedrooms have pretty patchwork covers and lovely wallpapers. Relax with a book in the conservatory, stroll through the magical, bird-filled garden or tackle a bit of the Cumbrian Way that meanders through the fields to the back. On sunny days you can have breakfast in the conservatory and enjoy the glorious views. History seeps from every pore, Sara is an engaging host and to stay here is a treat.

Over 12s welcome.

Rooms	1 twin; 1 twin with separate bath: £90. Singles from £45.
Meals	Packed lunch £7.50. Pubs 2-4 miles.
Closed	November-February.

	Sara Keegan
	Cockenskell Farm,
	Blawith, Ulverston, LA12 8EL
Tel	+44 (0)1229 885217
Mobile	+44 (0)7909 885086
Email	keegan@cockenskell.co.uk
Web	www.cockenskell.co.uk

Entry 85   Map 11

Cumbria

Broughton House

Down lanes edged with dry stone walls and hedges, with distant views of the Lakeland mountains… what peace! You feel instantly at home too, in a house full of books and colour. Bedrooms come with a jar of Cate's homemade brownies, a bowl of fruit and a deep mattress: owls hooting you to sleep in one, privacy in the wing, snug simplicity in Ben's Cabin. Wake to fresh juice, pancakes, homemade bread, local bacon and sausages, smoked salmon and scrambled eggs. Puffin the dog, Minty the cat, a host of hens and a large garden all add to the charm. Perfect for cycling, a hop from Windermere and eating out in pretty Cartmel is a treat.

Rooms	2 doubles: £90. 1 cabin for 2 (1 double, 1 single, kitchen & yurt sitting room): £60-£70. Singles £60.
Meals	Pub 1 mile.
Closed	29 November – 27 December.

	Cate Davies
	Broughton House,
	Field Broughton,
	Grange-over-Sands, LA11 6HN
Tel	+44 (0)1539 536439
Email	info@broughtonhousecartmel.co.uk
Web	www.broughtonhousecartmel.co.uk

Entry 86   Map 11

Derbyshire

Underleigh House

A Derbyshire longhouse in Brontë country built by a man called George Eyre. The position is unbeatable – field, river, hill, sky – but the stars of the show are Philip and Vivienne, dab hands at spoiling guests rotten. There's a big sitting room with maps for walkers, a dining room hall for hearty breakfasts, and tables and chairs scattered about the garden. Back inside, bedrooms vary in size, but all have super beds, goose down duvets and stunning views; a couple have doors onto the garden, the suites have proper sitting rooms. Fantastic walks start from the front door, Castleton Caves are on the doorstep and Chatsworth is close.

Minimum stay: 2 nights at weekends. Over 12s welcome.

Rooms	3 doubles: £90–£100.
	2 suites for 2: £105–£115.
	Singles £75–£90.
Meals	Packed lunches £6.
	Pubs/restaurants 0.5 miles.
Closed	Christmas & January.

Philip & Vivienne Taylor
Underleigh House,
Lose Hill Lane, Hope,
Hope Valley, S33 6AF
Tel   +44 (0)1433 621372
Email   underleigh.house@btconnect.com
Web   www.underleighhouse.co.uk

Entry 87   Map 12

Derbyshire

The Lodge at Dale End House

One of those places where you get your own annexe – in this case, the former milking parlour of the listed farmhouse. It certainly has scrubbed up nicely. The ground-floor bedroom has a finely dressed antique bed and magnificent chandelier while the well-equipped kitchen is a boon if you don't fancy venturing out for supper. Friendly, helpful Sarah takes orders for breakfasts – eggs from her hens, local sausages and bacon – and delivers to your door. No open fire but cosy underfloor heating warms you after a blustery yomp in any direction. Bring your four-legged friends – canine or equine – to this happy house.

Rooms	Lodge – 1 double with
	kitchen/dining/sitting room: £85–£95.
Meals	Pubs/restaurants 2.5 miles.
Closed	Rarely.

Sarah & Paul Summers
The Lodge at Dale End House,
Gratton,
Bakewell, DE45 1LN
Tel   +44 (0)1629 650380
Email   thebarn@daleendhouse.co.uk
Web   www.daleendhouse.co.uk

Entry 88   Map 8

Derbyshire

Old Shoulder of Mutton

The lively village of Winster is mega-pretty; the Old Shoulder of Mutton, once a pub, sits in its middle. Steven and Julie are welcoming and their home is as cosy as can be. Find a warm contemporary and traditional mix, framed clay pipes (found during renovations), a charming drawing room, luxurious bedrooms and snazzy en suite bathrooms. Breakfast is by the wood-burner: feast on eggs Benedict, homemade jam, local bacon and the famous Derbyshire oatcakes. There's a lovely and unexpected garden at the back; Bakewell, with its legendary Monday market and Chatsworth House, is a short drive, and the walking is dreamy.

Minimum stay: 2 nights. Over 12s welcome.

Rooms	2 doubles,
	1 twin/double: £115-£160.
Meals	Pubs in village.
Closed	Rarely.

Steven White
Old Shoulder of Mutton,
West Bank, Winster,
Matlock, DE4 2DQ
Tel +44 (0)1629 650005
Email steven@theoldshoulderofmutton.co.uk
Web www.oldshoulderofmutton.co.uk

Derbyshire

Manor Farm

Between two small dales, close to great houses (Chatsworth, Hardwick Hall, Haddon Hall), lies this cluster of ancient farms and a church; welcome to the 16th century! Simon and Gilly, warm, delightful and fascinated by the history, have restored the east wing to create big, beamy rooms in the old hayloft and a pretty garden room on the ground floor; a cosy and quaint bedroom overlooks the church. Wake to a scrumptious breakfast in the cavernous Elizabethan kitchen. There's a 'book exchange' in the old milking parlour and a lovely garden with sweeping views across the valley and distant hills.

Children over 6 welcome.

Rooms	1 double, 2 twin/doubles: £80-£90.
	1 family room for 2-4: £80-£140.
	Singles £55-£70.
Meals	Pubs within 10-minute drive.
Closed	Rarely.

Simon & Gilly Groom
Manor Farm,
Dethick, Matlock, DE4 5GG
Tel +44 (0)1629 534302
Mobile +44 (0)7944 660814
Email gilly.groom@w3z.co.uk
Web www.manorfarmdethick.co.uk

Derbyshire

Mount Tabor House

On a steep hillside between the Peaks and the Dales, a chapel in a pretty village with a peaceful aura and great views. Enter a hall where light streams through stained-glass windows – this is a relaxed, easy place to stay with a distinctive and original interior, a log-burner to keep you toasty and a sweet dog called Molly. Fay is charming and generous and breakfast, in a dining room with open stone walls, is delicious: mainly from the village shops and as organic as possible; you can eat on the balcony in summer. Walk to the pub for dinner, come home to a fabulous wet room and a big inviting bed.

Usually minimum stay: 2 nights at weekends.

Rooms	1 twin/double: £90-£95.
	Extra bed/sofabed available
	£10-£30 per person per night.
Meals	Occasional dinner £25.
	Pub 100 yds.
Closed	Rarely.

Fay Whitehead
Mount Tabor House,
Bowns Hill, Crich,
Matlock, DE4 5DG

Tel	+44 (0)1773 857008
Mobile	+44 (0)7813 007478
Email	mountabor@msn.com

Entry 91   Map 8

Derbyshire

Park View Farm

An extravagant refuge after a long journey, run by hospitable hosts. Daringly decadent, every inch of this Victorian farmhouse brims with flowers, sparkling trinkets, polished brass, plump cushions and swathes of chintz. Bedrooms with beautiful views dance in swirls of colour, frills, gleaming wood, lustrous glass, buttons and bows; fresh eggs, fresh fruits, homemade breads and their own rare-breed sausages accompany the grand performance. Have afternoon tea on the vine-covered terrace, roam the 370 organic acres. Kedleston Hall Park provides a stunning backdrop.

Rooms	2 four-posters; 1 four-poster with
	separate bath: £90.
	Singles £65-£70.
Meals	Pub/restaurant 1 mile.
Closed	Christmas.

Linda Adams
Park View Farm,
Weston Underwood,
Ashbourne, DE6 4PA

Tel	+44 (0)1335 360352
Mobile	+44 (0)7771 573057
Email	enquiries@parkviewfarm.co.uk
Web	www.parkviewfarm.co.uk

Entry 92   Map 8

Derbyshire

Hinchley Wood

Glorious Georgian house with the most engaging, friendly hosts: you're in for a treat. The pineapple-topped gateposts are a symbol of hospitality, and you arrive for tea and cake by the fire in the splendid drawing room. Sleep well in elegant bedrooms; beds are topped with good linen, there are interesting books to browse and the views are stunning. Rosemaré's breakfasts are "legendary" – a local, usually organic, spread with her wonderful Staffordshire oat cakes. Pretty villages, historic houses, Nordic walking, riding, fly fishing on the river Dove... the area is dreamy and Cedric is happy to arrange activities.

Minimum stay: 2 nights at weekends. Children over 10 welcome. Pets by arrangement.

Rooms	1 double, 1 four-poster: £120–£140.
Meals	Pubs/restaurants 3-minute walk.
Closed	1 December – 5 January.

Cedric & Rosemaré Stevenson
Hinchley Wood,
Mappleton,
Ashbourne, DE6 2AB
Tel   +44 (0)1335 350219
Email   rose-stevenson@hotmail.co.uk

Entry 93   Map 8

Derbyshire

Alstonefield Manor

Country manor house definitely, but delightfully understated and cleverly designed to look natural. This family home, sitting in walled gardens, is high in the hills above Dovedale. Local girl Jo spoils you with homemade scones and tea when you arrive, served on the lawns or by the fire in the elegant drawing room. Beautiful bedrooms have antiques, flowers, lovely fabrics, painted floors and garden views; wood panelled bathrooms have showers or a roll top tub. Wake to birdsong – and a candlelit breakfast with local bacon and Staffordshire oatcakes. After a great walk, stroll across the village green for supper at The George. A joy.

Minimum stay: 2 nights. Over 12s welcome..

Rooms	1 double; 2 doubles, each with separate bathroom: £110–£150. Singles from £95.
Meals	Pub 100 yds.
Closed	Christmas & occasionally.

Robert & Jo Wood
Alstonefield Manor,
Alstonefield,
Ashbourne, DE6 2FX
Tel   +44 (0)1335 310393
Email   stay@alstonefieldmanor.com
Web   www.alstonefieldmanor.com

Entry 94   Map 8

Derbyshire

Beechenhill Farm

Perched bang in the middle of the Peak District. Sustainable thinking has created this progressive family run, organic farm. Sue, an artist renowned for Swedish folk art, set targets to reduce their carbon footprint – so successfully she now guides others. Feed chickens, watch cows come home for milking, sit in a hot tub or eccentric sauna cave, even get married in a beautifully romantic hall. All is country-cosy, dotted with animal collections, tapestries and local art; views flood bedrooms (the family one has a pocket shower room). Organic breakfasts are a treat, and nippers will love Sue's adventure maps. Unwind and replenish...

Minimum stay: 2 nights. Children over 3 welcome.

Rooms	1 double: £88–£90. 1 family room for 3-4: £88–£130. Singles £52.
Meals	Pubs 2 miles.
Closed	November–March.

Sue Prince
Beechenhill Farm,
Ilam Moor Lane,
Ilam, DE6 2BD

Tel   +44 (0)1335 310274
Email   stay@beechenhill.co.uk
Web   www.beechenhill.co.uk

Entry 95   Map 8

Devon

Annapurna

Rural bliss: the garden of this pretty longhouse surrounded by fields of cows looks down the valley to the steeple of Modbury Church. Carol and Peter spoil you at breakfast with organic home-baked bread and eggs from their happy hens; if you're self-catering in the annexe you can join in or have continental in your own kitchen. Charming bedrooms have a fresh country feel, flowers, sparkling bathrooms and wonderfully comfy beds; the annexe suite has its own sitting room. The views stretch for miles, fabulous walking starts from the door and you are close to the watery delights of Salcombe and Dartmouth. Guests love this place!

Rooms	1 twin/double: £70–£80. Annexe – 1 suite for 3 with sitting room & kitchen: £95–£110. 1 single with separate bath: £35–£40. Self-catering available in the annexe (higher rate includes breakfast for up to 3).
Meals	Pubs/restaurants 1 mile.
Closed	Rarely.

Carol Farrand & Peter Foster
Annapurna,
Mary Cross, Modbury, PL21 0SA

Tel   +44 (0)1548 831299
Mobile   +44 (0)7977 200324
Email   carolfarrand@tiscali.co.uk
Web   www.annapurna-devon.co.uk

Entry 96   Map 2

Devon

Hooppells Torr

Brought up in Argentina, Serena is interesting, warm and friendly. Her home is just where you want to be... a quiet hamlet, a pink Georgian farmhouse with geraniums at the porch. Step in to find a lovely sitting room with squashy white sofas and wood-burner, stunning views over Dartmoor and a big welcoming kitchen; Serena will sit you down with a pot of tea. Bedrooms are large and traditional with a twist: French cane beds, a parasol collection, pots of flowers and understated chic. The garden is dreamy with colourful borders of bee-loving plants, well-stocked kitchen patch, natural spring and spots for sitting. A delight.

Devon

Seaview House

Morning sun pours into the dining room... tuck in to breakfast to the sound of seagulls and classical music. Your host is fun and well-travelled, and this house has heaps of personality: driftwood carvings above an open fire, a charcoal nude, a Rajasthani mirror embroidery hanging, white sofas, polished antiques and French style painted furniture. Your ground floor bedroom has a richly dressed bed, the bathroom a cheery seaside feel. Enjoy views from the living rooms to Bigbury Bay and Thurlestone Rock, walk to great beaches and across the river to Burgh Island; there's a cliff-top golf club and Kingsbridge and Salcombe (full of boats and cafés) are a short drive.

Rooms	1 double with separate bath; 1 double, 1 twin/double sharing bath: £90. Singles £50.
Meals	Pub 5-minute walk.
Closed	Mid-December to January.

Rooms	1 twin/double: £75-£90. Singles £60.
Meals	Pub 0.25 miles.
Closed	Rarely.

Serena Fraser
Hooppells Torr,
Kingston,
Kingsbridge, TQ7 4HA
Tel   +44 (0)1548 811187
Mobile   +44 (0)7982 309604
Email   serenafraser@btinternet.com
Web   www.hooppellstorr.co.uk

J Meredith
Seaview House,
Thurlestone,
Kingsbridge, TQ7 3NE
Mobile   +44 (0)7711 704193
Email   jan.meredith1@gmail.com

Devon

Keynedon Mill

Welcome to an ancient stone mill, and beautiful rooms in the old miller's house. There's a big friendly kitchen with stone floors and a cheerful red Aga, a beamed dining room with a long polished table, a guest sitting room with a wood-burner, and a pretty garden with a stream running through – picnic, read, enjoy a glass of wine in peaceful corners. Elegant bedrooms have superb beds, antique linen curtains, fresh flowers, morning tea trays and decanters of port. A delicious breakfast of home-baked bread and local produce will set you up for the day: walk the coastal path, discover secluded coves.

Over 12s welcome.

Rooms	2 doubles, each with separate bath/shower; 1 twin: £90–£110. 1 family room for 3: £110. Singles £55–£75.
Meals	Pub 0.5 miles.
Closed	Rarely.

Stuart & Jennifer Jebb
Keynedon Mill,
Sherford,
Kingsbridge, TQ7 2AS
Tel +44 (0)1548 531485
Mobile +44 (0)7775 501409
Email bookings@keynedonmill.co.uk
Web www.keynedonmill.co.uk

Entry 99   Map 2

Devon

Stokenham House

Lovely Stokenham House gazes at the sea and the bird-rich Slapton Ley. Iona and Paul – an energetic and thoughtful, imaginative couple – have created a super South Hams base: huge chill-out cushions on the lawn, summerhouse in the pretty banked garden, BBQ by the pool. It's grand yet laid-back, with a fine drawing room, big conservatory and a family-friendly feel. Learn to cook or grow veg, invite friends for dinner, host your own party: Iona is a superb cook. The funky large annexe suite is very private; generous bedrooms in the house are decked in vintage fabrics and papers, and have single rooms off.

Dogs welcome in downstairs room.

Rooms	1 twin/double sharing bath with single: £120. 1 suite for 2: £120. 1 family room for 4 (extra bed/cots available): £120–£210. 1 single: £60. Child over 5 £35. Cots & highchairs available.
Meals	Dinner from £30. Pubs/restaurants 2-minute walk.
Closed	Rarely.

Iona & Paul Jepson
Stokenham House,
Stokenham,
Kingsbridge, TQ7 2ST
Tel +44 (0)1548 581257
Mobile +44 (0)7720 443132
Email ionajepson@googlemail.com
Web www.stokenhamhouse.co.uk

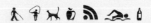

Entry 100   Map 2

Devon

Strete Barton House

Contemporary, friendly, exotic and exquisite: French sleigh beds and Asian art, white basins and black chandeliers, and a garden with sofas for the views. So much to love – and best of all, the coastal path outside the door. Your caring hosts live the dream, running immaculate B&B by the sea, in an old manor house at the top of the village. Breakfasts are exuberantly local (village eggs, sausages from Dartmouth, honey from the bay), there's a wood-burner in the sitting room, warm toasty floors and Kevin and Stuart know exactly which beach, walk or pub is the one for you. Heavenly.

Children over 8 welcome.

Rooms	3 doubles, 1 twin/double; 1 twin/double with separate shower: £105–£145. Cottage – 1 suite for 2 & sitting room: £150–£165.
Meals	Pub/restaurant 50 yds.
Closed	Rarely.

Stuart Litster & Kevin Hooper
Strete Barton House,
Totnes Road, Strete,
Dartmouth, TQ6 0RU
Tel   +44 (0)1803 770364
Email   info@stretebarton.co.uk
Web   www.stretebarton.co.uk

Entry 101   Map 2

Devon

Nonsuch House

The photo says it all! You are in your own crow's nest, perched above the flotillas of yachts zipping in and out of the estuary mouth: stunning. Kit and Penny are great fun and look after you well; ex-hotelier Kit smokes his own fish fresh from the quay and produces brilliant dinners. Further pleasures lie across the water… and a five-minute walk brings you to the ferry that transports you, and your car, to the other side. Breakfasts in the conservatory are a delight, bedrooms are big and comfortable, and fresh bathrooms sparkle.

Minimum stay: 2 nights at weekends. Children over 10 welcome.

Rooms	1 double, 3 twin/doubles: £130–£175. Singles £90–£145.
Meals	Dinner, 3 courses, £37.50 (not Tues/Wed/Sat). Pub/restaurant 5-minute walk & short boat trip.
Closed	Rarely.

Kit & Penny Noble
Nonsuch House,
Church Hill, Kingswear,
Dartmouth, TQ6 0BX
Tel   +44 (0)1803 752829
Email   enquiries@nonsuch-house.co.uk
Web   www.nonsuch-house.co.uk

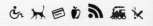

Entry 102   Map 2

Devon

Fingals

Fingals has been with us since our first B&B book. Much loved, it has always been beyond categorisation – and it's been going so long that some of the original guests' grandchildren now take their girlfriends. Richard and Sheila have been moving back into their Queen Anne manor farmhouse and winding down – but as ever doing it their own way. Stay in a best hotel room, or self-cater in rooms nattily converted into apartments. The old laissez-faire atmosphere remains: honesty bar, wood-panelled dining room (dinner on occasion), grass court, pool and gym. Not your run-of-the-mill B&B… but nor are Richard and Sheila.

Minimum stay: 2 nights at weekends.

Rooms	3 doubles: £110–£210.
	1 suite for 2: £300–£700 per week (self-catering).
	1 barn for 5, 1 barn for 6: £400–£1,200 per week (self-catering). Extra bed/sofabed available £15 per person per night.
Meals	Dinner £36.
	Pub 1 mile; restaurants 6 miles.
Closed	Mid-January to mid-March.

Richard & Sheila Johnston
Fingals,
Dittisham,
Dartmouth, TQ6 0JA
Tel   +44 (0)1803 722398
Email   info@fingals.co.uk
Web   www.fingals.co.uk

Devon

Beacon House

Perched above Brixham's bustling harbour (a scamper downhill for the sprightly) is this pretty Victorian villa and immaculate B&B. Here live Amanda, Nigel and Henry the springer spaniel, happily sharing garden, house and views. In 'Bay View' the bed is positioned so that you wake to the sun as it rises above the headland and shimmers across the bay… but every room is special and each gets the view. Torbay vistas compete with delicious breakfasts brought to small tables (Devon haddock; apricots stewed in tea and orange; local honey; Amanda's take on the old favourite, the 'Full Beacon'). Dartmouth is five miles, the coastal path a few steps.

Minimum stay: 3 nights on events weekends & bank holidays.

Rooms	3 doubles, 1 twin/double: £79–£129.
Meals	Pubs/restaurants 5-minute walk.
Closed	Rarely.

Nigel Makin
Beacon House,
Prospect Steps,
South Furzeham Road,
Brixham, TQ5 8JB
Mobile   +44 (0)7768 565656
Email   enquiries@beaconbrixham.co.uk
Web   www.beaconbrixham.co.uk

Devon

Kerswell Farmhouse

Close to Totnes yet out in the wilds, this house and barn sit on a ridge with glorious views to Dartmoor. The Devon longhouse was once in poor repair: you'd never know now! All has been transformed by oak – seasoned and new – while the front sports a gorgeous conservatory. Graham sells British art (on fabulous display), Nichola is an interior designer, together they run truly welcoming B&B. Bedrooms are super-comfortable with electronic slatted blinds, bathrooms are state of the art, and the suite comes with its own slice of garden. Books and DVDs are on tap, local tipples in the honesty bar.

Over 12s welcome.

Rooms	3 doubles: £110–£120.
	Barn – 1 twin/double: £110–£120.
	Barn – 1 suite for 2 with sitting room & private garden: £140.
	Singles available from £82.50–£105 per night.
Meals	Restaurants 2 miles.
Closed	22 December – 6 January.

Graham & Nichola Hawkins
Kerswell Farmhouse,
Kerswell,
Cornworthy,
Totnes, TQ9 7HH
Tel   +44 (0)1803 732013
Email   gjnhawkins@rocketmail.com
Web   www.kerswellfarmhouse.co.uk

Entry 105   Map 2

Devon

New Entry

Brooking

A whitewashed, wisteria-clad house in a gorgeous village… tea and cake will be waiting. Alison's is a relaxed and friendly home. You will sleep well in a peaceful, charming bedroom: luxurious linen on a brass bed, floral cushions, a jug of wild flowers on an antique wooden chest. Alison's breakfasts change with the seasons: homemade granola, jams and bread, fruit compotes and tasty cooked choices. The garden is walled, rambling and pretty with a tangle of climbers, a bright wooden summerhouse and places to sit in the sun. Head out for nearby Totnes (bustling and arty), great wood or moorland walks and fun on the river Dart.

Travel cot, high chair, toys and books in house! Babysitting happily available if needed.

Rooms	1 double: £80–£90. Extra room available (let to same party only).
Meals	Soup, bread & local cheeses (price on request).
	Children's meals available by arrangement.
	Pubs 2-minute walk.
Closed	Rarely.

Alison Carlyon
Brooking,
Ashprington,
Totnes, TQ9 7UL
Tel   +44 (0)1803 731037
Email   w.carlyon@btinternet.com

Entry 106   Map 2

Devon

Riverside House

The loveliest 18th-century house with the tidal river estuary bobbing past with boats and birds; dip your toes in the water while sitting in the garden. Felicity, an artist, and Roger, a passionate sailor, give you pretty bedrooms with paintings, poetry, little balconies, wide French windows and binoculars; spot swans at high tide, herons (perhaps a kingfisher) when the river goes down. Stroll to the pub for quayside barbecues and jazz in summer; catch the ferry from Dittisham to Agatha Christie's house; discover delightful Dartmouth. Kayaks and inflatables are welcome by arrangement.

Minimum stay: 2 nights at weekends.

Rooms	1 double; 1 double with separate shower: £80–£100. Singles £75. Extra bed/sofabed available £30 per person per night.
Meals	Pubs 100 yds.
Closed	Rarely.

Felicity & Roger Jobson
Riverside House,
Tuckenhay,
Totnes, TQ9 7EQ

Tel	+44 (0)1803 732837
Mobile	+44 (0)7710 510007
Email	felicity.riverside@hotmail.co.uk
Web	www.riverside-house.co.uk

Entry 107   Map 2

Devon

Avenue Cottage

The tree-lined approach is steep and spectacular; the cottage sits in 11 wondrous acres of rhododendron, magnolia and wild flowers with a lily-strewn pond, grassy paths and lovely views over the river. Find a quiet spot in which to read or simply sit and absorb the tranquillity. Richard is a gifted gardener, and the archetypal gardener's modesty and calm have penetrated the house itself — it is uncluttered, comfortable and warmed by a log fire. The old-fashioned twin room has a big bathroom with a walk-in shower and a balcony with sweeping valley views; the pretty village and pub are a short walk away.

Rooms	1 twin/double; 1 double sharing shower room with owner: £70–£90. Singles £55–£75.
Meals	Pub 0.25 miles.
Closed	Rarely.

Richard Pitts & David Sykes
Avenue Cottage,
Ashprington,
Totnes, TQ9 7UT

Tel	+44 (0)1803 732769
Mobile	+44 (0)7719 147475
Email	richard.pitts@btinternet.com
Web	www.avenuecottage.com

Entry 108   Map 2

Devon

Kilbury Manor

You can stroll down to the Dart from the garden and onto their little island, when the river's not in spate! Back at the Manor – a listed longhouse from the 1700s – are four super-comfortable bedrooms, the most private in the stone barn. Your genuinely welcoming hosts (with dogs Dillon and Buster) moved to Devon to renovate this big handsome house and open it to guests. Julia does everything beautifully so there's organic smoked salmon and delicious French toast for breakfast, baskets of toiletries by the bath, the best linen on the best beds and a drying room for wet gear – handy if you've come to walk the Moor. Spot-on B&B.

Rooms	1 double; 1 double with separate bath: £79–£95. Barn – 2 doubles: £79–£95. Singles from £65.
Meals	Pubs/restaurants 1.5–4 miles.
Closed	Rarely.

Julia & Martin Blundell
Kilbury Manor,
Colston Road,
Buckfastleigh, TQ11 0LN
Tel   +44 (0)1364 644079
Email   info@kilburymanor.co.uk
Web   www.kilburymanor.co.uk

Entry 109   Map 2

Devon

Mitchelcroft

Saunter down mown paths through meadow grass... The wooden verandah has pots of flowers, the pond attracts dragonflies and the magnificent garden is full of wildlife. Michael has done some stylish redesigning of this 1960s bungalow – and he and Deborah have created a friendly home. Bedrooms come with king-size beds, good linen, an abundance of flowers and personal touches; each has its own outside spot – sleep out on the terrace if you fancy some stargazing! Marvel at panoramic views while you tuck into a breakfast of fruits, cereals, nuts and the full works. Dartmoor National Park beckons, and it's a five-minute walk to a good pub.

Over 14s welcome.

Rooms	3 doubles: £80–£110. Singles £60.
Meals	Light supper from £5.50. Pub 5-minute walk. Hosted weekends with dinner & guided walking/cycling tours (min. 6).
Closed	Christmas.

Deborah Owen
Mitchelcroft,
Scoriton, Buckfastleigh, TQ11 0HU
Tel   +44 (0)1364 631336
Mobile   +44 (0)7841 342070
Email   mitchelcroft@hotmail.co.uk
Web   www.mitchelcroft.co.uk

Entry 110   Map 2

Devon

Penpark

Clough Williams-Ellis of Portmeirion fame did more than design an elegant house; he made sure it communed with nature. High on a hill overlooking the valley, light pours in to this lovely house from every window, and the views stretch across rolling farmland to Dartmoor and Hay Tor. One bedroom has a comfy sofa and its own balcony; the spacious private suite has arched French windows to gardens, pretty woodland beyond, and an extra room for young children. All is traditional and comforting: antiques, heirlooms, African carvings, silk and fresh flowers, richly coloured rugs. Your charming, generous hosts look after you well.

Rooms	2 twin/doubles, each with separate bath/shower: £76-£114. 1 family suite for 4 with separate shower (ground floor garden room, dogs welcome): £76-£114. Singles by arrangement.
Meals	Pubs/restaurants 3 miles.
Closed	Rarely.

	Madeleine & Michael Gregson Penpark, Bickington, Ashburton, TQ12 6LH
Tel	+44 (0)1626 821314
Email	maddy@penpark.co.uk
Web	www.penpark.co.uk

Entry 111 Map 2

Devon

Corndonford Farm

An ancient Devon longhouse and an engagingly chaotic haven run by warm and friendly Ann and Will, along with their Dartmoor ponies. Steep, stone circular stairs lead to bedrooms: bright colours, a four-poster with lacy curtains, gorgeous views over the cottage garden and a bathroom with a beam to duck. A place for those who want to get into the spirit of it all — maybe help catch an escaped foal, chatter to the farm workers around the table; not for fussy types or Mr and Mrs Tickety Boo! Delicious Aga breakfasts and good for walkers too — the Two Moors Way is on the doorstep.

Under 10s by arrangement.

Rooms	1 twin with separate bathroom; 1 four-poster: £80. Singles £40.
Meals	Pub 2 miles.
Closed	Rarely.

	Ann & Will Williams Corndonford Farm, Poundsgate, Newton Abbot, IQ13 7PP
Tel	+44 (0)1364 631595
Email	corndonford@btinternet.com

Entry 112 Map 2

Devon

South Harton Farm

High above the Wray valley in the Dartmoor National Park, and up the narrowest of lanes, sits this ancient immaculately restored farm with granite barns topped with thatch or slate. One barn is now a stylish cottage; the first-floor living/kitchen area is open-plan and uncluttered: pale stone walls, beams, modern pieces and a central wood-burner. Downstairs: a serene bedroom with a super soft bed. A tasty breakfast hamper is delivered at a time to suit you: bacon rolls or pancakes with maple syrup, juice, a pot of coffee. There's a garden, a timeless village pub and you can walk up to The Cleave for a spectacular 360° panorama. We loved it.

Minimum stay: 2 nights at weekends.

Rooms	1 cottage for 2 with sitting room & kitchen: £100–£125. Singles £90.
Meals	Breakfast hamper included, delivered to the cottage each morning. Dinner, 2-3 courses, £20–£30 (including carafe of wine, on request). Pubs/restaurants 2 miles.
Closed	Rarely.

	Bruce & Irene Gibson South Harton Farm, Lustleigh, Newton Abbot, TQ13 9SG
Tel	+44 (0)1647 277216
Mobile	+44 (0)7584 322523
Email	brgibson@btinternet.com

Entry 113   Map 2

Devon

Cyprian's Cot

A charming 16th-century terraced cottage filled with beams and burnished wood. The old stone fireplace is huge, the grandfather clock ticks, the views are stunning and Shelagh is warm and welcoming. Guests have their own sitting room with a crackling fire; up the narrow stairs and into cosy bedrooms – a small double and a tiny twin. Tasty breakfasts, served in the dining room, include free-range eggs, sausages and bacon from the local farm and garden fruits. Discover the lovely town with its pubs, fine restaurant and interesting shops. With the Dartmoor Way and the Two Moors Way on the doorstep, the walking is wonderful too.

Rooms	1 twin; 1 double with separate bath: £65–£75. Singles £32–£35.
Meals	Pubs/restaurants 4-minute walk.
Closed	Rarely.

	Shelagh Weeden Cyprian's Cot, 47 New Street, Chagford, Newton Abbot, TQ13 8BB
Tel	+44 (0)1647 432256
Email	shelaghweeden@btinternet.com
Web	www.cyprianscot.co.uk

Entry 114   Map 2

Devon

Devon

Rose Cottage

On a quiet country road on the edge of Peter Tavy is a pretty slate-hung cottage and a garden full of birds: Pippin's delight. Enter to find a dining room with a shining wooden floor, a fine Georgian table and a smart Aga to keep things cosy. Bedrooms are sunny; 'Blue Room' and 'Rose Room' have lovely fabrics, watercolours, luxuriously comfy king-size beds and TVs; the sweet twin shares a bathroom with 'Rose' so is perfect for families. After a generous breakfast, pull on your boots and stride onto Dartmoor — or visit Pippin's favourite gardens. Then it's home to a delicious dinner — and hot water bottles on chilly nights.

Minimum stay: 2 nights at weekends. Babes in arms and children over 8 welcome.

Wonwood Barton

A Thomas Hardy feel here… with stone barns wrapping around a pretty courtyard. In the middle is the Roundhouse, where you have breakfast — huge table, toasty stove and a bar in the corner. The three independent ground floor suites each have a wood-burner and sweet seating area, old beams and high ceilings, painted furniture and jaunty cushions; views stretch across the Tamar and beyond to Cornwall. Claudine and Bill (and their labradors) are charming and look after you well. Tamar Valley is stunning and so unspoilt; head off for walks, cycling, canoeing and good gardens. Return to snuggle by your fire — dinner can be made for you too.

Minimum stay: 2 nights at weekends & in high season.

Rooms	Blue Room – 1 double with separate bathroom: £70–£75. Rose Room – 1 double with separate bathroom (can form a family suite for 4 with an interconnecting twin): £70–£105. Singles £40.
Meals	Dinner, 2 courses, £20. Pubs/restaurants 0.5 miles.
Closed	Christmas.

Rooms	The Coach House – 1 double: £70–£90. The Cottage – 1 double: £70–£90. Swallow Barn – 1 twin/double: £70–£90.
Meals	Dinner, 2-3 courses, £15–£20. Pubs/restaurants 1 mile.
Closed	Rarely.

	Pippin Clarke
	Rose Cottage,
	Peter Tavey,
	Tavistock, PL19 9NP
Tel	+44 (0)1822 810500
Email	rose.pippin@gmail.com
Web	www.rosecottagedartmoor.co.uk/

	Claudine & Bill Sparks
	Wonwood Barton,
	Lamerton, Tavistock, PL19 8SE
Tel	+44 (0)1822 870533
Mobile	+44 (0)7970 128229
Email	booking.wonwood@gmail.com
Web	www.wonwoodbarton.com

Devon

Burnville House

Granite gateposts, Georgian house, rhododendrons, beechwoods and rolling fields of sheep: that's the setting. But there's more. Beautifully proportioned rooms reveal subtle colours, elegant antiques, squishy sofas and bucolic views, stylish bathrooms are sprinkled with candles, there are sumptuous dinners and pancakes at breakfast. Your hosts left busy jobs in London to settle here, and their place breathes life – space, smiles, energy. Swim, play tennis, walk to Dartmoor from the door, take a trip to Eden or the sea. Or... just gaze at the moors and the church on the Tor and listen to the silence, and the sheep.

Devon

New Entry

Langdale Farm

Victoria loves having people to stay, Cross the stream, then bump up the steep track to arrive at her friendly, whitewashed, slate-roofed farmhouse. It's a home full of art and quirky touches; the guest sitting room has a toasty wood-burner and gorgeous views; the big pretty bedrooms, up your own stairs, have sink-into linen, a posy of primroses, small bathrooms (mind your head here and there!) and chocs in a little basket. Wake to breakfast in the sun – inside or out on a terrace – fruits and yogurt, a tasty full English from the Aga, a pain au chocolat or two. Explore acres of fields and woodland, head off into Dartmoor National Park.

Rooms	3 doubles: £85–£95. Singles £65.
Meals	Dinner from £23. Pub 2 miles.
Closed	Rarely.

Rooms	1 double; 1 double with separate bath (let to same party only): £80. Singles £65.
Meals	Pubs 5 miles.
Closed	Rarely.

Victoria Cunningham
Burnville House,
Brentor,
Tavistock, PL19 0NE
Tel   +44 (0)1822 820443
Mobile   +44 (0)7881 583471
Email   burnvillef@aol.com
Web   www.burnville.co.uk

Victoria Machin
Langdale Farm,
Dunsford,
Exeter, EX6 7BQ
Tel   +44 (0)1392 811323
Email   victoriamachin@btinternet.com
Web   www.langdalefarm.co.uk

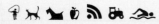

Entry 117   Map 2

Entry 118   Map 2

Devon

Brook Farmhouse

Tuck yourself up in the peace and quiet of Paul and Penny's whitewashed, thatched cottage, surrounded by glorious countryside. Inside find your own charming sitting room with a huge inglenook, good antiques, fresh flowers, and comfy sofa and chairs; breakfast here on homemade apple juice, eggs from the owners' hens and delicious local bacon and sausages. Up the ancient spiral stone stairs is your warm, beamed bedroom with smooth linen, chintzy curtains, lots of cushions. You are near Dartmoor and can reach Devon beaches and the north Cornish coast; perfect for hearty walkers, birdwatchers, surfers and picnic-lovers.

Rooms	1 double with separate bathroom: £80-£85. Singles £55-£65.
Meals	Pub 2 miles.
Closed	Rarely.

Paul & Penny Steadman
Brook Farmhouse,
Tedburn St Mary,
Exeter, EX6 6DS
Tel   +44 (0)1647 270042
Email   penny.steadman@btconnect.com
Web   www.brook-farmhouse.co.uk

Entry 119   Map 2

Devon

Coombe Farmhouse

Old and new blend perfectly here in this 400-year-old whitewashed farmhouse. Fenella and Simon's friendly thatched home is filled with books, beams and wonky stairs, polished wood and contemporary art. Your own private entrance opens into a guest sitting room with two cottagey bedrooms up above. Food is good! For breakfast, maybe pancakes or an egg, bacon, sausage extravaganza, with organic juice from garden apples and homemade soda bread. Supper starts with drinks and canapés by the log-burner. Cycle rides, walks, Dartmoor and arty Totnes are all on tap; children will love the Breeze hut – Pete and Dazzle the ponies too.

Children over 8 welcome.

Rooms	1 double; 1 twin with separate shower: £75-£90. Singles £60-£65.
Meals	Dinner £35. BYO. Pubs/restaurants 20-minute walk.
Closed	Rarely.

Fenella Hughes
Coombe Farmhouse,
Higher Ashton,
Exeter, EX6 7QS
Tel   +44 (0)1647 253434
Mobile   +44 (0)7557 307571
Email   fenellahughes@hotmail.co.uk

Entry 120   Map 2

Devon

Hannaford House

An inviting house with fabulous views across the valley to Haldon Forest. Kay and Simon give you your own comfy sitting room with wood-burner, bookcases stuffed with books and hare-inspired art and sculpture. Upstairs to a cosy bedroom: soft linen on a pretty iron bed, heaps of fluffy towels, lovely big shower. Breakfast includes lots of home-grown produce: sausage and bacon from the pigs, eggs from the hens, tomatoes in season, tasty home-baked bread and homemade jams. There are hammocks in the colourful garden in summer, the woods to explore, Exmouth estuary for boating fun and Dartmoor for hearty walks.

Rooms	1 double: £80–£100.
Meals	Pub 1.5 miles.
Closed	Rarely.

Kay & Simon Wisker
Hannaford House,
Kennford,
Exeter, EX6 7XZ
Tel +44 (0)1392 833577
Email kay@hannafordhouse.co.uk
Web www.hannafordhouse.co.uk

Entry 121   Map 2

Devon

Larkbeare Grange

Expectations rise as you follow the tree-lined drive to the immaculate Georgian house… to be warmly greeted with homemade cakes. The upkeep is perfect, the feel is chic and the whole place exudes well-being. Sparkling sash windows fill big rooms with light, floors shine and the grandfather clock ticks away the hours. Expect the best: good lighting, goose down duvets, luxurious fabrics and fittings, a fabulous suite for a small family, flexible (and delicious) breakfasts and lovely views from the bedrooms at the front. Charlie, Savoy-trained, and Julia are charming and fun and there are bikes to borrow. Exceptional B&B!

Rooms	2 doubles, 1 twin/double: £110–£140.
	1 suite for 4: £170–£195.
	Singles £85–£120.
Meals	Pub 1.5 miles.
Closed	Rarely.

Charlie & Julia Hutchings
Larkbeare Grange,
Larkbeare, Talaton, Exeter, EX5 2RY
Tel +44 (0)1404 822069
Mobile +44 (0)7762 574915
Email stay@larkbeare.net
Web www.larkbeare.net

Entry 122   Map 2

Devon

Lower Allercombe Farm

Horses in the paddock and no-frills bedrooms at this down-to-earth, friendly B&B. Susie, a retired eventer, lives at one end of the listed longhouse; a scented red rose rambles up one wall, and you step in to a sunny kitchen with a cat snoozing behind the Aga. There's a sitting room with horsey pictures and wood-burner, and bedrooms that reflect the fair price. You'll feast on home-grown fruit compote with Greek yogurt, homemade bread, garden tomatoes, home-laid eggs, honey from Susie's neighbour, rashers from local award-winning pigs. Handy for Exeter, the south coast and Dartmoor; the airport is ten minutes away, the A30 one mile.

Rooms	1 double;
	1 double with separate bath,
	1 twin: £60–£80.
	Singles £50.
Meals	Pub/restaurant 2 miles.
Closed	Rarely.

	Susie Holroyd
	Lower Allercombe Farm,
	Rockbeare, Exeter, EX5 2HD
Tel	+44 (0)1404 822519
Mobile	+44 (0)7980 255107
Email	holroyd.s@gmail.com
Web	www.lowerallercombefarm.co.uk

Entry 123   Map 2

Devon

The Dairy Loft

The lovely East Devon Way brings you almost to the door of this smart, new B&B for the independent-minded. Up the exterior stair is your bright, refreshingly opinionated room with its clever corner kitchen and double-headed shower room. The funky red leather sofa and big bed (or twins) opposite French windows invite lazing, star-gazing, Merlin-spotting. You're free to concoct your own lavish breakfast and eat beneath the Italian lamp. Oak-floored inside, larch clad out and with kind, interesting owners across the flowered yard who'll advise on all things local, from sea and river fishing to Exe Trail cycling. Great!

Minimum stay: 2 nights. Single night stays considered. Pets by arrangement. Arrive after 3pm and leave before 10am please.

Rooms	1 twin/double: £120.
	Stays of 2+ nights £80–£100.
Meals	Pubs/restaurants 2 miles.
Closed	Rarely.

	Rob & Annie Jones
	The Dairy Loft,
	Valley Barn, Hawkerland, Colaton
	Raleigh, Sidmouth, EX10 0JA
Tel	+44 (0)1395 568411
Email	robertjones@eclipse.co.uk
Web	www.thedairyloft.co.uk

Entry 124   Map 2

Devon

Glebe House

Set on a hillside with fabulous views over the Coly valley, this late-Georgian vicarage is now a heart-warming B&B. The views will entice you, the hosts will delight you and the house is filled with interesting things. Chuck and Emma spent many years at sea – he a Master Mariner, she a chef – and have filled these big light rooms with cushions, kilims and treasured family pieces. There's a sitting room for guests, a lovely conservatory with vintage vine, peaceful bedrooms with blissful views and bathrooms that sparkle. All this, two sweet pygmy goats, wildlife beyond the ha-ha and the fabulous coast a hike away.

Minimum stay: 2 nights July & August weekends & bank holidays.

Rooms	1 double, 1 twin/double: £80. 1 family room for 4: £80–£110. Singles £50.
Meals	Dinner, 3 courses, £25. Pubs/restaurants 2.5 miles.
Closed	Christmas & New Year.

	Emma & Chuck Guest Glebe House, Southleigh, Colyton, EX24 6SD
Tel	+44 (0)1404 871276
Mobile	+44 (0)7867 568569
Email	emma_guest@talktalk.net
Web	www.guestsatglebe.co.uk

Entry 125　Map 2

Devon

West Colwell Farm

Devon lanes, pheasants, bluebell walks *and* sparkling B&B. The Hayes clearly love what they do; ex-TV producers, they have converted this 18th-century farmhouse and barns into a snug and stylish place to stay. Be charmed by original beams and pine doors, heritage colours and clean lines. Bedrooms are very private and luxurious, two have terraces overlooking the wooded valley and the most cosy is tucked under the roof. Linen is tip-top, showers are huge and breakfasts (Frank's pancakes, lovely bacon, eggs from next door) are totally flexible. A welcoming glass of wine, starry night skies, beaches nearby, peace all around. Bliss.

Rooms	3 doubles: £105. Singles £85.
Meals	Restaurants 3 miles.
Closed	1 December – 28 February.

	Frank & Carol Hayes West Colwell Farm, Offwell, Honiton, EX14 9SL
Tel	+44 (0)1404 831130
Email	stay@westcolwell.co.uk
Web	www.westcolwell.co.uk

Entry 126　Map 2

Devon

Barton View

The feel is contemporary with a hint of brocante and breakfast is… whenever! There's a happy self-catering twist to this bright B&B. As well as a pretty bedroom and shower room, you've a sitting room — sofa and leather chair by the log-burner — and a kitchen area stocked with good homemade and local breakfast choices and all the kit for you to rustle it up. The Magranes, in the adjoining house, are relaxed and on hand to pop in. Views are of 15th-century Shute Barton and richly rolling AONB countryside. Train and bike here, walk along the Jurassic Coast from Beer to Branscombe, be a birder — and try the many good eateries in the area.

Minimum stay: 2 nights.

Rooms	Apartment – 1 double with sitting room & kitchen area (child's bed available): £95. Reduced rates for stays longer than 2 nights. Book 4 nights & get a 5th for free.
Meals	Pub 30-minute walk.
Closed	Rarely.

Paddy & Di Magrane
Barton View,
Shute,
Axminster, EX13 7QR
Tel   +44 (0)1297 35197
Email   paddymagrane@onetel.com
Web   www.bartonview.co.uk

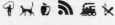

Devon

The Stables

Herb garden, veg patch, forests and a wild swimming lake… head down the track to this organic farm and education centre — an inspirational place. You stay in their eco converted stables — solar panels, natural spring water, timbers from the land. Bedrooms are simple and white, the living area is big with high rafters, long communal table and a seating area. Breakfast is laissez-faire (brought over to you or ingredients provided) and all is homemade, home-grown and seasonal. Lots to do too: a wooden yoga stage for early bird sessions, natural remedy courses, a zip-wire (book well in advance)… and walks galore.

Rooms	2 twin/doubles; 1 twin/double with separate bath: £100. Singles £55.
Meals	Pubs/restaurants 1-3 miles.
Closed	Rarely.

Zoe Haigh
The Stables,
Trill Farm, Musbury,
Axminster, EX13 8TU
Tel   +44 (0)1297 631113
Email   zoe@trillfarm.co.uk
Web   www.trillfarm.co.uk

Devon

Applebarn Cottage

A tree-lined drive leads to a long white wall, and a gate opening to an explosion of colour – the garden. Come for a deliciously restful place and the nicest, most easy-going hosts; the wisteria-covered 17th-century cottage is full of books, paintings and fresh flowers. Bedrooms – one in an extension that blends in beautifully – are large, traditional, wonderfully comfortable, and the views down the valley are sublime. Patricia trained as a chef and dinners at Applebarn are delicious and great fun. Breakfast, served in a lovely oak-floored dining room, includes honey from the neighbour's bees.

Minimum stay: 2 nights.

Rooms	2 suites for 2: £78–£83. Dinner, B&B option (dinner & aperitif) £41.50–£67 p.p.
Meals	Dinner, 3 courses with aperitif, £28.
Closed	November to mid-March.

Patricia & Robert Spencer
Applebarn Cottage,
Bewley Down,
Axminster, EX13 7JX
Tel   +44 (0)1460 220873
Email   paspenceruk@yahoo.co.uk
Web   www.applebarn.wordpress.com

Entry 129   Map 2

Devon

Pounds Farm

A flock of white geese trot across the field, the cottage garden is a summer-blooming feast of colour and the Blackdown Hills are the green backdrop. Inside is just as good: polished wood, original lithographs, oil paintings, comfy seats by the fire, airy bedrooms in apple-pie order and freshly picked flowers in every room. Enjoy the pool, wander the gorgeous gardens, chat to Georgia the spaniel and Molly the horse, have breakfast (free-range and delicious) outside in the sun – Diana wants you to feel at home. Exmoor is close and you can wander down the hill for a pint in the local. A friendly house with a timeless charm.

Rooms	1 double; 1 double with separate bath: £60–£70.
Meals	Pubs/restaurants 10-minute walk.
Closed	Rarely.

Diana Elliott
Pounds Farm,
Hemyock,
Cullompton, EX15 3QS
Tel   +44 (0)1823 680802
Email   diana@poundsfarm.co.uk
Web   www.poundsfarm.co.uk

Entry 130   Map 2

Devon

The Linhay

Your own peaceful hideaway. The open valley has a running stream, views are of orchard, friendly sheep and a bright yellow vintage tractor. Andrei and Holly live in the main house, and they've created a quirky, natural feel in the lovely old barn: jaunty red rocking chairs by a wood-burner, art, flowers; up spiral steps to a colourfully clad bed in the eaves, down to a little kitchen area. They bring over a cooked breakfast: home-laid eggs, sausages from the pigs; help yourself to organic muesli, artisan bread, homemade jams – out on the balcony if you want. Borrow wellies and maps, return from Dartmoor to a great value supper. Bliss.

Arrival after 3pm, departure by 12 noon if possible. With a bit of notice can collect guests from the local stations.

Rooms	The Linhay Annexe – 1 suite for 2 with kitchenette: £85.
Meals	Dinner, 2 courses, £10 per person. Pubs/restaurants 3 miles.
Closed	Rarely.

	Holly Carter & Andrei Szerard
	The Linhay,
	Brendon Cottage, Copplestone,
	Crediton, EX17 5NZ
Tel	+44 (0)1363 84386
Email	hescarter@gmail.com
Web	www.smilingsheep.co.uk

Entry 131   Map 2

Devon

Sannacott

On the southern fringes of Exmoor you're in peaceful rolling hills, hidden valleys and a Designated Dark Sky area. The Trickeys breed horses from their Georgian style farmhouse; find roaring log fires, antiques, pretty fabrics, fresh flowers and a relaxed feel. Bedrooms are traditional and comfortable (one in an annexe), some with views over the garden and countryside. Generous breakfasts include homemade bread and jams and organic or local goodies. There's a pretty bird-filled garden to wander, walkers can enjoy the North Devon coastal path, birdwatchers and riders will be happy and there are well-known gardens to visit.

Pets by arrangement. Stabling available and arrangements can be made for riding to West Liscombe B&B.

Rooms	1 double, 1 twin/double sharing bath/shower (let to same party only); Annexe – 1 twin with kitchenette: £80. Singles £45.
Meals	Occasional dinner, 3 courses, £25. Pub 2.5 miles.
Closed	Rarely.

	Clare Trickey
	Sannacott,
	North Molton, EX36 3JS
Tel	+44 (0)1598 740203
Email	mct@sannacott.co.uk
Web	www.sannacott.co.uk

Entry 132   Map 2

Devon

Tabor Hill Farm

From nearly 1,000-feet up the moorland views roll away to the south and down to the church spire in the village. Bring walking boots, perhaps even your horse, and enjoy being well away from it all in this beautiful Exmoor National Park spot. Smart rooms come with super-comfortable Hypnos beds, new oak floors and a stylish country feel; bathrooms are modern and spotless. A woodburner warms the dining room and you may tinkle the Bechstein if you wish as sociable Astley fries eggs from her own hens. There are trails to walk, romantic Exmoor to explore, a wildlife hide and the clearest night skies. Wonderful.

Over 14s welcome. Pets by arrangement.

Rooms	1 double, 1 twin: £90.
	Singles £55.
Meals	Dinner £20.
	Pubs/restaurants 2-6 miles.
Closed	Rarely.

Astley Shilton Barlow
Tabor Hill Farm,
Heasley Mill,
South Molton, EX36 3LQ
Tel   +44 (0)1598 740528
Email   taborhillfarm@btinternet.com
Web   www.taborhillfarm.co.uk

Devon

North Walk House

Sea views, brass bedsteads and big rooms at this calm retreat, perfectly positioned on a cliff-top path – super for walkers and foodies. Ian and Sarah welcome you with homemade cake in a cosy guest lounge, and give you light bedrooms with sparkling bathrooms and seductive beds. Enjoy the coastal and Exmoor walks, or genteel Lynton and Lynmouth; return to log fire and armchairs. Take your tea on a sea-view terrace, or be tempted by Sarah's four-course dinner, seasonal and mostly organic. Everything here has been carefully thought out, from the welcome to the décor and the refreshments: arrive, unpack, unwind…

Rooms	4 doubles, 1 twin: £86-£162.
	Singles £50-£100.
Meals	Dinner, 4 courses, from £27.
	Pub/restaurant 0.25 miles.
Closed	Rarely.

Ian & Sarah Downing
North Walk House,
North Walk,
Lynton, EX35 6HJ
Tel   +44 (0)1598 753372
Email   walk@northwalkhouse.co.uk
Web   www.northwalkhouse.co.uk

Devon

Victoria House

Beachcombers, surfers and walkers will be in their element here. You stay in the beach-hut annexe with a big romantic deck facing the sea; complete with funky daybed and a magnificent view. The owners live next door in the Edwardian seaside villa: Heather is lively and fun; she and David are ex-RAF. They go out of their way to give you the best tour de force breakfasts – fruits, yogurts, waffles, eggs Benedict or the full Monty. Sip a sundowner on the deck or stir yourself to go further; you are on the coastal road to Woolacombe (of surfing and kite-surfing fame) and the beach is a ten-minute walk. A top spot for couples.

Check-in 4pm-9pm, unless arranged. Special diets catered for.

Rooms	1 double: £100-£115. Singles £70-£80.
Meals	Pubs/restaurants 200 yds.
Closed	Rarely.

	Heather & David Burke Victoria House, Chapel Hill, Mortehoe, Woolacombe, EX34 7DZ
Tel	+44 (0)1271 871302
Email	heatherburke59@fsmail.net
Web	www.victoriahousebandb.co.uk

Entry 135   Map 2

Devon

Beachborough Country House

Welcome to this gracious 18th-century rectory with stone-flagged floors, lofty windows, wooden shutters and glorious rugs. Viviane is vivacious and spoils you with dinners and breakfasts from the Aga; dine in the elegant dining room before a twinkling fire. Hens cluck, horses whinny but otherwise the peace is deep. Ease any walker's pains away in a steaming roll top tub; lap up country views from big airy bedrooms. There's a games room for kids in the outbuildings and a stream winds through the garden – a delicious three acres of vegetables and roses. Huge fun.

Rooms	2 doubles, 1 twin/double (extra single bed): £80-£90. Singles £60. Extra bed/sofabed available £10-£20 per person per night.
Meals	Dinner, 2-3 courses, £20-£25. Catering for house parties. Pub 3 miles.
Closed	Rarely.

	Viviane Clout Beachborough Country House, Kentisbury, Barnstaple, EX31 4NH
Tel	+44 (0)1271 882487
Mobile	+44 (0)7732 947755
Email	viviane@beachboroughcountryhouse.co.uk
Web	www.beachboroughcountryhouse.co.uk

Entry 136   Map 2

Devon

Hollamoor Farm

If it's a civilised retreat you're after then head to where the Taw and Torridge meet… to Tarka country, and this rambling 300-year-old farm. Roses ramble, swallows swoop and there are 500 acres to explore. One bedroom is in a barn next to the house and combines stone rusticity and country house grandeur with aplomb; the soft furnishings are exquisite. The bedroom in the house is equally plush and both have fun bathrooms. There's a huge fireplace in the dining room and a well-loved sitting room where you can meet the Wreys (past and present). A real family home where the door is always open – elegant informality at its very best.

Rooms	1 twin/double with separate bath; Barn – 1 twin/double: £90. Singles £45.
Meals	Dinner, 3 courses, £35. Pubs/restaurants 3 miles.
Closed	Rarely.

Sir George & Lady Caroline Wrey
Hollamoor Farm,
Tawstock,
Barnstaple, EX31 3NY
Tel   +44 (0)1271 373466
Mobile   +44 (0)7766 700904
Email   carolinewrey@gmail.com

Entry 137   Map 2

Devon

South Yeo

Down windy lanes with tall grassy banks and the smell of the sea is a lovely Georgian country house with two walled gardens and barns at the back. You'll fall for this place the moment you arrive, and its owners: Jo runs an interiors business; Mike keeps the cattle and sheep that graze all around. Bedrooms are inviting; the double, overlooking the valley, has a cream French bed, a pretty quilted cover, a claw-foot bath and a little sitting room (adjoining) with TV. There's an elegant drawing room with a real fire too. Delicious breakfasts with home-laid eggs and homemade jams are brought to a snug room that catches the morning sun.

Rooms	1 double with sitting room; 1 twin/double with separate bath: £85–£105. Singles £75.
Meals	Pub 1.5 miles.
Closed	Rarely.

Joanne Wade
South Yeo,
Yeo Vale, Bideford, EX39 5ES
Tel   +44 (0)1237 451218
Mobile   +44 (0)7766 201191
Email   stay@southyeo.com
Web   www.southyeo.com

Entry 138   Map 2

Devon

Beara Farmhouse

The moment you arrive at the whitewashed farmhouse you feel the affection your hosts have for their home and gardens. Richard is a lover of wood and a fine craftsman – every room echoes his talent; he also created the pond that's home to mallards and geese. Ann has laid brick paths, stencilled, stitched and painted, all with an eye for colour; bedrooms and guest sitting room are delectable and snug. Open farmland all around, sheep, hens in the yard, the Tarka Trail on your doorstep and hosts happy to give you 6.30am breakfast should you plan a day on Lundy Island. Guests love this place.

Minimum stay: 2 nights at weekends, bank holidays & June-September.

Rooms	1 double, 1 twin: £80.
	Singles by arrangement.
Meals	Pub 1.5 miles.
Closed	20 December – 5 January.

Ann & Richard Dorsett
Beara Farmhouse,
Buckland Brewer,
Bideford, EX39 5EH
Tel   +44 (0)1237 451666
Web   www.bearafarmhouse.co.uk

Entry 139   Map 2

Devon

Leworthy Barton

Biscuits, scones, sweet vases of hedgerow flowers. Breakfasts are left for you to cook and come courtesy of Rupert's Tamworth pigs and happy hens; bread and jams are homemade, wellies and waxed jackets are on tap. Rupert is a busy farmer and designer who chooses to give guests what he would most like himself. So… you have the whole of the stables, tranquil, beautifully restored and with field and sky views. Downstairs is open-plan, with kitchen and log-burner; up are sloping ceilings, wooden floors, big bed, soft towels. It's cosy yet spacious, stylish yet homely, and the Atlantic coast is the shortest drive.

Rooms	Barn – 1 double with sitting room
	& kitchen: £80-£100.
	Singles £60.
Meals	Pub 3 miles.
Closed	Rarely.

Rupert Ashmore
Leworthy Barton,
Woolsery,
Bideford, EX39 5PY
Tel   +44 (0)1237 431140

Entry 140   Map 2

Dorset

Arty BnB By the Sea

Hugh & Candida – busy, travelled artists and environmentalists – make this place very special. You'll be at ease in a blink if you go for easy-going, arty, ramshackling in places, inspiring in others. Revel in the creativity of it all, from Hugh's bold paintings and wallpaper to great homemade bread and jam. You share the dining room, the lawn and veranda (with a nod to Cape Cod), looking sideways to the sea and Golden Cap, and could help in the veg garden. Rooms don't have sea views but plenty of comfort and charm; one has a handsome four-poster; both have brand new shower rooms. Plenty to do in Lyme on foot; forget the car.

Please check owners' website for availability before enquiring.

Rooms	2 doubles: £100.
Meals	Restaurant 5-minute walk.
Closed	Rarely.

Candida & Hugh Dunford Wood
Arty BnB By the Sea,
The Little Place,
Silver Street,
Lyme Regis, DT7 3HR

Mobile	+44 (0)7932 677540
Email	hugh@dunfordwood.com
Web	www.artybnbbythesea.com

Entry 141   Map 2

Dorset

Denhay Corner House

Charlie runs a cut flower business, so her mellow stone cottage has beautiful blooms in every corner. The garden is dreamy, awash with colour. Step inside to find fantastic fabrics and artwork, wall hangings from all over the world, kilims and antiques. Bedrooms have down duvets, a morning tea tray if you wish, and the scent from jugs of old fashioned roses; dated bathrooms are spotless. Expect scrumptious Aga breakfasts – sausages and bacon from friends' pigs, homemade bread, orchard compotes. You can read in the garden, good walks start from the door, Bridport is arty and foodie and it's a short drive to the sea. Wonderfully relaxed.

Rooms	1 double; 1 double with separate bath: £90–£100. Singles £65. Dinner, B&B £65 per person.
Meals	Dinner, 2 courses, £15. Pubs/restaurants 2.5 miles.
Closed	January/February.

Charlie Ryrie
Denhay Corner House,
Denhay Corner,
Broadoak,
Bridport, DT6 5NN

Tel	+44 (0)1308 427355
Email	charlie@cutflowergarden.co.uk
Web	www.denhaycorner.co.uk

Entry 142   Map 3

Dorset

Urless Farm

In its own beautiful valley, this extended, refurbished 19th-century family house does seriously smart B&B. You'll want to linger over breakfast – local bacon, their hens' eggs, homemade jams, their own tomato sauce – in the light-filled orangery with breathtaking views across rich farmland to the distant Mendips. Luxuriate in traditional bedrooms with antiques and colourful rugs on polished floors; sensors control the lighting in peerless bathrooms with heated floors. Watch for wildlife by the ponds in the large, well-kept grounds. It's a short walk to a good pub and Dorset's delights surround you.

Over 16s welcome.

Rooms	2 doubles, 1 twin; 1 double with separate shower: £100–£120.
Meals	Pubs/restaurants 15-minute walk.
Closed	Rarely.

	Charlotte Hemsley
	Urless Farm,
	Corscombe,
	Dorchester, DT2 0NP
Tel	+44 (0)1935 891528
Email	charlie@urless.co.uk
Web	www.urlessdorset.com

Entry 143   Map 3

Dorset

Wooden Cabbage House

Leafy lanes and a private drive lead you to Martyn and Susie's beautifully restored hamstone house, hidden in rolling West Dorset. Leave the hubbub behind, savour the stunning valley views, relax in this spacious stylish home amongst flowers, fine antiques and paintings. Cosy bedrooms have country-house charm. A delicious breakfast is served in the garden room – homemade muesli, a fresh fruit platter, local eggs and sausages – and French windows open to a productive potager and terraced gardens. Walks are good and the Jurassic coast is half an hour away; return to comfy sofas by the log fire. Fabulous hosts – nothing is too much trouble.

Minimum stay: 2 nights at weekends.

Rooms	2 doubles, 1 twin: £110. Singles £90.
Meals	Dinner, 3 courses with wine, £40. Supper, 2 courses with wine, £30. Pubs/restaurants 3 miles.
Closed	Rarely.

	Martyn & Susie Lee
	Wooden Cabbage House,
	East Chelborough,
	Dorchester, DT2 0QA
Tel	+44 (0)1935 83362
Email	relax@woodencabbage.co.uk
Web	www.woodencabbage.co.uk

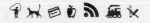

Entry 144   Map 3

Dorset

Old Forge

Snug in a stream-tickled hamlet, deep in Hardy country, this B&B is as pretty as a painting – and wonderfully peaceful. That is, until owner Judy starts to giggle: she is full of smiles and laughter. This is a happy place, a real country home, a no-rules B&B. The one guest double, sharing the former forge with a self-catering pad for two, is neat, warm and cosy with yellow hues, thick carpets and trinkets from travels. The 17th-century farmhouse opposite is where you breakfast: Prue Leith-trained Judy serves a neighbour's eggs and a friend's sausages, in an eclectically furnished room with bucolic views to garden, meadows and hills.

Rooms	Old Forge – 1 double: £80–£100. Extra person £15.
Meals	Restaurant 1.5 miles.
Closed	Rarely.

Judy Thompson
Old Forge,
Lower Wraxall Farmhouse,
Lower Wraxall,
Dorchester, DT2 0HL
Tel   +44 (0)1935 83218
Email   judyjthompson@hotmail.co.uk
Web   www.lowerwraxall.co.uk

Entry 145   Map 3

Dorset

Holyleas House

In a lovely village, a fabulous house, comfortable, peaceful and easy – and Tia and her two friendly dogs give the warmest welcome. You breakfast in an elegant dining room, by a log fire in winter, on free-range eggs, bacon and sausages from the farmers' market, homemade jams and marmalade. Sleep in light, softly coloured bedrooms with lovely views across well-tended gardens; bathrooms are spotless. Walkers and explorers will be happy to roam the Dorset Downs, then return to a roaring fire and a cosy book in the drawing room.

Minimum stay: 2 nights in high season & at weekends.

Rooms	1 double: £80–£90. 1 family room for 3: £100–£120. 1 single with separate bath: £40.
Meals	Pub a short walk.
Closed	Christmas & New Year.

Tia Bunkall
Holyleas House,
Buckland Newton,
Dorchester, DT2 7DP
Tel   +44 (0)1300 345214
Mobile +44 (0)7968 341887
Email   tiabunkall@holyleas.fsnet.co.uk
Web   www.holyleashouse.co.uk

Entry 146   Map 3

Dorset

Fullers Earth

Such an English feel: the village with pub, post office and stores, the rose-filled walled garden with fruit trees beyond, the tranquil church view. This listed house – its late-Georgian frontage added in 1820 – is a treat: flowers and white linen, a lovely sitting room where you settle with tea and cake by the fire, roomy bedrooms with comfortable beds, books and views. At breakfast enjoy perfect compotes and jams from the garden, homemade muesli and local produce. Friendly Ian and Wendy will plan great walks with you in this AONB, the Jurassic coast is 20 minutes away and you can walk to the pub through the garden.

Rooms	1 double; 1 double sharing bath/shower room with single (let to same party only): £100–£110. 1 single: £40–£45
Meals	Pub within 5-minute walk.
Closed	Christmas.

Wendy Gregory
Fullers Earth,
Cattistock,
Dorchester, DT2 0JL

Tel	+44 (0)1300 320190
Mobile	+44 (0)7792 654543
Email	stay@fullersearth.co.uk
Web	www.fullersearth.co.uk

Entry 147   Map 3

Dorset

Manor Farm

Pheasants stroll along grassy lanes, kestrels fly overhead and this stunning stone manor house is a delight. Ashley is easy-going and you have your own wing as well as a private courtyard next to the orangery; take a book and sit by the koi ponds. Bedrooms come in comfy country style; the Rose suite with antique linen and pretty wallpaper is charming. The dining room gleams with antiques, silver and flowers; feast on a breakfast of home-laid eggs, homemade jams and local sausages. Climb Eggardon Hill, visit Bridport and Sherborne; Lyme Regis and the Jurassic Coast are a short drive. Friendly lurchers add to the relaxed feel.

Minimum stay: 2 nights. Coarse fishing available on estate lake.

Rooms	1 double, 1 twin, each with separate bath/shower: £120–£150. 1 suite for 2: £150–£175. Singles £80. Extra bed/sofabed available £50 per person per night.
Meals	Pubs within 3 miles.
Closed	Rarely.

Ashley Stewart
Manor Farm,
West Compton,
Dorchester, DT2 0EY

Tel	+44 (0)1300 320400
Email	ashley@manorfarmwestcompton.com
Web	www.westcomptonmanor.co.uk

Entry 148   Map 3

Dorset

Tudor Cottage

There are gentle walks from this thatched cottage along the river Frome valley, and rugged coastal paths nearby for heartier souls. Return to homemade scones, a sitting room with lots of art and a roaring fire on chilly days – architecture buffs will swoop upon the medieval over mantle and ancient stone archway. Sleep soundly in crisp white linen with thick fabrics at the windows (you are on the road but it's quiet at night); bathrooms are gleaming. Charming Louise can make anybody feel at home and cooks delicious breakfasts and dinners from local ingredients. Fossils abound and you can track down public gardens too.

Over 12s welcome.

Rooms	1 double, 1 twin: £85-£110.
Meals	Dinner, 2-3 courses, £22-£27. Afternoon tea £7.50 (complimentary on arrival). Pub 2 miles.
Closed	Rarely.

Louise Clarke
Tudor Cottage,
9 Dorchester Road, Frampton,
Dorchester, DT2 9NB
Tel   +44 (0)1300 320382
Mobile +44 (0)7970 282151
Email   stay@tudorcottagedorset.co.uk
Web   www.tudorcottagedorset.co.uk

Entry 149   Map 3

Dorset

Manor Farm

You are high up on the chalk hills that fall to the Jurassic Coast. Tessa's family have lived in the flint and stone house since 1860 and it is crammed with history: solid antiques, books galore, pictures, maps and photographs. From all the windows views soar to sheep-dotted hills. Settle by the wood-burner in the dining room for your Aga-cooked breakfast or supper; in the summer you can eat outside in the garden; cooking is one of Tessa's passions so food is good! Bedrooms are without frills but clean and comfortable; the bathroom is large and sparkling. Outdoor heaven is yours; find a pet pig called Pork!

Rooms	1 double, 1 twin sharing bath (let to same party only): £80-£100.
Meals	Dinner, 2-3 courses, from £15. Pub/restaurant 4 miles.
Closed	Rarely.

Tessa Russell
Manor Farm,
Compton Valence,
Dorchester, DT2 9ES
Tel   +44 (0)1308 482227
Mobile +44 (0)7818 037184 (signal unreliable)
Email   tessa.nrussell@btinternet.com
Web   www.manor-farm.uk.com

Entry 150   Map 3

Dorset

The White Cottage

Strolling distance from lovely old Athelhampton House and its gardens is this thatched cottage where Lindsay and Mark are slowly becoming self-sufficient. You will be well fed: home-grown vegetables, bacon from the pigs, eggs from Pru the chicken. It's a lively family-friendly household with gorgeous bedrooms: super linen, plump pillows; generous bathrooms with thick towels and eco-friendly lotions. The suite has its own entrance and a big comfortable sitting room. Help feed the animals, admire the new flock of sheep and enjoy the river Piddle running through the garden – fish for brown trout but please put them back!

Rooms	1 double; 1 twin/double with separate bath: £75-£85. 1 suite for 2-4 (with sofabed): £100-£120. Singles from £55.
Meals	Pubs 1 mile.
Closed	Rarely.

Lindsay & Mark Piper
The White Cottage,
Athelhampton,
Dorchester, DT2 7LG
Tel   +44 (0)1305 848622
Mobile   +44 (0)7788 166322
Email   bookings@white-cottage-bandb.co.uk
Web   www.white-cottage-bandb.co.uk

Entry 151   Map 3

Dorset

Yoah Cottage

Rose and Furse are ceramic sculptors; she makes delicate, sometimes humorous, pieces, he creates bold animals and birds; their thatched, rambling house is a jaw-dropping gallery of modern art, ceramics and fabrics. The prettiest of cottage gardens brims with colour and scent – lots of seats and a summerhouse for sitting and admiring. Originally two cottages, you sleep on one side in lovely bedrooms under the eaves, sharing (with friends or family) a bathroom and a sitting room with log fire. Breakfast (full English, homemade jams) is next to the couple's studio. Such warm-hearted, artistic owners – and you're deep in Hardy country.

Minimum stay: 2 nights.

Rooms	1 double, 1 twin sharing bath (let to same party only): £70-£90. Singles £40-£50.
Meals	Pub/restaurant next door.
Closed	Christmas & Easter.

Furse & Rosemary Swann
Yoah Cottage,
West Knighton,
Dorchester, DT2 8PE
Tel   +44 (0)1305 852087
Email   roseswann@tiscali.co.uk
Web   www.yoahcottage.co.uk

Entry 152   Map 3

Dorset

Marren

On the Dorset coastal path overlooking Weymouth Bay – a blissful spot for Jurassic Coast adventures. The owners have transformed this 1920s house, set in six acres of terraced and wooded garden, and their style reflects their penchant for natural materials and country life. Bedrooms are elegant and comfortable; one has a door onto the garden; from the other you can marvel at the sun setting over the sea. Enjoy superb spreads of farm produce and homemade bread, then head off to the secluded beach below and a turquoise sea swim. There's a sense of slow living here. Leave the low-slung Morgan at home: the track is steep!

Minimum stay: 2 nights at weekends. Over 12s welcome.

Rooms	2 doubles: £95–£135.
Meals	Pub 1 mile.
Closed	Rarely.

Peter Cartwright
Marren,
Holworth,
Dorchester, DT2 8NJ
Tel	+44 (0)1305 851503
Mobile	+44 (0)7957 886399
Email	marren@lineone.net
Web	www.marren.info

Entry 153   Map 3

Dorset

Old Harbour View

Perch in the bow-fronted window and gaze down on the harbour where the fishing boats dock. What a position – at the heart of Old Weymouth. As for the house, built in 1805, it is uniquely 12 feet wide, yet all is spacious inside, and brimming with light. Imagine stained-glass windows, huge gilt mirrors, fragrant lilies, amusing etchings and posters, sumptuous sofas, and the most delightful hosts. Boat trips, seafood restaurants galore… then it's back home to ivory-white beds in soft-carpeted rooms. Wake to Anna's breads and jams, and locally-smoked haddock: outstanding breakfasts served on lovely china.

Ask about permits for parking, on booking. Minimum stay: 2 nights.

Rooms	1 double, 1 twin/double: £98. Singles £80.
Meals	Pubs/restaurants within walking distance.
Closed	Rarely.

Peter Vincent
Old Harbour View,
12 Trinity Road,
Weymouth, DT4 8TJ
Tel	+44 (0)1305 774633
Email	info@oldharbourview.co.uk
Web	www.oldharbourviewweymouth.co.uk

Entry 154   Map 3

Dorset

Lulworth House

Down through hills, wild heaths and pine forests to beautiful Lulworth. Carole and John's home is set back from this popular cove in a peaceful lane; artist and garden designer, their 1980s house is a creative treasure, inside and out. The garden has a tropical feel with banana trees, ferns, deep borders and abundant grapes over a pergola. Inside is a sparkling white canvas dotted with colour: paintings, glass vases, antique desk, an old grandfather clock, cubist furniture. Garden bedrooms are delightful – one opens to its own terrace; breakfast is upstairs in the stunning open-plan living space. Walks galore from the door.

Minimum stay: 2 nights at weekends. Over 12s welcome.

Rooms	1 double; 1 double with separate shower room: £85-£110.
Meals	Pubs/restaurants within walking distance.
Closed	Occasionally.

John & Carole Bickerton
Lulworth House,
Bindon Road, West Lulworth,
Wareham, BH20 5RU
Tel +44 (0)1929 406192
Email info@lulworthhousebandb.co.uk
Web www.lulworthhousebandb.co.uk

Entry 155   Map 3

Dorset

Gold Court House

Anthea and Michael have created a mood of restrained luxury and uncluttered, often beautiful, good taste in their Georgian townhouse. Restful bedrooms have antiques, beams, linen armchairs, radios and TVs. There's an eye-catching collection of aquamarine glass, interesting art, and a large drawing room and pretty walled garden in which to relax after a day out. Views are soft and lush yet you are in the small square of this attractive town with cafes and galleries a short walk. Your hosts are delightful – "they do everything to perfection" says a guest; both house and garden are a refuge.

Children over 10 welcome.

Rooms	1 double, 2 twin/doubles, each with separate bath: £85. Singles £60.
Meals	Restaurants 50 yds.
Closed	Rarely.

Anthea & Michael Hipwell
Gold Court House,
St John's Hill,
Wareham, BH20 4LZ
Tel +44 (0)1929 553320
Email info@goldcourthouse.co.uk
Web www.goldcourthouse.co.uk

Entry 156   Map 3

Dorset

Bering House

Fabulous in every way. Renate's attention to detail reveals a love of running B&B: the fluffy dressing gowns and bathroom treats, the biscuits, fruit and sherry... she and John are welcoming and delightful. Expect pretty sofas, golden bath taps, a gleaming breakfast table, and a big sumptuous suite with views across sparkling Poole harbour to Brownsea Island and Purbeck Hills. Breakfasts are served on blue and white Spode china: exotic fruits with Parma ham, smoked salmon with poached eggs and muffins, kedgeree, smoked haddock gratin, warm figs with Greek yogurt and honey: the choice is superb. An immaculate harbourside retreat.

Rooms	1 twin/double: £85.
	1 suite for 2 with kitchenette: £100.
	Singles £75-£90.
Meals	Pub 400 yds.
	Restaurant 500 yds.
Closed	Rarely.

	Renate & John Wadham
	Bering House,
	53 Branksea Avenue,
	Hamworthy,
	Poole, BH15 4DP
Tel	+44 (0)1202 673419
Email	johnandrenate1@tiscali.co.uk
Web	www.beringhouse.co.uk

Entry 157   Map 3

Dorset

7 Smithfield Place

Valerie is creative and her home an elegant blend of old and new: tapestries and art, large restored mirrors, antiques and modern pieces in your own sitting room. She's also unstinting with treats, from wine to shortbread, kettle chips and chocolates. And breakfast is equally lavish: fruits and yogurts, excellent coffee, pastries, kedgeree or the full works served outdoors on sunny days. Built in 1880, the house sits on a quiet cul-de-sac off the high street, two miles from Bournemouth town centre with easy public transport. The garden is lit up in spring by blooming camellias and cherry blossom, and the whole house sparkles.

Rooms	1 double: £85-£90.
	Singles £60.
Meals	Packed lunch £15.
	Pub/restaurant 100 yds.
Closed	Christmas.

	Valerie Johns
	7 Smithfield Place,
	Winton,
	Bournemouth, BH9 2QJ
Tel	+44 (0)1202 520722
Mobile	+44 (0)7743 481671
Email	valeriejohns@btinternet.com
Web	www.smithfieldplace.co.uk

Entry 158   Map 3

Dorset

The Old Mill

Ancient willow trees cast shade over stretches of lawn as kingfishers flit from branch to branch. A secret paradise unfurls before you, as through the Mill's gardens the Stour and its tributaries flow, their banks a-shimmer with hostas, irises, day lilies, gunneras and ferns. Find privacy and independence in your own comfortably contemporary bolthole above the detached garage; a chandelier sparkles in the sun, a mini kitchen hides behind louvre doors, and relaxed Caroline brings you a fine continental breakfast. Walk across the water meadows to little Spetisbury for a pint; discover the delights of Brownsea Island and Blandford Forum.

Minimum stay: 2 nights at weekends during high season & bank holidays. Self-catering by arrangement.

Rooms	1 family room for 2 (self-contained with sofabed & kitchenette): £95. Singles £80 (mid-week only). £12 per child per night.
Meals	Continental breakfast. Pub 10-minute walk.
Closed	Rarely.

Caroline Ivay
The Old Mill,
Spetisbury,
Blandford Forum, DT11 9DF
Tel   +44 (0)1258 456014
Mobile +44 (0)7786 096803
Email   c.ivay@btinternet.com
Web   www.theoldmillspetisbury.com

Entry 159   Map 3

Dorset

Crawford House

Below, the river Stour winds through the valley and under the medieval, nine-arched bridge. Above, an Iron Age hill fort; between is Crawford House. Elegant and Georgian, it sits in an acre of attractive walled gardens full of roses; inside is pretty too, with an easy, relaxed atmosphere. Bedrooms with period furnishings are homely and warm; one room has flowery four-poster twin beds. The sun streams through the tall windows of the downstairs rooms, and charming oil paintings hang in the dining room. Andrea is fun, and a great host, with lots of local knowledge; the North Dorset Trailway starts from her garden.

One night stays available.

Rooms	1 twin/double, 1 twin with separate bath; 1 twin with separate shower: £75-£80. Singles £40.
Meals	Pub in village.
Closed	Rarely.

Andrea Lea
Crawford House,
Spetisbury,
Blandford Forum, DT11 9DP
Tel   +44 (0)1258 857338
Email   andrea@lea8.wanadoo.co.uk

Entry 160   Map 3

Dorset

Launceston Farm

Farmhouse chic in the most glorious of surroundings. The bedrooms, all named after the fields, are an exquisite blend of contemporary and traditional; two have roll tops in the room itself. Take tea by the open fire or find a secluded spot in the ornamental, walled gardens. Breakfast and candlelit dinner are farm-sourced and deliciously rustic. Sarah, who was born in this listed house, provides a truly relaxing stay; son Jimi's organic farm tours are a must and there are footpaths through the surrounding AONB from the door. You will leave this country retreat feeling completely rejuvenated.

Over 12s welcome. Dogs welcome in the warm boot room.

Rooms	4 doubles, 2 twin/doubles: £100-£125. Singles £70-£125.
Meals	Dinner, 3 courses, £30 (Mon & Fri only). Pub 10-minute walk.
Closed	Rarely.

Sarah Worrall
Launceston Farm,
Tarrant Launceston,
Blandford Forum, DT11 8BY
Tel   +44 (0)1258 830528
Email   info@launcestonfarm.co.uk
Web   www.launcestonfarm.co.uk

Entry 161   Map 3

Dorset

Stickland Farmhouse

Charming Dorset… welcome to a soft, delightful thatched cottage in an enviably rural setting. Sandy and Paul have poured love into this listed farmhouse and garden, the latter bursting with lupins, poppies, foxgloves, clematis, delphiniums. Sandy gives you delicious breakfasts with homemade muesli, eggs from the hens and soda bread from the Aga. Pretty, cottagey bedrooms have crisp white dressing gowns and lots of books and pictures – one room opens onto your own seating area in the garden. The village has a good pub, and Cranborne Chase, rich in barrows and hill forts, is close by.

Minimum stay: 2 nights at weekends in summer. Children over 10 welcome.

Rooms	2 doubles, 1 twin: £70-£75. Singles £60-£65.
Meals	Pub 3-minute walk.
Closed	Rarely.

Sandy & Paul Crofton-Atkins
Stickland Farmhouse,
Winterborne Stickland,
Blandford Forum, DT11 0NT
Tel   +44 (0)1258 880119
Mobile   +44 (0)7932 897774
Email   sandysticklandfarm@gmail.com
Web   www.sticklandfarmhouse.co.uk

Entry 162   Map 3

Dorset

Higher Melcombe Manor

You will thrill to this manor house of local stone and far-reaching views. Lorel and Michael are delightful, their home supremely comfortable and relaxed. The two acres appear to blend into the countryside, Highland cattle are sometimes seen grazing in the pastures and the garden is a colourful work in progress. Chic bedrooms have sumptuous linens, chalky white walls and painted furniture; bathrooms are simply stunning. There's a guest kitchen on the landing, and a big sitting room with duck egg blue sofas, bean bags, books and TV. Stretch out with a Bucks Fizz, a hot chocolate or whatever you fancy: you'll be pampered here.

Minimum stay: 2 nights. Check-in 5pm-6pm.

Rooms	3 doubles: £120.
	Singles from £75.
Meals	Supper, £15. Pub 1.5 miles.
Closed	Christmas.

Lorel Morton & Michael Woodhouse
Higher Melcombe Manor,
Melcombe Bingham, DT2 7PB

Tel	+44 (0)1258 880251
Mobile	+44 (0)7973 920119
Email	lorel@lorelmorton.com
Web	www.highermelcombemanor.co.uk

Entry 163   Map 3

Dorset

Glebe House

Clematis and wisteria cover much of the mellow brickwork of this spacious and uncluttered 1950s house, down a quiet lane in a tiny hamlet in the heart of stunning Blackmore Vale. From the hall look right through to the mature pretty garden; it's open house and David and Barbara love having guests to stay. Enjoy tea and scones in the garden room, neat-as-a-pin bedrooms and bathrooms, and wide views from every window. Tuck into all sorts of tasty choices at breakfast, by the fire in the dining room. Magnificent castle and abbey are close, and walks from the door are outstanding – you could stay a week and never do the same one twice!

Rooms	1 double, 1 twin/double: £70-£85.
	Singles £55.
Meals	Pub/restaurant within 1 mile.
Closed	Rarely.

David & Barbara Fifield
Glebe House,
Folke, Sherborne, DT9 5HP

Tel	+44 (0)1963 210337
Mobile	+44 (0)7980 864033
Email	glebe.house@hotmail.com
Web	www.glebehouse-dorset.co.uk

Entry 164   Map 3

Dorset

Caundle Barn

Take the pretty route… ramble through rich pasture, tiny hamlets and woodland to reach this attractive 17th-century stone barn. All is spotless, from the oak stairs and galleried landing to the antiques and exquisite curtains; Sarah has blended old and new beautifully. Your bedroom is sunny and sumptuous; the little shower room has scented oils and luxurious towels. Sarah cooks with the seasons and you'll enjoy homemade marmalade, fruits, local eggs, bacon and sausages. Views and walks are sublime, Sherborne is fun, there are gourmet pubs galore and Poppy the Jack Russell adds her charm to this friendly home.

Rooms	1 double: £80–£110.
	Singles £50.
Meals	Pubs/restaurants 4 miles.
Closed	Rarely.

	Sarah Howes
	Caundle Barn,
	Purse Caundle,
	Sherborne, DT9 5DY
Tel	+44 (0)1963 251264
Email	howes20@btinternet.com

Entry 165   Map 3

Dorset

Munden House

This is a super B&B — a couple of farm cottages and assorted outbuildings beautifully stitched together. It's run with great warmth by Colin and Annie, who buy and sell colourful rugs and have travelled the world to do it. Outside, long views shoot off over open country; inside, airy interiors, pretty bedrooms and lots of colour. The garden studios are bigger and more private; one has a galleried bedroom above a lovely sitting room. Annie cooks fantastic food — local meat, fish from Brixham — but her vegetarian dishes will seduce die-hard carnivores. You eat at smartly dressed tables; breakfast is on the terrace in good weather.

Rooms	3 doubles, 1 twin/double,
	1 four-poster: £85–£130.
	Garden studios – 3 doubles: £85–£130.
	Singles from £70.
Meals	Dinner, 3 courses, £27.
	Pub 0.5 miles.
Closed	Christmas.

	Annie & Colin Fletcher
	Munden House,
	Mundens Lane, Alweston,
	Sherborne, DT9 5HU
Tel	+44 (0)1963 23150
Email	stay@mundenhouse.co.uk
Web	www.mundenhouse.co.uk

Entry 166   Map 3

Dorset

Lower Fifehead Farm

A passion for cooking here! The dramatic dining room has church pews at an oak refectory table; the log fire will be lit in winter, and you can eat on the terrace in summer. Hearty breakfasts include bacon and sausages from home-reared pigs, devilled mushrooms or eggs Benedict; Jessica makes the bread and preserves, and there's always freshly squeezed orange juice. It's a gorgeous house too – it's been in Jasper's family for years and shines with pretty fabrics, antiques, hand-painted furniture, vintage pieces, rich colour – and seriously comfortable brass beds. Don't miss the candlelit dinners.

Minimum stay: 2 nights at weekends.

Rooms	2 doubles, 1 twin/double: £75–£95. Singles from £55.
Meals	Dinner, 2-3 courses, £20–£30. Pubs/restaurants 2 miles.
Closed	Christmas & New Year.

Jessica Miller
Lower Fifehead Farm,
Fifehead St Quinton,
Sturminster Newton, DT10 2AP
Tel +44 (0)1258 817335
Email lowerfifeheadfm@gmail.com
Web www.lowerfifeheadfarm.co.uk

Entry 167   Map 3

Dorset

Golden Hill Cottage

Deep in the countryside lies Stourton Caundle and this charming thatched cottage. You have the peace and privacy of your own sitting room, traditionally furnished with antiques, paintings and open fire; up a private stair is your carpeted twin room with its own shower room. Anna, courteous and kind, brings you splendid platefuls of local bacon and sausage, homemade jams and Dorset honey for breakfast; nothing is too much trouble for these hosts. There are glorious walks from the village, a good pub that serves lunches (check when the kitchen's open) and real ales, and Sherborne, Montacute and Stourhead for landscape, culture and history.

Babes in arms welcome.

Rooms	1 twin with sitting room: £90–£100. Singles £50.
Meals	Pubs/restaurants within 3 miles.
Closed	Rarely.

Anna & Andrew Oliver
Golden Hill Cottage,
Stourton Caundle,
Sturminster Newton, DT10 2JW
Tel +44 (0)1963 362109
Email anna@goldenhillcottage.co.uk
Web www.goldenhillcottage.co.uk

Entry 168   Map 3

Dorset

The Old Forge, Fanners Yard

Step back in time in this beautifully restored forge: retro signs, museum pieces, ponies in the paddock and a slower way of life... Tim and Lucy's smallholding gives you a taste of harmonious living with the seasons, and they recycle everything. This includes Tim's classic cars, cosy gypsy caravan and vintage shepherd's hut. Attic bedrooms in the main house are snug with Lucy's quilts, antiques, sparkling bathrooms. Breakfasts are renowned: eggs from the hens, organic bacon and sausages, home-grown jams, orchard apple juice; if you stay in the Smithy, a tasty hamper is left for you so rise when you want. A happy place, a tonic to stay.

Children over 8 welcome. Minimum stay: 2 nights in caravan, hut and Smithy.

Rooms	1 double with separate bath; Smithy – 1 double with kitchen: £60–£125. 1 family room for 3: £70–£125. 2 shepherd's huts for 2 (shower/wc close by): £95. Singles £60–£75
Meals	Pub/restaurant within 1 mile.
Closed	Rarely.

	Tim & Lucy Kerridge
	The Old Forge, Fanners Yard,
	Compton Abbas,
	Shaftesbury, SP7 0NQ
Tel	+44 (0)1747 811881
Email	theoldforge@ymail.com
Web	www.theoldforgedorset.co.uk

Entry 169   Map 3

Dorset

Lawn Cottage

In a quiet village in Blackmore Vale, the path to this spacious cottage is lined with tulips and vegetables. Easy-going June is a collector of pretty things; art, antiques and china blend charmingly with soft colours and zingy kilims. Bedrooms are sunny – one is downstairs (en suite) with a private entrance; there's a sweet very comfy shepherd's hut too if you fancy a night under the stars and sunset views. Breakfasts are generous; hut dwellers can come in to the dining room or have a hamper delivered. Visit Sherborne (abbey, castle, smart shops), walk from the gate to Duncliffe Wood. Return to a tiny snug sitting room. Perfect Dorset B&B!

Rooms	1 double with separate bathroom; 1 twin/double: £80. 1 shepherd's hut for 2 (separate bathroom in main house): £90. Singles £40. Dinner, B&B £80–£90 per person. Extra bed/sofabed available at no charge.
Meals	Pub/restaurant 1 mile.
Closed	Rarely.

	June Watkins
	Lawn Cottage,
	Stour Row, Shaftesbury, SP7 0QF
Tel	+44 (0)1747 838719
Mobile	+44 (0)7809 696218
Email	enquiries@lawncottagedorset.co.uk
Web	www.lawncottagedorset.co.uk

Entry 170   Map 3

Dorset

Glebe Farm

You're in Dorset's highest village – views from the house sprawl for miles. Ian farms 1,000 acres, Tessa does shoot catering and is a part-time model. Their home, newly built, comes with green oak, soaring ceilings and walls of glass that frame spectacular views ("Emmerdale meets Grand Designs" to quote a happy guest). Aga-cooked breakfasts include local bacon and home-laid eggs, while bedrooms, one up, one down, have warm colours, big beds, beautiful views, super bathrooms. The Wessex Ridgeway starts in the village, so follow it over to magnificent Hambledon Hill, an Iron Age hill fort. Dine on the terrace in summer.

Over 14s welcome.

Rooms	2 twin/doubles: £100–£120. Singles from £60.
Meals	Dinner, 2 courses, £25 (by prior arrangement). Pubs 2 miles.
Closed	Christmas & New Year.

Tessa & Ian Millard
Glebe Farm,
High Street, Ashmore,
Salisbury, SP5 5AE

Tel	+44 (0)1747 811974
Mobile	+44 (0)7799 858961
Email	stay@glebefarmbandb.co.uk
Web	www.glebefarmbandb.co.uk

Entry 171   Map 3

Durham

The Coach House

There's so much to gladden your heart – the cobbled courtyard that evokes memories of its days as a coaching inn, the river running through the estate, the drawing room's log fire, the delicious breakfasts, the blackberry crumbles with cream... and Peter and Mary, your kind, unstuffy, dog-adoring hosts (they have one well-behaved one). All your creature comforts are attended to in this small, perfect, English country house: lined chintz, pure cotton linen, cushioned window seats looking onto a lovely garden, heated towel rails, cut flowers. Friendly, delightful, and the perfect stepping stone to Scotland or the south.

Rooms	1 twin/double; 1 twin/double with separate bath/shower: £90. Singles £60.
Meals	Dinner, 3 courses, £25. Pub/restaurants within 3 miles.
Closed	Rarely.

Peter & Mary Gilbertson
The Coach House,
Greta Bridge,
Barnard Castle, DL12 9SD

Tel	+44 (0)1833 627201
Email	info@coachhousegreta.co.uk
Web	www.coachhousegreta.co.uk

Entry 172   Map 12

Essex

32 The Hythe

The Thames barge in all her glory: the Gibbs' garden runs almost into the river Blackwater where these majestic old craft are moored and the mudflats are a bird watcher's dream. Summer breakfast on the deck – local smoked kippers and free-range eggs – watching the barges sail up the river is a rare treat. Beneath wide limpid skies this sensitively extended fisherman's cottage looks out to 12th-century St Mary's at the back where Kim and Gerry ring the Sunday bells. It's immaculate and comfortable inside, an inspired mix of modern and antique lit by myriad candles, among other romantic touches.

Over 14s welcome.

Rooms	2 doubles: £100.
	Singles £80.
Meals	Pub 100 yds.
Closed	Christmas & Boxing Day.

	Kim & Gerry Gibbs
	32 The Hythe,
	Maldon, CM9 5HN
Tel	+44 (0)1621 859435
Mobile	+44 (0)7753 135108
Email	gibbsie@live.co.uk
Web	www.thehythemaldon.co.uk

Entry 173   Map 10

Essex

Caterpillar Cottage

Traditional brick and clapboard, dormer windows, tall chimney – this looks like the real thing. But Caterpillar Cottage was built in 2004 – in the grounds of Patricia's former grand 14th-century house. Filled with fine furniture, family photos and *objets* from far-flung travels, it invites relaxation. The double-height, vaulted sitting room brims with sofas and books, logs crackle on chilly nights. Bedrooms are simple and comfortable; the family room has plenty of space for little ones. Patricia, a lively grandmother, loves having children to stay. Enjoy the big peaceful garden with pretty terrace and vine-covered pergola.

Camp bed & travel cot available. Ample parking.

Rooms	1 double with separate
	bath/shower: £70–£75.
	1 triple: £75–£85.
	10% off for 3 nights or more.
	Singles from £45.
Meals	Packed lunch available
	(with prior warning).
	Pubs 50 yds.
Closed	Rarely.

	Patricia Mitchell
	Caterpillar Cottage,
	Fordstreet, Aldham,
	Colchester, CO6 3PH
Tel	+44 (0)1206 240456
Email	bandbcaterpillar@tiscali.co.uk
Web	www.caterpillarcottage.co.uk

Entry 174   Map 10

Essex

Hill House

The Romer-Lees converted this listed brick Coach House and it's rather special: light and airy with pale beams, oatmeal carpets and merry gingham blinds. Downstairs is a private entrance hall; upstairs is a generous open-plan bedroom/living area with a queen-sized bed and en suite bathroom. On the other side of the room, separated by the stairs, are two cream sofas that open into double beds, a TV, DVDs and board games. No garden but you get a balcony with stunning views across the Colne Valley, breakfast (all the usuals plus bacon and sausages from the owners' rare-breed pigs) is served here on warm days. Cambridge is close.

Minimum stay: 2 nights at weekends.

Rooms	Coach House – 1 suite for 2 with sitting room & sofabeds (can sleep up to 6 people): £95–£120. Extra bed/sofabed available £15 per person per night.
Meals	Pub/restaurant 5-minute walk.
Closed	Rarely.

Hattie Romer-Lee
Hill House,
Chappel Hill, Chappel,
Colchester, CO6 2DX

Tel	+44 (0)1787 221561
Mobile	+44 (0)7802 601144
Email	hattieromerlee@yahoo.co.uk
Web	www.hillhousechappel.com

Entry 175   Map 10

Gloucestershire

The Moda House

A fine house and a big B&B, but one that retains a deeply homely feel; Duncan and Jo are hugely well-travelled and have filled it with pictures and artefacts from all over the world. Bedrooms differ (three are in a neat annexe) but all are cosy and well decorated with lovely colours, good fabrics, pocket sprung mattresses and bright bathrooms with thick towels. Breakfast – locally sourced, cooked on the Aga and brought to round tables – sets you up for fabulous walks: you are a mile from the Cotswold Way. Return to a basement sitting room with comfy armchairs and lots of books, and a bustling town full of restaurants and shops.

Minimum stay: 2 nights over busy weekends & 3 nights during Badminton.

Rooms	8 doubles: £82–£95. 3 singles: £62–£67.
Meals	Pubs/restaurants within 100 yards.
Closed	Rarely.

Duncan & Jo MacArthur
The Moda House,
1 High Street,
Chipping Sodbury, BS37 6BA

Tel	+44 (0)1454 312135
Email	enquiries@modahouse.co.uk
Web	www.modahouse.co.uk

Entry 176   Map 3

Gloucestershire

Pauntley Court

If a rural hideaway is what you seek then beat a path here and prepare to be enchanted. The house is a historical corker and was home to the Whittington family for 300 years – Dick is reputed to have been born here. Plush traditional rooms with beautiful beds look over unspoilt countryside; smart bathrooms have Neal's Yard toiletries. Breakfast in the ballroom on fresh local produce, some from the garden, and enjoy the special juice of the day. Surrounded by romantic gardens you can wander at will amidst the yew 'ruins' or gaze at Pan over a glass of Chablis. Delightful Melissa adds the finishing touch to a blissful place.

Fishing & stable available.

Rooms	2 twin/doubles: £125–£140. Singles £80.
Meals	Pub 6 miles.
Closed	Rarely.

Mark & Melissa Hargreaves
Pauntley Court,
Pauntley Court Drive, Redmarley,
Gloucester, GL19 3JA
Tel   +44 (0)1531 828627
Mobile   +44 (0)7798 865979
Email   melissa@pauntleycourt.com
Web   www.pauntleycourt.com

Entry 177   Map 8

Gloucestershire

Ashley Barn

On the edge of a hamlet... a beautifully restored, traditional converted barn. Huge doorways and floor to ceiling timber-framed windows let the light flood in. You have your own entrance and can come and go as you please. Your suite has good linen, plump pillows, flowers and views onto the garden; the roomy bathroom is gleaming. Walk through for breakfast by a log fire in the huge dining hall in the main barn: local sausages and bacon, eggs from the hens on pretty Poole pottery; Amanda is happy to cook dinner too. Badminton Horse Trials are a hop, Cirencester too; return for a wander round the rose garden, and a snooze by the fire.

Rooms	1 suite: £100–£110. Singles £75.
Meals	Dinner, 3 courses, £25. Pub/restaurant 5-minute drive.
Closed	Rarely.

Amanda Montgomerie
Ashley Barn,
Ashley,
Tetbury, GL8 8SU
Tel   +44 (0)1666 575156
Mobile   +44 (0)7785 505548
Email   amanda@montgomerie.org
Web   www.ashleybarn.co.uk

Entry 178   Map 3

Gloucestershire

Frampton Court

Deep authenticity in this magnificent Grade I-listed house. The manor of Frampton on Severn has been in the Clifford family since the 11th century and although Rollo and Janie look after the estate, it is cooking enthusiasts Polly and Craig who greet you on their behalf and look after you. There are exquisite examples of decorative woodwork and, in the hall, a cheerful log fire; perch on the Mouseman fire seat. Bedrooms are traditional with antiques, panelling and long views. Beds have fine linen, one with embroidered Stuart hangings. Stroll around the ornamental canal, soak up the old-master views. An architectural masterpiece.

Children over 10 welcome.

Rooms	1 double, 1 twin/double, 1 four-poster: £150–£250.
Meals	Dinner from £45. Pub across the green. Restaurant 3 miles.
Closed	Christmas.

Polly Dugdale & Craig Kempson
Frampton Court,
Frampton on Severn, GL2 7EX
Tel   +44 (0)1452 740267
Email   framptoncourt@
           framptoncourtestate.co.uk
Web   www.framptoncourtestate.co.uk

Entry 179   Map 8

Gloucestershire

The Close

Up a hill of pretty Cotswold-stone houses, this large Queen Anne house with handsome sash windows delivers what it promises. Step into a stone-flagged hall with grandfather clock and Georgian oak staircase; take welcoming tea with Karen in the drawing room – all gracious sofas and charming chandelier; then upstairs to three light and airy bedrooms softly furnished with antiques. Window seats, shutters and views over garden or pretty street add to the restful atmosphere. Karen, as gracious and relaxed as her house, serves excellent breakfasts in the polished dining room. An elegantly hospitable base for exploring the Cotswolds.

Rooms	2 doubles, 1 twin: £80–£90. Singles £55–£65.
Meals	Pubs/restaurants 1-minute walk.
Closed	January.

Karen Champney
The Close,
Well Hill,
Minchinhampton,
Stroud, GL6 9JE
Tel   +44 (0)1453 883338
Email   theclosebnb@gmail.com
Web   www.theclosebnb.co.uk

Entry 180   Map 8

Gloucestershire

Well Farm

Perhaps it's the gentle, unstuffy attitude of Kate and Edward. Or the great position of the house with its glorious views across the valley. Whichever, you'll feel comforted and invigorated by your stay. It's a real family home and you get both a fresh, pretty bedroom that feels very private and the use of a comfortable, book-filled sitting room opening to a flowery courtyard; Kate is an inspired gardener. Sleep soundly on the softest of pillows, wake to the deep peace of the countryside and the delicious prospect of eggs from their own hens, local sausages and good bacon. The area teems with great walks – lovely pubs too.

Rooms	1 twin/double with sitting room: £95.
Meals	Dinner from £25. Pubs nearby.
Closed	Rarely.

Kate & Edward Gordon Lennox
Well Farm,
Frampton Mansell,
Stroud, GL6 8JB
Tel   +44 (0)1285 760651
Email   kategl@btinternet.com
Web   www.well-farm.co.uk

Entry 181   Map 8

Gloucestershire

Mayfield Studio

A small lane runs past the studio, and oak doors open to a stylish interior. Slate floors are warmed from beneath and the double height ceiling lends an airy feel. A lime-washed staircase leads to a mezzanine bedroom of uncluttered simplicity with views across the valley. Quirky industrial lighting, stone walls, 1930s woodcut prints, and Ercol furniture all marry superbly. There's no garden – although with permission you may use Sara's next door; choose to stay on a B&B or self-catering basis, with breakfasts delivered or left for you as you wish. Walk to Laurie Lee's favourite pub or dine locally, it's all on your doorstep.

Minimum stay: 2 nights at weekends.

Rooms	Studio – 1 double: £100-£125. Extra bed/sofabed available £40 per person per night.
Meals	Breakfast arranged on booking. Pubs/restaurants 2-4-minute walk.
Closed	Rarely.

Sara Kirby
Mayfield Studio,
Vicarage Street,
Painswick,
Stroud, GL6 6XP
Tel   +44 (0)1452 814858
Email   sara.kirby@mac.com

Entry 182   Map 8

Gloucestershire

St Annes

Step straight off the narrow pavement into a sunny hall and a warm and welcoming family home. Iris and Greg have made their pretty 17th-century house, in the heart of this bustling village, as eco-friendly as possible. Comfy bedrooms are charming; the four-poster room has a tiny en suite shower room. Farmers' market breakfasts are a feast, the Aga kitchen is a friendly space and Rollo the dog (who has his own sofa) loves children. Painswick is known as 'the Queen of the Cotswolds': enjoy superb walks through orchid meadows and beech woods carpeted with bluebells; visit good pubs on the way. Great value and perfect for walkers without a car.

Rooms	1 double, 1 twin, 1 four-poster: £75.
Meals	Packed lunch £6.
	Pubs/restaurants in village.
Closed	Rarely.

Iris McCormick
St Annes,
Gloucester Street,
Painswick, Stroud, GL6 6QN
Tel   +44 (0)1452 812879
Email iris@st-annes-painswick.co.uk
Web   www.st-annes-painswick.co.uk

Entry 183   Map 8

Gloucestershire

27 Sheep Street

An evocative address and a handsome, wonderfully idiosyncratic Cotswold townhouse. Alex grew up in this rambling Georgian home of time-worn elegance and pushes the breakfast boat out with good things homemade and local. Eat outside, attended by bantams and Pudding, the dog; or in, overlooking the lovely walled garden (with croquet). The feel is unselfconsciously quirky: modern canvasses hang next to demure family portraits under a spectacular Regency ceiling. Sink into cotton sheets and feather duvets on comfy mattresses in delightfully old-fashioned bedrooms; curl up with a book in the fire-warmed sitting room. A truly characterful place.

Rooms	2 doubles: £95.
	Singles £75.
Meals	Pubs/restaurants 5-minute walk.
Closed	Rarely.

Alex Norman-Walker
27 Sheep Street,
Cirencester, GL7 1QW
Tel   +44 (0)1285 653226
Email alexnorma@hotmail.com
Web   www.27sheepstreet.co.uk

Entry 184   Map 8

Gloucestershire

The Old Rectory

English to the core – and to the bottom of its lovely garden, with a woodland walk and plenty of quiet places to sit. Sweep into the circular driveway to this beautiful, 17th-century high gabled house. Inside, all is comfortably lived-in with an understated décor, antiques, creaky floorboards and a real sense of atmosphere and history. The bedrooms, one with a garden view, have good beds, TVs and a chaise longue or easy chair; bathrooms are vintage and functional but large. Caroline is charming and serves breakfasts with eggs from friends' hens and local bacon at the long table in the rich red dining room. A welcoming place.

Rooms	1 double, 1 twin/double (extra bed available): £85-£100. Extra bed & cot for children available. Singles £60-£100.
Meals	Pub 200 yds.
Closed	December/January.

Roger & Caroline Carne
The Old Rectory,
Meysey Hampton,
Cirencester, GL7 5JX
Tel   +44 (0)1285 851200
Email   carocarne13@gmail.com
Web   www.meyseyoldrectory.co.uk

Entry 185   Map 8

Gloucestershire

Poulton Hill Estate

A stately drive sweeps up to the Cotswold stone house and vineyard, past a huge stag sculpture and paddocks on either side. All is immaculate – inside and out. Lawned grounds have topiary, a walled kitchen garden with trim lines of lettuces and tulips, a French fountain in the Cloister Garden to sit by. Step in to find hide rugs draped over big arm chairs, masses of art and more huge sculptures; bedrooms are lavishly comfortable with views over vines or orchard. Wake for Caroline's organic breakfast set on a vast table: croissants, yogurt, fresh fruit, eggs from the local farm, delicious bread. Head off for a game of tennis or a walk round the grounds.

Minimum stay: 2 nights. Children over 10 welcome.

Rooms	2 doubles; 1 double with separate bathroom: £95-£150. Singles £95-£110. Whole house available, £345-£410 per night.
Meals	Pubs/restaurants 15-minute walk.
Closed	Christmas & New Year.

Caroline & Max Thomas
Poulton Hill Estate,
Poulton,
Cirencester, GL7 5JA
Tel   +44 (0)1285 850700
Email   caroline.poultonhill@gmail.com
Web   www.poultonhillestate.co.uk

Entry 186   Map 8

Gloucestershire

The Old Bear

Step through the cool antiques showroom into a beautiful old house. Anne-Marie. charming and Danish, and Allan have filled their home with colour, polished antiques (of course) and vases of flowers. Upstairs to huge bedrooms with a sofa and armchair or two, books and tea tray with fresh coffee; beds have fine linen and bathrooms are pretty. Breakfast is at a lovely long sycamore table, with blue and white china in the dresser, gorgeous linen curtains at the window (looking onto the road); feast on French pastries, homemade jams, a neighbour's eggs, local bacon and sausages. Passing cars but quiet at night, so you sleep well.

Rooms	2 doubles (Z-beds & extra small double available): £95. Singles £75.
Meals	Pub/restaurant 1 mile.
Closed	Christmas.

Anne-Marie Hare
The Old Bear,
Perrotts Brook,
Cirencester, GL7 7BP
Tel   +44 (0)1285 831131
Email   annemarie.eaton1@btinternet.com
Web   www.hares-antiques.com

Entry 187   Map 8

Gloucestershire

The Guest House

Your own timber-framed house with masses of light and space, a sunny terrace, and spectacular valley and woodland views... A peaceful secluded place, it's full of books and mementoes of Sue's treks across the world; the large living room has wooden floors, lovely old oak furniture and French windows onto the rose-filled garden. Sue brims with enthusiasm and is a flexible host: breakfast can be over in her kitchen with delicious farm shop sausages and bacon, or continental in yours at a time to suit you. There's a wet room downstairs, and you hop up the stairs to your charming up-in-the-eaves bedroom with oriental rugs and a big comfy bed. Wonderful!

Rooms	1 double with sitting room & kitchenette: £140-£160. 3-6 night breaks £133-£152 per night, 7 nights £935.
Meals	Dinner, 2 courses, from £15; 3 courses, from £20. Pub 1 mile.
Closed	Christmas.

Sue Bathurst
The Guest House,
Manor Cottage, Bagendon,
Cirencester, GL7 7DU
Tel   +44 (0)1285 831417
Email   thecotswoldguesthouse@gmail.com
Web   www.cotswoldguesthouse.co.uk

Entry 188   Map 8

Gloucestershire

Clapton Manor

Karin and James's 16th-century manor is as all homes should be: loved and lived-in. And, with three-foot-thick walls, rich Persian rugs on flagstoned floors, sit-in fireplaces and stone-mullioned windows, it's gorgeous. The garden, enclosed by old stone walls, is full of birdsong and roses. One bedroom has a secret door leading to a fuchsia-pink bathroom; the other room, smaller, has a Tudor stone fireplace and wonderful garden views. Wellies, dogs, a comfy guest sitting room with lots of books... and breakfast by a vast fireplace: homemade bread, award-winning marmalade and eggs from the hens. A happy, charming family home.

Rooms	1 double, 1 twin/double: £110–£130. Singles from £100.
Meals	Pub/restaurants within 15-minute drive.
Closed	Rarely.

Karin & James Bolton
Clapton Manor,
Clapton-on-the-Hill, GL54 2LG
Tel   +44 (0)1451 810202
Mobile   +44 (0)7967 144416
Email   bandb@claptonmanor.co.uk
Web   www.claptonmanor.co.uk

Entry 189   Map 8

Gloucestershire

Calcot Peak House

A treat to stay in such a handsome old house with such relaxed owners – lovely Alex is full of enthusiasm for her B&B enterprise. There's an excellent butcher in Northleach so breakfasts are tip-top, and the bedrooms are a sophisticated mix of traditional and contemporary: Farrow & Ball colours, rich florals, fresh flowers, and fluffy white robes for trots to the bathroom. You also have your own charming drawing room: tartan carpet, pink sofas, family oils. Outside: 19 acres for Dexie the dog and a bench on the hill for the view. Tramp the Salt Way, dine in Cirencester, let the owls hoot you to sleep.

Dogs very welcome to sleep in utility room (comfortable and warm!) but not in bedrooms.

Rooms	1 double, 1 twin sharing bathroom & drawing room (let to same party only; children's room available): £95. Singles £75.
Meals	Pub 2 miles.
Closed	Rarely.

Tom & Alexandra Pearson
Calcot Peak House,
Northleach,
Cheltenham, GL54 3QB
Tel   +44 (0)1285 721047
Mobile   +44 (0)7738 468798
Email   pearsonalex5@gmail.com

Entry 190   Map 8

Gloucestershire

The Priest House

This romantic, ancient cottage is all yours. Tucked behind the owners' farm, and next to the Saxon church of St Andrew, part remains an atmospheric ruin. You sleep under soaring oak beams in the airy attic bedroom: sumptuous feather mattress, white linen, flowers; downstairs, you'll find a bathroom, and a big swish open-plan kitchen/sitting area. Delightful Jo leaves all you need to rustle up a full breakfast – or you can walk over to the main house if you'd like her to cook. The medieval-style vegetable garden is a perfect spot for a sundowner – the views are glorious – and it's a short drive to a good pub for supper.

Rooms	Cottage – 1 double with kitchen/sitting room: £110.
Meals	Pub 1 mile.
Closed	Rarely.

Joanna Davies
The Priest House,
Coln Rogers,
Cirencester,
Cheltenham, GL54 3LB
Tel   +44 (0)1285 720246
Email   joannadavies29@gmail.com

Entry 191   Map 8

Gloucestershire

Aylworth Manor

Set in a peaceful Cotswolds valley and surrounded by attractive gardens, John and Joanna's gorgeous manor is immaculate. Sit beside the wood-burner in the comfy snug or play the piano in a grand drawing room, rich with art and family photos: your hosts have that happy knack of making you feel instantly at home. Large sunny bedrooms come with garden and valley views, perfect linen on seriously cushy beds, antiques and lavish bathrooms. Wake refreshed for breakfast in the dining room: homemade bread, eggs from the ducks and hens, coffee in a silver pot. The Windrush Way passes the gate at the end of the drive. What a treat!

Over 12s welcome.

Rooms	1 double; 1 twin/double with separate bath: £90–£110. Singles £60.
Meals	Pub 1 mile.
Closed	Rarely.

John & Joanna Ireland
Aylworth Manor,
Naunton, Cheltenham, GL54 3AH
Tel   +44 (0)1451 850850
Mobile +44 (0)7768 810357
Email   enquiries@aylworthmanor.co.uk
Web   www.aylworthmanor.co.uk

Entry 192   Map 8

Gloucestershire

North Farmcote

Step back 50 years, to a solid 19th-century farmhouse high on the escarpment, and views falling away to the west; on a clear day you can see Hay Bluff. A brilliant spot for North Cotswolds' exploration, it is run by charming and gently self-deprecating David – farmer of cereals and sheep, keen walker, good shot. The exploits of his family decorate the walls (racing at Brooklands, hunting in Africa), there's a floral three-piece to sink into, a terrace with outstanding views, and a great pub you can stride to across fields. Bedrooms and bathrooms are old-fashioned, spacious, comfortable and spotless.

Rooms	1 double, 1 twin; 1 twin with separate bath: £85–£100. Singles £60.
Meals	Pub 2 miles.
Closed	January/February.

	David Eayrs
	North Farmcote,
	Winchcombe,
	Cheltenham, GL54 5AU
Tel	+44 (0)1242 602304
Email	davideayrs@yahoo.co.uk
Web	www.northfarmcote.co.uk

Entry 193   Map 8

Gloucestershire

Hanover House

The former home of Elgar's wife, in a Victorian terrace in Cheltenham's heart, is warm, elegant, inviting and surprisingly peaceful. There are big trees all around and the river Chelt laps at the foot of the garden. Inside, find a graceful period décor enlivened by exuberant splashes of colour; the delectable drawing room, with pale walls and a trio of arched windows, is the perfect foil for great art, books and rugs. Bedrooms are beautiful in vibrant red and amber; bathrooms are simply stylish. Breakfast is superb and served in the dining room window. Best of all are Veronica and James: musical, well-travelled, irresistible.

Rooms	1 double; 1 double with separate bath, 1 twin: £100–£120. Singles £70.
Meals	Pubs/restaurants 200 yds.
Closed	Rarely.

	Veronica & James Ritchie
	Hanover House,
	65 St George's Road,
	Cheltenham, GL50 3DU
Tel	+44 (0)1242 541297
Email	info@hanoverhouse.org
Web	www.hanoverhouse.org

Entry 194   Map 8

Gloucestershire

Detmore House

Down a private drive, surrounded by seven acres, this smart shiny house has been the home of poets, artists and writers. Gill carries on the creativity with her cooking, interior design, jewellery, gardening and chickens; she and Hugh are easy natural hosts. Supremely comfortable bedrooms have a smart hotel feel, bathrooms are immaculate and you and your dinner party guests will be spoiled with organic produce from the garden. There are wide lawns and mature trees and you can lap up the views across Charlton Hills from lots of lovely sitting spots. Cheltenham and the Cotswold Way are on the doorstep.

Rooms	2 twin/doubles, 1 twin: £85–£95. 1 family room for 3: £120–£150. Singles from £65.
Meals	Dinner from £28.50 (for groups of 6+). Packed lunch £6. Pub 1 mile.
Closed	Christmas & New Year.

Gill Kilminster
Detmore House,
London Road,
Charlton Kings,
Cheltenham, GL52 6UT

Tel	+44 (0)1242 582868
Email	gillkilminster@btconnect.com
Web	www.detmorehouse.com

Gloucestershire

The Courtyard Studio

This smart first-floor studio, attractive in reclaimed red brick, is reached via its own wrought-iron staircase; you are beautifully private. The friendly owners live next door, and will cook you a delicious breakfast in the house, or leave you a continental one in your own fridge. Find a clever, compact, contemporary space with a light and uncluttered living area, a mini window seat opposite two very comfortable boutiquey beds, fine linen, wicker armchair, and a patio area for balmy days. A 20-minute walk brings you to the centre of Cheltenham and you're a two-minute canter from the races.

Minimum stay: 2 nights.

Rooms	Studio – 1 twin: £85.
Meals	Restaurants/pubs within 1 mile.
Closed	Rarely.

John & Annette Gill
The Courtyard Studio,
1 The Cleevelands Courtyard,
Cleevelands Drive,
Cheltenham, GL50 4QF

Tel	+44 (0)1242 573125
Mobile	+44 (0)7901 978917
Email	courtyardstudio@aol.com

Gloucestershire

Rectory Farmhouse

Once a monastery, now a farmhouse with style. Passing a development of converted farm buildings to reach the Rectory's warm Cotswold stones makes the discovery doubly exciting. More glory within: Sybil, a talented designer, has created something immaculate, fresh and uplifting. A wood-burner glows in the sitting room, bed linen is white, walls cream; beds are superb, bathrooms sport cast-iron slipper baths and power showers and views are to the church. Your hosts are naturally friendly; Sybil used to own a restaurant and her breakfasts — by the Aga or in the conservatory under a rampant vine — are a further treat.

Over 14s welcome.

Rooms	2 doubles: £104–£110.
	Singles £85–£95.
Meals	Pubs/restaurants 1 mile.
Closed	Christmas & New Year.

Sybil Gisby
Rectory Farmhouse,
Lower Swell,
Stow-on-the-Wold, Cheltenham,
GL54 1LH
Tel   +44 (0)1451 832351
Email   rectoryfarmhouse@yahoo.com
Web   www.rectoryfarmhouse.yolasite.com

Entry 197   Map 8

Gloucestershire

Wren House

Barely two miles from Stow-on-the-Wold, this peaceful house sits charmingly on the edge of a tiny hamlet. It was built before the English Civil War and Kiloran spent two years stylishly renovating it; the results are a joy. Downstairs, light-filled, elegant rooms with glowing rugs on pale Cotswold stone; upstairs, delicious bedrooms, spotless bathrooms and a doorway to duck. Breakfast in the vaulted kitchen is locally sourced and organic, where possible, and the well-planted garden, in which you are encouraged to sit, has far-reaching views. Explore rolling valleys and glorious gardens; Kiloran can advise.

Minimum stay: 2 nights.

Rooms	1 twin/double; 2 twin/doubles, each with separate bath/shower: £110.
	Singles from £85.
	Well-behaved dogs welcome, one at a time, and only downstairs, £25.
Meals	Pubs/restaurants 1 mile.
Closed	Rarely.

Mrs Kiloran McGrigor
Wren House,
Donnington,
Stow-on-the-Wold, GL56 0XZ
Tel   +44 (0)1451 831787
Mobile   +44 (0)7802 676673
Email   enquiries@wrenhouse.net
Web   www.wrenhouse.net

Entry 198   Map 8

Gloucestershire

Donnington Manor

Through the pillared entrance find a slice of English life – old-fashioned grandeur in the Cotswolds. Kat and Henry, affable and interesting, keep their own chickens, bake their own bread, and breakfasts are delicious. Bedrooms (floral drapes, sinks in the room) have high ceilings and wonderful views, bathrooms (baths not showers) are a leisurely size and the drawing room and snug are to share: cosy log fires and plush sofas to melt into. In summer, the natural gardens come into their own and the views from the terrace reach for miles. Walkers rejoice: the Heart of England Way runs right by.

Rooms	1 double, 1 twin, each with separate bath: £120–£140. Singles £85.
Meals	Pub/restaurant 2 miles.
Closed	Rarely.

Katherine & Henry Dennis
Donnington Manor,
Donnington,
Moreton-in-Marsh, GL56 0YB
Mobile +44 (0)7913 461551
Email   katdnns@gmail.com

Entry 199   Map 8

Gloucestershire

Trinity House

Meet Zelie: generous, charming, and passionate about the Cotswolds. Off a lane in dreamy Upper Oddington is a smart modern house with a crisp gravel drive and newly planted borders. Inside, a country elegance prevails. Antique furniture shines with care and polish, walls are covered with 20th-century art and splendid sofas front the fire. Bedrooms and bathrooms ooze comfort and joy: one with a private balcony, another with its own terrace, all with village views. But don't snuggle under the goose down for too long: breakfast verges on the sinful and is locally sourced and delicious. Prepare to be thoroughly spoiled!

Rooms	1 double, 2 twin/doubles: £110–£120. Singles £70–£85.
Meals	Pubs within walking distance.
Closed	Rarely.

Zelie Mason
Trinity House,
Upper Oddington,
Moreton-in-Marsh, GL56 0XH
Tel   +44 (0)1451 831284
Mobile +44 (0)7809 429365
Email   info@trinityhousebandb.co.uk
Web   www.trinityhousebandb.co.uk

Entry 200   Map 8

Gloucestershire

The Old School

So comfortable and filled with understated style is this 1854 Cotswold stone house. Wendy and John are generous, beds are huge, linen is laundered, towels and robes are fluffy. Your own mini fridge is carefully hidden and pretty lamps cast a warm glow. Best of all is the upstairs sitting room: a chic, open-plan space with church style windows letting light flood in and super sofas, good art, lovely fabrics. A wood-burner keeps you toasty, Wendy is a grand cook and all is flexible. A gorgeous, relaxing place to stay – on the A44 but peaceful at night – that positively hums with hospitality. Guests say "even better than home!"

Minimum stay: 2 nights at weekends & in high season. Over 12s welcome.

Rooms	3 doubles, 1 twin/double: £120–£150. Singles £96–£125. Extra bed/sofabed available.
Meals	Dinner, 4 courses, £32. Supper, 2 courses, £18. Supper tray £12. Pub 0.5 miles.
Closed	Rarely.

Wendy Veale & John Scott-Lee
The Old School,
Little Compton,
Moreton-in-Marsh, GL56 0SL

Tel	+44 (0)1608 674588
Mobile	+44 (0)7831 098271
Email	wendy@theoldschoolbedandbreakfast.com
Web	www.theoldschoolbedandbreakfast.com

Entry 201   Map 8

Hampshire

Meadow Lodge

A summerhouse treat, tucked away beside the handsome Lodge, overlooking a pool and pretty landscaped gardens. French windows open to a terrace of tumbling wisteria, shrubs and pots. The huge bedroom is elegant and light, the bathroom luxurious; beds are well-dressed, there are books to read, rattan sofa and chairs, wide-screen TV, CDs and a lovely mix of family pieces, antiques and Liza's art. An English beakfast with home-laid eggs is brought over; help yourself to cereals, patisserie, toast, coffee… and your fridge is stocked with nibbles and drinks. Amble over the trout-filled river Anton and meadows for a pub supper.

Rooms	Summerhouse: 1 double, 2 singles (single room and extra beds available too): £75–£200. £140 for 3; £180 for 4; £200 for 5. Singles £85.
Meals	Dinner, 2 courses, £20. Pubs 5-minute walk.
Closed	Rarely.

Elizabeth Butterworth
Meadow Lodge,
Green Meadow Lane, Goodworth
Clatford, Andover, SP11 7HH

Tel	+44 (0)1264 352965
Mobile	+44 (0)7930 532822
Email	liza.butterworth@googlemail.com
Web	www.greenmeadowlodge.co.uk

Entry 202   Map 3

Hampshire

Yew Tree House

Philip and Janet's house is artistic and tranquil. The views, the house and the villagers are said to have inspired Dickens, who escaped London for the peace of the valley. The exquisite red brick house was there 200 years before him; the rare dovecote in the next door churchyard, to which you may have the key, 300 years before that. Thoughtful hosts, interesting to talk to, have created a home of understated elegance: a yellow-ochre bedroom with top quality bed linen, cashmere/silk curtains designed by their son, enchanting garden views, flowers in every room, a welcoming log fire. Breakfast with good coffee is delicious too.

Rooms	1 double: £85.
	Twin by arrangement.
Meals	Pub within 50 yds.
Closed	Rarely.

Philip & Janet Mutton
Yew Tree House,
Broughton,
Stockbridge, SO20 8AA
Tel   +44 (0)1794 301227
Email   pandjmutton@onetel.com

Entry 203   Map 3

Hampshire

Vinegar Hill Pottery

A sylvan setting, stylish pottery, a young and talented family. The cobalt blues and rich browns of David's ceramics fill the old stables of a Victorian manor house. Take pottery courses (one hour to a long weekend) or just enjoy the creative Mexican-inspired décor. A narrow staircase spirals up to a modern loft: crisp whites, cathedral ceiling with sunny windows, brilliant shower. The ground-floor garden suite has a patio (with a gorgeous Showman's wagon!), sitting room, painted bed and optional children's beds. Lucy brings breakfast to your room. Stroll to the beach: stretch out and you almost touch the Isle of Wight.

Minimum stay: 2 nights at weekends (April-October), 3 on bank holidays.

Rooms	1 double: £85.
	1 suite for 2-4: £95.
	1 wagon for 2 (available in summer, with separate wet room): £80.
	Singles from £60.
Meals	Pub/restaurant 0.25 miles.
Closed	Rarely.

Lucy Rogers
Vinegar Hill Pottery,
Vinegar Hill,
Milford on Sea, SO41 0RZ
Tel   +44 (0)1590 642979
Email   info@vinegarhillpottery.co.uk
Web   www.vinegarhillpottery.co.uk

Entry 204   Map 3

Hampshire

Bay Trees

The Isle of Wight and the Needles loom large as you approach Milford on Sea: the beach is shingle, the views are amazing. Mark and Sarah have become dab hands at B&B and welcome you in to a sun-filled conservatory with Ercol elm and beech tables and chairs; the home-bakes and award-winning breakfasts are delicious. Comfortable bedrooms, with good linen, are spotless and warm; bathrooms ooze white towels. One room opens to the lush garden: magnolias, weeping willow and pond; and chickens that lay your breakfast eggs! With Mark's background in hospitality and Sarah's passion for cooking the service here is second to none.

Minimum stay: usually 2 nights at weekends.

Rooms	1 double, 1 four-poster, 1 family room for 3: £100–£115. Singles £80–£90.
Meals	Restaurants 100 yds.
Closed	Rarely.

Mark & Sarah Clayson
Bay Trees,
8 High Street, Milford on Sea,
Lymington, SO41 0QD
Tel   +44 (0)1590 642186
Email   mark.clayson@btinternet.com
Web   www.baytreebedandbreakfast.co.uk

Entry 205   Map 3

Hampshire

Broadcroft

Tucked down a leafy lane, the Howards happy home is full of art, porcelain, antiques and traditional furnishings. Comfy bedrooms with new digital shower rooms are in a separate wing and face south over the pretty garden. Relax in the large, light and lovely drawing room which leads outside – perfect for children and dogs on sunny days. Breakfast on the terrace in summer, or in the conservatory – a colourful spot with grandchildren's drawings and Heather's collection of wire/pottery chickens topping the windowsills. Tuck into a hearty continental or full English. Lymington is fun: restaurants, shops and a great Saturday market.

Very pet friendly with secure garden. Minimum stay: 2 nights preferred at weekends.

Rooms	1 double, 1 twin: £75–£85. (Both rooms make a family suite.) Singles £60–£65.
Meals	Pubs/restaurants 0.5 miles.
Closed	Rarely.

Heather Howard
Broadcroft,
28 Broad Lane,
Lymington, SO41 3QP
Tel   +44 (0)1590 672741
Email   whoward@uwclub.net
Web   www.broadcroft-lymington.co.uk

Entry 206   Map 3

Hampshire

Garden Room at Furze Cottage

Your own peaceful garden escape with a fresh, sunny feel. Heather brings you a breakfast basket with toast, sourdough crumpets, croissants or hot sausage rolls, and you can help yourself to muesli, porridge and coffee. Her studio/workshop is next door – producing an amazing range of cards. Take an open top bus tour through the New Forest National Park, visit the local Wildlife Park to see otters and badgers, explore the coast. There are heaps of good restaurants nearby, and you can stroll to the oldest inn in the New Forest for a pint – serving drinks since 1096! Return to a gleaming shower room, sumptuous king-size bed and organic chocolates.

Minimum stay: 2 nights (April-October).

Rooms	1 suite for 2-4 with bunk bed: £100-£120. Extra £15 per additional person per night.
Meals	Pubs/restaurants 2 miles.
Closed	Rarely.

Heather Marten
Garden Room at Furze Cottage,
Holly Lane, Pilley,
Lymington, SO41 5QZ
Tel +44 (0)1590 672778
Email info@heathermarten.co.uk
Web www.newforestboutiquebandb.co.uk

Hampshire

Brymer House

Complete privacy in a B&B is rare. Here you have it, just a 12-minute walk from town, cathedral and water meadows. Relax in your own half of a Victorian townhouse immaculately furnished and decorated, and with a garden to match – all roses and lilac in the spring. Breakfasts are sumptuous, there's a log fire in the guests' sitting room and fresh flowers abound. An 'honesty box' means you may help yourselves to drinks. Bedrooms are small and elegant, with antique mirrors, furniture and bedspreads; bathrooms are warm and spotless. Guy and Fizzy have charmed Special Places guests for many years.

Children over 7 welcome.

Rooms	1 double, 1 twin: £85-£95. Singles £65-£70. Extra bed/sofabed available £20 per person per night.
Meals	Pubs/restaurants nearby.
Closed	Rarely.

Guy & Fizzy Warren
Brymer House,
29-30 St Faith's Road, St Cross,
Winchester, SO23 9QD
Tel +44 (0)1962 867428
Email brymerhouse@aol.com
Web www.brymerhouse.co.uk

Hampshire

Beechwood

In a popular residential area of town you find the best of both worlds: a bedroom that overlooks a huge garden, and the joys of Winchester a walk away – the Cathedral is 15 minutes. Tony and Cecile love their big Victorian house, offer you a cosy room with an elegant bed, a private sitting room (Dickens on the shelves, glowing coals in the grate), and a claw-foot bath for a luxurious soak. It's a family home, a place to relax, and flexible too; if you'd like breakfast outside you can have it. Catch the bus to Jane Austen's house at Chawton, dine finely in Winchester, pop into the local pub.

Rooms	1 double: £75.
	Singles £60.
Meals	Pub 5-minute walk.
Closed	Rarely.

Cecile Pryor
Beechwood,
Worthy Road,
Winchester, SO23 7AG
Tel   +44 (0)1962 869561
Email   tony_cecile@yahoo.co.uk
Web   www.beechwood-winchester.com

Hampshire

Bridge House

A beautifully tended garden, with a paved breakfast area, surrounds this 1920s family home and the Grettons couldn't be more hospitable: tea, cake and good talk on arrival; stacks of local knowledge. Family photos and evidence of Michael's naval career personalise the elegant sitting room, with its open fire and doors onto the garden. Bedrooms – Yellow and Blue – are comfortable, pretty, immaculate, and the double overlooks the garden. Steph's breakfasts are a happy mix of good things homemade and local. The old Watercress Line is nearby, Winchester is a draw and have you been to Jane Austen's Chawton?

Rooms	1 double; 1 twin with separate bath: £90-£105.
Meals	Pubs/restaurants 5-minute drive.
Closed	Rarely.

Stephanie & Michael Gretton
Bridge House,
Chillandham Lane, Martyr Worthy,
Winchester, SO21 1AS
Tel   +44 (0)1962 779379
Email   bh@itchenvalleybandb.com
Web   www.itchenvalleybandb.com

Hampshire

Shafts Farm

The 1960s farmhouse has many weapons in its armoury: a tremendous South Downs thatched-village setting, owners who know every path and trail, comfortable generous bedrooms and a stunning rose garden designed by David Austin Roses (parterres, obelisks, meandering paths). The two bedrooms are fresh in cream, florals and plaids, each with a shower room with heated floors to keep toes toasty. Homemade granola, garden fruit and the full English make a fine start to the day; the airy, cane-furnished conservatory is the place for afternoon tea and a read. Your hosts are both geographers and have created an intriguing display of maps.

Quiet village — motorbikes not encouraged.

Rooms	2 twins: £90.
	Singles £55.
Meals	Pubs/restaurants 500 yds.
Closed	Rarely.

Rosemary Morrish
Shafts Farm,
West Meon,
Petersfield, GU32 1LU

Tel	+44 (0)1730 829266
Email	info@shaftsfarm.co.uk
Web	www.shaftsfarm.co.uk

Entry 211   Map 4

Hampshire

Browninghill Farm

Complete independence here: your own prettily converted threshing barn down an oak-lined lane. Hattie lives in the farm next door and looks after you well; breakfasts and dinners are rustled up for you in your little kitchen — eggs from the hens, homemade bread and jams and local produce. The attractive dining/sitting space has a soaring ceiling, beams, a duck egg blue dresser holding cheerful crockery and a picture window with views across the fields. Bedrooms (one up, one down) are cosy with comfy feather pillows and white linen; bathrooms are small yet perfect with robes and big towels. Snug and romantic.

Minimum stay: 2 nights.

Rooms	Barn - 1 double: £110.
	1 single: £50.
Meals	Supper, 2 courses, £25.
	Pubs/restaurants 0.5 miles.
Closed	Rarely.

Hattie Pigot
Browninghill Farm,
Browninghill Green, Baughurst,
Tadley, RG26 5JZ

Tel	+44 (0)1189 815537
Mobile	+44 (0)7789 431220
Email	hattie@browninghillfarm.com
Web	www.browninghillfarm.com

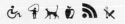

Entry 212   Map 4

Hampshire

Little Cottage

Just 45 minutes from Heathrow but the peace is deep, the views are long and the wildlife thrives – watch fox and deer, listen out for the rare nightjar. Chris and Therese grow summer salads and soft fruits and give you superb home cooking; eat in a big conservatory filled with greenery. Guests have a lovely sitting room with an eclectic mix of modern and antique furniture, and a pretty terrace overlooks the garden; bedrooms, likewise, are on the ground-floor, fresh and light, the double with distant views. Perfect for walkers and those who seek solace from urban life but don't want to stray too far.

Minimum stay: 2 nights at weekends (April-October). Over 12s welcome.

Rooms	1 double, 1 twin/double: £80–£95. 1 single: £55.
Meals	Dinner from £25. Pub 1.5 miles.
Closed	Christmas, New Year & occasionally.

Chris & Therese Abbott
Little Cottage,
Hazeley Heath, Hartley Wintney,
Hook, RG27 8LY

Tel	+44 (0)1252 845050
Mobile	+44 (0)7721 462214
Email	info@little-cottage.co.uk
Web	www.little-cottage.co.uk

Entry 213   Map 4

Herefordshire

Grendon Manor

The best of traditional meets modern country living: this 16th-century manor house is a super mix of the very old and very new. A working sheep and cattle farm is wrapped around it and you can walk over fields and down to a pretty Norman church. Jane is easy company and looks after you well. Guests in their own wing will rejoice in bedrooms with old beams, crisply comfortable linen and new bathrooms, while the guest sitting room downstairs has marvellous dark oak panelling, rich colours and glowing lamps. A farmhouse-tasty breakfast sets you up for beautiful Herefordshire walks, and Ludlow is close.

Rooms	2 doubles, 1 twin: £100. Singles £50.
Meals	Dinner £25 (groups only). Pub/restaurant 2 miles.
Closed	Rarely.

Jane Piggott
Grendon Manor,
Bredenbury,
Bromyard, HR7 4TH

Tel	+44 (0)1885 482226
Mobile	+44 (0)7977 493083
Email	jane.piggott@btconnect.com
Web	www.grendonmanor.com

Entry 214   Map 7

Herefordshire

Wickton Court

At the end of a no-through road, two miles from little Stoke Prior, is a rambling old place steeped in history, a courthouse that dates from the 15th century; ask Sally to show you the wig room! Be welcomed by ducks on the pond, sheep in the field, dogs by the fire, and lovely hosts who make you feel at home. The hallway is flagged, the sitting room panelled, the fireplace huge and often lit; all feels authentic and atmospheric. Visit Hampton Court Castle, antique-browse in Leominster, play golf, walk to the pub. Return to cosseting bedrooms with generous curtains, big bathrooms, wonky floors and ancient beams; one room even has a wood-burner.

Rooms	1 four-poster; 1 twin with separate bathroom: £95.
Meals	Dinner, 2 courses, £25. Cold platter for late arrivals, £12.50. Pubs/restaurants 5 miles.
Closed	Rarely.

Sally Kellard
Wickton Court,
Stoke Prior,
Leominster, HR6 0LN
Mobile +44 (0)7812 602122
Email sally@wickton.co.uk

Herefordshire

Bunns Croft

The timbers of this medieval yeoman's house are quite possibly a thousand years old. Little of the structure has ever been altered and it is sheer delight. Stone floors, rich colours, a piano, dogs, books, cosy chairs – all give a homely, warm feel. Cruck-beamed bedrooms are snugly small, the stairs are steep, and the twin's bathroom has its own sweet fireplace. The countryside is 'pure', too, with 1,500 acres of National Trust land a short hop away. Anita is charming, loves to look after her guests, grows her own fruit and vegetables and makes fabulous dinners. Just mind your head.

Rooms	1 twin; 1 double sharing bath with 2 singles (let to same party only): £80–£90. 2 singles: £40.
Meals	Dinner, 3 courses, £25. Pub 7 miles.
Closed	Rarely.

Anita Syers-Gibson
Bunns Croft,
Moreton Eye,
Leominster, HR6 0DP
Tel +44 (0)1568 615836

Herefordshire

The Old House

Dutch Andrea and Rick have poured love into their 16th-century house, restoring with traditional materials, using local craftspeople. It's now a home with an open house vibe brimming with dark beams, books, art, Delft Blue china and flowers. Bedrooms are colourful, comfortable and cottagey. Wake for a vegetarian spread with homemade jams, local honey and fruit salads or opt for traditional English with a twist; Andrea will do dinner too, often Ottolenghi-inspired – she's a great cook. It's a stroll to the village green and the local pubs. The rose-filled garden has a natural swimming pond, and a library in a shed.

Rooms	1 double; 1 twin/double with separate bath: £80. Singles £45.
Meals	Dinner, 3 courses with drinks, £17. Pub 5-minute walk.
Closed	Rarely.

Rick & Andrea Noordegraaf-Teeuw
The Old House,
Kingsland,
Leominster, HR6 9QS
Tel +44 (0)1568 709120
Email andrea@teacosy.nl
Web www.teacosy.nl

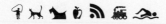

Entry 217 Map 7

Herefordshire

Staunton House

This handsome Georgian rectory has a traditional, peaceful feel. Step into light, colourful and well-proportioned rooms that brim with family photographs, antiques, china and masses of books. The original oak staircase leads to inviting bedrooms with comfortable beds, pretty fabrics and garden posies; the blue room looks onto garden and pond. Wander through the beautiful garden, drive to Hay or Ludlow, stride across ravishing countryside, play golf near Offa's Dyke; return to Rosie and Richard's lovely home to relax in their drawing room before enjoying a delicious dinner in the elegant dining room. You will be well looked after here.

Pets by arrangement.

Rooms	1 double, 1 twin/double: £85–£95. Singles £55–£65.
Meals	Dinner, 3 courses, £30. Pub/restaurant 2.5 miles.
Closed	Rarely.

Rosie & Richard Bowen
Staunton House,
Staunton-on-Arrow, Pembridge,
Leominster, HR6 9HR
Tel +44 (0)1544 388313
Mobile +44 (0)7780 961994
Email rosbown@aol.com
Web www.stauntonhouse.co.uk

Entry 218 Map 7

Herefordshire

Hall's Mill House

Quiet lanes bring you to this most idyllic spot – a stone cottage in a light and open valley. The sitting room is snug with a wood-burner and sofas but the kitchen is the hub of the place, and delicious breakfasts and dinners are cooked on the Aga. Grace, chatty and easy-going, obviously enjoys living in her modernised mill house. Bedrooms are small and sunny, with exposed beams and slate sills, candles and pretty old pine chests; only the old mill interrupts the far-reaching, all-green views. Drift off to sleep to the sound of the Arrow burbling by – a blissful tonic for walkers and nature lovers. Great value, too.

Rooms	1 double; 1 double, 1 twin sharing bath: £60-£75. Singles £30-£40.
Meals	Dinner from £15. Pub/restaurant 3 miles.
Closed	Christmas.

Grace Watson
Hall's Mill House,
Huntington,
Kington, HR5 3QA
Tel   +44 (0)1497 831409
Email   hallsmillhouse@hotmail.co.uk

Entry 219   Map 7

Herefordshire

Ty-Mynydd

Six miles over open heathland from Hay-on-Wye, it is a remote approach up the mountainside to Ty-Mynydd, and this renovated, stone-flagged farmhouse is absolutely gorgeous. Sheep graze the hillside, the views are simply the best. Relax by the log burner on leather sofas wrapped in a cosy Welsh blanket. Turn on the taps and taste water straight from your hosts' own mountain stream; awake to delicious rare-breed sausages and eggs produced in the fields around you (this is a working organic farm). The lovely young family give you two sweetly restful rooms on the ground floor, one with 'that view', and a simple country bathroom complete with roll top bath. The sunsets are magical.

Minimum stay: 2 nights at weekends.

Rooms	2 doubles sharing bathroom (2nd room let to same party only): £90. Singles £60.
Meals	Pubs 6-8 miles.
Closed	Christmas & New Year.

Niki Spenceley
Ty-Mynydd,
Llanigon,
Hay-on-Wye, HR3 5RJ
Tel   +44 (0)1497 821593
Mobile   +44 (0)7896 020459
Email   nikispenceley@gmail.com
Web   www.tymynydd.co.uk

Entry 220   Map 7

Herefordshire

Rock Cottage

Birds, books and beautiful Black Mountain views highlighted by morning sun, turning to an inky black line at dusk; the cottage glows. There's an instant feeling of warmth and friendliness as you step into the snug hall; find rich autumnal colours, old rugs, a big wood-burner and comfy sitting rooms. Local art and photos line the walls, bedrooms have sumptuous beds, perfect linen and garden posies. You eat (very well) en famille at the communal oak table, or out on the pretty terrace. Thoughtful Chris and Sue will take you to hear the dawn chorus and there are food and literary festivals, bookshops and walks galore.

Minimum stay: 2 nights. Pets by arrangement.

Rooms	2 doubles: £70–£90.
Meals	Packed lunch £6.
	Dinner, 1 course, £15; 3 courses, £23.
	Pub/restaurant 4 miles.
Closed	Christmas & New Year.

Chris & Sue Robinson
Rock Cottage,
Newton St Margarets,
Hereford, HR2 0QW
Tel   +44 (0)1981 510360
Email   robinsrockcottage@googlemail.com
Web   www.rockcottagebandb.co.uk

Entry 221   Map 7

Herefordshire

The Bridge Inn

Getting here is half the fun, down by the river in the wilds of Herefordshire. The 16th-century inn and farmhouse sit beneath the Black Hill of Bruce Chatwin fame and willows line the footbridge. Walkers descend, as do local farmers and shooting parties, and Glyn is a brilliant host. Comfy country bedrooms lie in the farmhouse; find antiques, flagstone floors and a dark panelled sitting room below. Breakfast in the farmhouse kitchen or hop over to the beamed pub for an outstanding full English spiced up with chorizo, served at scrubbed pine tables by the wood-burner. Dinner is very good too – and pints of Butty Bach will slip down nicely.

Rooms	1 double, 1 twin/double: £95.
	Hay Festival price for 2 per night: £165.
Meals	Lunch £8–£22.
	Dinner £12–£22.
Closed	Rarely.

Glyn Bufton & Gisela Vargas
The Bridge Inn,
Michaelchurch Escley,
Hereford, HR2 0JW
Tel   +44 (0)1981 510646
Email   contact@thebridgeinnmichaelchurch.co.uk
Web   www.thebridgeinnmichaelchurch.co.uk

Entry 222   Map 7

Yew Tree House

Sue and John's gorgeous 19th-century home is surrounded by gardens bejewelled with roses and fruit trees – plus stunning views across the Golden Valley to Hay Bluff. Meet these delightful people over tea and homemade cake in a tastefully decorated guest sitting room with comfy sofas, an open fire and shelves groaning with books. Generous bedrooms in pretty pastels are supremely comfortable, bathrooms have plenty of fluffy towels. Wake to the smell of baking bread, hasten to the dining room for a delicious breakfast of local produce. Dore Abbey's down the road, and Hay-on-Wye a half hour jaunt. The countryside is glorious.

New Inn at Brilley

Daphne is delightful, and spiritual and kind. Her ancient drovers inn shines brightly in the hills above Hay with its tattered Tibetan flags, wonky overgrown garden and words of wisdom at every turn. Enter a kingdom of peace, sleep in the house or the yurt, help yourself to supper or let yourself be cooked for. Spotless bedrooms (up steep steps) are pink or yellow, one with a teeny, sweet bathroom, one without (but Daphne can provide a potty). Homemade yogurt and plum jam at breakfast with eggs from her bantams, a warm and history-filled house crammed with collectibles and with views from every window. Unusual and uplifting.

Rooms	1 double, 1 twin: £80–£100. 1 suite for 3: £80–£100.
Meals	Dinner, 3 courses, £25. Pub/restaurant 3.5 miles.
Closed	Rarely.

Rooms	2 doubles sharing bathroom: £60–£70. 1 yurt for 6 with separate shower room: £70–£90. Singles £45.
Meals	Dinner with dessert £12.50. Pub 4 miles.
Closed	Rarely.

John & Susan Richardson
Yew Tree House,
Batcho Hill,
Vowchurch,
Hereford, HR2 9PF
Tel   +44 (0)1981 251195
Email   enquiries@yewtreehouse-hereford.co.uk
Web   www.yewtreehouse-hereford.co.uk

Daphne Tucker
New Inn at Brilley,
Brilley, Whitney-on-Wye,
Hereford, HR3 6HE
Tel   +44 (0)1497 831284
Email   karmadaphne@onetel.com
Web   www.newinnbrilley.co.uk

Entry 223   Map 7

Entry 224   Map 7

Herefordshire

East Friars

Laid back, lively and on the banks of the river Wye... Polly and Roger's family house will scoop you up and make you feel at home. Find a jumble of books, music and art in every corner, comfy armchairs in the lived-in sitting room and generous sunny bedrooms. Watch swans and ducks from the conservatory or terrace, while you tuck into Polly's local, seasonal, yummy breakfast with homemade bread and marmalade; she's a chef and holds pop-up restaurant nights in the conservatory too. Fish from the pontoon, borrow a canoe, bounce on trampolines, stroll to the city centre. Ted Hughes the Jack Russell and Bea the Cockerton love guests too!

Rooms	1 twin/double: £75–£115.
	1 family room for 4: £85–£120.
Meals	Pubs/restaurants 10-minute walk.
Closed	Rarely.

Polly Ernest
East Friars,
Greyfriars Avenue,
Hereford, HR4 0BE
Tel +44 (0)1432 276462
Email polly@eastfriars.co.uk
Web www.eastfriars.co.uk

Herefordshire

New Entry

Orchard Ridge

Pass pretty well-kept hedges, fruit trees and sheep and arrive at this lovely Georgian farmhouse for tea and homemade cake – in the sitting room or under an apple tree in the garden. The views towards the Malvern Hills are magnificent. Inside is lived-in and friendly: wood fires, family photos, comfy sofas and inviting bedrooms with goose down duvets. Breakfast includes homemade granola and lots of local produce: fruit, honey, bacon from happy pigs. Malvern Three Counties Showground is close, there's stabling and grazing if you fancy bringing your horse, and the Herefordshire trail runs past the end of the garden.

Rooms	2 doubles: £65–£100.
Meals	Dinner £30.
	Restaurants 1.5 miles away.
Closed	Rarely.

Belinda McMullen
Orchard Ridge,
Hill End, Rushall,
Ledbury, HR8 2PB
Mobile +44 (0)7759 975951
Email bel42@btinternet.com
Web www.orchard-ridge.co.uk

Herefordshire

The Coach House

Pots of flowers by the front door and Farne the friendly terrier greet you. Iola and Michael are warm, friendly, and give you a continental breakfast of homemade breads and preserves, eggs from Michael's hens, croissants from the local bakery. Their house is airy and pleasing with comfy sofas and an open fire in the sitting room, a huge dining room overlooking farmland and an inviting bedroom with painted beams, good linen and a bookcase full of novels. Sit in the garden and admire the glorious views to the south; head off for Ross-on-Wye, Ledbury, the music festival in Malvern, Cheltenham races and Wye valley walks.

Hertfordshire

Number One

It's worth hopping out of bed for Annie's breakfast: luxury continental with raspberry brioche or the full delicious Monty. Her house is a sparkling Aladdin's cave of mirrors, bunches of white twigs with birds atop, candles, cherubs, painted wooden floors, big open fires and generous bunches of roses. Bedrooms are lavishly done; nifty bathrooms have Italian tiles – and more roses! Close to the centre, this good-looking Georgian terrace house featured in Pevsner's guide to Hertfordshire, and the market town is busy with theatre, shops and galleries. Return for a gourmet dinner in the magical courtyard garden – when the sun is shining!

Over 12s welcome.

Rooms	1 double: £85.
	Singles £55.
Meals	Continental breakfast.
	Pubs/restaurants 1 mile.
Closed	Rarely.

Rooms	1 double with separate bath/shower;
	2 twin/doubles: £105-£130.
Meals	Dinner £40. BYO.
	Pubs/restaurants 5-minute walk.
Closed	Rarely.

Iola & Michael Fass
The Coach House,
Old Gore,
Ross-on-Wye, HR9 7QT
Tel   +44 (0)1989 780339
Email iolafass@btinternet.com
Web   www.thecoachhousebandb.com

Annie Rowley
Number One,
1 Port Hill, Hertford, SG14 1PJ
Tel   +44 (0)1992 587350
Mobile +44 (0)7770 914070
Email   annie@numberoneporthill.co.uk
Web   www.numberoneporthill.co.uk

Isle of Wight

Westbourne House

Watch the yachts go by from this elegant townhouse on the waterfront. A welcoming drink and chat with Richard in the drawing room sets you up well: antiques, oil paintings, a bevy of guitars, family photos – and stunning views. Bedrooms (one downstairs) have WiFi, home-baked biscuits, cosy well-dressed beds. Kate gives you breakfast: with the view: lots of choice, homemade marmalade – and Bucks Fizz too; if you're an early bird you can help yourself to a continental spread. You're between the two main marinas and close to the high street, so attractive shops, bars and restaurants (as well as the Southampton ferry) are all a saunter.

Over 13s welcome.

Rooms	2 doubles: £110.
Meals	Pubs/restaurants 1-minute walk.
Closed	Rarely.

Kate Gough
Westbourne House,
43 Birmingham Road,
Cowes, PO31 7BH
Tel   +44 (0)1983 290009
Email   katec56@gmail.com
Web   www.westbournehousecowes.co.uk

Entry 229   Map 4

Isle of Wight

Arreton Manor

A dream of a manor… Jacobean, grand and gorgeous. Owned by a parade of English monarchs, including Edward the Confessor and Henry VIII, it rests peacefully in five acres of landscaped gardens. Snooze by a fire in the atmospheric Old Hall, breakfast in the wonderful dining room: ancient oak panelling, polished table and gilt-framed pictures of nobility. Gleaming bedrooms have rich fabrics and excellent linen. Wake for Julia's award-winning breakfast: local sausages and bacon, famous Arreton tomatoes, homemade jams. Village pubs are a stroll, festival sites a short drive; it's a treat to stay in this friendly, very special home.

Rooms	2 doubles: £115-£130.
Meals	Pubs 5-minute walk.
Closed	Rarely.

Julia Gray-Ling
Arreton Manor,
Main Road,
Newport, PO30 3AA
Tel   +44 (0)1983 522604
Email   julia@arretonmanor.co.uk
Web   www.arretonmanor.co.uk

Entry 230   Map 4

Isle of Wight

Redway Farm

Immerse yourself in the rolling landscape of the sunny Arreton Valley... up a winding lane find a handsome, south-facing Georgian farmhouse and friendly Linda. Bedrooms are quiet, large, light and sumptuous with thick mattresses, gorgeous linen and lovely views over the gardens; warm bathrooms sparkle. Downstairs is delightful with antiques, roaring fires and fresh flowers. You breakfast on fresh croissants from the Aga – or the full works with eggs from the hens, in the sun-filled morning room or the dining room with wood-burner. Explore acres of bird-sung garden, cycle to sandy beaches. Bliss.

Rooms	2 doubles, each with separate bath: £89–£99. Extra bed/sofabed available £20 per person per night.
Meals	Pub 3 miles.
Closed	Rarely.

Linda James
Redway Farm,
Budbridge Lane, Merstone,
Newport, PO30 3DJ

Tel	+44 (0)1983 865228
Mobile	+44 (0)7775 480830
Email	lindajames.redway@gmail.com
Web	www.bedbreakfast.redwayfarm.co.uk

🐦 🐈 🐎 📶 🚂 🐃 ✕

Isle of Wight

New Hill Farm

We've had to wrestle this one from Canopy & Stars, so taken were their team by this deeply unusual B&B. A bit like an iceberg in that you only see the tip, below is a veritable labyrinth of guest rooms made from wattle and daub (without the wattle) and all decorated in Sawday's favourite, 'Mole's Breath' by Farrow & Ball (of course). If you're lucky you may meet owner Mo as she scurries past dressed head to toe in brown velvet, lorgnettes perched on her nose – she loves to dish the dirt on fellow guests. So successful has her self-build concept been that she has plans for more – expect to see them sprouting up all over the place.

Price	Dig deep.
Rooms	24 at time of going to press.
Meals	None but humus and mud pies available all day.
Closed	Occasionally if nearby neighbours have anything to do with it.
Directions	Cross the perfect lawn and you can't miss it.

Mo Leskine
New Hill Farm
Old Sodbury
SOD OFF

Tel	Nope
Email	Too busy
Web	www.noplacelikeloam.co.uk

Isle of Wight

Lisle Combe

How many gardens sport tall palms, miniature donkeys and lawns that slope down to woods, fields and beach — with Botanic Gardens next door? The grounds are huge, the position is uplifting and upper rooms have views of the sea. Author Alfred Noyes lived here in the 1930s and the feel is timeless; today grandson Robert, wife Ruth and their young family, run gentle, charming, traditional B&B. After a day exploring Ventnor and all the coves and beaches, return to carpeted corridors, faded satin sofas, delightful gilt-framed oils and old-fashioned tranquillity. Bedrooms are homely, lofty, with floral cotton bedspreads.

Minimum stay: 2 nights July & August.

Rooms	1 double; 1 double with separate bath/shower: £90-£110. 1 triple with separate bath/shower: £90-£120. Child £25.
Meals	Pubs/restaurants 2 miles.
Closed	December-February.

	Robert & Ruth Noyes
	Lisle Combe,
	Undercliff Drive,
	St Lawrence,
	Ventnor, PO38 1UW
Tel	+44 (0)1983 852582
Email	enquiries@lislecombe.co.uk
Web	www.lislecombe.co.uk

Isle of Wight

Gotten Manor

Miles from the beaten track and bordered by old stone barns, the guest wing of this Saxon house is charmingly simple. Up steep stone steps (you must be nimble!) and through a low doorway find big bedrooms in laid-back rustic, funky French style: beams, limewashed stone, wooden floors, Persian rugs and a sweet window. Sleep on a rosewood bed and bathe by candlelight — in a roll top tub in your room. Friendly, informal Caroline serves breakfast in the old creamery: homemade yogurts, compotes and organic produce. There's a walled garden and a guest living room with cosy wood-burner.

Minimum stay: 2 nights at weekends. Over 12s welcome.

Rooms	2 doubles: £95-£105.
Meals	Pub 1.5 miles.
Closed	Rarely.

	Caroline Gurney-Champion
	Gotten Manor,
	Gotten Lane,
	Chale, PO38 2HQ
Tel	+44 (0)1983 551368
Mobile	+44 (0)7746 453398
Email	as@gottenmanor.co.uk
Web	www.gottenmanor.co.uk/bed-breakfast

Isle of Wight

Northcourt

A Jacobean manor in matchless grounds: 15 acres of terraced gardens, exotica and subtropical flowers. The house is magnificent too; huge but a lived-in home with big comfortable guest bedrooms in one of the wings. The formal dining room has separate tables, where delicious homemade bread and jams, garden fruit, honey and local produce are served. There's a snooker table in the library, a chamber organ in the hall and a grand piano in the vast music room. Groups are welcome and John offers garden tours. The peaceful village is in lovely downland – and you can walk from the garden to the Needles.

Rooms	3 twin/doubles: £78–£105. Singles £50–£68.
Meals	Pub 3-minute walk through gardens.
Closed	Rarely.

John & Christine Harrison
Northcourt,
Shorwell, PO30 3JG
Tel   +44 (0)1983 740415
Mobile   +44 (0)7955 174699
Email   christine@northcourt.info
Web   www.northcourt.info

Entry 235   Map 4

Kent

Dadmans

Once the dower house to Lynsted Park, Dadmans sits in parkland with nearby orchards and grazing cattle and sheep. Your breakfast eggs are laid by rare-breed hens and Amanda sources fantastic local produce for dinner, served in the dining room on gleaming mahogany or in the Aga-warmed kitchen. There's an elegant drawing room to enjoy, and lovely bedrooms have indulgent beds, flowers, views and good bathrooms. Pretty outside too with ancient trees, walled areas, a nuttery and box-edged herb garden, and plenty of castles and cathedrals to visit nearby. A special retreat where you feel part of the family.

Children over 4 welcome.

Rooms	1 twin; 1 double with separate bath: £70–£100. Singles by arrangement.
Meals	Dinner, 4 courses, £35. Supper from £15. Pubs/restaurants nearby.
Closed	Rarely.

Amanda Strevens
Dadmans,
Lynsted, Sittingbourne, ME9 0JJ
Tel   +44 (0)1795 521293
Mobile   +44 (0)7931 153253
Email   amanda.strevens@btopenworld.com
Web   www.dadmans.co.uk

Entry 236   Map 5

Huntingfield House

A sleepy setting... a long drive through parkland brings you to this Georgian-fronted manor house and delightful host Emma. It's a friendly family home with chickens, ponies and two stable cats who like to go for walks with the basset hounds. Classic country-house bedrooms have garden views, flowers and tea trays. Hop down for breakfast in the sunny elegant dining room: home-reared bacon and sausages, homemade bread and marmalade. Lots of treats nearby will keep you happy: Leeds Castle, Sissinghurst, shopping in Canterbury... Emma is a keen cook – so you might return to a tasty informal supper (or three-course spread) too.

Minimum stay: 2 nights in high season.

Rooms	1 double, 1 twin: £90–£100. Singles £60–£70. Dinner, B&B £110–£140 per person. Extra bed/sofabed available £30 per person per night.
Meals	Supper, 2 courses, £20. Dinner, 3 courses, £30. Pubs/restaurants 2 miles.
Closed	Rarely.

	Emma Norwood
	Huntingfield House,
	Stalisfield Road,
	Eastling,
	Faversham, ME13 0HT
Tel	+44 (0)1795 892138
Email	emma@huntingfieldhouse.co.uk
Web	www.huntingfieldhouse.co.uk

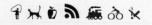

The Linen Shed

A weatherboard house with a winding footpath to the front door and a pot-covered veranda out the back: sit here and nibble something delicious and homemade while you contemplate the pretty garden with its gypsy caravan. Vickie, wreathed in smiles, has created a 'vintage' interior: find wooden flooring, reclaimed architectural pieces, big old roll tops, a mahogany loo seat. Bedrooms (two up, one down) are painted in the softest colours, firm mattresses are covered in fine cotton or linen, dressing gowns hang in the smart bathrooms. Food is seriously good here, and adventurous – try a seaside picnic hamper!

Rooms	2 doubles with separate bath/shower, 1 double with separate bath (occasionally shared with family): £85–£110. Singles from £75.
Meals	Picnic hamper from £20. Pub/restaurant 300 yds.
Closed	Rarely.

	Vickie Hassan
	The Linen Shed,
	104 The Street,
	Boughton-under-Blean,
	Faversham, ME13 9AP
Tel	+44 (0)1227 752271
Mobile	+44 (0)7714 646469
Email	bookings@thelinenshed.com
Web	www.thelinenshed.com

Kent

Northwood Lodge

Emma is happy to share her friendly home. Bedrooms have pretty beds and rugs on painted floors; the huge guest bathroom is gorgeous: freestanding bath, fluffy towels, scented lotions, a jug of flowers. A delicious breakfast with a dish of the day and homemade jam is served in the big, bright kitchen, or outside in the sun. You can settle in the drawing room for a film/dinner night (book beforehand), and there's another sitting room with heaps of books, open fire and large antique mirrors. Head out for seaside walks, Whitstable Oyster Festival and Faversham with its medieval market place; Canterbury and Margate are a short drive too.

Minimum stay: 2 nights at weekends & in high season. Children over 8 welcome.

Rooms	2 doubles sharing bathroom: £110. Singles £85.
Meals	Dinner from £25. Dinner & movie from £35. Pubs/restaurants 5 miles.
Closed	Rarely.

Emma Clarke
Northwood Lodge,
Bullockstone Road,
Herne Bay, CT6 7NR
Tel   +44 (0)1227 634549
Email   emma@stellarproductions.co.uk

🐈 🐾 📶 🚂 ✕

Entry 239   Map 5

Kent

7 Longport

A delightful, unexpected hideaway bang opposite the site of St Augustine's Abbey and a five-minute walk to the Cathedral. You pass through Ursula and Christopher's elegant Georgian house to emerge in a pretty courtyard, with fig tree and rambling rose, to find your self-contained cottage. Downstairs is a cosy sitting room with pale walls, tiled floors and plenty of books, and a clever, compact wet room with mosaic tiles. Then up steep stairs to a swish bedroom with crisp cotton sheets on a handmade bed and views of magnolia and ancient wisteria. You breakfast in the main house or in the courtyard on sunny days. Perfect.

Rooms	Cottage - 1 double with sitting room: £90-£100. Singles £70.
Meals	Restaurants 5-minute walk.
Closed	Rarely.

Ursula & Christopher Wacher
7 Longport,
Canterbury, CT1 1PE
Tel   +44 (0)1227 455367
Email   info@7longport.co.uk
Web   www.7longport.co.uk

🐾 📶 🚂 ✕

Entry 240   Map 5

Kent

Waterlock House

A stylish Georgian town house with your own airy loft apartment on two floors. Judith gives you a key to a separate entrance, so come and go as you please. The vast bedroom/sitting room has French antique quirky pieces, a painted black and white diamond floor, a sink-into sofa and a very comfortable big bed with a colourful cover. Hop downstairs for a continental breakfast with croissants, local ham, boiled eggs – and the papers too. There's a fantastic, authentic Provençal-style walled garden behind, Sophie and Judith's decorative antique shop next door – have a browse – and you're surrounded by pretty villages and marvellous walks.

Well-behaved pets welcome (no access to garden).

Rooms	1 apartment for 2 with sitting room & kitchenette: £120.
Meals	Continental breakfast. Pubs/restaurants 2-minute walk.
Closed	Rarely.

Sophie Norton
Waterlock House,
Canterbury Road, Wingham,
Canterbury, CT3 1BH
Tel   +44 (0)1227 721792
Email   branchingoutwingham@gmail.com
Web   www.branchingoutwingham.co.uk

Entry 241   Map 5

Kent

Park Gate

Peter and Mary are a generous team and their conversation is informed and easy. Behind the wisteria-clad façade are two sitting rooms with inglenook fireplaces, ancient beams and polished wood. Fresh comfortable bedrooms have TVs, gorgeous views over the garden to the fields beyond and gleaming bathrooms. Meals are delicious! More magic outside: croquet, tennis and thatched pavilions, wildlife and roses and a sprinkling of sheep to mow the paddock. The house dates back to 1460 and has a noble history: Sir Anthony Eden lived here and Churchill visited during the war. Great value, and convenient for Channel Tunnel and ferries.

Rooms	2 twin/doubles: £85. 1 single with separate shower: £45.
Meals	Occasional dinner, 3 courses, £30. Simple supper £17.50. Pubs/restaurants 1 mile.
Closed	Christmas, New Year & January.

Peter & Mary Morgan
Park Gate,
Elham,
Canterbury, CT4 6NE
Tel   +44 (0)1303 840304
Email   marylmorgan@hotmail.co.uk

Entry 242   Map 5

Kent

Farthingales

Deep in rural Kent (yet 15 minutes from Canterbury and Dover) is a village hall-house of great character with a Victorian draper's shop addition. Overlooking Nonington Church and fields beyond, inside all is warm and inviting. The twin in the main house has colourful rugs on wooden floors, and a big bathroom with freestanding blue tub; the bedrooms in the 'old shop' wing have comfy beds and headphones for the TV; sitting rooms are delightful with pretty sofas and cosy wood-burner. Ex-radio presenter Peter brings a fine breakfast to your table overlooking beautiful gardens and orchard; you can breakfast outside on balmy days.

Cots & highchairs available.

Rooms	Main house - 1 twin: £75-£95. Old shop wing - 1 double, 2 twins: £75-£95. Singles £65.
Meals	Pub 0.5 miles (discounted meals for Farthingales guests).
Closed	Rarely.

Peter Deeley
Farthingales,
Old Court Hill, Nonington,
Dover, CT15 4LQ
Tel +44 (0)1304 840174
Email farthingalesbandb@yahoo.co.uk
Web www.farthingales.co.uk

Entry 243   Map 5

Kent

Kingsdown Place

A huge white Italianate villa set in terraced gardens running down to the sea – on clear days you can see France! Tan has renovated house and garden with panache: modern art festoons the walls, statues lurk and all is light and contemporary. Upstairs are superb bedrooms: one four-poster with garden views, and, up a spiral staircase in the loft, a private suite with a sitting room, terrace and view of the sea. All have Conran mattresses and white linen. Breakfast on scrambled eggs, smoked salmon or the full works, out on the terrace in good weather. Relaxed seaside chic and a mere hop from Deal, Dover, Walmer and Sandwich.

Rooms	1 double, 1 four-poster, each with separate bath & sitting room: £95-£100. 1 suite for 2 with sitting room & terrace: £120-£130. Singles from £75.
Meals	Packed lunch £10. Dinner £25. Restaurant 500 yds. Pub 0.5 miles.
Closed	Christmas & New Year.

Tan Harrington
Kingsdown Place,
Upper Street,
Kingsdown, CT14 8EU
Tel +44 (0)1304 380510
Email tan@tanharrington.com

Entry 244   Map 5

Stowting Hill House

A classic manor house in an idyllic setting, close to Canterbury and the North Downs Way. This warm, civilised home mixes Tudor beams with Georgian proportions; find a huge conservatory full of greenery, a guest sitting room with sofas and log fire, and breakfasts fresh from the Aga. Traditional bedrooms are carpeted and cosily furnished. Your charming, country-loving hosts welcome you with tea and flowers from the garden – a perfect spot with its lawns, tree-lined avenue, bluebell woods and stone obelisk. Not much more than a half hour train ride from London – and ten minutes from the Chunnel, but this is worth more than one night.

Rooms	1 twin/double, 1 twin: from £100. Singles from £65.
Meals	Dinner from £30. Pub 1 mile.
Closed	Christmas & New Year.

Richard & Virginia Latham
Stowting Hill House,
Stowting,
Ashford, TN25 6BE

Tel	+44 (0)1303 862881
Email	lathamvj@gmail.com
Web	www.stowtinghillhouse.co.uk

Entry 245   Map 5

The Old Rectory

On a really good day (about once every year) you can see France. But you'll be more than happy to settle for the superb views over Romney Marsh, the Channel in the distance. The big, friendly house, built in 1845, has impeccable, elegant bedrooms and good bathrooms; the large, many-windowed sitting room is full of books, pictures and flowers from the south-facing garden. Marion and David are both charming and can organise transport to the Channel Tunnel for you. It's remarkably peaceful – perfect for walking (right on the Saxon Shore path), cycling and bird watching.

Children over 10 welcome.

Rooms	1 twin; 1 twin with separate bath/shower: £80–£90. Singles £60.
Meals	Pubs within 4 miles.
Closed	Christmas & New Year.

Marion & David Hanbury
The Old Rectory,
Ruckinge,
Ashford, TN26 2PE

Tel	+44 (0)1233 732328
Email	oldrectory@hotmail.com
Web	www.oldrectoryruckinge.co.uk

Entry 246   Map 5

Kent

Snoadhill Cottage

You'll feel at home the moment you arrive at Yvette and Philip's friendly cottage. Once a medieval 'hall house', it's awash with huge oak beams. Up steep stairs and past shelves of books find fresh, sunny bedrooms with lovely views. Enjoy a flagstone terrace for summery breakfasts or a fireside spot in the dining room; expect eggs from the hens, homemade jams, kippers perhaps or a full English. You're surrounded by glorious open countryside, walks and cycle rides start from the door and it's just 25 minutes from the Channel Tunnel. Dip in the swimming pond, chat to Rocky the labrador... and wander the blooming gardens.

Rooms	1 double with separate shower, 1 twin with separate bath: £80–£85. Singles £65.
Meals	Pub 1 mile.
Closed	Rarely.

Yvette James
Snoadhill Cottage,
Snoadhill, Bethersden,
Ashford, TN26 3DY
Tel   +44 (0)1233 820245
Email   enquiries@snoadhillcottage.co.uk
Web   www.snoadhillcottage.co.uk

Entry 247   Map 5

Kent

Romden

Guarded by tall trees and songbirds, lording it over meadows and lanes, this rambling 'castle' with its 16th-century tower has a charmingly lived-in feel. Lovely laid-back Miranda and Dominic make you feel at home; help yourself to cereals while they drum up your bacon and eggs, play croquet or use their pool and tennis court (by arrangement). Bedrooms, sitting room and hall are decked out with pretty wallpapers, antiques, paintings, rugs and throws; log fires keep things toasty; kids can gambol with the dogs on a flower filled terrace and lawn. And if you're hankering after a real castle, Sissinghurst and Leeds are down the road.

Rooms	1 double, 1 twin; 1 twin with separate bath: £70–£95. Singles £55–£75.
Meals	Pubs/restaurants 1.5 miles.
Closed	Rarely.

Miranda Kelly
Romden,
Smarden,
Ashford, TN27 8RA
Tel   +44 (0)1233 770687
Email   miranda_kelly@hotmail.com
Web   www.romdencastle.co.uk

Entry 248   Map 5

Kent

Hereford Oast

Jack the Jack Russell will meet you, swiftly followed by Suzy who'll bring you tea and cake in the garden: sheer heaven in summer. The 1876 oast house, set back from a country road and gazing on lush fields, has become the loveliest B&B. Downstairs is the dining room, as unique as it is round. Upstairs is the guest room, sunny, fresh and bright, with a blue and white theme and a rural view. As for the village – white-clapboard cottages, pubs, fine church – it's the prettiest in Kent. Sausages from Pluckley and homemade soda bread set you up for cultured jaunts: Leeds Castle, Sissinghurst, Great Dixter… all marvellously close.

Rooms	1 twin/double: £85–£90.
	Singles £50–£55.
Meals	Pubs 1 mile.
Closed	Rarely.

	Suzy Hill
	Hereford Oast,
	Smarden Bell Road,
	Smarden,
	Ashford, TN27 8PA
Tel	+44 (0)1233 770541
Email	suzy@herefordoast.fsnet.co.uk
Web	www.herefordoast.co.uk

Entry 249   Map 5

Kent

Merzie Meadows

This lovely ranch-style house has huge windows, pergolas groaning with climbers and a Mediterranean-style swimming pool. Sitting in landscaped gardens, paddocks and woodland there are horses, hens, wild flowers and lots of twittering birds. Pamela gives you a locally sourced breakfast with fruits, organic bread and just-laid eggs. Bedrooms are beautifully dressed with pretty fabrics, handmade mattresses are topped with good linen and goose down pillows; the suite has a sitting area looking onto the garden, a study and a bathroom sleek with Italian marble and plump towels. All is peaceful; garden and nature lovers will adore it here.

Minimum stay: 2 nights at weekends April-September.

Rooms	1 double: £110.
	1 suite for 2-3: £110–£115.
	Singles £100. Extra bed/sofabed
	available £50 per person per night.
Meals	Pub 2.5 miles.
Closed	Mid-December to February.

	Pamela Mumford
	Merzie Meadows,
	Hunton Road, Marden,
	Maidstone, TN12 9SL
Tel	+44 (0)1622 820500
Mobile	+44 (0)7762 713077
Email	merziemeadows@me.com
Web	www.merziemeadows.co.uk

Entry 250   Map 5

Kent

Reason Hill

Brian and Antonia's 200-acre fruit farm is perched on the edge of the Weald of Kent, with stunning views over orchards and oast houses. The farmhouse has 17th-century origins (low ceilings, wonky floors, stone flags) and a conservatory for sunny breakfasts; colours are soft, antiques gleam, the mood is relaxed. Pretty bedrooms have garden views, TVs and magazines; there's a comfy sitting room too. Come in spring for the blossom, in summer for the fruit and veg from the garden; chickens roam free. The Greensand Way runs along the bottom of the farm, you're close to Sissinghurst Castle and 45 minutes from the Channel Tunnel.

Rooms	1 double, 2 twins: £85–£90.
	1 single, sharing shower with double
	(let to same party only): £50.
Meals	Pubs within 1 mile.
Closed	Christmas & New Year.

Brian & Antonia Allfrey
Reason Hill,
Linton,
Maidstone, ME17 4BT

Tel	+44 (0)1622 743679
Mobile	+44 (0)7775 745580
Email	antonia@allfrey.net
Web	www.reasonhill.co.uk

Entry 251   Map 5

Kent

Ightham

Lord it through electric oak gates to find B&B in your own modern barn. Gardening enthusiast Caroline's house is close but not hugely visible: you're wonderfully independent. Bedrooms on the ground floor are eclectic and appealing, with pine floors, dazzling white walls and slatted wooden blinds for a moody light; the bathroom is big and contemporary with a walk-in shower. Upstairs: an enormous family space for sitting, eating, playing, and glass doors on to a terrace for outdoor fun. Breakfast is delivered: eggs from the hens, pancakes, French toast. Great walks start from the door; return for supper — Caroline loves to cook.

Rooms	Barn – 1 double, 1 twin (let to
	same party only): £115–£125.
	Extra bed/sofabed available £25 per
	person per night.
Meals	Pub/restaurant 5-minute walk.
Closed	Rarely.

Caroline Standish
Ightham,
Hope Farm,
Sandy Lane, Ightham,
Sevenoaks, TN15 9BA

Tel	+44 (0)1732 884359
Email	clstandish@gmail.com
Web	www.ighthambedandbreakfast.co.uk

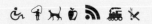

Entry 252   Map 5

Kent

Eggpie B&B at Pond Cottage

Afternoon tea and cake is offered on arrival – in the sunken garden in summer. Hard to believe that this stunning house in the middle of Eggpie Lane is just minutes from the A21. It started life in 1580 as a gamekeeper's cottage; now it is listed and loved, by delightful hosts Graham and Mandy. Settle in amongst low beams, standing timbers, ancient slabs, and a charming medley of armchairs and sofas around the inglenook. Three lovely bedrooms are decorated in keeping with the country cottage feel, and an inspired Kentish breakfast is served in the oldest part of the house. Visit Chartwell, Knole, Hever, Penshurst Place.

Minimum stay: 2 nights during busy periods.

Rooms	2 doubles; 1 double sharing bath (let to same party only): £90–£150. Singles £90–£135.
Meals	Restaurant 1 mile.
Closed	Rarely.

	Amanda Webb
	Eggpie B&B at Pond Cottage,
	Eggpie Lane, Weald,
	Sevenoaks, TN14 6NP
Mobile	+44 (0)7768 020201
Email	enquiries@eggpiebandb.com
Web	www.eggpiebandb.com

Entry 253   Map 5

Kent

Charcott Farmhouse

The 1750s farmhouse is rustic and family orientated, and if you don't come expecting an immaculate environment you will enjoy it here. In the old bake house there's a small sitting room with original beams and bread oven, TV and WiFi; relax in here on cooler days, with cats and a dog to keep you company. On sunny days tea is served in the garden. Bedrooms are pretty and comfy with blankets and eiderdowns, oriental rugs and antique furniture. Nicholas – a tad eccentric for some – is half French and cooks amazing breakfasts on the Aga, while Ginny's great grandfather (Arnold Hills) founded West Ham football team. Come and go as you please.

Rooms	2 twins; 1 twin with separate bath: £75–£90. Price varies according to season. Singles from £55.
Meals	Pub 5-minute walk.
Closed	Rarely.

	Nicholas & Ginny Morris
	Charcott Farmhouse,
	Charcott, Leigh,
	Tonbridge, TN11 8LG
Tel	+44 (0)1892 870024
Mobile	+44 (0)7734 009292
Email	charcottfarmhouse@btinternet.com
Web	www.charcottfarmhouse.com

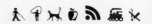

Entry 254   Map 5

22 Lansdowne Road

Built in 1861, this house in leafy Tunbridge Wells "has never been as Victorian as it is now". So says Harold, whose devotion to Victoriana knows no bounds. Deep colours, rich velvets, marble tables, authentic wallpapers, tasselled lamps, portraits of Queen Victoria, tea and scones by the fire… be prepared to take a serious step back in time. Bedrooms have antique lace-edged sheets; the largest has a six foot bed, a sitting area – and an amazing Victorian style bathroom with slipper bath and Victorian toilet all hidden behind what appears to be a wardrobe door! Breakfast is a locally sourced spread, and Harold is the perfect host.

Off-road parking.

Rooms	1 double, 2 twin/doubles: £100–£120. Singles £80.
Meals	Dinner, 3 courses, £35. Pubs/restaurants within 5-minute walk.
Closed	Rarely.

	Harold Brown
	22 Lansdowne Road,
	Tunbridge Wells, TN1 2NJ
Tel	+44 (0)1892 533633
Mobile	+44 (0)7714 264489
Email	info@thevictorianbandb.com
Web	www.thevictorianbandb.com

Entry 255   Map 5

Kent

New Entry

Barclay Farmhouse

Lynn's breakfasts are fabulous: fresh fruit, warm croissants, home-baked breads and a daily changing twist on the traditional English. The weatherboarded guest barn may be in perfect trim but it has a been-here-forever feel; you have country-cosy dining tables for breakfast, a patio for summer, a big peaceful garden. Gleaming bedrooms have handmade oak bedheads, chocolates, slippers, discreet fridges, radios, TVs; shower rooms are in perfect order. Couples, honeymooners, garden lovers – many would love it here (but no children: the garden pond is deep). Warm-hearted B&B, and glorious Sissinghurst nearby.

Minimum stay: 2 nights at weekends in high season.

Rooms	Barn - 3 doubles: £95. Singles from £70.
Meals	Pubs/restaurants 1 mile.
Closed	Rarely.

	Lynn Ruse
	Barclay Farmhouse,
	Woolpack Corner,
	Biddenden, TN27 8BQ
Tel	+44 (0)1580 292626
Email	info@barclayfarmhouse.co.uk
Web	www.barclayfarmhouse.co.uk

Entry 256   Map 5

Ramsden Farm

The views across the Wealds are stunning! These former farm buildings have been renovated with flair, and Sally has created a gorgeous, comfortable home. Unhurried, very good breakfasts are eaten in the huge kitchen by the jaunty lemon Aga, and floor to ceiling glass doors open on to a wooden deck; spill outside on warm days. After a hearty walk you can doze in front of a tree-devouring inglenook. Find lovely sunny bedrooms with more of that view from each, natural colours, tip-top mattresses and the crispest white linen – chocolates too; bathrooms have travertine marble and underfloor heating. Friendly, spoiling and completely peaceful.

Pullington Barn

Up a private drive and straight in to a vast, beamed expanse of bright light, warm colours, beautiful art and a cheery welcome from Gavin and Anne in their converted barn. There are endless books to choose: settle in the comfy drawing room with its grand piano, or sit in the pretty south-facing garden on a fine day. On the other side, views from the orchard spread over oast houses and church spires. Big bedrooms (one on the ground floor) have good mattresses, coordinated bed linen and feather pillows. You breakfast well on local and homemade produce, served at the travertine table in the dining hall. Lovely walks from the door.

Children over 9 welcome, younger ones by arrangement.

Rooms	1 double, 1 twin; 1 double with separate bath: £95-£120.
Meals	Pub 1 mile.
Closed	Rarely.

Rooms	1 double, 1 twin: £85-£100. Singles £60-£80.
Meals	Pub/restaurant 0.5 miles.
Closed	Christmas.

	Sally Harrington
	Ramsden Farm,
	Dingleden Lane,
	Benenden, TN17 4JT
Tel	+44 (0)1580 240203
Email	sally@ramsdenfarmhouse.co.uk
Web	www.ramsdenfarmhouse.co.uk

	Gavin & Anne Wetton
	Pullington Barn,
	Benenden, TN17 4EH
Tel	+44 (0)1580 240246
Mobile	+44 (0)7849 759929
Email	anne@wetton.info
Web	www.wetton.info/bandb

Entry 257   Map 5

Entry 258   Map 5

Kent

Beacon Hall House

A family home and Julie truly enjoys having guests. Aga breakfasts are full of delicious homemade, home-grown things; dinner too, perhaps cottage pie or Hastings sea bass with veg from the garden. Find sweet herbs on your pillow, home-baked biscuits, flowers and beautiful eclectic furnishings in comfortable bedrooms. Explore seven acres of paddocks, cutting garden and mature elevated terraces, with gorgeous views across rolling Kent and Sussex. Sissinghurst and Great Dixter, castles and pretty villages are close. Return to a sitting room with huge relaxing sofas and fat cushions; Buster and Hetty the spaniels are an added boon.

Rooms	1 double, 1 twin/double: £95–£110. 1 family room for 4: £110–£140. Singles £75–£95.
Meals	Supper from £20. Pubs within 10 miles.
Closed	Christmas.

Julie Jex
Beacon Hall House,
Rolvenden Road,
Benenden, TN17 4BU
Tel   +44 (0)1580 240434
Email   julie.jex@btconnect.com
Web   www.beaconhallhouse.co.uk

Entry 259   Map 5

Kent

Lamberden Cottage

Down a farm track find two 1780 cottages knocked into one, with flagstone floors, a cheery wood-burner in the guest sitting room and welcoming Beverley and Branton. There's a traditional country-cottage feel with pale walls, thick oak beams, soft carpeting and very comfortable bedrooms (the twin has an adjoining bedroom); views from all are across the Weald of Kent. Wander the lovely gardens to find your own private spot, sip a sundowner on the terrace, eat a hearty breakfast in the family dining room: home-grown fresh fruits, homemade marmalades and yogurts. Near to Sissinghurst, Great Dixter and many historic places.

Rooms	1 double, 1 twin with adjoining twin room: £75–£100. Singles from £65.
Meals	Pub 1 mile.
Closed	Christmas & New Year.

Beverley & Branton Screeton
Lamberden Cottage,
Rye Road, Sandhurst,
Cranbrook, TN18 5PH
Tel   +44 (0)1580 850743
Mobile +44 (0)7768 462070
Email   thewalledgarden@lamberdencottage.co.uk
Web   www.lamberdencottage.co.uk

Entry 260   Map 5

Lancashire

Sagar Fold House

In a spectacular setting, a 17th-century dairy and two perfect studios, one up, one down. Private entrances lead to big beamed spaces that marry immaculate efficiency with unusual beauty. A gorgeous Indian door frame serves as the en suite door upstairs, soft colours and contemporary touches lift the spirit, plentiful books and DVDs entertain you and a continental breakfast is supplied – homemade and organic whenever possible. The gardens are amazing with lovely places to sit, a sweet old summer house and an Italian knot garden – very Wolf Hall! Take walks in deeply peaceful countryside; top-notch places to eat are an easy drive.

Rooms	2 studios for 2, each with kitchenette: £90.
Meals	Continental breakfast in fridge. Pubs/restaurants 1-2 miles.
Closed	Rarely.

	Helen & John Cook
	Sagar Fold House,
	Higher Hodder,
	Clitheroe, BB7 3LW
Tel	+44 (0)1254 826844
Mobile	+44 (0)7850 750709
Email	helencook14@gmail.com
Web	www.sagarfoldhouse.co.uk

Lancashire

Challan Hall

The wind in the trees, the boom of a bittern and birdsong. That's as noisy as it gets. On the edge of the village, delightful Charlotte's former farmhouse overlooks woods and Haweswater Reservoir; deer, squirrels and Leighton Moss Nature Reserve are your neighbours. The Cassons are well-travelled and the house, filled with a colourful collection of mementos, is happily and comfortably traditional. Expect a sofa-strewn sitting room, a smart red and polished-wood dining room and two freshly floral bedrooms (one with a tiny shower room). Morecambe Bay and the Lakes are on the doorstep – come home to lovely views and stunning sunsets.

Rooms	1 twin/double; 1 twin/double with separate bath: £75. 2 nights or more: £70 (Mon-Fri). Singles from £50.
Meals	Dinner, 2 courses, £25. Packed lunch available. Pubs 1 mile.
Closed	Rarely.

	Charlotte Casson
	Challan Hall,
	Silverdale, LA5 0UH
Tel	+44 (0)1524 701054
Mobile	+44 (0)7790 360776
Email	cassons@btopenworld.com
Web	www.challanhall.co.uk

Leicestershire

Breedon Hall

Through high brick walls find a listed Georgian manor house in an acre of garden, and friendly Charlotte and Charles. Make yourselves at home in the fire-warmed drawing room full of fine furniture and pictures; carpets and curtains are in the richest, warmest reds and golds. Charlotte is a smashing cook and gives you homemade granola, jams and marmalade with local eggs, bacon and sausages; you'd kick yourself if you didn't book dinner. Bedrooms are painted in soft colours, fabrics are thick, beds covered in goose down; bathrooms are immaculate. Borrow a bike and discover the glorious countryside right on the cusp of two counties.

Check availability calendar on owners' website.

Rooms	5 doubles: £75–£150.
Meals	Supper £25.
	Dinner, 3 courses, £35.
	Pub/restaurant 1-minute walk.
Closed	Occasionally.

Charlotte Meynell
Breedon Hall,
Main Street,
Breedon-on-the-Hill,
Derby, DE73 8AN
Tel +44 (0)1332 864935
Mobile +44 (0)7973 105467
Email charlottemeynell1963@gmail.com
Web www.breedonhall.com

Entry 263   Map 8

Leicestershire

Curtain Cottage

A pretty village setting for this cottage on the main street, next door to Sarah's interior design shop. You have your own entrance by the side and through a large garden, which backs onto fields with horses and the National Forest beyond. A conservatory is your sitting room: wicker armchairs, wooden floors, a contemporary take on the country look. Bedrooms are light and fresh: linen from The White Company on sumptuous beds, slate-tiled bathrooms, stunning fabrics. Breakfast is full English with eggs from the hens or fresh fruit and croissants from the local shop – all is delivered to you. Perfect privacy.

Rooms	1 double, 1 twin: £85–£90.
	Singles £60–£70.
Meals	Pubs/restaurants 150 yds.
Closed	Rarely.

Sarah Barker
Curtain Cottage,
92-94 Main Street,
Woodhouse Eaves, LE12 8RZ
Tel +44 (0)1509 891361
Mobile +44 (0)7906 830088
Email sarah@curtaincottage.co.uk
Web www.curtaincottage.co.uk

Entry 264   Map 8

Leicestershire

Kicklewell House

The last house in the village overlooks miles of fields and the garden includes paddocks and stables. Fiona, easy, hospitable, great fun, loves horses, dogs and fine art; her cream walls glow with artwork, much of which she frames and sells. The house is warm, inviting and a visual delight: big deep sofas, bright ethnic rugs, a trusty Aga, heaps of books. After a scrumptious local breakfast, stride off to the lovely Foxton Canal, or visit one of the big local houses and gardens like Cottesbrooke Hall and Holdenby. Bedrooms are as peaceful and as charming as can be; good dogs are welcomed with open arms.

Rooms	1 double, 1 twin: £90.
	Singles £50.
Meals	Dinner, 3 courses, £25.
	Packed lunch £7.50.
	Pubs 2 miles.
Closed	Christmas & Easter.

Fiona Shann
Kicklewell House,
Laughton,
Lutterworth, LE17 6QF
Tel   +44 (0)1162 404173
Email   fonishann@gmail.com

Entry 265   Map 8

Leicestershire

The Gorse House

Passing cars are less frequent than passing horses – this is a peaceful spot in a pretty village. Lyn and Richard's 17th-century cottage has a feeling of lightness and space; there's a fine collection of paintings and furniture, and oak doors lead from dining room to guest sitting room. Country style bedrooms have green views and are simply done. The garden layout was designed by Bunny Guinness, you can bring your horse (there's plenty of stabling) and it's a stroll to a good pub dinner. The house is filled with laughter, breakfasts with home-grown fruits are tasty and the Cowdells are terrific hosts who love having guests to stay.

Rooms	1 double: £75.
	1 family room for 4: £90-£125.
	Stable - 1 triple with kitchenette: £75-£112.
	Singles £45.
Meals	Packed lunch £5.
	Pub 75 yds (closed on Sun eves).
Closed	Rarely.

Lyn & Richard Cowdell
The Gorse House,
33 Main Street, Grimston,
Melton Mowbray, LE14 3BZ
Tel   +44 (0)1664 813537
Mobile +44 (0)7780 600792
Email   cowdell@gorsehouse.co.uk
Web   www.gorsehouse.co.uk

Entry 266   Map 9

Lincolnshire

Baumber Park

Lincoln red cows and Longwool sheep surround this attractive rosy-brick farmhouse – once a stud that bred a Derby winner. The old watering pond is now a haven for frogs, newts and toads; birds sing lustily. Maran hens conjure delicious eggs, and charming Clare, a botanist, is hugely knowledgeable about the area. Bedrooms are light and traditional with mahogany furniture; two have heart-stopping views. Guests have their own wisteria-covered entrance, sitting room with an open fire, dining room with local books and the lovely garden to roam. This is good walking, riding and cycling country; seals and rare birds on the coast.

Minimum stay: usually 2 nights at weekends in high season.

Rooms	2 doubles; 1 twin with separate shower: £65–£75. Singles £35–£60.
Meals	Pubs 1.5 miles.
Closed	Christmas & New Year.

Clare Harrison
Baumber Park,
Baumber,
Horncastle, LN9 5NE

Tel	+44 (0)1507 578235
Mobile	+44 (0)7977 722776
Email	mail@baumberpark.com
Web	www.baumberpark.com

Entry 267   Map 9

Lincolnshire

The Grange

Wide open farmland and an award-winning farm on the edge of the Lincolnshire Wolds. This immaculately kept farm has been in the family for generations; Sarah and Jonathan are delightful and make you feel instantly at home. Find acres of farmland and a two-mile farm trail to explore, a trout lake to picnic by and an open fire to warm you in an elegant drawing room with Georgian windows. Sarah gives you delicious homemade cake on arrival and huge Aga breakfasts with home-laid eggs and local produce. Comfortable bedrooms have TVs, tea trays and gleaming bathrooms. Fabulous views stretch to Lincoln Cathedral and the walks are superb.

Rooms	2 doubles: £72–£78. Singles £49–£50.
Meals	Supper from £18. Dinner, 2 courses, from £25. BYO. (No meals during harvest.) Pub/restaurant 1 mile.
Closed	Christmas & New Year.

Sarah & Jonathan Stamp
The Grange,
Torrington Lane,
East Barkwith, LN8 5RY

Tel	+44 (0)1673 858670
Mobile	+44 (0)7951 079474
Email	sarahstamp@farmersweekly.net
Web	www.thegrange-lincolnshire.co.uk

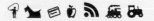

Entry 268   Map 9

Lincolnshire

Grayingham Lodge

An attractive stone farmhouse surrounded by fields. Jane and Peter's house is a working sheep farm, and you arrive to a welcoming cup from a silver teapot and delicious cake by the fire. If you're peckish later too, there are homemade flapjacks in pretty, very comfortable bedrooms. In the morning, the sideboard holds an impressive spread: homemade marmalade, fruit salad, compote, cereals – and a tasty cooked breakfast to follow. Have a day sightseeing in Lincoln – the Cathedral is magnificent and the castle has a copy of the Magna Carta; explore the Lincolnshire Wolds and coast; head off early for some exciting racing at Blyton Park.

Rooms	3 doubles: £85.
	Singles £55.
Meals	Pubs/restaurants 3 miles.
Closed	Rarely.

Jane Summers
Grayingham Lodge,
Gainsborough Road, Northorpe,
Gainsborough, DN21 4AN
Tel   +44 (0)1652 648544
Email   janesummers@btinternet.com
Web   www.grayinghamlodge.co.uk

Entry 269   Map 13

Lincolnshire

The Manor House

At the end of a neatly raked gravel drive, a new manor house with wide views and stunning sunsets over the peaceful Trent valley. The Days have farmed in the village since 1898 and look after you with rich warm comfort and friendly ease. You have your own entrance hall leading to a bedroom with opulent curtains, period furniture, comfy sofa and rural art. There's a sunny patio outside your annexe, and the beautiful gardens are awash with roses, ducks on the pond, horses in the paddock. Shooting can be arranged and you can fish for carp in the lake, or play golf nearby; there are music and art festivals, antique fairs and walks in abundance too.

Rooms	Annexe - 1 twin/double with kitchenette: £75.
	Singles £50.
Meals	Pub/restaurant 3.5 miles.
Closed	Christmas & New Year.

Judy Day
The Manor House,
Manton, Kirton Lindsey,
Gainsborough, DN21 4JT
Tel   +44 (0)1652 649508
Mobile +44 (0)7712 766347
Email   enquiries@manorhousebedandbreakfast.co.uk
Web   www.manorhousebedandbreakfast.co.uk

Entry 270   Map 13

Lincolnshire

The Old Farm House

You will feel at home in this rambling, quirky house — Nicola loves having guests to stay. Three cottages combined, the house is 300 years old and it's said that Dick Turpin, on the run, once hid in the roof. Read the papers by a winter fire, flop into worn leather chairs, sip an evening glass of wine in the garden, sleep soundly on a fine brass bed. Rooms are named after the men of the extended family — King Henry, George and James — and all are colourful, comfortable and cushioned. There are cycle routes, walks and golf courses galore (Nicola has all the info), racing at Market Rasen, quaint churches to visit and an annual classic car rally.

Rooms	2 doubles: £80.
	1 family room for 4: £120
	(£90 for 3, £80 for 2).
	Singles £55.
Meals	Pub 2.5 miles.
Closed	Christmas, New Year &
	occasionally.

Nicola Clarke
The Old Farm House,
Low Road, Hatcliffe,
Grimsby, DN37 0SH
Tel   +44 (0)1472 824455
Mobile   +44 (0)7818 272523
Email   clarky.hatcliffe@btinternet.com
Web   www.oldfarmhousebandbgrimsby.com

Entry 271   Map 13

London

37 Trevor Square

A three-minute walk from Hyde Park or Harrods — a fabulous find. The square is peaceful, private, exquisite, so find a pretty corner and enjoy. Margaret ran an interior design company — rather successfully, by the look of things — and serves a superb full English breakfast in the kitchen/diner; there's also a small conservatory you are welcome to use. Bedrooms (one downstairs has an enormous bed and a little patio) have goose down pillows, cashmere duvets, electric blankets and a mini fridge; slip on your robe, listen to some music or watch a DVD — it's all here. Blissful luxury in the middle of Knightsbridge.

Tube: Knightsbridge. Nearest car park £25 for 24 hrs (closed overnight).

Rooms	1 twin/double; 1 double sharing
	shower with single (let to same
	party only): £200.
	1 single: £50–£75.
	Single in twin/double £120.
Meals	Restaurants 200 yds.
Closed	Occasionally.

Margaret & Holly Palmer
37 Trevor Square,
Knightsbridge, SW7 1DY
Tel   +44 (0)20 7823 8186
Email margaret@37trevorsquare.co.uk
Web   www.37trevorsquare.co.uk

Entry 272   Map 22

London

90 Old Church Street

In a quiet street facing the Chelsea Arts Club is an enticing, contemporary haven. Softly spoken Nina is passionate about the arts, knows Chelsea inside out and takes real pleasure in looking after her guests. Antique shop spoils stand alongside more modern delights, the attention to detail is amazing and there are plentiful bunches of flowers. A lush carpet takes you up to the second floor and your super-private, surprisingly peaceful and deliciously designed bedroom and bathroom. Breakfast – fruit platters, yogurt and croissants – is shared with Nina in the kitchen. We love No. 90 – and the little black poodles!

Minimum stay: 2 nights on weekdays, 3 nights at weekends, 4 nights in high season.

Rooms	1 double: £120–£150. Singles £100–£130.
Meals	Continental breakfast £10. Restaurants nearby.
Closed	Occasionally.

Nina Holland
90 Old Church Street,
Chelsea, SW3 6EP

Tel	+44 (0)20 7352 4758
Mobile	+44 (0)7831 689167
Email	ninastcharles@gmail.com
Web	www.chelseabedbreakfast.com

Entry 273   Map 22

London

21 Barclay Road

A great city find. All is swish and contemporary here: polished oak floors, beautifully done bedrooms with decanters of sherry and luxuriously dressed beds (one a splendid king), and smart, sparkling Philippe Starck bathrooms. There's a grand piano and delightful Charlotte and Adrian occasionally host lively social music evenings. Help yourself to good espresso and a light breakfast tray in your room before setting off to tour London. Charlotte, who does something unspeakably high-powered by day, will happily advise you on the best restaurants and places to visit.

Minimum stay: usually 3 nights, 4 nights in high season.

Rooms	2 doubles: £135–£160. Singles £110–£125. Extra bed/sofabed available £15 per person per night.
Meals	Continental breakfast. Food & music evenings occasionally. Pubs/restaurants 2-minute walk.
Closed	Occasionally.

Charlotte Dexter
21 Barclay Road,
Fulham, SW6 1EJ

Tel	+44 (0)20 7384 3390
Mobile	+44 (0)7767 420943
Email	info@barclayhouselondon.com
Web	www.barclayhouselondon.com

Entry 274   Map 22

London

London

8 Parthenia Road

Caroline, an interior designer, mixes the sophistication of the city with the feel of the countryside and her handsome big kitchen is the engine-room of the house. It leads through to a light breakfast room with doors onto a pretty brick garden with chairs and table – hope for fine days. The house is long and thin, Fulham style, and reaches up to a big sloping-ceilinged bedroom in the eaves, cosy, sunny and bright. A remarkably quiet place to stay in an accessible part of town, near the King's Road with all its antique and designer shops, and Chelsea Football ground.

Tube: Parsons Green, 4-minute walk. Parking £17.60 per day in street (9am-5pm), free on Sunday. Bus 22, 2-minute walk.

22 Marville Road

Smart railings help a pink rose climb, orange lilies add a touch of colour, and breakfast is in the pretty back garden on sunny days. Ben, the springer and Tizzie the cocker spaniel, and Christine – music lover, traveller, rower – make you feel at home. Your big light-filled bedroom is high up in the eaves and comes in elegant French grey with comfortable beds, crisp linen, pretty lamps, a smart bathroom and a chaise longue for lounging and reading. The house is friendly with treasures from Christine's travels and gentle music at breakfast; there's a baby grand to play too. Restaurants and shops are a stroll away and the Boat Race down the river.

Children over 10 welcome.

Rooms	1 twin/double: £100–£140. Singles from £85.
Meals	Continental breakfast. Restaurants nearby.
Closed	Rarely.

Rooms	1 twin/double: £95–£105. Singles £95.
Meals	Continental breakfast. Pubs/restaurants nearby.
Closed	Rarely.

	Caroline & George Docker
	8 Parthenia Road,
	Fulham, SW6 4BD
Tel	+44 (0)20 7384 1165
Email	dockercaroline@gmail.com

	Christine Drake
	22 Marville Road,
	Fulham, SW6 7BD
Tel	+44 (0)20 7381 3205
Email	chris@christine-drake.com
Web	www.londonguestsathome.com

Entry 275   Map 22

Entry 276   Map 22

London

35 Burnthwaite Road

Near Queen's Club and Wimbledon for tennis and Fulham Broadway's tube, a sweet terraced house on the sunny side of the street. A fresh aqua carpet ushers you up to a bright bedroom on the second floor, and a spotless white bathroom squeezed under the eaves. It's as peaceful as can be. No sitting room but a rather smart dining table for breakfast – croissants, cereals, fresh fruit salad. A traditional and civilised feel prevails, thanks to lovely family pieces, fine china, touches of chintz – and friendly Diana who helps you plan your day. Buses to Piccadilly and Westminster, a stroll to the Thames, all of London at your feet.

Tube: Fulham Broadway, 6-minute walk. Parking pay & display. Bus 211, 414, 14.

Rooms	1 twin/double: £100–£120. Singles £85–£105.
Meals	Pubs/restaurants within walking distance.
Closed	Rarely.

Diana FitzGeorge–Balfour
35 Burnthwaite Road,
Fulham, SW6 5BQ
Tel   +44 (0)20 7385 8081
Mobile   +44 (0)7831 571449
Email   diana@dianabalfour.co.uk
Web   www.dianabalfour.co.uk

Entry 277   Map 22

London

15 Delaford Street

A pretty Victorian, terraced Fulham home, inside all charming and spacious. In a tiny, sun-trapping courtyard you can have continental breakfast in good weather – tropical fruits are a favourite and the coffee is very good; a second miniature garden bursts with life at the back. The bedroom, up a spiral staircase, looks down on it all. Expect perfectly ironed sheets on a comfy bed, a quilted throw, books in the alcove, a sunny bathroom and fluffy white towels. The tennis at Queen's is in June and on your doorstep. Tim and Margot – she's from Melbourne – are fun, charming and happy to pick you up from the nearest tube.

Tube: West Brompton. Parking free eves & weekends; otherwise pay & display. 74 bus to West End nearby.

Rooms	1 double: £100–£105. Singles £80.
Meals	Restaurants nearby.
Closed	Occasionally.

Margot & Tim Woods
15 Delaford Street,
Fulham, SW6 7LT
Tel   +44 (0)20 7385 9671
Email   woodsmargot@hotmail.co.uk

Entry 278   Map 22

London

Colet Gardens

This smart Victorian terraced house is an easy base for Kensington and a ten-minute walk from the hustle of Hammersmith. A home of art, sculptures, books and music, and Jane and Rod offer you a large modern loft studio with floor to ceiling windows, colourful rug and a day bed, or a smaller comfy double on the first floor; both have little shower rooms. A continental breakfast is served at the kitchen table; French windows lead out to a palm-dotted courtyard where you can have your coffee in the sun. Convenient for tube or bus, and close to the Lyric Theatre, Riverside Studios, and a Thames riverside amble with good pubs along the way.

Minimum stay: 2 nights.

Rooms	1 studio room with kitchenette: £60–£105. Garden Room - 1 double: £60–£105.
Meals	Pub/restaurant 5-minute walk.
Closed	Rarely.

Jane Kennard
Colet Gardens,
West Kensington, W14 9DH
Mobile   +44 (0)7958 932749
Email   janekennard@btinternet.com
Web   www.guestinlondon.com

Entry 279   Map 22

London

31 Rowan Road

Terrific value for money in leafy Brook Green. The two studios are fantastic spaces: one under the eaves (comfy twin beds and armchairs, a deep cast-iron bath from which you can gaze at the birds), the other larger and more contemporary in style, on the lower ground floor, with its own wisteria-clad entrance. All independent with a continental breakfast popped in your fridge. Or join in with family life and stay in the little pink bedroom with books and hats, and take breakfast in the pretty conservatory with Vicky and Edmund. A friendly home with flowers, art, photos and a relaxed vibe – Tiger the terrier and a blossoming garden too.

Tube: Hammersmith. Off-street parking £20 a day.

Rooms	1 double with separate bath/shower; 2 studios with kitchenette: £75–£130. Singles £75. Extra bed/sofabed available £20 per person per night.
Meals	Continental breakfast. Pubs/restaurants 2 minutes.
Closed	Occasionally.

Vicky & Edmund Sixsmith
31 Rowan Road,
Brook Green,
Hammersmith, W6 7DT
Tel   +44 (0)20 8748 0930
Mobile   +44 (0)7966 829359
Email   vickysixsmith@me.com
Web   www.abetterwaytostay.co.uk

Entry 280   Map 22

London

101 Abbotsbury Road

The area is one of London's most desirable and Sunny's family home is opposite the borough's loveliest park, with open-air opera in summer. The top floor is for visitors. Warm, homely bedrooms are in gentle beiges and greens, with pale carpets, white duvets, pelmeted windows and a pretty dressing table for the double. The bathroom, marble-tiled and sky-lit, shines. You are well placed for Kensington High Street, Olympia, Notting Hill, Portobello Market, Kensington Gardens, the Albert Hall, Knightsbridge and Piccadilly! Relax, unwind, feel free to come and go.

Children over 6 welcome. Tube: Holland Park, 7-minute walk. Off-street parking sometimes available.

Rooms	1 double, sharing bath with single: £110–£120. 1 single: £60–£65.
Meals	Continental breakfast. Pubs/restaurants 5-minute walk.
Closed	Occasionally.

Sunny Murray
101 Abbotsbury Road,
Holland Park, W14 8EP
Tel   +44 (0)20 7602 0179
Mobile +44 (0)7768 362562
Email sunny.murray@googlemail.com

Entry 281 Map 22

London

1 Peel Street

Pretty, gabled and surprisingly quiet with central London on your doorstep. Fascinating old maps, photos from Susie's world travels and objets d'art all create an unusual and elegant feel. The top floor is all yours: the bedroom is full of character, framed by the slanting angles of the roof and soothingly decorated in neutral shades; the shelf above the snug-looking bed is crammed with interesting reads. Breakfast is at a table overlooking the patio: organic bread, pastries, fruit and excellent coffee. Just a stroll to good tapas, wine bars, Hyde Park and Notting Hill. Hop on a bus or tube to explore further. Guests love it here.

Rooms	1 double with separate bath/shower: £125. Singles £95.
Meals	Continental breakfast. Pubs/restaurants 2-minute walk.
Closed	Occasionally.

Susan Laws
1 Peel Street,
Kensington, W8 7PA
Tel   +44 (0)20 7792 8361
Mobile +44 (0)7776 140060
Email susan@susielaws.co.uk

Entry 282 Map 22

London

Keslake Towers

Well-travelled Duncan and Barbro love having guests. Their house is in a peaceful, leafy terrace – step in to cool, calm interiors alive with bright modern art, classic travel posters, books and a relaxed feel. Bedrooms, one with garden views, are stylish yet homely; bathrooms sparkle – one compact and one with a funky LED-embedded mirror. Breakfast is a fabulous feast with everything from Swedish cheeses, porridge and smoked salmon to 'Duncan's Ilsington Scrambled Eggs'. Oxford Circus and Portobello Market are a short tube ride, the Park is fun-filled and the sun-trap garden has deck chairs, roses and parrots flying over.

On-street parking. Over 12s welcome. Smoking permitted in the garden or on the patio.

Rooms	1 double, 1 twin/double: £150. Singles £90.
Meals	Pubs/restaurants nearby.
Closed	Rarely.

Duncan McAusland
Keslake Towers,
35 Keslake Road,
Queen's Park, NW6 6DJ
Tel   +44 (0)20 8960 0535
Email   duncan@keslaketowers.co.uk
Web   www.keslaketowers.co.uk

Entry 283   Map 22

London

The Roost

The immaculate pale blue-painted front door sets the tone for this large and lofty Victorian home. This is boutique B&B and you get smart hotel-standard rooms at a fraction of the price. The furniture is excellent: fine family pieces and clever Liz's handsome finds. There is a conservatory for continental breakfast, a delightful Parson Russell dog and art everywhere. Liz, a former fashion pattern cutter and dancer, is a natural and lovely hostess. The Roost is brilliantly positioned for whizzing into town, yet here you have a lovely park, an irresistible bakery, great restaurants and a farmers' market on Sundays. Marvellous.

Minimum stay: 2 nights at weekends. Free parking weekends. Tube & overground within walking distance.

Rooms	3 doubles (2 with bath/shower, 1 with shower): £110-£125. Singles £90-£110.
Meals	Pubs/restaurants 5-minute walk.
Closed	Rarely.

Liz Crosland
The Roost,
37 Lynton Road,
Queen's Park, NW6 6BE
Tel   +44 (0)20 7625 6770
Mobile   +44 (0)7967 354477
Email   liz@boutiquebandblondon.com
Web   www.boutiquebandblondon.com

Entry 284   Map 22

London

30 King Henry's Road

Shops, restaurants and sublime views of Primrose Hill are a five-minute stroll from this interesting 1860s house; walls are covered in a lifetime collection of watercolours, drawings and maps. Your room on the top floor has a comfortable brass bed, a sisal floor, fine pieces of furniture, a wall of books, digital TV and a smart new bathroom. Breakfast on homemade bread and jams, bagels, croissants, yogurts and fresh fruit salad in the large kitchen/dining room with a big open fire and garden views. There's open-air theatre in Regent's Park in summer; Carole and Ted know London well and will happily advise.

Min stay: 2 nights at weekends. Tube: Chalk Farm, 5-minute walk. Private parking not available, but parking free on street 6pm to 8.30am & all weekend.

Rooms	1 double: £130.
	Singles £115.
Meals	Pubs/restaurants 2-minute walk.
Closed	Occasionally.

Carole & Ted Cox
30 King Henry's Road,
Primrose Hill, NW3 3RP

Tel	+44 (0)20 7483 2871
Mobile	+44 (0)7976 389350
Email	carole.l.cox@gmail.com

London

66 Camden Square

A modern, architect designed house made of African teak, brick and glass. Climb wooden stairs under a glazed pyramid to light-filled, Japanese-style bedrooms with low platform beds, modern chairs and private sitting room/study. Sue and Rodger have travelled widely so there are pictures, photographs and ethnic pieces everywhere – and a burst of colour from Peckam the parrot. Share their lovely open-plan dining space overlooking a verdant bird-filled courtyard at breakfast – a delicious start to the day. Cool Camden's bustling market is close, along with theatres, restaurants, bars and zoo.

Children over 7 welcome.

Rooms	1 double: £110-£120.
	1 single, sharing bath with double
	(let to same party only): £65-£75.
Meals	Pubs/restaurants nearby.
Closed	Occasionally.

Sue & Rodger Davis
66 Camden Square,
Camden Town, NW1 9XD

| Tel | +44 (0)20 7485 4622 |
| Email | rodgerdavis@btopenworld.com |

London

Arlington Avenue

This 1848 townhouse is a real find – from here you can follow the canal up to Islington. Inside you find a world of books and art; immaculate bedrooms (the double very spacious) are colourful and filled with pictures, etchings and pretty furniture, with views over several gardens to the back. The grey marble shared guest bathroom is two flights down, but if you don't mind that, you've struck gold. Shop locally, eat picnic suppers in the red and gold dining room, chill drinks in the fridge. You help yourself to breakfast in a lemon coloured country-style kitchen; this is laissez-faire B&B and fantastic value.

Tube: Angel & Old Street (15-minute walk). Buses: 5 minutes to stops for City, St Paul's, Tate Modern. Limited parking (by arrangement).

Rooms	1 double, sharing bath with single: £55–£70.
	1 single: £45–£65.
Meals	Pubs/restaurants 100 yds.
Closed	Rarely.

Thomas Blaikie
Arlington Avenue,
Islington, N1 7AX
Mobile   +44 (0)7711 265183
Email   thomas@arlingtonavenue.co.uk
Web   www.arlingtonavenue.co.uk

Entry 287   Map 22

London

Russell's

Be in the thick of edgy, vibrant, multi-cultural London in this pink Victorian terraced house bang on the high street. Lovely Annette gives you imaginative breakfasts: try mushrooms cooked in truffle oil. You enjoy a funky guest sitting room with vintage furniture, a friendly whippet called Reggie, interesting book shelves and an easy-going feel. Lovely uncluttered bedrooms (those overlooking the garden are quieter) have good art and great 60s and 70s pieces. Sparkling bathrooms have powerful showers. Very good cafes on the doorstep, a 20-minute walk to the Olympic Stadium, and near Hackney Marshes, with grazing cows!

Rooms	2 doubles, 1 twin/double;
	1 double, 1 twin/double sharing
	bath: £98–£115.
	1 single: £103.
Meals	Pubs/restaurants 5-minute walk.
Closed	Rarely.

Annette Russell
Russell's,
123 Chatsworth Road,
Clapton, E5 0LA
Mobile   +44 (0)7976 669906
Email   annette@russellsofclapton.com
Web   www.russellsofclapton.com

Entry 288   Map 4

London

20 St Philip Street

Come to retreat from the frenzy of city life. In the 1890 Victorian cottage all is peaceful and calm and Barbara looks after you beautifully. The dining room, with the odd oriental piece from past travels, is where you have your full English breakfast – unusual for London – and across the hall is the elegant sitting room, with gilt-framed mirrors, sumptuous curtains, and a piano. Upstairs is a bright and restful bedroom with pretty linen and a cloud of goose down. The large, sparkling bathroom next door is all yours – fabulous. Nothing has been overlooked and the tiny courtyard garden is a summer oasis.

Train: 6-min Waterloo, 3-min Victoria. Bus: 137, 452 (Sloane Sq) & 156 (Vauxhall). Tube: 10 mins. Parking: £2.50 per hour 9.30am-5.30pm weekdays or £10 day permit. Free at weekends.

Rooms	1 double with separate bath & shower: £115. Singles £85. Stays of 2 nights or more: £110 double; £80 singles.
Meals	Pubs/restaurants 200 yds.
Closed	Occasionally.

Barbara Graham
20 St Philip Street,
Battersea, SW8 3SL
Tel   +44 (0)20 7622 5547
Email   batterseabedandbreakfast@gmail.com
Web   www.batterseabandb.co.uk

London

26 Montefiore Street

Step off a quiet street into a hall of rich golds and a charming, elegant and comfortable bolthole. There's a little bird-filled garden where you can breakfast in summer: an organic spread with homemade jams and bread. This house is brimful of books – your bedroom too. Find white linen on a generous-sized handmade bed, dressing gowns and, down steps, a fresh chic bathroom with fluffy towels and bath oils. No sitting room but there are wicker chairs in a corner of the library/dining room facing the pretty garden. Walk to Battersea Arts Centre and Battersea Park with its festivals and art fairs; not far from Chelsea Flower Show too.

Parking available for £7 per day at weekdays, free at weekends.

Rooms	1 double with separate bath/shower (1 single in attached study, suitable for a child): £110–£115. Singles £80–£85. Extra bed/sofabed available £50–£55 per person per night.
Meals	Restaurants 300 yds.
Closed	Occasionally.

D Porter
26 Montefiore Street,
Battersea, SW8 3TL
Tel   +44 (0)20 7720 0939
Email   bedandbreakfast.london.sw8@gmail.com

London

The Glebe House

Surely one of London's most village-y spots? Find a pretty Georgian house snuggling up to the church, a community pottery and beehives and allotments in a walled garden. Alix writes for interiors magazines and has weaved her magic into every corner of her home. The sitting room, with velvet and linen sofas on toasty stone floors, was once an archway for horses and carriages; now it's a lofty space with huge doors onto a courtyard. Your bed is antique, your room deeply peaceful, the bathroom bright with white Metro brick tiles. Help yourself to a continental breakfast of cereal, fruit, and artisan breads in the funky kitchen. Alix, son and dog are a delight.

Rooms	2 doubles sharing family bathroom (let to same party only, extra futon available): £110. Singles £80.
Meals	Continental breakfast. Pubs/restaurants 0.2 miles.
Closed	Rarely.

Alix Bateman
The Glebe House,
Clapham Old Town, SW4 0DZ

Tel	+44 (0)20 7720 3844
Email	talixjones@hotmail.com
Web	www.theglebehouselondon.com

Entry 291   Map 22

London

28 Old Devonshire Road

In a quiet part of Balham – close to leafy common, tube and train – are Georgina's lovely home and award-winning garden. Enjoy breakfast under the pear tree, or at the long wooden table in the dining room, with a marble fireplace and a friend's watercolours. You have the top floor to yourself: a sunny, cosy bedroom, with city views, a TV, lots of books; a big bathroom too, with a fab shower and comforting waffle robes to pad about in. Georgina lays on a special breakfast and all sorts of thoughtful extras. She loves to chat (speaks French and Italian too) really knows her London and will help plan your stay.

Minimum stay: 2 nights. 7 minute-walk from Balham mainline and tube stations. Visitors' Parking Permits available £7 per day excluding Sunday.

Rooms	1 double: £100–£105. Singles £80–£85.
Meals	Pubs/restaurants 500 yds.
Closed	Rarely.

Georgina Ivor
28 Old Devonshire Road,
Balham, SW12 9RB

Tel	+44 (0)20 8673 7179
Mobile	+44 (0)7941 960199
Email	georgina@balhambandb.co.uk
Web	www.balhambandb.co.uk

Entry 292   Map 22

London

The Coach House

A rare privacy: you have your own coach house, separated from the Notts' home by a stylish terracotta-potted courtyard with Indian sandstone paving and various fruit trees (peach, pear, nectarine). Breakfast in your own sunny kitchen, or let Meena treat you to a full English in hers (she makes great porridge, too). The lovely big attic bedroom has beams, cream curtains, rugs on polished wood floors; the brick-walled ground-floor twin is pleasant and airy; both look over the peaceful garden. Urban but bucolic – just perfect as a romantic retreat, or a family getaway.

Minimum stay: 3 nights; 2 nights January & February. Tube: Balham Station to Leicester Square & Oxford Street or train to Victoria.

Rooms	1 twin with separate shower (same-party bookings only): £120–£200. 1 family room for 2-3: £190–£200. £200 for the whole Coach House.
Meals	Pub/restaurant 200 yds.
Closed	Occasionally.

Meena & Harley Nott
The Coach House,
2 Tunley Road,
Balham, SW17 7QJ
Tel   +44 (0)20 8772 1939
Email   coachhouse@chslondon.com
Web   www.coachhouse.chslondon.com

London

108 Streathbourne Road

It's a handsome house in a conservation area that manages to be both elegant and cosy. The cream-coloured double bedroom has an armchair, a writing desk, pretty curtains and a big comfy walnut bed; the twin is light and airy. The dining room overlooks a secluded terrace and garden and there are newspapers at breakfast. You can eat in – David, who works in the wine trade, always puts a bottle on the table – or out, at one of the trendy new restaurants in Balham. A friendly city base on a quiet, tree-lined street – maximum comfort, delicious food and good value for London. Delightful.

Minimum stay: 2 nights. Tube: Tooting Bec, 7-minute walk. Bus: 319 from Sloane Square. British Rail Balham to Victoria. Free parking weekends, otherwise meters of £7.40 daily permit.

Rooms	1 double, 1 twin: £95–£100. Singles £80–£85.
Meals	Dinner £35. Restaurants 5-minute walk.
Closed	Occasionally.

Mary & David Hodges
108 Streathbourne Road,
Balham, SW17 8QY
Tel   +44 (0)20 8767 6931
Email   davidandmaryhodges@gmail.com
Web   www.southwestlondonbandb.co.uk

London

38 Killieser Avenue

On a quiet leafy street, the Haworths have brought country-house chic to South London. Philip and Winkle have filled their elegant Victorian townhouse with stunning fabrics, sunny colours and treasures from far-flung travels. The house glows, the garden is ravishing, breakfasts are delicious (so are the scones – book a cream tea course!) and bedrooms are spacious: fine linen, lambswool throws, waffle robes, the scent of roses. Few people do things with as much natural good humour as Winkle, whose passions are cooking, gardening and garden history (tours can be arranged). Transport is close and you can be in Victoria in 15 minutes.

Minimum stay: 2 nights at weekends. Free and unrestricted parking on street outside the house.

Rooms	1 twin: £115–£120.
	1 single with separate bath: £95–£100.
	Stays of 2 or more nights:
	£110 double; £90 single.
Meals	Dinner £30–£35.
Closed	Occasionally.

Winkle Haworth
38 Killieser Avenue,
Streatham Hill, SW2 4NT
Tel   +44 (0)20 8671 4196
Email winklehaworth@hotmail.com
Web www.thegardenbedandbreakfast.com

Entry 295 Map 22

London

113 Pepys Road

This Victorian terraced house overlooks the first landscaped park of its kind in south-east London; the pretty garden, designed by David's father, is graced with majestic magnolias. Find a quirky mix of classic British furniture and oriental antiques. Picking up from his Chinese mother Anne, David has now taken on the B&B (helped by his housekeeper) and breakfast can be English or oriental. It's a convivial, lived-in home full of family portraits, batiks and books; the Chinese 'Peony' room downstairs has a huge bed, bamboo blinds, kimonos for the bathroom. A short walk to buses and tubes… and blissfully quiet for London.

Rooms	1 double, 1 twin/double;
	1 twin with separate bath: £110.
	Singles £85.
Meals	Restaurant 0.5 miles.
Closed	Rarely.

David Marten
113 Pepys Road,
New Cross, SE14 5SE
Tel   +44 (0)20 7639 1060
Email pepysroad@gmail.com
Web www.pepysroad.com

Entry 296 Map 22

16 St Alfege Passage

The peaceful approach is along the passage between Hawksmoor church and its graveyard, away from Greenwich hubbub. At the end of the lane is a 'cottage' set about with greenery, lamp posts and benches; inside, bold art and antiques – and tea with flapjack awaiting you in an eccentrically furnished (stuffed cat on dentist chair, huge parasol) sitting room. Bedrooms are cosy and colourful, with double beds (not huge) that positively encourage intimacy. Breakfast – delicious – is in the basement, another engagingly furnished room awash with character. Robert, an actor, is easy, funny, chatty – and has created an unusual, attractive place.

3-min walk from Greenwich train & Docklands Light Railway station or Cutty Sark DLR station. Parking free from 5pm (6pm Sundays) to 9am.

24 Fox Hill

This part of London is full of sky, trees and wildlife; Pissarro captured on canvas the view up the hill in 1870 (the painting is in the National Gallery). There's good stuff everywhere – things hang off walls and peep over the tops of dressers; bedrooms are stunning, with antiques, textiles, paintings and big, firm beds. Sue, a graduate from Chelsea Art College, employs humour and intelligence to put guests at ease and has created a special garden too. Tim often helps with breakfasts: eggs to order, good coffee. Owls hoot at night, woodpeckers wake you in the morning, in this lofty, peaceful retreat.

Train: Crystal Palace. Underground: East London line. Collection possible. Good buses to West End & Westminster. Victoria 20 minutes by train.

Rooms	1 double, 1 four-poster: £110–£150. 1 single: £90.
Meals	Pubs/restaurants 2-minute walk.
Closed	Rarely.

Rooms	1 twin/double; 1 double, 1 twin sharing bath: £90–£120. Singles £60. Dinner, B&B £100 per person. Extra bed/sofabed available £30 per person per night.
Meals	Dinner £35. Pubs/restaurants 5-minute walk.
Closed	Rarely.

	Nicholas Mesure & Robert Gray 16 St Alfege Passage, Greenwich, SE10 9JS
Tel	+44 (0)20 8853 4337
Email	info@st-alfeges.co.uk
Web	www.st-alfeges.co.uk

	Sue & Tim Haigh 24 Fox Hill, Crystal Palace, SE19 2XE
Tel	+44 (0)20 8768 0059
Email	suehaigh@hotmail.co.uk
Web	www.foxhill-bandb.co.uk

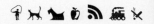

Heacham House

Rebecca is a dab hand at soft furnishings and creating delicious things. Step in to a home full of pretty fabrics and flowers. All is homemade from the welcoming cake to the granola, potato farls and home-grown roasted tomatoes on brioche; honey, bacon and eggs are sourced from local suppliers, hand-knitted tea cosies and hand-embroidered tablecloths add a thoughtful touch. Immaculate, comfortable bedrooms have all sorts of extra goodies. It's paradise for bird watchers, you can take a boat trip to spot seals, and it's a short walk to the beach. Norfolk Lavender is minutes away too – buy some pots to take home. Lovely!

Minimum stay: 2 nights.

Rooms	2 doubles; 1 twin/double with separate bathroom: £85–£95.
Meals	Pubs/restaurants 5-minute walk.
Closed	Christmas & New Year.

	Rebecca Bradley
	Heacham House,
	18 Staithe Road, Heacham,
	King's Lynn, PE31 7ED
Tel	+44 (0)1485 579529
Email	info@heachamhouse.com
Web	www.heachamhouse.com

Entry 299   Map 9

Holland House

Oak-smoked kippers from Cley, meat from Walsingham, eggs from the hens, veg from the garden… prepare yourself for some glorious pampering. Once the dower house to Docking Hall, this red-brick, roadside, 1750s house is deceptively large inside. Find fabric pelmets, shining wood floors, interesting curios and pictures. Melanie and Steve, cooks, gardeners and homemakers, have created three bedrooms for guests, all on the first floor, fabulously comfortable and rather grand. Enjoy a sherry by the drawing room fire, linger by the lavender, and splash out on the Holkham suite – the bathroom is delectable.

Minimum stay: 2 nights.

Rooms	1 suite; 1 double, 1 twin/double, each with separate bathroom: £105–£170.
Meals	Dinner from £15. Pubs/restaurants 8-minute walk.
Closed	Occasionally.

	Steve Lewis
	Holland House,
	Chequers Street, Docking,
	King's Lynn, PE31 8LH
Tel	+44 (0)1485 518295
Mobile	+44 (0)7976 910272
Email	stevelewisart917@gmail.com
Web	www.hollandhousebandb.co.uk

Entry 300   Map 9

Norfolk

Tudor Lodgings

A treasured family home on the site of Castle Acre's medieval defences, with dogs, ducks and views of the lovely Nar valley. A cosy guest sitting room leads to the ancient, dark-beamed dining room hung with portraits, where you breakfast on good things homemade and local; do try a Swaffham Sizzler. Cottagey bedrooms are cream-carpeted and have coordinated fabrics, attractive wildlife prints and small shower rooms. Julia is passionate about garden history, Gus is a keen fisherman; both know their history and horses. Peddars Way runs close by and you're not far from the coast — or the village pub!

Rooms	2 twins: £80.
	Singles £60.
Meals	Pub within walking distance.
Closed	Rarely.

Julia Stafford-Allen
Tudor Lodgings,
Castle Acre,
King's Lynn, PE32 2AN
Tel   +44 (0)1760 755334
Email   jstaffordallen@btinternet.com
Web   www.tudorlodgings.co.uk

Norfolk

Litcham Hall

For the whole of the 19th century this was Litcham's doctor's house; the Hall is still at the centre of the community. The big-windowed guest bedrooms look onto stunning gardens with yew hedges, a lily pond and herbaceous borders. This is a thoroughly English home with elegant proportions — the hall, drawing room and dining room are gracious and beautifully furnished, and there's a large sitting room for guests. The garden fills the breakfast table with soft fruit in season and John and Hermione are friendly and most helpful. Close to Fakenham, and only 30 minutes from Burnham Market and the coast.

Children & pets by arrangement. Outside pool heated in high summer; use by arrangement.

Rooms	2 doubles; 1 twin with separate bath: £75–£95.
	Singles by arrangement.
Meals	Pub in village & 5 miles.
Closed	Christmas.

John & Hermione Birkbeck
Litcham Hall,
Litcham,
King's Lynn, PE32 2QQ
Tel   +44 (0)1328 701389
Email   hermionebirkbeck@hotmail.com
Web   www.litchamhall.co.uk

Norfolk

Meadow House

Handmade oak banisters, period furniture: this new-build is beautifully traditional, the conservatory full of light. Breakfast is served in the lovely large drawing room, where you find a warm, sociable atmosphere with squashy sofas and comfy chairs for anytime use. One bedroom is cosy and chintzy, the other is larger and more neutral; brand-new bathrooms gleam. Amanda knows B&B and does it well; she's lived in Norfolk most of her life and is delighted to advise. There are footpaths from the door and plenty to see, starting with Walpole's Houghton Hall, a short walk. A bucolic setting for a profoundly comfortable stay, perfect for country enthusiasts.

Rooms	2 twin/doubles: £70-£80. Singles £40-£45.
Meals	Packed lunch £5-£7. Pub 9-minute walk.
Closed	Rarely.

Amanda Case
Meadow House,
Harpley, King's Lynn, PE31 6TU
Tel   +44 (0)1485 520240
Mobile   +44 (0)7890 037134
Email   amandacase@amandacase.plus.com
Web   www.meadowhousebandb.co.uk

Entry 303   Map 10

Norfolk

Bagthorpe Hall

Ten minutes from Burnham Market, yet here you are immersed in peaceful countryside. Tid is a pioneer of organic farming and the stunning 700 acres include a woodland snowdrop walk. Gina's passions are music, dance and gardens and she organises open days and concerts for charity. Theirs is a large, elegant house with a fascinating hall mural chronicling their family life; bedrooms – one with a tiny en suite shower room – have big comfy beds and lovely views. Breakfasts are delicious with local sausages and bacon, homemade jams and raspberries from the garden. Birdwatching, cycling and walking are all around.

Rooms	1 double; 1 twin/double with separate shower: £90. Singles £50.
Meals	Pubs/restaurants 2 miles.
Closed	Rarely.

Gina & Tid Morton
Bagthorpe Hall,
Bagthorpe, Bircham,
King's Lynn, PE31 6QY
Tel   +44 (0)1485 578528
Mobile   +44 (0)7979 746591
Email   dgmorton@hotmail.com
Web   www.bagthorpehall.co.uk

Entry 304   Map 10

Norfolk

1 Leicester Meadows

Up among 13 acres of wild meadow and woodland – not another building in sight. It's all so relaxed and unhurried: barn owls roosting in the outhouse, hens strutting, geese pottering up from the pond. The 19th-century cottages have been imaginatively restored; Bob was an architect, Sara an art teacher, and both are immensely friendly and helpful. Polished wood and old brick are topped with bright rugs; paintings and ceramics engage the eye; bedrooms have flowers and colourful covers. Hop downstairs for a superb breakfast at the big convivial table: rare breed bacon, homemade jams and bread, fruits from the kitchen garden.

Minimum stay: 2 nights.

Rooms	1 double with sitting room; 1 twin/double: £80-£95. Singles £65.
Meals	Supper by arrangement from £20. Pub 1 mile.
Closed	Rarely.

Bob & Sara Freakley
1 Leicester Meadows,
South Creake,
Fakenham, NR21 9NZ

Tel	+44 (0)1328 823533
Email	rf@freakley.com
Web	www.leicestermeadows.com

Norfolk

The Merchants House

The oak four-poster – a beauty – came with the house. Part of the building (1400) is the oldest in Wells; in those days, the merchant could bring his boats up to the door. Liz and Dennis know the history, and happily share it. Inside is friendly and inviting: the mahogany shines, bathrooms sparkle, there are books to borrow and pretty sash windows overlook salt marshes. Breakfasts are a treat: homemade bread and jams, local produce and flowers on the table. As for Wells, it's on the famous Coastal Path, has a quay bustling with boats and 16 miles of sands. Birdwatch by day, dine out at night – easy when you're in the centre.

Minimum stay: 2 nights in July & August.

Rooms	1 double; 1 four-poster with separate bath/shower: £90-£100. Singles £70-£75.
Meals	Pubs/restaurants 300 yds.
Closed	Rarely.

Elizabeth & Dennis Woods
The Merchants House,
47 Freeman Street,
Wells-next-the-Sea, NR23 1BQ

Tel	+44 (0)1328 711877
Mobile	+44 (0)7816 632742
Email	denniswoods@talktalk.net
Web	www.the-merchants-house.co.uk

Norfolk

The Control Tower

A unique slice of history. This iconic landmark on the former RAF North Creake airfield was built in the 1940s to command 199 and 171 Squadrons. The restoration has been a labour of love and Ni and Claire's attention to detail is remarkable: modernism and Art Deco design in full flow. Be greeted with tea or locally roasted coffee in the art-filled sitting room; sink into goose down in bright bedrooms; enjoy shiny bathrooms with period fittings and lavender soaps. Vegetarian breakfasts are good! House tours include the open roof deck; you can lunch al fresco in the wild flower garden; Wells-next-the-Sea and Blakeney seal trips are close.

Rooms	2 doubles: £110–£120.
Meals	Restaurants 3 miles.
Closed	Rarely.

Claire Nugent & Nigel Morter
The Control Tower,
Bunkers Hill,
Eymere,
Walsingham, NR22 6AZ
Tel   +44 (0)1328 821574
Email   mail@controltowerstays.com
Web   www.controltowerstays.com

Entry 307   Map 10

Norfolk

Green Farm House

This Norfolk farmhouse has been beautifully restored. Choose to stay in the 'Garden Room' wing, or upstairs in the main house – both well-dressed bedrooms have smart bathrooms. Sun streams in through the French windows of the garden room; find books, DVDs, rugs on slate floors, art, pots of flowers and a comfy sofa by the wood-burner. The 'Guest Room' has field views and morning sun. Breakfast in the conservatory on local sausages, bacon and eggs, homemade marmalade and muesli – or in the pretty, sheltered garden on sunny days. Friendly Lucy can arrange sailing; good for walkers, cyclists and birdwatchers too

Cyclists welcome; secure bike shed available.

Rooms	House - 1 double: £80–£120.
	Garden Room - 1 double: £80–£120.
	Singles £80.
Meals	Pub within 2 miles.
Closed	Rarely.

Lucy Jupe
Green Farm House,
Balls Lane, Thursford,
Fakenham, NR21 0BX
Tel   +44 (0)1328 878507
Mobile   +44 (0)7768 542645
Email   ljupe@nnv.org.uk
Web   www.greenfarmbarns.co.uk

Entry 308   Map 10

Norfolk

Holly Lodge

The whole place radiates a lavish attention to detail, from the spoilingly comfortable beds to the complimentary bottle of wine. It's perfect for those who love their privacy: these three snug guest 'cottages' have their own entrances as well as smart bedsteads and rugs on stone tiles, neat little shower rooms and tapestry-seat chairs, and books, music and TVs. Enjoy the Mediterranean garden, the handsome conservatory and the utter peace; Holt and historic Little Walsingham are nearby. Your hosts are delightful: ex-restaurateur Jeremy who cooks enthusiastically, ethically and with panache, and Canadian-raised Gill.

Rooms	3 cottages for 2: £90–£120. Singles £70–£100
Meals	Dinner, 2-3 courses with wine, £16–£19.50. Pubs/restaurants 1 mile.
Closed	Rarely.

Jeremy Bolam
Holly Lodge,
Thursford Green, NR21 0AS
Tel   +44 (0)1328 878465
Email   info@hollylodgeguesthouse.co.uk
Web   www.hollylodgeguesthouse.co.uk

Entry 309   Map 10

Norfolk

Burgh Parva Hall

Sunlight bathes the Norfolk longhouse on sunny afternoons; the welcome from the Heals is as warm. The listed house is all that remains of the old village of Burgh Parva, deserted after the Great Plague. It's an inviting, handsome home… old furniture, rugs, books, pictures and Magnet the terrier-daschund. Large guest bedrooms face the sunsets and the garden flat makes a delightful hideaway, especially in summer. Breakfast eggs come from the garden hens, vegetables and fruits are home-grown, fresh fish is locally sourced and the game may have been shot by William: settle down by the fire and tuck in!

Dogs welcome in the garden-flat twin, but not in the main house.

Rooms	1 double; 1 twin with separate bath: £70–£90. Garden flat - 1 twin (self-catering option): £70–£90. Singles £45–£55.
Meals	Dinner £24. BYO. Pub/restaurant 4 miles.
Closed	Rarely.

Judy & William Heal
Burgh Parva Hall,
Melton Constable, NR24 2PU
Tel   +44 (0)1263 862569
Email   judyheal@dsl.pipex.com

Entry 310   Map 10

Cleat House

A fantastic welcome in a peaceful street, a short walk from town and beach. This attractive late-Victorian seaside villa, built for a London merchant, has been sumptuously renovated inside. Bedrooms have original fireplaces and sash windows, upbeat fabrics and original art, and a warm inviting mix of antique and traditional. The guest sitting room comes with an honesty bar, games, books, DVDs and guides – set off for Holkham or Sandringham! Rob and Linda greet you with homemade treats and serve a tasty breakfast at separate tables: very good coffee, kippers, smoked salmon and lots more. You're beautifully cared for here.

Minimum stay: 2 nights at weekends.

The Old Rectory

Conservation farmland all around; acres of wild heathland busy with woodpeckers and owls; the coast two miles away. Relax in the spacious drawing room of this handsome 17th-century rectory and friendly family home, set in lovely mature gardens (NGS) full of trees and unusual planting. Fiona loves to cook and bakes her bread daily, food is delicious, seasonal and locally sourced, jams are homemade. Comfortable bedrooms have *objets* from diplomatic postings and the spacious suite comes with mahogany furniture and armchairs so you can settle in with a book. Super views, friendly dogs, tennis in the garden and masses of space.

Self-catering available in the Garden Room.

Rooms	2 suites for 2; 1 suite for 2 with separate bath: £90–£120. Singles £70–£100.
Meals	Pubs/restaurants within 0.5 miles.
Closed	Mid-November to mid-March.

Rooms	1 suite for 2; 1 double with kitchenette, separate bath & shower: £70–£85. Singles £50.
Meals	Dinner from £25. Pubs 2 miles.
Closed	Rarely.

Rob & Linda Ownsworth
Cleat House,
7 Montague Road,
Sheringham, NR26 8LN
Tel   +44 (0)1263 822765
Mobile +44 (0)7557 356952
Email   roblinda@cleathouse.co.uk
Web   www.cleathouse.co.uk

Peter & Fiona Black
The Old Rectory,
Ridlington, NR28 9NZ
Tel   +44 (0)1692 650247
Mobile +44 (0)7774 599911
Email   ridlingtonoldrectory@gmail.com
Web   www.oldrectorynorthnorfolk.co.uk

Sutton Hall

Sweep up the gravel drive to a red-brick Victorian country house, in quiet parkland near the Norfolk Broads and coast. Sue serves delicious breakfasts in the chandelier'd dining room with bay windows to the morning sun. Enjoy local produce, tomatoes from the kitchen garden, and knobbly apples from an orchard where deer and ducks roam free… Rooms are in keeping with the home's comfortable elegance – tall sash windows, a four-poster, fireplace, power showers, an extra bed for children; a Chinese screen adorns the high-ceilinged sitting room. Spend the day on the Broads with the binoculars.

Hoveton Hall

A Regency house snoozing in beautiful parkland and gardens. Formal and grand, yet comfortably friendly, Harry and Rachel's home brims with wonderful woodwork, decorated ceilings, art old and new. Their children are keen to play with visiting young ones, there's a lovely collection of hare sculptures up the stairs and the views over the 620 acres are stunning. Airy bedrooms have well-dressed beds, tea trays, biscuits and flowers. Morning sun lights up the panelled library/sitting room where you have breakfast, shelves are crammed with books and there's a large fire to sit by. Explore the estate, head off for beaches and The Broads.

Minimum stay: 2 nights at weekends.

Rooms	2 doubles: £90–£120.
	Singles £70–£90.
Meals	Pubs/restaurant 1.5 miles.
Closed	Rarely.

Rooms	1 double: £120.
	1 family room for 4: £140.
Meals	Pubs/restaurants 1 mile.
Closed	Rarely.

	Sue Berry
	Sutton Hall,
	Hall Road, Sutton,
	Norwich, NR12 9RX
Tel	+44 (0)1692 584888
Mobile	+44 (0)7977 575788
Email	enquiries@suttonhallnorfolk.co.uk
Web	www.suttonhallnorfolk.co.uk

	Rachel Buxton
	Hoveton Hall,
	Hoveton Hall Estate,
	Hoveton,
	Norwich, NR12 8RJ
Tel	+44 (0)1603 784 297
Email	rachel@hovetonhallestate.co.uk
Web	www.hovetonhallestate.co.uk

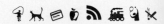

Norfolk

Sloley Hall

A grand and gracious yellow-brick Georgian house with formal gardens, tree-studded parkland and glorious views from every window. It has also been beautifully renovated, with flagstoned floors, Persian rugs, gleaming circular tables and vases of garden-grown flowers. Your hosts are delightful – Barbara and Simon were married here and are easy-going and helpful. A huge light-flooded dining room is perfect for breakfast; the drawing room is comfy and uncluttered with a marble fireplace and long views. Bedrooms are large and elegant with sumptuous bed linen; generous bathrooms glow with warmth.

Minimum stay: 2 nights on bank holidays.

Rooms	1 suite for 2; 1 double with separate bath, 1 double with separate shower: £80–£90. Singles from £50. Child bed available.
Meals	Pubs/restaurants 2-4 miles.
Closed	Rarely.

Barbara Gorton
Sloley Hall,
Sloley,
Norwich, NR12 8HA
Tel   +44 (0)1692 538582
Mobile   +44 (0)7748 152079
Email   babsgorton@hotmail.com
Web   www.sloleyhall.com

Entry 315   Map 10

Norfolk

Gothic House

Silver tea and coffee pots and Portmeirion china, pictures and prints from far-flung places, and an unexpected peace in the centre of the city – welcome to Gothic House. The building is listed and Regency and your host, enthusiastic, charming, knows the history. As for breakfast, it is fresh, lavish and locally sourced; in short, a treat. Bedrooms are stylish and spacious with a strong period feel, the double and the two bathrooms on the first floor, and the twin above. Norwich is blessed with culture, character and pubs, and a cathedral with the second tallest spire in England. Fabulous!

Parking space available.

Rooms	1 double with separate bathroom, 1 twin with separate bathroom & wc: £95. Singles £65.
Meals	Pubs/restaurants 5-minute walk.
Closed	Rarely.

Clive Harvey
Gothic House,
King's Head Yard,
42 Magdalen Street,
Norwich, NR3 1JE
Tel   +44 (0)1603 631879
Email   charvey649@aol.com
Web   www.gothic-house-norwich.com

Entry 316   Map 10

Norfolk

Washingford House

Tall octagonal chimney stacks and a Georgian façade give the house a stately air. In fact, it's the friendliest of places to stay and Paris gives you a delicious, locally sourced breakfast including plenty of fresh fruit. The house, originally Tudor, is a delightful mix of old and new. Large light-filled bedrooms have loads of good books and views over the four-acre garden, a favourite haunt for local birds. Bergh Apton is a conservation village seven miles from Norwich and you are in the heart of it; perfect for cycling, boat trips on the Norfolk Broads and the twelve Wherryman's Way circular walks.

Rooms	1 twin/double: £65–£85.
	1 twin/double with separate bath & shower: £60–£75.
	1 single with separate bath: £35–£50.
Meals	Pubs/restaurants 4–6 miles.
Closed	Christmas.

Paris & Nigel Back
Washingford House,
Cookes Road, Bergh Apton,
Norwich, NR15 1AA
Tel   +44 (0)1508 550924
Mobile   +44 (0)7900 683617
Email   parisb@waitrose.com
Web   www.washingford.com

Entry 317   Map 10

Norfolk

The Buttery

Down a farm track, a treasure: your own thatch-and-flint octagonal dairy house perfectly restored by local craftsmen and as snug as can be. You get a jacuzzi bath, a little kitchen and a fridge stocked with delicious bacon and ground coffee so you can breakfast when you want; take it to the sun terrace in good weather. The sitting room is terracotta-tiled and has a music system, a warming fire and a sofabed for those who don't want to tackle the steep wooden stair to the cosy bedroom on the mezzanine. You can play a game of tennis, and walk from the door into peaceful parkland and woods. Lovely!

Minimum stay: 2 nights at weekends.

Rooms	1 double with sitting room & small kitchen: £90–£110.
Meals	Pub 10-minute walk.
Closed	Rarely.

Deborah Meynell
The Buttery,
Berry Hall,
Honingham,
Norwich, NR9 5AX
Tel   +44 (0)1603 880541
Email   thebuttery@paston.co.uk
Web   www.thebuttery.biz

Entry 318   Map 10

Norfolk

Stable Cottage

Sarah's home is set in the grounds of Heydon, one of Norfolk's finest Elizabethan houses. In the Dutch-gabled stable block, fronted by Cromwell's Oak, is her cottage – fresh, sunny and enchanting. Each room is touched by her warm personality and love of beautiful things: seagrass floors, crisp linen and pretty china; the cosy sitting room is set with tea and biscuits for your arrival. Bedrooms are cottagey and immaculate; bathrooms have baskets of treats. Sarah serves a delicious breakfast with golden eggs from her hens, homemade marmalade and garden fruit. Thursford is close and you're 20 minutes from the coast.

Minimum stay: 2 nights at weekends.

Rooms	2 twin/doubles: £100.
	For stays of 2 nights or more: £90 per night.
	Singles from £50.
Meals	Pub 1 mile.
Closed	Christmas.

Sarah Bulwer-Long
Stable Cottage,
Heydon Hall, Heydon,
Norwich, NR11 6RE

Tel	+44 (0)1263 587343
Mobile	+44 (0)7780 998742
Web	www.heydon-bb.co.uk

Norfolk

Norfolk Courtyard

Walk straight in through French windows to your own, underfloor-heated room in the courtyard; independence from the main house where friendly Simon and Catherine live. The rooms are decorated in soft colours, mattresses are perfect, cotton sheets are smooth and your handsome bathroom has limestone tiles – all rather luxurious; there's a welcome tea tray and a fridge to cool a bottle too. Continental breakfast is next door in the old, beamed barn – help yourself to croissants, crumpets, homemade jams, compotes and muesli – and home-laid eggs that you cook in an easy egg steamer: very popular! Stunning walks await on the coast.

Minimum stay: 2 nights (peak season weekends).

Rooms	3 doubles, 1 twin/double: £105–£110.
	Singles £60. Extra bed/sofabed available £10 per person per night.
Meals	Pub/restaurant 0.5 miles.
Closed	Rarely.

Simon & Catherine Davis
Norfolk Courtyard,
Westfield Farm, Foxley Road,
Foulsham, Dereham, NR20 5RH

Tel	+44 (0)1362 683333
Mobile	+44 (0)7969 611510
Email	info@norfolkcourtyard.co.uk
Web	www.norfolkcourtyard.co.uk

Norfolk

Carrick's at Castle Farm

This warm-bricked farmhouse is up a long drive and surrounded by 720 acres; John's family have lived here since the 1920s. He and Jean are passionate about conservation and the protection of wildlife, and here you have absolute quiet — for birdwatching, fishing or walking. Return to the drawing room with its open fire, books, and decanter of sherry. Your friendly hosts give you coffee and cake, or wine, when you arrive, and bedrooms are light and luxurious with pretty fabrics and homemade biscuits. Breakfasts and candlelit dinners are delicious, and the garden leads to a footpath alongside the river.

Norfolk

College Farm

Katharine is a natural at making guests feel like friends. Her beautiful farmhouse tucks itself away on the edge of the village and the big friendly kitchen is filled with delicious smells of home baking. Meals are served by the large wood-burner in the grand Jacobean dining room, filled with good antiques, period furnishings and cosy places to sit; food is home-grown, seasonal and local. Sleep well in charming bedrooms with smooth linen, pretty furniture and garden views; bathrooms are small and simple. A fascinating area teeming with pingos, wildlife, old churches… and glorious antique shops.

Over 12s welcome.

Rooms	1 double, 2 twin/doubles; 1 double with separate bath: £95. Singles £65.
Meals	Dinner, 3 courses, £30. BYO. Pub 0.5 miles.
Closed	Rarely.

Rooms	3 twin/doubles: £100–£125. Singles £50–£75.
Meals	Dinner from £20. Pub 1 mile.
Closed	Rarely.

	Jean Wright
	Carrick's at Castle Farm,
	Castle Farm,
	Swanton Morley,
	Dereham, NR20 4JT
Tel	+44 (0)1362 638302
Email	jean@castlefarm-swanton.co.uk
Web	www.carricksatcastlefarm.co.uk

	Katharine Wolstenholme
	College Farm,
	Thompson,
	Thetford, IP24 1QG
Tel	+44 (0)1953 483318
Email	info@collegefarmnorfolk.co.uk
Web	www.collegefarmnorfolk.co.uk

Entry 321   Map 10

Entry 322   Map 10

Northamptonshire

Staverton Hall

Through impressive iron gates to a grand house in a spectacular setting. Find masses of room, and friendly owners who have young children of their own; they love having families to stay. Relaxed breakfasts at flexible times are served at one table; all is local and delicious. Large, light bedrooms and super-modern bathrooms are upstairs, have good views and feel private. Relax in the huge, creamy-yellow guest sitting room with sash windows, log fire, board games and comfy sofas; there's also a heated pool, a play area, acres of garden, and the pub a walk away. Family heaven.

Minimum stay: 2 nights in high season.

Rooms	2 doubles, each with separate private bathroom: £90. 2 singles, each with separate private bathroom: £60. Extra bed/sofabed available.
Meals	Pub 3-minute walk.
Closed	Rarely.

Serena Frost
Staverton Hall,
Manor Road,
Staverton, Daventry, NN11 6JD

Tel	+44 (0)1327 878296
Email	rupert@frostsgroup.com
Web	www.stavertonhall.co.uk

Entry 323   Map 8

Northamptonshire

Colledges House

Huge attention to comfort here, and a house full of laughter. Liz clearly derives pleasure from sharing her 300-year-old stone thatched cottage, immaculate garden, conservatory and converted barn with guests. Sumptuous bedrooms have deep mattresses with fine linen, sparkling bathrooms are a good size. The house is full of interesting things: a Jacobean trunk, a Bechstein piano, mirrors and pictures, pretty china, bright fabrics, a beautiful bureau. Cordon Bleu dinners are elegant affairs – and great fun. Stroll around the conservation village of Staverton – delightful.

Babes in arms & children over 8 welcome.

Rooms	Cottage - 1 double, 1 twin; 1 double with separate bath: £99. 1 single: £70. Stays of 3 nights or more: £95 for 2 per night.
Meals	Dinner, 3 courses, £35. Pub 4-minute walk.
Closed	Rarely.

Liz Jarrett
Colledges House,
Oakham Lane, Staverton,
Daventry, NN11 6JQ

Tel	+44 (0)1327 702737
Mobile	+44 (0)7710 794112
Email	liz@colledgeshouse.co.uk
Web	www.colledgeshouse.co.uk

Entry 324   Map 8

Northamptonshire

The Old Vicarage

A golden ironstone vicarage overlooking the 12th-century church. The pretty porch leads you into Tim and Alison's traditional home of family portraits, antiques, books and cosy armchairs. There's a trio of comfortable bedrooms; all are fresh and light with well-dressed beds and a private bath or powerful shower. The main double has a neat basin in a cupboard; another flight of stairs takes you to the lovely room at the top. Breakfast with a leafy view is in the dining room at a long polished table. Sunny seats in the garden, Silverstone a short drive, plenty of handsome houses to visit and you can join the Macmillan Way from the door.

Pets by arrangement.

Rooms	1 double; 1 double, 1 twin, each with separate bath: £90. Singles £60.
Meals	Pubs 2 miles.
Closed	Christmas & New Year.

Tim Eastwood
The Old Vicarage,
Banbury Road,
Moreton Pinkney,
Daventry, NN11 3SQ

Tel	+44 (0)1295 760057
Email	tjs.eastwood@btinternet.com
Web	www.theoldvicaragemp.com

Entry 325   Map 8

Northamptonshire

The Vyne

Weighed down by wisteria, this 16th-century cottage rests in a honey-hued conservation village on the cusp of Oxfordshire. Beams and wonky lines abound; rooms are filled with good antiques and eclectic art. The twin overlooking the garden is enchanting, tucked under the rafters, its beds decorated in willow-pattern chintz, its walls glinting with gilded frames; the double has a Georgian four-poster and a sampler-decorated bathroom that's a quick flit next door. Warm and charming, Imogen not only works in publishing but is a contented gardener and Cordon Bleu cook – enjoy supper in her sunny secluded garden.

Babies welcome.

Rooms	1 twin; 1 four-poster with separate bath: £80. Singles £50–£55.
Meals	Supper £20. Dinner £30. BYO. Pub 2-minute walk.
Closed	Rarely.

Imogen Butler
The Vyne,
High Street,
Eydon,
Daventry, NN11 3PP

Tel	+44 (0)1327 264886
Mobile	+44 (0)7974 801475
Email	imogen@ibutler2.wanadoo.co.uk

Entry 326   Map 8

Northamptonshire

Northamptonshire

The Old House

Northamptonshire is the county of spires and squires. And here, on the through-road of this fascinating medieval town, is a listed squire's house — once home to a merchant who traded in the marketplace opposite. Enter the heavy oak door and step back 400 years. William, courteous, hospitable and renovating with aplomb, is full of plans. Facing the courtyard at the back (furnished for summery breakfasts and aperitifs) are the quietest rooms; all have sumptuous fabrics and wallpapers, dramatic touches and divine beds. Delightfully quirky, spanking new bathrooms with roll top tubs are as special as all the rest.

Bridge Cottage

A truly peaceful place, yet only a few miles from Peterborough. Sip a glass of wine on the decking down by the Willowbrook; beautiful countryside envelops you, the cattle doze, kingfishers flash by and you may see a red kite (borrow some binoculars). Inside find pretty bedrooms with sloping ceilings, the purest cotton sheets and proper blankets; bathrooms are thickly towelled and full of lovely lotions and bubbles. Breakfast is local and scrumptious and served in the friendliest kitchen facing that heavenly view. There's a tranquil conservatory for a quiet read, and Judy and Rod are brilliant hosts. A hidden gem.

Rooms	3 doubles, 1 twin/double: £70. Singles £55.
Meals	Pubs/restaurants 150 yds.
Closed	Rarely.

Rooms	1 double, 1 twin; 1 double with separate bath: £83-£90. Singles £55-£60. Extra bed/sofabed available £5-£10 per person per night.
Meals	Pub/restaurant 500 yds.
Closed	Christmas.

William Evans
The Old House,
5 Market Square,
Higham Ferrers,
Rushden, NN10 8BP
Tel +44 (0)1933 314006
Email theoldhousehighamferrers@gmail.com
Web www.theoldhousehighamferrers.co.uk

Judy Young
Bridge Cottage,
Oundle Road, Woodnewton,
Peterborough, PE8 5EG
Tel +44 (0)1780 470860
Mobile +44 (0)7979 644864
Email enquiries@bridgecottage.net
Web www.bridgecottage.net

Northumberland

Matfen High House

Bring the wellies – and jumpers! You are 25 miles from the border and the walking is a joy. Struan and Jenny are good company, love sporting pursuits and will advise on where to eat locally (and drive you there if needed). The sturdy stone house of 1735 is a lived-in, happily shabby-chic kind of place: the en suite bedrooms have fine fabrics and pictures, bathrooms are well-kept and the drawing room has books and choice pieces. Enjoy local bacon and sausages at breakfast, with Struan's marmalade and bread warm from the oven. The countryside is stunning, Hadrian's Wall and the great castles (Alnwick, Bamburgh) beckon.

Rooms	1 double, 2 twins; 1 double, 1 twin sharing bath: £60-£80. Singles £45.
Meals	Packed lunch £4.50. Restaurant 2 miles.
Closed	Rarely.

Struan & Jenny Wilson
Matfen High House,
Matfen,
Corbridge, NE20 0RG
Tel   +44 (0)1661 886592
Email   struan@struan.enterprise-plc.com
Web   www.matfenhighhouse.co.uk

Entry 329   Map 12

Northumberland

Emley Farm

You will be happy here, deep in the rural bliss of Northumberland with its bleating sheep and spectacular views. The Smarts look after you beautifully in their elegant Georgian farmhouse surrounded by a charming garden and on the edge of the village. You have your own comfortable sitting room with open fire, and delicious meals are taken in the handsome dining room; do stay in for dinner – local lobster, fish or game perhaps? Margaret is an accomplished cook. Sleep soundly in your view-filled bedroom under a proper eiderdown and savour the total peace. Hadrian's Wall is near, and the Lakes close enough for a bracing day out.

Rooms	1 suite for 2 with separate bath: £95-£100.
Meals	Dinner on request. Pubs less than a mile away.
Closed	Rarely.

Margaret Smart
Emley Farm,
Whitfield,
Hexham, NE47 8HB
Tel   +44 (0)1434 345776
Email   margiecook2001@yahoo.co.uk

Entry 330   Map 12

Northumberland

The Hermitage

A magical setting, three miles from Hadrian's Wall, in a house of friendship and comfort. Through ancient woodland, up the drive, over the burn and there it is: big, beautiful and Georgian. Interiors are comfortable country-house, full of warmth and charm; bedrooms, carpeted, spacious and delightful, are furnished with antiques, paintings and superb beds; bathrooms have roll top baths. Outside are lovely lawns, a walled garden, wildlife, and breakfasts on the terrace in summer. Katie – who was born in this house – looks after you brilliantly.

Babes in arms & children over 7 welcome.

Rooms	1 double, 1 twin; 1 double with separate bath: £85–£90. Singles from £55.
Meals	Pub 2 miles.
Closed	October–February.

Simon & Katie Stewart
The Hermitage,
Swinburne,
Hexham, NE48 4DG
Tel   +44 (0)1434 681248
Mobile +44 (0)7708 016297
Email   katie.stewart@themeet.co.uk

Entry 331   Map 16

Northumberland

The Grange

You're only seven miles away from Newcastle city centre but this couldn't be more peaceful. Kind owners let you wind down in their elegant Georgian house on the private Blagdon Estate, surrounded by mature trees and lovely gardens. Nod off in cosy, airy bedrooms with pale carpets (quiet at night), wake to eat like a lord at separate tables with Blagdon bacon, award-winning sausages and all the trimmings. There's a gentle woodland walk on the doorstep, rugged countryside and the nearby coast to explore. Newcastle airport is only four miles away (owners can arrange drop off and collection) and you can return to a roaring log fire.

Rooms	3 doubles: £100–£150. Extra bed/sofabed available £20–£40 per person per night.
Meals	Pubs/restaurants 1 mile.
Closed	Rarely.

Paul Wappat & Penny Dane
The Grange,
Great North Road, Seaton Burn,
Newcastle upon Tyne, NE13 6DF
Tel   +44 (0)1670 789666
Email info@thegrangebandb.co.uk
Web   www.thegrangebandb.co.uk

Entry 332   Map 16

Northumberland

Shieldhall

The converted 18th-century farm buildings are charming. Step in through your own entrance off the central courtyard to cosy bedrooms, flowers and homemade biscuits. Family run and friendly, it's a treat to stay. Stephen and his sons make bespoke, and restore antique, furniture, and the rooms are named after the different woods they use. Daughter Sarah and her husband John are great hosts; you pop over to the main house for meals. Delicious Aga-cooked breakfasts include homemade bread and eggs from the hens; Celia helps with the dinners — have a glass of wine in the beautiful library beforehand: the views over garden and parkland are stunning.

Rooms	1 double, 1 twin, 1 four-poster: £80. Singles £60.
Meals	Dinner, 4 courses, £28. Pub 7 miles.
Closed	Rarely.

Celia & Stephen Robinson-Gay
Shieldhall,
Wallington,
Morpeth, NE61 4AQ
Tel   +44 (0)1830 540387
Email   stay@shieldhallguesthouse.co.uk
Web   www.shieldhallguesthouse.co.uk

Entry 333   Map 16

Northumberland

Thistleyhaugh

The family thrives on hard work and humour, and if Enid's not the perfect B&B hostess, she's a close contender. Her passions are pictures, cooking and people, and certainly you eat well — local farm eggs at breakfast and their beef at dinner. Choose any of the five large, lovely bedrooms and stay the week; they are awash with old paintings, silk fabrics and crisp linen. Wake refreshed and nip downstairs, past the log fire, to a laden and sociable table, head off afterwards to find 720 acres of organic farmland and a few million more of the Cheviots beyond. Wonderful hosts, a glorious region, a happy house.

Rooms	3 doubles, 1 twin: £100. 1 single: £70–£85. Extra bed/sofabed available £15 per person per night.
Meals	Dinner, 3 courses, £25. Pub/restaurant 2 miles.
Closed	Christmas, New Year & January.

Henry & Enid Nelless
Thistleyhaugh,
Longhorsley,
Morpeth, NE65 8RG
Tel   +44 (0)1665 570629
Email   thistleyhaugh@hotmail.com
Web   www.thistleyhaugh.co.uk

Entry 334   Map 16

Northumberland

Bilton Barns

A solidly good farmhouse B&B whose lifeblood is still farming. The Jacksons know every inch of the surrounding countryside and coast; it's a pretty spot. They farm the 400 acres of mixed arable land that sweeps down to the sea yet always have time for guests. Dorothy creates an easy and sociable atmosphere with welcoming pots of tea and convivial breakfasts – all delicious and locally sourced. Comfortable, smartly done bedrooms have a traditional feel, bathrooms have underfloor heating, the huge conservatory is filled with sofas and chairs and there's an elegant guest sitting room with an open fire and views to the sea.

Rooms	1 double, 1 twin, 1 four-poster: £80–£88. Singles £40–£65.
Meals	Packed lunch £4–£6. Pub/restaurant 2 miles.
Closed	Christmas.

Brian & Dorothy Jackson
Bilton Barns,
Alnmouth,
Alnwick, NE66 2TB

Tel	+44 (0)1665 830427
Mobile	+44 (0)7939 262028
Email	dorothy@biltonbarns.com
Web	www.biltonbarns.com

Entry 335   Map 16

Northumberland

Redfoot Lea

Prepare to be thoroughly spoiled. This fine renovation of an old farmsteading lies just off the A1 up a quiet lane – perfect for touring the county or a great stopover. Amiable Philippa gives you a super south-facing sitting room and ground-floor bedrooms with comfortable beds, crisp linen, fluffy bathrobes and heated floors; bathrooms are smart and spotless. You breakfast at a large table in the magnificent open-plan hall, scented with glorious flower arrangements; enjoy freshly squeezed orange juice, homemade compotes, local produce, excellent coffee. A short hop from Alnwick Castle and gardens, and stunning beaches.

Rooms	1 double, 1 suite for 2: £90–£100. Singles £65.
Meals	Pubs/restaurants 0.25 miles.
Closed	Rarely.

Philippa Bell
Redfoot Lea,
Greensfield Moor Farm,
Alnwick, NE66 2HH

Tel	+44 (0)1665 603891
Mobile	+44 (0)7870 586214
Email	info@redfootlea.co.uk
Web	www.redfootlea.co.uk

Entry 336   Map 16

Northumberland

Northumberland

Courtyard Garden

In the county town of Northumberland, with its grand castle and innovative gardens, step directly off the pavement and enter a courtyard surrounded by shrubs and pretty pots; sit out here on sunny days and sip a glass of something cool. Bedrooms (one overlooking the church, the other the garden) are traditional and immaculate; bathrooms, one with a roll top bath, have original wooden floors, thick towels. Friendly Maureen gives you breakfast in the comfortable sitting room at a round Georgian table underneath the window. Explore the town on foot, stride along white beaches, discover more castles; history is all around you.

Old Rectory Howick

Christine and David's house on the edge of the village is surrounded by fields and woods, and is only minutes from the beautiful Northumberland coast, a designated AONB. Breakfasts are hearty: Craster kippers from down the road, eggs from Erica, Sylvia and Ella. Scamper about with wide beaches, stunning castles, rugged walks, golf courses and Holy Island, return to a cosy sitting room with a wood-burner. Sleep well in large, airy bedrooms with good bouncy mattresses, chintzy fabrics, top-of-the-range cotton sheets, warm showers and white towels. Wander the peaceful garden – there's a tree house and a croquet lawn.

Minimum stay: 2 nights.

Rooms	1 double, 1 twin/double: £80–£90. Singles £65.
Meals	Pub/restaurant within 300 yds.
Closed	Rarely.

Rooms	2 doubles; 1 twin with separate bathroom: £75–£95. 1 suite for 4 with separate bathroom: £140–£160. Singles £65–£75.
Meals	Pubs/restaurants 1 mile.
Closed	December/January.

	Maureen Mason Courtyard Garden, 10 Prudhoe Street, Alnwick, NE66 1UW
Tel	+44 (0)1665 603393
Email	maureenpeter10@btinternet.com
Web	www.courtyardgarden-alnwick.com

	Christine & David Jackson Old Rectory Howick, Howick, Alnwick, NE66 3LE
Tel	+44 (0)1665 577590
Mobile	+44 (0)7879 681753
Email	stay@oldrectoryhowick.co.uk
Web	www.oldrectoryhowick.co.uk

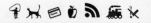

Entry 337   Map 16

Entry 338   Map 16

Northumberland

Tuggal Hall

Once owned by Lord Beveridge... a lovely stone hall surrounded by fields of horses. Your host is charming and very happy for guests to feel at home. Relax by the log fire in the guest sitting room, cosy with books and magazines, antiques and paintings. Bedrooms are comfortably traditional (with garden views and simple bathrooms) – and you can enjoy a full English, black pudding or Craster kippers for breakfast. The gardens are full of mature trees and the productive kitchen garden provides fresh vegetables for dinner. House martins nest under the eaves, the terriers are friendly, the beautiful Northumbrian coast is just down the road.

Over 15s welcome.

Rooms	1 double, 1 twin, each with separate bath: £90–£95. Singles £45–£50.
Meals	Dinner £35. Pubs/restaurants 5 miles.
Closed	November to mid-March.

Naomi Barrett
Tuggal Hall,
Chathill, NE67 5EW
Tel   +44 (0)1665 589229
Email   naomibarrett23@btinternet.com

🐱 🐴 🔊 ⚔

Entry 339   Map 16

Northumberland

Laundry Cottage

History lovers, peace seekers and observers of nature will mellow further in this glorious spot overlooking the Cheviot hills. On arrival enjoy cake and tea with the evening sun – in the sun room, or in the garden on warm days. Douse yourself in one of Ginia's wonderful big breakfasts, stride through iron age forts and the remains of Saxon palaces or visit long, white beaches; return to Welsh slate floors, wood-burners, a delicious dinner, feather and down on deep comfy mattresses and fluffy towels; the twin beds have cheerful patchwork quilts made by Ginia. She and Peter are amiable hosts and the super garden is filled with roses in summer.

Over 14s welcome. Pets by arrangement.

Rooms	1 double, 1 twin: £70–£75. Singles £50–£70.
Meals	Dinner £18–£22, coffee included. Pub/restaurant 5 miles.
Closed	December–March.

Peter & Ginia Gadsdon
Laundry Cottage,
East Horton,
Wooler, NE71 6EZ
Tel   +44 (0)1668 215383
Email   peter@gadsdon.me.uk
Web   www.laundry-cottage-bnb.co.uk

🐱 🐴 🔊 🚂 🚜 ⚔

Entry 340   Map 16

Northumberland

Chain Bridge House

Overlooking an idyllic stretch of the river Tweed is the last house in England – Scotland is 100 yards away across the magnificent Union Chain Bridge. In the sitting room: a log fire and books galore. In the bedrooms: goose down duvets and a fresh, airy feel. Livvy, a professional cook, is an active supporter of the Slow Food movement and local producers. Visit the neighbouring honey farm, glorious Bamburgh, Holy Island, the Farnes, or the unspoilt borders beyond: return to a revolving summerhouse in the garden for tea. Children and dogs get a generous welcome in this delightful family home.

Children over 2 welcome.

Rooms	1 double, 1 twin: £90–£95. Singles £60–£65.
Meals	Dinner £30. Supper £15. Packed lunch from £7.50. Pubs/restaurants 5-7 miles.
Closed	Rarely.

Livvy Cawthorn
Chain Bridge House,
Horncliffe,
Berwick-upon-Tweed, TD15 2XT
Tel +44 (0)1289 382541
Email info@chainbridgehouse.co.uk
Web www.chainbridgehouse.co.uk

Entry 341 Map 16

Northumberland

West Coates

Slip through the gates of this Victorian townhouse and you're in the country. Two acres of leafy gardens, with pretty spots to relax, belie the closeness of Berwick's centre. From the lofty ceilings and sash windows to the soft colours, paintings and gleaming furniture, the house has a calm, ordered elegance. Bedrooms have antiques and garden views; one has a roll top bath; fruit, homemade cakes, flowers welcome you. Warm, friendly Karen is a stunning cook, inventively using local produce and spoiling you – she runs a cookery school here too. The coastline is stunning and there are castles and country houses galore to visit.

Minimum stay: 2 nights at weekends & in high season.

Rooms	2 twin/doubles: £90–£120. Singles £70.
Meals	Pub/restaurant 15-minute walk.
Closed	December/January.

Karen Brown
West Coates,
30 Castle Terrace,
Berwick-upon-Tweed, TD15 1NZ
Tel +44 (0)1289 309666
Mobile +44 (0)7814 281973
Email westcoatesbandb@gmail.com
Web www.westcoates.co.uk

Entry 342 Map 16

Nottinghamshire

Compton House

Two minutes from Newark's antique shops and old market, seek out this terraced Georgian townhouse where the mayor once lived. Naturally elegant, and overlooking Fountain Gardens, the drawing room has an open fire and books. Lisa – who won 'Friendliest Landlady of the Year' – has filled the place with lovely personal touches and rooms are named after friends, from red-gold Judy's room to Harry's bijou single; the best is Cooper's, with a four-poster, a roll top bath through a draped archway and a wall hand-painted by a local artist. Pad down to the sunny basement for Lisa's feast of a breakfast. Hotel comforts but a truly homely feel.

Dogs by arrangement.

Rooms	2 doubles, 1 twin/double, 2 twins, 1 four-poster: £95-£130. 1 single with separate shower: £50.
Meals	Packed lunch £5. Dinner, 3 courses, from £25. Pub/restaurant 0.5 miles.
Closed	Christmas.

Lisa Holloway
Compton House,
117 Baldertongate,
Newark, NG24 1RY

Tel	+44 (0)1636 708670
Mobile	+44 (0)7817 446485
Email	info@comptonhousenewark.com
Web	www.comptonhousenewark.com

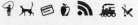

Entry 343   Map 9

Nottinghamshire

Willoughby House

A smart three-storey farmhouse with a fascinating mix of traditional and modern. Find meat hooks in the scullery-turned-sitting room, huge canvases of modern art, and heaps of atmosphere. Beautifully decorated bedrooms have perfect linen and homemade flapjacks; climb up to Harry's room with its brass bed and toy soldiers over the fireplace; Edward's and George's share a raftered loft space and swish bathroom. Sarah rustles up delicious breakfasts in a dining room with poppy red walls and shutters. Unspoilt Georgian town Newark is close – come for the huge annual antiques fair – and you can walk to the village gastropub for supper.

Rooms	4 twin/doubles, 1 suite for 4; 1 double with separate bath/shower: £85-£105. Singles £65-£75.
Meals	Packed lunch £7.50. Pub 3-minute walk.
Closed	Rarely.

Andrew & Sarah Nesbitt
Willoughby House,
Main Street, Norwell,
Newark, NG23 6JN

Tel	+44 (0)1636 636266
Mobile	+44 (0)7789 965352
Email	willoughbyhousebandb@gmail.com
Web	www.willoughbyhousebandb.co.uk

Entry 344   Map 9

Oxfordshire

Primrose Hill Farm

Surrounded by 80 acres dotted with munching sheep and horses… you've landed in a peaceful spot. All is polished and immaculate inside. Bedrooms are inviting: some have vaulted elm beams, all have deep beds, fat feather pillows, pretty lamps, vases of flowers. Elegant sitting and dining rooms look uphill to the woods; find silver pheasants atop a gleaming table, a trio of colourful sofas. Expect a hearty breakfast with compotes and a myriad of teas. The area teems with places to visit: Stratford, Warwick Castle, National Trust gems, Compton Verney art. John is warm and engaging – Trouble the terrier will help you feel at home too.

Rooms	2 doubles, 1 twin/double, 1 twin: £80–£90.
	Singles £65–£70.
Meals	Pubs/restaurants 3 miles.
Closed	Rarely.

	John Jeffries
	Primrose Hill Farm,
	Arlescote,
	Banbury, OX17 1DQ
Mobile	+44 (0)7956 328359
Email	stay@primrose-hill-farm.com
Web	www.primrose-hill-farm.com

Entry 345   Map 8

Oxfordshire

Uplands House

Come to be spoiled at this handsome house, built in 1875 for the Earl of Jersey's farm manager. All is elegant and lavishly furnished; expect large light bedrooms, crisp linen, thick towels and vases of flowers. There are long views from the orangery, where you can have tea and cake; relax here with a book as the scents of the pretty garden waft by. Chat to Poppy while she creates delicious dinner – a convivial occasion enjoyed with your hosts. Breakfast is Graham's domain – try smoked salmon with scrambled eggs and red caviar. You're well placed for exploring – Moreton-in-Marsh and Stratford are close, Oxford just under an hour.

Rooms	1 double, 1 twin/double,
	1 four-poster: £100–£180.
	Singles £70–£110
	(Monday to Thursday).
Meals	Dinner, 2–4 courses, £20–£35.
	Pub 1.25 miles.
Closed	Rarely.

	Poppy Cooksey & Graham Paul
	Uplands House,
	Upton, Banbury, OX15 6HJ
Tel	+44 (0)1295 678663
Mobile	+44 (0)7836 535538
Email	poppy@cotswolds-uplands.co.uk
Web	www.cotswolds-uplands.co.uk

Entry 346   Map 8

Oxfordshire

Home Farmhouse

This 400-year-old house is charming...
beams, inglenooks and winding stairs.
Rosemary and Nigel have been welcoming
guests for over 20 years; their gently faded
home brims with character, antiques and
chintz. Pretty bedrooms have eiderdowns
and traditional blankets; bathrooms are small
and a little dated. Hop up old stone steps and
enjoy independence in the barn room – a
simple space with a mixture of family pieces.
Breakfast is generous with garden compotes,
homemade bread and conserves. The family's
travels are evident all over, Samson the wire-
haired dachshund is friendly and it's all so
laid-back you'll find it hard to leave.

Rooms	1 double, 1 twin/double: £94.
	Barn - 1 twin/double: £94.
	Singles £65.
Meals	Pub 100 yds.
Closed	Christmas.

Rosemary & Nigel Grove-White
Home Farmhouse,
Charlton, Banbury, OX17 3DR

Tel	+44 (0)1295 811683
Mobile	+44 (0)7795 207000
Email	grovewhite@lineone.net
Web	www.homefarmhouse.co.uk

Entry 347   Map 8

Oxfordshire

Minehill House

Wind your way up the farm track to the top
of a beautiful hill and you arrive at a gorgeous
family farmhouse with views for miles and
warm, energetic Hester to care for you.
Children will have fun with the ping-pong
table and trampoline; their parents will
enjoy the gleaming old flagstones, vibrant
contemporary oils, wood-burning stove and
seriously sophisticated food. Rest well in the
big double room with its gloriously
comfortable bed, verdant leafy wallpaper and
stunning views; there's a cubby-hole door to
extra twin beds (children love it!) and the
bathroom is sparkling and spacious. Bracing
walks start straight from the door.

Rooms	1 double with adjoining twin room:
	£110–£150.
	Singles £75.
Meals	Dinner, 3 courses, £35.
	Pubs 1-5 miles.
Closed	Christmas & New Year.

Hester & Ed Sale
Minehill House,
Lower Brailes, Banbury, OX15 5BJ

Tel	+44 (0)1608 685594
Mobile	+44 (0)7890 266441
Email	hester@minehillhouse.co.uk
Web	www.minehillhouse.co.uk

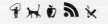

Entry 348   Map 8

Oxfordshire

Buttslade House

Choose between a gorgeous ground-floor retreat across the courtyard, or a very pretty twin in the 17th-century farmhouse with barns and stables. The guest sitting room is a clever melody of ancient and contemporary styles: Spanish art, antique sofas, velvet cushions. Beds have seriously good mattresses, feather and down pillows and crisp white linen; bathrooms are smart and sparkling – one with a Victorian roll top. Diana is lovely and will pamper you or leave you, there's a blissful garden to stroll through, breakfast is a feast of fruits and homemade bread and it's a hop to the village pub. A fun and stylish treat.

Rooms	1 double; 1 twin with separate bath: £80–£90. Singles £50.
Meals	Dinner, 3 courses, £25. Lunch £7. Pub 100 yds.
Closed	Rarely.

Diana Thompson
Buttslade House,
Temple Mill Road,
Sibford Gower,
Banbury, OX15 5RX

Tel	+44 (0)1295 788818
Email	diana@buttsladehouse.co.uk
Web	www.buttsladehouse.co.uk

Entry 349   Map 8

Oxfordshire

The Old Post House

Great natural charm in the 17th-century Old Post House, where shiny flagstones, rich dark wood and mullion windows combine with handsome fabrics and furniture. Bedrooms are big, with antique wardrobes, oak headboards and a comfortably elegant feel. The walled gardens are lovely – with espaliered fruit trees, and a pool for sunny evenings. Christine, a well-travelled ex-pat, has an innate sense of hospitality; breakfasts are delicious (homemade granola, eggs Benedict, blueberry pancakes perhaps). There's village traffic but your sleep should be sound. Deddington is delightful – you will love Harry the friendly terrier too!

Over 12s welcome.

Rooms	1 twin/double; 1 double with separate bath, 1 four-poster with separate shower: £95. Singles £65.
Meals	Occasional dinner from £20. Pubs/restaurants within 5-minute walk.
Closed	Rarely.

Christine Blenntoft
The Old Post House,
New Street,
Deddington, OX15 0SP

Tel	+44 (0)1869 338978
Mobile	+44 (0)7713 631092
Email	kblenntoft@aol.com
Web	www.oldposthouse.co.uk

Entry 350   Map 8

Oxfordshire

Manor Farm

An attractive old farmhouse dating from the 17th century with a warm friendly atmosphere. Jeannette and Andrew are generous hosts; Andrew built his own heating system, which runs on pallets and linseed straw – now he's finished a four-seater plane! Elegant, light bedrooms with garden views have pretty lamps and fabrics, sofas and comfortable beds. Wake for a full English served around a big table in an immaculate kitchen: homemade bread, eggs from the hens. There's a wood-burner in the snug sitting room, the garden has a pond and lots of birds, the little village is peaceful and Oxford is a half hour drive.

Rooms	2 doubles, 1 twin: £85-£90. Singles £40-£50.
Meals	Pubs/restaurants 3 miles.
Closed	Rarely.

Andrew & Jeannette Collett
Manor Farm,
Main Street, Poundon,
Bicester, OX27 9BB
Tel +44 (0)1869 277212
Mobile +44 (0)7974 753772
Email ajcollett@live.co.uk
Web www.manorfarmpoundon.co.uk

Entry 351   Map 8

Oxfordshire

Heyford House

Old church and handsome house face each other down a village lane – and then the road runs out. In this timeless Oxfordshire valley, the white gate leads into gardens where pathways weave between borders to a kitchen garden and orchards. The house, warm-hearted and well-proportioned, has been in the family for years; your hosts (he a personal trainer, she a chef) live in one wing. Find contemporary art, bright old rugs and open fires – a happy mix of traditional and new. Bedrooms are handsome and comfortable, with excellent bath and shower rooms; Sonja's breakfasts, served by the Aga, are a treat.

Rooms	2 doubles, 2 twin/doubles: £100-£120. Singles £60-£80. Extra bed/sofabed available £25 per person per night.
Meals	Dinner for larger parties available, 2 courses from £20; 3 courses from £27 (enquire for further catering). Picnic from £10. Pubs/restaurants 4 miles.
Closed	Rarely.

Leo Brooke-Little
Heyford House,
Church Lane,
Lower Heyford,
Bicester, OX25 5NZ
Tel +44 (0)1869 349061
Email info@stayatheyfordhouse.co.uk

Entry 352   Map 8

Oxfordshire

Rectory Farm

This big country house has a wonderfully settled, tranquil feel – the family have farmed here for three generations. Find large, light bedrooms, floral and pretty, with bold chintz bed covers, draped dressing tables, thick mattresses and tea trays with delicious chocolate shortbread; all have garden views. Sink into comfortable sofas flanking a huge fireplace in the drawing room, breakfast on local bacon and sausage with free-range eggs, stroll the lovely garden, or grab a rod and try your luck on one of the trout lakes. Elizabeth knows her patch well, walkers can borrow maps and lively market town Chipping Norton is close.

Rooms	1 double, 1 twin/double; 1 twin/double with separate bath: £95–£120. Singles £65–£75.
Meals	Pub/restaurant 1.5 miles.
Closed	December–January.

Elizabeth Colston
Rectory Farm,
Salford,
Chipping Norton, OX7 5YY

Tel	+44 (0)1608 643209
Mobile	+44 (0)7866 834208
Email	enquiries@rectoryfarm.info
Web	www.rectoryfarm.info

Entry 353 Map 8

Oxfordshire

Corner House at Churchill

Peter and Caroline, London escapees keen on the fine detail, have turned this handsome listed house into an immaculate home. All is beamed and inviting with warm colours, smart furniture, limestone floors, white linen on the refectory table; carbon-neutral too. Bedrooms are in a separate wing and named after local villages; find a headboard clad in tweed, Welsh rugs, plump pillows on comfy beds. Peter cooks you a generous classic breakfast along with compotes, yogurt, smoked salmon, pancakes with fruit. The Cotswolds is foodie heaven; there are literary and music festivals to attend, National Trust gems to visit. It's a treat to stay.

Minimum stay: 2 nights on bank holidays.

Rooms	2 doubles, 1 twin/double: £95–£125. Singles £85–£115.
Meals	Breakfast served until 10am. Pubs 2-minute walk.
Closed	Rarely.

Caroline & Peter Dunnicliffe
Corner House at Churchill,
Church Road,
Churchill,
Chipping Norton, OX7 6NJ

Tel	+44 (0)1608 658432
Email	cornerhousepeter@icloud.com
Web	www.cornerhousechurchill.co.uk

Entry 354 Map 8

Oxfordshire

York House

On a country road between villages, surrounded by open garden, lake and trees, is this freshly painted and peaceful house. Its old cottage heart has become a delicious low-ceilinged sitting room with a log fire; new and 'deceptively spacious' is the rest. Ewa, warm, fun and full of good taste, has made it all delightful with swagged curtains, gold embossed antique books, delicate china, ancestral pieces and elegant glass. Bedrooms are comfortable, pretty and traditional. There are stately houses and gardens to visit and gastropubs to try, but if you've come with a party and decide to dine in, Ewa's cooking is a joy.

Whole house available for Christmas & New Year: decorations, meals & butler plus lifts to local pubs.

Rooms	2 doubles (extra double available); 1 double, 1 twin sharing bath: £100–£130.
Meals	Dinner £40 (min. 8). BYO. Pubs within 2 miles.
Closed	Rarely.

Ewa Lewis
York House,
Kingham,
Chipping Norton, OX7 6UL

Tel	+44 (0)1608 659341
Mobile	+44 (0)7747 784830
Email	ewa.lewis2@virgin.net
Web	www.cotswolds-yorkhouse-bandb.co.uk

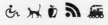

Entry 355 Map 8

Oxfordshire

Upper Court Farm

In a quiet, gently hilly spot in the Cotswolds, the super smart Edwardian farmhouse comes with groomed gardens, 30 acres of grassland for Chloë's horses and woodland walks. A dressage rider, she and Tim are interesting hosts and their home is laden with country art and family pieces. Charming bedrooms have madly comfy beds, TVs, drenching showers; there's a cosy sitting room too; the Dove apartment has its own entrance and little garden. Breakfast is generous, local and delicious with fruit salad, and homemade bread and jams. Relax in the rose garden with drinks or tea and home-baked cakes – two sweet dogs will join you.

Minimum stay: 2 nights. Children over 8 welcome.

Rooms	1 double, 1 twin/double: £85–£120. Dove Apartment – 1 double for 2-3 with kitchen, sitting room and futon (self-catering option also available): £95–£120. Singles £65–£95. Extra bed/sofabed available £20 per person per night.
Meals	Pub 200 yds & 3 miles, café 5-minute walk.
Closed	Rarely.

Chloë Robson
Upper Court Farm,
Mill End, Chadlington,
Chipping Norton, OX7 3NY

Tel	+44 (0)1608 676296
Mobile	+44 (0)7717 571792
Email	chloe.uppercourt@gmail.com
Web	www.uppercourtfarm.co.uk

Entry 356 Map 8

Oxfordshire

Star Cottage

Classic Cotswolds — from the cottagey stone walls to the flower-bright garden — and swathes of open countryside for cyclists and walkers. Step inside to hand-sewn fabrics, cute lampshades, country furniture, fresh flowers and calm, pretty bedrooms: Sally delights in details. She and Peter, a plant biologist, love their winding stone-walled garden with its herbs, climbers and medlar tree; its jelly appears at breakfast, alongside smoked haddock and local sausages. The pub (yards away) offers dinner, Burford market town is a ten-minute walk, Cheltenham and Oxford a half-hour drive. Or kind Peter will fetch from the station.

Rooms	1 double, 1 family room for 3: £80–£110. Barn – 1 family room for 3 with kitchen: £80–£110. Singles £70–£80.
Meals	Pubs/restaurants within walking distance.
Closed	Rarely.

Peter & Sally Wyatt
Star Cottage,
Meadow Lane, Fulbrook,
Burford, OX18 4BW

Tel +44 (0)1993 822032
Email wyattpeter@btconnect.com
Web www.burfordbedandbreakfast.co.uk

Entry 357   Map 8

Oxfordshire

The Glove House

Handmade chocolates from Turin (Francesco is Italian) and espresso machines in the bedrooms show proper respect for the important things in life. This handsome Georgian house in the heart of Woodstock combines calm contemporary comfort with warm smiles. The sitting room is panelled in golden oak; the suites, overlooking rooftops at the back, are discreet and delicious. Upholstered headboards, best feather duvets, Cotswolds wool throws, books, magazines and small buttoned armchairs... Enjoy a chilled prosecco by the garden's fountain before venturing out for supper; this lovely old town is awash with treats.

Ask about parking. Children over 10 welcome.

Rooms	1 double: £140–£175. 2 suites for 3: £150–£220. Extra bed/sofabed available £55 per person per night.
Meals	Pubs/restaurants nearby.
Closed	Rarely.

Francesco & Caroline Totta
The Glove House,
24 Oxford Street,
Woodstock, OX20 1TS

Tel +44 (0)1993 813475
Email info@theglovehouse.co.uk
Web www.theglovehouse.co.uk

Entry 358   Map 8

Oxfordshire

Manor Farmhouse

This old Cotswold stone farmhouse is tucked down a quiet lane and was once part of the Blenheim estate. Helen and John are good humoured and have been happily welcoming guests for years. Find comfortable, traditional furnishings, lots of water colours and nothing overdone. The two doubles are in a private area of the house. Breakfast is at a polished oak table by the fire – cheerful wading birds from Italy sit at the window, pretty hand-painted Portuguese plates on the dresser. Wander in the lovely garden, have tea in the Victorian-style garden house or under an apple tree. Oxford is an easy drive and it's a stroll to the village pub.

Rooms	2 doubles sharing shower (let to same party only): £80-£94. Singles £75.
Meals	Pub 5-minute walk.
Closed	Christmas.

Helen Stevenson
Manor Farmhouse,
Manor Road, Bladon,
Woodstock, OX20 1RU
Tel +44 (0)1993 812168
Email helstevenson@hotmail.com
Web www.oxtowns.co.uk/woodstock/manor-farmhouse/

Entry 359   Map 8

Oxfordshire

New Entry

Green Close

This trim idyllic village abuts Blenheim Park and the parish church is famous for its medieval wall paintings. The Freelands' old stone house sits on the edge of one of the greens. The feel inside is harmonious and airy: high rafters, polished wood, a hall dining room with light streaming through mullioned windows, a winter fire in the lived-in sitting room, simple spotless bedrooms. Your hosts are easy-going, the retriever is smiley and children are welcome. An Aga breakfast will include compote, yogurt, eggs from the hens, homemade bread and good coffee. Woodstock and Oxford are a hop, and you can walk to supper at the pub.

Pets by arrangement.

Rooms	2 doubles; 1 twin with separate bath: £85. Singles £50.
Meals	Pubs/restaurants 75 yds.
Closed	Rarely.

Caroline Freeland
Green Close,
West End, Combe,
Witney, OX29 8NS
Tel +44 (0)1993 891223
Email julian.freeland@btinternet.com
Web www.greenclose.net

Entry 360   Map

Oxfordshire

Rectory Farm

Come for the happy relaxed vibe, and Mary Anne's welcome with tea and homemade shortbread. There's a wood-burner in the guest sitting room, and bedrooms have beautiful arched mullion windows. The huge twin with ornate plasterwork overlooks the garden and church, the pretty double is cosier and both have good showers and big fluffy towels. Wake for an excellent Aga breakfast with eggs from the hens, garden and hedgerow compotes, home or locally produced bacon and homemade jams. A herd of Red Ruby Devon cattle are Robert's pride and joy; the family have farmed for generations and you can buy the beef. It's a treat to stay.

Minimum stay: 2 nights at weekends & high season.

Rooms	1 double, 1 twin: £86–£88. Singles £65–£67.
Meals	Pub 2-minute walk.
Closed	Christmas & New Year.

	Mary Anne Florey
	Rectory Farm,
	Northmoor, Witney, OX29 5SX
Tel	+44 (0)1865 300207
Mobile	+44 (0)7974 102198
Email	pj.florey@farmline.com
Web	www.oxtowns.co.uk/rectoryfarm

🐾 ✉ 🍃 📶 🚜 🍴

Oxfordshire

Oxford University

Oxford at your fingertips – at a fair price. In the city's ancient heart are Wadham and Keble; in leafy North Oxford is friendly St Hugh's. Keble's sleeping quarters, functional though a good size, stand in stark contrast to the neo-gothic grandeur of its dining hall – pure Hogwarts! Wadham's hall, 17th century, soaring, is yet more glorious – with top breakfasts. Its student-simple bedrooms are reached via crenellated cloisters and lovely walled gardens; ask for a room facing the beautiful quad. At St Hugh's: three residences (one historic), a student café, 14 acres of romantic gardens and a 15-minute walk into town.

23 colleges in total.

Rooms	52 doubles, 121 twins: £69–£120. 12 family rooms for 3-4: £90–£165. 1052 singles: £35–£85.
Meals	Breakfast included. Keble: occasional supper £22.50. Restaurants 2-15 minutes' walk.
Closed	Mid-January to mid-March, May/June, October/November; Christmas. A few rooms available throughout year.

	University Rooms
	Oxford University,
	Oxford
Web	www.universityrooms.com/ en/city/oxford/home

 🍶

Oxfordshire

Willow Cottage

You are a short step from a village with an excellent pub (return across fields with a torch). Or treat yourself to dinner at Le Manoir aux Quat'Saisons. Katrina's delicious thatched cottage sits down a quiet lane. Through your own entrance find a guest dining room with armchairs by the old range, interesting prints and paintings, an eclectic mix of antiques and contemporary furniture. Bedrooms are warm, comfortable and stylish with views over the garden; shower rooms (not huge) are brand new and deeply smart. Breakfast, unhurried and bristling with local produce, sets walkers up for the Chiltern Way and the Ridgeway.

Rooms	2 doubles: £90.
	Singles £60.
Meals	Pubs/restaurants 0.5 miles.
Closed	Rarely.

	Katrina Sheldon
	Willow Cottage,
	Denton,
	Oxford, OX44 9JG
Tel	+44 (0)1865 874728
Email	katrinasheldon@aol.com
Web	www.willowcottage.info

Entry 363 Map 8

Oxfordshire

Fyfield Manor

A fabulous house in Oxfordshire (once owned by Simon de Montfort) with vast water gardens, providing a most romantic setting. The Browns have added solar panels too. From the grand wood-panelled hall enter a beamed dining room with high-backed chairs, brass rubbings, wood-burner and pretty 12th-century arch; breakfast on eggs from the hens, garden fruit, organic bacon. Charming bedrooms have views, slippers and comfy sofas. Oxford Park & Ride is nearby, there's walking from the door and delightful Christine has wangled you a free glass of wine in the local pub if you walk or cycle to get there! Superb.

Children over 10 welcome.

Rooms	1 twin/double: £85–£90.
	1 family room for 2–4 with sofabed
	& separate bath (£20 extra per
	person): £85–£90.
	Singles £60–£70. Family room £20
	extra per person, after first 2.
Meals	Pubs within 1 mile.
Closed	Rarely.

	Christine Brown
	Fyfield Manor,
	Benson,
	Wallingford, OX10 6HA
Tel	+44 (0)1491 835184
Email	chris_fyfield@hotmail.co.uk
Web	www.fyfieldmanor.co.uk

Entry 364 Map 4

Rutland

Old Rectory

Jane Austen fans will swoon. This elegant 1740s village house was used as Mr Collins's 'humble abode' by the BBC: you breakfast in the beautiful dining room that was 'Mr Collins's hall', and you can sleep in 'Miss Bennett's bedroom'. Victoria is wonderful – feisty, fun and gregarious – and looks after you beautifully with White Company linen in chintzy old-fashioned bedrooms, a log fire in the drawing room, fruit from the lovely garden, homemade jams and Aga-cooked local bacon and eggs. Guests love it here. You are near to some pleasant market towns and good walking and riding country. Don't forget the smelling salts!

Pets by arrangement.

Rooms	1 double, 1 twin: £85. Singles £45.
Meals	Pubs within 3 miles.
Closed	Rarely.

Victoria Owen
Old Rectory,
Teigh,
Oakham, LE15 7RT

Tel	+44 (0)1572 787681
Mobile	+44 (0)7717 223678
Email	torowen@btinternet.com
Web	www.teighbedandbreakfast.co.uk

Entry 365   Map 9

Rutland

Old Hall Coach House

A rare and special setting; the grounds of the house meet the edge of Rutland Water, with far-reaching lake and church views. There's a terrace with table and chairs, a stunning garden and a croquet lawn. Inside: high ceilings, stone archways, antiques, a log fire to sit by. Comfortable and traditional bedrooms have smart, handsome bathrooms; the twin has glorious views from both windows. Wake for an Aga-cooked spread of home-laid eggs, sausages and homemade marmalade. Rutland is a mini-Cotswolds of stone villages and gentle hills; Georgian Stamford, Burghley House and Belvoir Castle are all near. Cecilie is a well-travelled, interesting host.

Minimum stay: 2 nights at weekends.

Rooms	1 double; 1 twin with separate bath: £95. Singles from £45.
Meals	Dinner £30. Pub/restaurant 5-minute walk.
Closed	Occasionally.

Cecilie Ingoldby
Old Hall Coach House,
31 Weston Road, Edith Weston,
Oakham, LE15 8HQ

Tel	+44 (0)1780 721504
Mobile	+44 (0)7767 678267
Email	cecilieingoldby@aol.com
Web	www.oldhallcoachhouse.co.uk

Entry 366   Map 9

Shropshire

Tybroughton Hall

Off a winding country lane, surrounded by 40 acres of grassland, find a pretty white listed farmhouse and a wonderful welcome from Daisy, her family and two dear dogs. Step into the hallway with its polished antique table and bright garden flowers and you know you've made the right choice: this is a house to unwind in. After a day's hiking or biking, bliss to return to bedrooms cosy and comfortable – the traditional double with its country view or the large lovely twin. Breakfasts are worth getting up for: Tim makes the preserves, bees make the honey, hens lay the eggs and the pigs (five beauties!) provide the bacon.

Rooms	1 double; 1 twin with separate bath: £80–£100. Singles £50–£65.
Meals	Dinner £20–£25. Pub 4 miles.
Closed	Rarely.

Daisy Woodhead
Tybroughton Hall,
Tybroughton,
Whitchurch, SY13 3BB
Tel   +44 (0)1948 780726
Mobile   +44 (0)7850 395885
Email   daisy.woodhead@btinternet.com
Web   www.tybroughtonhall-
         bedandbreakfast.co.uk

Entry 367   Map 7

Shropshire

Brimford House

Beautifully tucked under the Breidden Hills, farm and Georgian farmhouse have been in the Dawson family for four generations. Views stretch all the way to the Severn; the simple garden does not try to compete. Spotless bedrooms have flowers, and pretty china for morning tea; there's a half-tester with rope-twist columns, a twin with Victorian wrought-iron bedsteads, a double with a brass bed, a big bathroom with a roll top bath. Liz serves you farm eggs and homemade preserves at breakfast, and there's a food pub just down the road. Sheep and cattle outdoors, a lovely black lab in, and wildlife walks from the door. Good value.

Minimum stay: 2 nights at weekends.

Rooms	2 doubles, 1 twin: £70–£80. Singles £50–£60.
Meals	Packed lunch £4.50. Pub 3-minute walk.
Closed	Rarely.

Liz Dawson
Brimford House,
Criggion,
Shrewsbury, SY5 9AU
Tel   +44 (0)1938 570235
Mobile   +44 (0)7801 100848
Email   info@brimford.co.uk
Web   www.brimford.co.uk

Entry 368   Map 7

Shropshire

Whitton Hall

Down a long private drive with fields on either side is a lovely 18th-century farmhouse, elegant but not intimidating, with a sense of timelessness. A large open hallway and a cosy sitting room where tea and a drinks tray are provided are peaceful spaces for relaxing with a book. You breakfast in the dining room, on local muesli, bread, marmalades and jams, milk from their Jersey cows, soft fruit from their garden, sausages and bacon from down the road. Peaceful, light and large bedrooms in an adjacent wing have modern bathrooms, country house furniture and long views to glorious gardens. Unwind in the peace.

Over 12s welcome.

Rooms	1 double with separate bathroom, 1 twin/double with separate shower: £100. 1 family room for 4 with separate bathroom: £140. Singles £60.
Meals	Supper in dining room £25 a head for 4+ guests. Cold supper tray in room or garden £15 for 2, £10 for 1. Restaurant 1.5 miles.
Closed	Christmas, New Year & Easter.

Christopher & Gill Halliday & Kate Boscawen
Whitton Hall,
Westbury, Shrewsbury, SY5 9RD
Tel   +44 (0)1743 884270
Mobile   +44 (0)7974 689629
Email   accommodation@whittonhall.com
Web   www.whittonhall.co.uk

Entry 369   Map 7

Shropshire

Hardwick House

On a quiet street in the heart of Shrewsbury, this fine Georgian house has been in Lucy's family for generations. The dining room (oak panelling, a huge fireplace) is a lovely space to breakfast on locally sourced produce and homemade bread; vases of garden flowers are dotted all around this cheerful family home. Bedrooms are traditional and comfortable with pretty china tea cups; bathrooms are old-fashioned. The walled garden is fabulous; take tea in an 18th-century summerhouse. Birthplace of Darwin, this is a fascinating historic town; walk to the abbey, castle, theatre, festivals and great shops. Lucy is delightful.

Rooms	2 twin/doubles (1 with adjoining twin can form a large suite): £85-£100. Singles £55-£75.
Meals	Pubs/restaurants 150 yds.
Closed	Christmas & New Year.

Lucy Whitaker
Hardwick House,
12 St John's Hill,
Shrewsbury, SY1 1JJ
Tel   +44 (0)1743 350165
Email   gilesandlucy@btinternet.com
Web   www.hardwickhouseshrewsbury.co.uk

Entry 370   Map 7

Shropshire

Shropshire

North Farm

Peaceful green Shropshire and a stunning garden surround this classic white farmhouse. Chickens, ducks and geese are happily dotted about and the veg patch blooms. Tess and family look after you well. Bedrooms have flowery fabrics, tip-top linen, Lloyd Loom chairs and pretty tea trays. Wake for a delicious breakfast served on Portmeirion china: homemade marmalade, compotes, eggs from the hens, bacon and sausages from home-reared pigs. Lots to do close by: historic Shrewsbury, Ironbridge, Ludlow, Powis Castle – and the walks are a treat. Settle by the log-burner on your return: books to browse, a glass of wine... lovely.

Lawley House

A lovely calm sense of the continuity of history and family life emanates from this large, comfortable Victorian home. Jackie and Jim are delightful hosts and great fun. Bedrooms welcome you with flowers, duck down pillows – and stupendous views of the Stretton Hills, even from bed. Tea and cake on arrival in the spectacular conservatory set the scene for a spoiling stay, there are binoculars for bird watchers and a drawing room with a huge variety of books. Awake to birdsong and a royal breakfast in the elegant dining room; enjoy the lushly planted garden – brimming with scents and seating spots. A charming and friendly place.

Over 12s welcome.

Rooms	1 double, 1 twin; 1 double with separate bath: £85. Singles £55.	Rooms	1 double, 1 twin/double: £70-£80. Singles £55-£65. One-night weekend stay, small extra charge.
Meals	Pubs/restaurants 4-minute drive.	Meals	Pub/restaurant 1.5 miles.
Closed	Rarely.	Closed	Christmas & New Year.

	Tess Bromley		**Jackie & Jim Scarratt**
	North Farm,		Lawley House,
	Eaton Mascot, Cross Houses,		Smethcott,
	Shrewsbury, SY5 6HF		Church Stretton, SY6 6NX
Tel	+44 (0)1743 761031	Tel	+44 (0)1694 751236
Mobile	+44 (0)7956 817705	Mobile	+44 (0)7980 331792
Email	tessbromley@ymail.com	Email	jscarratt@onetel.com
Web	www.northfarm.co.uk	Web	www.lawleyhouse.co.uk

Entry 371   Map 7

Entry 372   Map 7

Shropshire

Clun Farm House

A relaxed country feel here, with heavenly hills all around. Friendly hosts Susan and Anthony are enthusiastic collectors of country artefacts and have filled their listed 15th-century farmhouse with eye-catching things; the cowboy's saddle by the old range echoes Susan's roots. Bedrooms have aged and oiled floorboards, fun florals and bold walls; there is space for children in the extra bunk room; bathrooms are small and simple. Walk Offa's Dyke and the Shropshire Way; return to rescue hens wandering the garden, a warm smile and a glass of wine by the cosy wood-burner — before supper at one of the local pubs. Good value.

Horses welcome.

Rooms	1 double with extra bunk bedroom; 1 twin/double with separate shower: £80. Singles by arrangement.
Meals	Packed lunch £4. Pubs/restaurants nearby.
Closed	Occasionally.

Anthony & Susan Whitfield
Clun Farm House,
High Street, Clun,
Craven Arms, SY7 8JB
Tel   +44 (0)1588 640432
Mobile   +44 (0)7885 261391
Email   anthonyswhitfield0158@btinternet.com
Web   www.clunfarmhouse.co.uk

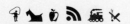

Entry 373   Map 7

Shropshire

Hopton House

Karen looks after her guests wonderfully and even runs courses on how to do B&B! Unwind in this fresh and uplifting converted granary with old beams, high ceilings and a sun-filled dining/sitting room overlooking the hills. The bedroom above has its own balcony; those in the barn, one up, one down, each with its own entrance, are as enticing: beautifully dressed beds, silent fridges, good lighting, homemade cakes. Bathrooms have deep baths (and showers) — from one you can lie back and gaze at the stars. Karen's breakfasts promise Ludlow sausages, home-laid eggs, fine jams and homemade marmalade.

Minimum stay: 2 nights. Over 16s welcome.

Rooms	1 double; Barn - 2 doubles: £110-£120.
Meals	Restaurant 3 miles.
Closed	19-27 December.

Karen Thorne
Hopton House,
Hopton Heath,
Craven Arms, SY7 0QD
Tel   +44 (0)1547 530885
Email   info@shropshirebreakfast.co.uk
Web   www.shropshirebreakfast.co.uk

Entry 374   Map 7

Shropshire

Lower Buckton Country House

You are spoiled here in house-party style; Carolyn – passionate about Slow Food – and Henry, are born entertainers. Kick off with homemade cake in the drawing room with its oil paintings, antique furniture and old rugs; return for delicious nibbles when the lamps and wood-burner are flickering. Dine well at a huge oak table (home-reared pork, local cheeses, dreamy puddings), then nestle into the best linen and the softest pillows; bedrooms feel wonderfully restful. This is laid-back B&B: paddle in the stream, admire the stunning views, find a quiet spot with a good book. Great fun!

Minimum stay: 2 nights at weekends.

Rooms	2 doubles; 1 twin/double with separate bath: £100. Singles £75–£100. Dinner, B&B £85 per person. Extra bed/sofabed available £25–£45 per person per night.
Meals	Dinner, 4 courses, £35. BYO wine. Pub/restaurant 4 miles.
Closed	Rarely.

Henry & Carolyn Chesshire
Lower Buckton Country House,
Buckton, Leintwardine, SY7 0JU

Tel	+44 (0)1547 540532
Mobile	+44 (0)7960 273865
Email	carolyn@lowerbuckton.co.uk
Web	www.lowerbuckton.co.uk

Entry 375   Map 7

Shropshire

Walford Court

Come for a break from clock-watching and a spot of fresh air. Large bedrooms delight with the comfiest mattresses on king-size beds, scented candles, antiques, books, games and double-end roll top baths – one under a west facing window. Aga-cooked breakfasts include eggs from 'the ladies of the orchard'; candlelit dinners may be served outside on fine evenings. Wander through apple, plum and pear trees, find a motte and bailey, strike out for a long hike. Craig and Debbie are thoughtful and hugely keen on wildlife (you get binoculars) and this is the perfect place to bring a special person – and a bottle of champagne.

Older children by arrangement.

Rooms	1 double; 2 doubles, each with sitting room: £95–£105. Extra bed/sofabed available £30 per person per night.
Meals	Dinner, 2-3 courses, £25–£31. Cold platters & packed lunch available. Pubs/restaurants 1-3 miles.
Closed	Christmas & Boxing Day.

Debbie & Craig Fraser
Walford Court,
Walford, Leintwardine,
Ludlow, SY7 0JT

Tel	+44 (0)1547 540570
Email	info@romanticbreak.com
Web	www.romanticbreak.com

Entry 376   Map 7

Rosecroft

A pretty, quiet, traditional house with charming owners, well-proportioned rooms, an elegant sitting room and not a trace of pomposity. Breakfasts are huge enough to set you up for the day: Pimhill organic muesli, smoked or unsmoked local bacon, black pudding, delicious jams. The garden is a delight to stroll through – in summer you can picnic here – while serious walkers are close to the Welsh borders. Bedrooms and bathrooms are polished to perfection; there are fresh flowers, plenty of interesting books, home-baked cakes when you arrive. The village has a super pub and Ludlow is close by.

Over 12s welcome.

35 Lower Broad Street

You're almost at the bottom of the town, near the river and the bridge. Elaine's terraced Georgian cottage is spotless and cosy; her office doubles as a sitting area for guests with leather armchairs, TV and a desk space for workaholics. Upstairs are two good-sized doubles with a country crisp feel, king-size beds and a pretty blue and white bathroom. Walkers, shoppers, antique- and book-hunters can fill up on a superb breakfast of homemade potato scones, black pudding, organic eggs and good coffee before striding out to explore. This is excellent value, comfortable B&B and can be enjoyed without a car.

Rooms	1 double; 1 double with separate bath: £80–£90. Singles £65–£75.
Meals	Packed lunch £4. Pub 200 yds.
Closed	Rarely.

Rooms	1 double with sitting room & separate bathroom; 1 double sharing bathroom (let to same party only): £75. Singles £50.
Meals	Pubs/restaurants 100 yds.
Closed	Rarely.

	Gail Benson
	Rosecroft,
	Orleton,
	Ludlow, SY8 4HN
Tel	+44 (0)1568 780565
Email	gailanddavid@rosecroftorleton.co.uk
Web	www.rosecroftbedandbreakfast.co.uk

	Elaine Downs
	35 Lower Broad Street,
	Ludlow, SY8 1PH
Tel	+44 (0)1584 876912
Mobile	+44 (0)7970 151010
Email	a.downs@tesco.net

Cleeton Court

Rare peace: a tiny lane leads to this part 14th-century farmhouse, immersed in the countryside with views over meadows and heathland. You have your own entrance, and the use of the pretty drawing room, elegantly comfortable with sofas and a log fire. Beamed bedrooms are delightfully furnished, one with a magnificent, chintzy four-poster and a vast bathroom; recline in the cast-iron bath with a glass of wine, gaze on views from the window as you soak. Bring your boots: the walking is superb, and charming Ros gives you a smashing, locally sourced breakfast to get you going.

Timberstone Bed & Breakfast

The house is young and engaging – as are Tracey and Alex, new generation B&Bers. Come for charming bedrooms – two snug under the eaves, two in the smart oak-floored extension – roll top baths, pretty fabrics, thick white cotton, beams galore… and reflexology or a sauna in the garden studios; Tracey, once in catering, is a reflexologist. In the warm guest sitting/dining room find art, books, comfortable sofas and glass doors onto the terrace. Breakfasts are special with croissants and local eggs and bacon; suppers are delicious too, or you can head off to Ludlow and its clutch of Michelin stars.

Whole house available for self-catering.

Rooms	1 twin/double, 1 four-poster: £80–£90. Singles £65.
Meals	Pubs/restaurants 1.5-4 miles.
Closed	Christmas & New Year.

Rooms	2 doubles, 1 double, with sofabed: £85–£120. 1 family room for 4: £115–£120. Summerhouse - 1 double (summer only): £85–£120. Singles £50–£90.
Meals	Dinner, 3 courses, £25. Pubs/restaurants 5 miles.
Closed	Rarely.

Rosamond Woodward
Cleeton Court,
Cleeton St Mary,
Ludlow, DY14 0QZ
Tel   +44 (0)1584 823379
Mobile   +44 (0)7778 903136
Email   roswoodward1@gmail.com
Web   www.cleetoncourt.co.uk

Tracey Baylis & Alex Read
Timberstone Bed & Breakfast,
Clee Stanton,
Ludlow, SY8 3EL
Tel   +44 (0)1584 823519
Mobile   +44 (0)7905 967263
Email   timberstone1@hotmail.com
Web   www.timberstoneludlow.co.uk

Entry 379   Map 7

Entry 380   Map 7

Shropshire

The Old Rectory

With its own spring water, horses, dogs and slow pace this Georgian rectory is comfortable country living at its best. Izzy and Andy are charming and interesting and give you scones and tea by the fire in a drawing room full of family photos, plump sofas and books. Elegant bedrooms have fluffy hot water bottles; smart bathrooms have scented lotions in pretty bottles, robes and slippers. Candlelit dinner will often be fish or game with garden vegetables; breakfast is local and leisurely with homemade granola and jams. There's a bootroom for muddy feet and paws, stabling and seven acres to roam.

Pets welcome, sleeping in bootroom.

Rooms	1 double, 1 twin/double; 1 double with separate bathroom: £85–£125. Singles £70–£110.
Meals	Dinner, 3 courses with coffee, drinks & canapés, £35. Supper tray (soup & sandwich) £10. Pubs 1.25–4 miles.
Closed	Rarely.

Isabel Barnard
The Old Rectory,
Wheathill,
Ludlow,
Bridgnorth, WV16 6QT
Tel   +44 (0)1746 787209
Email   enquiries@theoldrectorywheathill.com
Web   www.theoldrectorywheathill.com

Entry 381   Map 7

Somerset

Glen Lodge

Come for the food and Meryl and David's open house vibe. Their secluded Victorian home is spacious, comfy and surrounded by high banks of woodland. Enjoy delicious meals with an American slant using local venison, lamb, honey, cheeses and fish; they grow fruit and veg, make jams and serve tea and cakes every day — perfect brownies! Polished oak floors are dotted with oriental rugs and log fires burn. Wander the 21 acres, play croquet, sip a sunset drink on the terrace overlooking the wide bay. Exmoor and popular Porlock are on the doorstep; sandy beaches, harbours, boat trips — and a hot tub with an ice bucket — will keep you happy too.

Rooms	3 doubles; 1 double, 1 twin, each with separate bath: £90–£95. Singles £60.
Meals	Dinner, 3 courses, £30. Supper £20. Packed lunch £8. Pub/restaurant 0.5 miles.
Closed	Rarely.

Meryl Salter
Glen Lodge,
Hawkcombe,
Porlock, TA24 8LN
Tel   +44 (0)1643 863371
Mobile   +44 (0)7786 118933
Email   glenlodge@gmail.com
Web   www.glenlodge.net

Entry 382   Map 2

Higher Orchard

A little lane tumbles down to the centre of lovely old Dunster. The village is a two-minute walk, yet here you have open views of fields, sheep and sea. Exmoor footpaths start behind the house and Janet encourages explorers, by bike or on foot: ever helpful and kind, she is a local who knows the patch well. The 1860s house keeps its Victorian features, bedrooms are quiet and simple and the double has a view to Blue Anchor Bay and Dunster castle and church. All is homely, with stripped pine, cream curtains, fresh flowers, garden fruit and home-laid eggs for breakfast.

Cider Barn

Set back from the lane is a newly converted and refurbished barn. Step in to find fine old proportions, heated oak floors and heaps of character. Louise's stunning living quarters spread under the beams and bedrooms lie privately below on the ground floor. One opens to the courtyard, and all are airy and peaceful with modern fabrics and cream walls. There's a sunny guest sitting room leading onto the garden, and delightful Louise, a great cook, serves breakfast at a long table by the wood-burner. You can walk through fields to the river or hills, stroll to the pub for supper – and alternative therapies can be arranged locally.

Pets may be considered.

Rooms	1 double, 2 twin/doubles: £70. Singles from £35.
Meals	Packed lunch from £3.50. Restaurants 2-minute walk.
Closed	Christmas.

Rooms	1 double, 1 twin/double: £75–£85. Singles £50–£65.
Meals	Pub 1 mile.
Closed	Rarely.

	Janet Lamacraft
	Higher Orchard,
	30 St George's Street,
	Dunster, TA24 6RS
Tel	+44 (0)1643 821915
Mobile	+44 (0)7896 464420
Email	lamacraft@higherorchard.fsnet.co.uk
Web	www.higherorchard-dunster.co.uk

	Louise Bancroft
	Cider Barn,
	Runnington,
	Wellington, TA21 0QW
Tel	+44 (0)1823 665533
Email	louisegaddon@btinternet.com
Web	www.runningtonciderbarn.co.uk

Somerset

Brook House

A relaxed home with no rules; arrive to tasty cake and tea or a tipple, settle in the sitting room by one of the wood-burners, chat in the kitchen, wander mown paths in the garden. The sunny open-plan kitchen/living room is the heart of the house; Becky is a keen cook so food is good, local, homemade; Crumpet, one of the terriers, snoozes by the Aga. Quiet, comfy bedrooms have tip-top linen, painted furniture, pots of flowers, garden views; the larger twin has a sofa by tall windows. Next door Cider Mill has a farm shop, museum and tea rooms, the walks are great, the Jurassic coast is a short drive. A friendly place, a treat to stay.

Over 12s welcome.

Rooms	1 double, 1 twin/double: £85-£95. Singles £65-£75.
Meals	Dinner, 3 courses, from £20. Pub 3 miles.
Closed	Occasionally.

Becky Jam
Brook House,
Dowlish Wake,
Ilminster, TA19 0NY
Tel   +44 (0)1460 250860
Mobile   +44 (0)7841 594342
Email   becky@brookhousesomerset.com
Web   www.brookhousesomerset.com

Entry 385   Map 3

Somerset

The Beeches

Grown ups will love this relaxed, beautiful old house filled with interesting furniture, good art and family photos, thick curtains, flickering fires and views from every window. Children will adore running wild on the wide lawns, pottering to collect eggs from the chickens and playing with all the games. Gentle Abby encourages unwinding: sleep on the fattest hand-stitched mattresses, choose pretty much what you want for breakfast (try panettone eggy bread), help yourself to homemade cake in the sitting room at teatime, or head off for the Jurassic coast. On sunny days you can just loll in Abby's pretty garden if you prefer.

Rooms	1 double, 1 twin/double: £80. Singles £50. Extra bed/sofabed available £10-£15 per person per night.
Meals	Pubs/restaurants 2-minute walk.
Closed	Rarely.

Abby Norton
The Beeches,
Water Street,
Seavington St Michael,
Ilminster, TA19 0QH
Tel   +44 (0)1460 241123
Email   abigail@southsomersetbandb.co.uk
Web   www.southsomersetbandb.co.uk

Entry 386   Map 3

Somerset

Fairways

The food, the views – amazing! Tim is a passionate cook, and he and Sarah want you to enjoy their friendly open house. Settle in with tea and Tim's high-rise scones and look out over Seaborough Hill. Their 1960s bungalow is immaculate: white walls, gleaming oak floors, toasty wood-burner and French windows onto the garden. Perfect bedrooms have inviting beds and pots of sweet peas; bathrooms sparkle. Pad through to breakfast in the airy sitting/dining room – or out on the sunny deck: eggs from across the valley, smoked salmon, homemade bread, granola and jams; dinner is equally good with organic local veg and charcuterie. A treat!

Over 16s welcome.

Rooms	2 doubles: £90.
	Singles £75.
Meals	Dinner, 3 courses with tea/coffee, £25.
	BYO. Pub/restaurant 3 miles.
Closed	Rarely.

Sarah & Tim Dommett
Fairways,
Hewish Lane,
Crewkerne, TA18 8RN
Tel   +44 (0)1460 271093
Email   info@fairwaysbandb.co.uk
Web   www.fairwaysbandb.co.uk

Entry 387   Map 3

Somerset

Causeway Cottage

Robert and Lesley are ex-restaurateurs, so guests heap praise on their food, most of which is sourced from a local butcher and fishmonger; charming Lesley is an author, runs cookery courses and once taught at Prue Leith's. This is the perfect, pretty Somerset cottage, with an apple orchard and views to the church across a cottage garden and a field. The bedrooms are light, restful and have a country-style simplicity with their green check bedspreads, white walls and antique pine furniture; guests have their own comfortable sitting room. Easy access to the M5 yet with a rural feel. Very special.

Children over 10 welcome.

Rooms	1 double, 2 twins: £80-£85.
	Singles £60.
Meals	Dinner from £28.
	Pub/restaurant 0.75 miles.
Closed	Christmas.

Lesley & Robert Orr
Causeway Cottage,
West Buckland, Taunton, TA21 9JZ
Tel   +44 (0)1823 663458
Mobile +44 (0)7703 412827
Email   orrs@causewaycottage.co.uk
Web   www.causewaycottage.co.uk

Entry 388   Map 2

Somerset

Frog Street Farmhouse

Through a pastoral landscape, past green paddocks and fine thoroughbreds, to a beautiful longhouse set in pretty secluded gardens surrounded by 130 acres. Its heart dates back to 1436 and its renovation is remarkable, highlighting beamed ceilings, Jacobean panelling and open fireplaces. Louise and David, brimful of enthusiasm for both house and visitors, give you four exquisite bedrooms in French country style, one with its own sitting room – very romantic. Louise happily does evening meals and hosts small house parties with ease. After a day out, return to great leather sofas and a wood-burning stove. Guests love it here!

Rooms	3 doubles: £90–£120. 1 family room for 4: £120–£160. Singles £80–£120. Extra bed/sofabed available £15 per person per night.
Meals	Dinner, 3 courses, £27.50 (for parties of 6 or more). Pubs within 2.5 miles.
Closed	Christmas.

Louise & David Farrance
Frog Street Farmhouse,
Hatch Beauchamp,
Taunton, TA3 6AF

Tel	+44 (0)1823 481883
Mobile	+44 (0)7811 700789
Email	frogstreet@hotmail.com
Web	www.frogstreet.co.uk

Entry 389   Map 2

Somerset

Brook Farm

The front door is open for your arrival… Step into the rich red hallway of this traditional Georgian-fronted farmhouse, and find cosy corners for reading, period prints, polished wood, and open fires in the winter. Maria gives you breakfast in a sunny dining/sitting room, where doors open out to the patio and garden beyond; the guest sitting room is snug with comfy sofas and plenty of books. Sink into luxurious beds in immaculate bedrooms; TVs are smart, WiFi is on tap, bathrooms gleam and views are green and peaceful. The Somerset Levels surround you, Glastonbury and Wells are close and there's a good pub in the village too.

Over 12s welcome.

Rooms	1 double, 1 twin/double: £90–£95. Singles £70–£75.
Meals	Pubs/restaurants 1.2 miles.
Closed	Rarely.

Maria Laing
Brook Farm,
Newport Road,
North Curry,
Taunton, TA3 6DJ

Tel	+44 (0)1823 491124
Email	maria.follett@hotmail.co.uk
Web	www.brookfarmbb.com

Entry 390   Map 2

Bashfords Farmhouse

A feeling of warmth and happiness pervades this exquisite 17th-century farmhouse in the Quantock Hills. The Ritchies love doing B&B – even after over 20 years! – and interiors have a homely feel with well-framed prints, natural fabrics, comfortable sofas, and a sitting room with inglenook, sofas and books. Bedrooms are pretty, fresh and large and look over the cobbled courtyard or open fields. Charles and Jane couldn't be nicer, know about local walks (the Macmillan Way runs by) and love to cook: local meat and game, tarte tatin, homemade bread and jams. A delightful garden rambles up the hill; the pub is just a minute away.

Huntstile Organic Farm

Catapult yourself into country life in the foothills of the Quantocks; make that connection between the rolling green hills, the idyllic munching animals and the delicious, organic food on your plate; here it is understood. Lizzie and John buzz with energy in this gorgeous old house with Jacobean panelling and huge walk-in fireplaces, two sitting rooms, sweet and cosy rustic bedrooms, a café, and a restaurant serving their own meat, eggs and vegetables. House parties, weddings, team building, a stone circle for hand-fasting ceremonies – all come under Lizzie's happy and efficient umbrella. And there are woodlands to roam.

Minimum stay: 2 nights in high season.

Rooms	1 twin/double; 2 twin/doubles, both with separate bath: £75. Singles £45.
Meals	Dinner £27.50. Supper £22.50. Pub 75 yds.
Closed	Rarely.

Rooms	7 doubles: £60–£150. 3 family rooms for 4: £95–£150. Apartment - 1 double, 1 twin with sitting room: £60–£150. Singles £55–£75. Extra bed/sofabed £15–£25 per person per night.
Meals	Dinner, 3 courses, £22.50–£27. Packed lunch from £6.50. Pub/restaurant 3 miles.
Closed	Rarely.

	Charles & Jane Ritchie
	Bashfords Farmhouse,
	West Bagborough,
	Taunton, TA4 3EF
Tel	+44 (0)1823 432015
Email	info@bashfordsfarmhouse.co.uk
Web	www.bashfordsfarmhouse.co.uk

	Lizzie Myers
	Huntstile Organic Farm,
	Goathurst,
	Bridgwater, TA5 2DQ
Tel	+44 (0)1278 662358
Email	huntstile@live.co.uk
Web	www.huntstileorganicfarm.co.uk

Somerset

Blackmore Farm

Come for atmosphere and architecture: the Grade I-listed manor-farmhouse is remarkable. Medieval stone, soaring beams, ecclesiastical windows, giant logs blazing in the Great Hall. Ann and Ian look after guests and busy dairy farm with equal enthusiasm. Furnishings are comfortable, décor is rich, bedrooms are cavernous and the oak-panelled suite (with secret stairway) takes up an entire floor. The rooms in the stables are simpler with green oak and wide doorways. Breakfast is generous and organic and eaten at the 20-foot polished table in baronial splendour. Visit the calves in the dairy and don't miss the excellent farm shop.

Rooms	1 double, 1 four-poster, 1 suite for 2: £110–£120. Extra room available. Courtyard stables - 1 double, 1 twin: £110–£120. Singles £60.
Meals	Occasional dinner from £26 for parties (min. 15). Pubs/restaurants 5-minute walk.
Closed	Rarely.

Ann Dyer
Blackmore Farm,
Cannington,
Bridgwater, TA5 2NE

Tel	+44 (0)1278 653442
Email	dyerfarm@aol.com
Web	www.dyerfarm.co.uk

Entry 393   Map 2

Somerset

Parsonage Farm

The Quantock Hills are wonderful for walking and cycling, with the Coleridge Way starting down the lane. In this 17th-century farmhouse relaxed hosts give you easy comfort with quarry floors, books, a cosy log-fired sitting room and spacious bedrooms with tranquil country views. Suki, from Vermont, has turned a stable into a studio — her pots and paintings add charm to the décor. Breakfast by the fire is a feast: homemade bread and jam, eggs from the hens, juice from the orchard, porridge and pancakes with maple syrup. Relax in the beautiful walled kitchen garden; there's an outdoor wood-fired pizza oven too!

Children over 2 welcome.

Rooms	1 double, 1 twin/double, each with extra sofabed; 1 double with separate bathroom & extra sofabed: £65–£85. Singles £50–£70.
Meals	Supper £11. Dinner, 2–3 courses, £20–£25. Pub/restaurant 1 mile.
Closed	Christmas Day.

Susan Lilienthal
Parsonage Farm,
Over Stowey,
Nether Stowey, TA5 1HA

Tel	+44 (0)1278 733237
Mobile	+44 (0)7928 368836
Email	suki@parsonfarm.co.uk
Web	www.parsonfarm.co.uk

Entry 394   Map 2

Somerset

Barwick Farm House

A 17th-century farmhouse sitting in organically managed land dotted with hens, horses and Dorset sheep. Angela is delightful and works wonders with gorgeous limewash colours in every room. Step into a beautiful hall to find a house full of ancient elm boards, colourful rugs, open fires, books, china and pots of flowers. Pretty bedrooms have good linen on comfy beds; the downstairs one has its own breakfast room and garden entrance, and a big copper tub; one bathroom is cleverly clad in reclaimed grain store panels. Wake to birdsong and sizzling local bacon; excellent walking and cycling start from the door.

Rooms	2 doubles, 1 twin/double: £80–£90. Singles £50–£60.
Meals	'Early Bird' packed breakfasts also available. Restaurant 100 yds.
Closed	Rarely.

Angela Nicoll
Barwick Farm House,
Barwick,
Yeovil, BA22 9TD

Tel	+44 (0)1935 410779
Mobile	+44 (0)7967 385307
Email	info@barwickfarmhouse.co.uk
Web	www.barwickfarmhouse.co.uk

Somerset

Church Byres

Meander down lanes and a tree-lined drive to a courtyard flanked by farm buildings: four solid stone farm byres. One side is your hosts', the other is yours, so you have your own wing; it's great value for a family - and your dog is very welcome too. Peter and Jenny, attentive and fun, give you breakfast out on a terrace on sunny mornings, and can direct you to some good local country pubs for supper. It's a treat to come home to your own wood-burner and deep sofas, white bathrobes and muted tones: the mood is warmly contemporary. Take a chilled beer from your own fridge to the guest terrace by the front lawn – lovely!

Children under 12 half price.

Rooms	1 double, 1 twin sharing bathroom (let to same party only): £80–£100. Singles £50.
Meals	Pubs/restaurants 3 miles.
Closed	Christmas.

Jenny Cox
Church Byres,
South Barrow,
Yeovil, BA22 7LN

Mobile	+44 (0)7765 175058
Email	bookings@somerset-bb.co.uk
Web	www.somerset-bb.co.uk

Somerset

The Lynch Country House

Peace and privacy at this immaculate Regency house in a Somerset valley. First-floor bedrooms are traditionally grand, attic rooms are smaller but pretty; those in the coach house have a more modern feel. Rich colours prevail, fabrics are flowery and linen best Irish. You'll feel as warm as toast and beautifully looked after. A stone staircase goes right to the top where the observatory lets in cascading light; the flagged hall, high ceilings, long windows and private tables at breakfast create a country-house hotel feel. The lovely garden has black swans on a lake, hundreds of trees and a terrace from which to drink it all in.

Somerset

Studio Farrows

An appealingly quirky studio hidden in the luxuriant garden of artists Paul and Tracey. They live in the main house and are relaxed, helpful hosts. They'll arrange a swim in a friend's walled pool, and all sorts of courses from baking to glass blowing; or you can simply relax in this comfy, peaceful retreat. You have a big living space with giant wood-burner, books, and eclectic art and furniture (including an Anglia!); bedrooms are colourful, bathrooms sleek. Breakfasts are gorgeous, a continental feast and scrambled eggs to die for! Sit out on the veranda, light the fire baskets, gaze at the stars... Bliss.

Minimum 4 person booking. Minimum stay: 2 nights. Pets by arrangement. Smoking permitted on the veranda.

Rooms	1 double, 1 four-poster, 2 twin/doubles with extra single bed; 1 double with separate bath & extra single bed: £80–£115. Coach House – 2 doubles, 2 twin/doubles: £90. Singles £70–£95.
Meals	Pubs 5-minute walk.
Closed	Rarely.

Rooms	2 doubles with sitting room and kitchen: £114. Price per person per night £57 including breakfast. 15% discount for weekly stays. Sofabed, in its own space available on request, £40 per person.
Meals	Vegetarian & vegan meals available on request. Pub 3 miles.
Closed	Rarely.

	Lynne Vincent
	The Lynch Country House,
	4 Behind Berry,
	Somerton, TA11 7PD
Tel	+44 (0)1458 272316
Email	thelynchcountryhouse@gmail.com
Web	www.thelynchcountryhouse.co.uk

	Tracey Baker
	Studio Farrows,
	Aller,
	Langport, TA10 0QW
Tel	+44 (0)1458 252599
Email	tracey@studiofarrows.com
Web	www.studiofarrows.com

Somerset

Yarlington House

A mellow Georgian manor surrounded by impressive parkland, romantic rose gardens, apple tree pergola and laburnum walk. Your hosts are friendly and flexible artists with an eye for quirky detail; Carolyn's embroideries are everywhere, and there's something to astound at every turn: fine copies of 18th-century wallpapers, elegant antiques, statues with hats atop and tremendous art. Traditional bedrooms with glorious garden views and proper 50s bathrooms have a faded charm. Enjoy a full English breakfast, grape juice from the glasshouse vines, log fires and lovely local walks. Surprising, unique.

Rooms	1 double, 1 twin: £140. Singles £70.
Meals	Pubs/restaurants within 0.5 miles.
Closed	25 July - 23 August.

Carolyn & Charles de Salis
Yarlington House,
Yarlington,
Wincanton, BA9 8DY
Tel +44 (0)1963 440344
Email carolyn.desalis@yarlingtonhouse.com
Web www.yarlingtonhouse.com

Somerset

Cary Place

In the heart of town yet sitting in three acres… a honey-stoned gem. Debra's home has an open-house vibe – helped along perfectly by Humphrey the terrier. Step into a generous hall to find an elegant sitting room for guests, polished floors, original art and gorgeous colours in every room. Bedrooms are a delight: sofas at the end of sleigh beds, tip-top linen and pretty fabrics. Hop down for breakfast in the airy dining room, or out on a sunny terrace: fruits from the orchard, croissants, organic sausages and bacon. Come and go as you want – walk to cafés, delis and independent shops; Glastonbury and Stourhead are close.

Rooms	1 double, 1 twin; 1 double with separate bath: £105. Extra room available.
Meals	Pubs/restaurants within walking distance.
Closed	Rarely.

Debra Henderson
Cary Place,
4 Upper High Street,
Castle Cary, BA7 7AR
Tel +44 (0)1963 359269
Email info@caryplace.co.uk
Web www.caryplace.co.uk

Somerset

Ansford Park Cottage

An old farmworker's house, modernised and freshly spruced, stands proud in verdant countryside. Long views from the clipped garden drift into the distance; warm Sue (plus cute Jack Russells) greets you. You sleep in the extension to the front of the house; one bedroom has valley views, the other has views over the Mendips. Both have comfy beds, books, homely touches and peacefulness. Breakfast is a leisurely affair of local bacon and eggs. Tramp off on an inspiring walk – Leland trail, Macmillan Way – you're spoilt for choice. Escape London by train (95 minutes) – collection from the station can be arranged.

Rooms	1 twin/double; 1 twin/double with separate bath: £75.
Meals	Dinner £25. Packed lunch £5. Pub/restaurant 1 mile.
Closed	Christmas & rarely.

Susan Begg
Ansford Park Cottage,
Ansford Park, Maggs Lane,
Castle Cary, BA7 7JJ
Tel +44 (0)1963 351066
Email nigelbegg@lineone.net
Web www.ansfordparkcottage.co.uk

Entry 401   Map 3

Somerset

Culverwell House

Cynthia and Barry's friendly old house is tucked down a little track in this sleepy village. Step into your own sitting room, with mezzanine bedroom upstairs: eclectic art, 60s and 70s pieces, huge funky mobile, a comfy bed with pretty Indian cover, pots of flowers on window sills (and snoozing Cortina the cat perhaps). Breakfast where you want: sitting room, pretty dining room next door, vine-clad conservatory or out in the flowery garden in a sunny spot. Delicious choices – garden grapes and figs, bagels with bacon or smoked salmon and cream cheese, organic scrambled eggs. Wells and Glastonbury are a hop, walks start from the door.

Children over 10 welcome.

Rooms	1 double: £100–£120.
Meals	Dinner £25. Pubs/restaurants 5 miles.
Closed	Rarely.

Cynthia Taylor
Culverwell House,
Top Street, Pilton,
Shepton Mallet, BA4 4DF
Tel +44 (0)1749 890437
Email cynthiafroutrou@sky.com
Web www.culverwellhouse.co.uk

Entry 402   Map 3

Somerset

Broadgrove House

Head down the long, private lane and arrive at Sarah's peaceful 17th-century stone house with its pretty walled cottage garden and views to Alfred's Tower and Longleat. Inside is just as special. Beams, flagstones and inglenook fireplaces have been sensitively restored; rugs, pictures, comfy sofas and polished antiques add warmth and serenity. The twin, at the end of the house, has a little shower room and its own sitting room. Breakfast on homemade and farmers' market produce before exploring Stourhead, Wells, Glastonbury. Sarah, engaging, well-travelled and a great cook, looks after you warmly.

Children by arrangement. Minimum stay: 2 nights at weekends in the summer season.

Rooms	1 twin with sitting room, 1 double with separate bath: £85–£95. Singles £65.
Meals	Pub/restaurant 1 mile.
Closed	Christmas.

Sarah Voller
Broadgrove House,
Leighton, Frome, BA11 4PP

Tel	+44 (0)1373 836296
Mobile	+44 (0)7775 918388
Email	broadgrove836@tiscali.co.uk
Web	www.broadgrovehouse.co.uk

Entry 403   Map 3

Somerset

Penny's Mill

The old part of Nunney village, with its small pretty streets, has a shop, a café and Rosie's gorgeous old stone millhouse down in the river valley. You are greeted warmly with tea and biscuits at a large wooden table in the kitchen, or in the drawing room upstairs with family photos, paintings and a big window looking over the millpond. Sunny bedrooms painted in gentle blues and greens have a mix of antique and modern furniture; bathrooms have Molton Brown soaps and white fluffy towels. You can book one of Rosie's cookery courses, and her fine breakfast sets you up for a short walk to Nunney Castle, or a yomp further afield.

Rooms	1 double, 1 twin/double with own living room: £90. 1 family room for 4: £150.
Meals	Dinner £25–£35. Pub 300 yds.
Closed	Rarely.

Rosie Davies
Penny's Mill,
Horn Street, Nunney,
Frome, BA11 4NP

Tel	+44 (0)1373 836210
Email	stay@pennysmill.com
Web	www.stayatpennysmill.com

Entry 404   Map 3

Somerset

Old Reading Room

Mells is a treasure with its medieval centre and liberal sprinkling of charming cottages; you'll find Vicky and John's attractive house down a track in the quiet wooded valley. It's a home with a friendly feel: books, art, pots of flowers, intriguing finds from family travels, comfy sofas around the wood-burner. Beds are wrapped in fine cotton and colourful quilts; sweet bathrooms have scented candles. Come down for breakfast in the kitchen — homemade bread, eggs from happy hens — delivered by a friend on a pony! Sunny cottage garden, walks from the door, a five-minute drive to Babington House… and entertaining hosts.

Rooms	2 doubles: £95. Singles £75.
Meals	Pubs/restaurants 5-minute walk.
Closed	Rarely.

	Vicky & John Macdonald
	Old Reading Room,
	Mells, Frome, BA11 3QA
Tel	+44 (0)1373 813487
Email	johnmacdonaldm@gmail.com

Entry 405   Map 3

Somerset

Claveys Farm

For the artistic seeker of inspiration, not those who thrill to standardised luxury. Fleur is a talented artist, Francis works for English Heritage, both have a passion for art, gardening and lively conversation. Rugs are time-worn, panelling and walls are distempered with natural pigment, bedrooms are better than simple, bathrooms old. From the Aga-warm kitchen of this lived-in, historic farmhouse come eggs from the hens, honey from the bees, oak-smoked bacon from Fleur's rare-breed pigs and homemade bread and jams. Fields, footpaths and woodland for walks, and a garden for children to adore. Bring your woolly jumpers!

Rooms	1 double with separate bath (sometimes shared with twin), 1 twin with separate bath (sometimes shared with double or owner): £75. Singles £50.
Meals	Dinner, 3 courses, £25. BYO. Packed lunch £7. Pub in village.
Closed	Rarely.

	Fleur & Francis Kelly
	Claveys Farm,
	Mells, Frome, BA11 3QP
Tel	+44 (0)1373 814651
Mobile	+44 (0)7968 055398
Email	bandb@fleurkelly.com

Entry 406   Map 3

Somerset

Jericho

'Jericho' means in the middle of nowhere and here above lovely Mells you have space around your ears and long views. Babington House and excellent pubs are close, yet sybarites may just want to wallow in the generous bedroom and sitting room with doors to a vine-hung loggia and parterre, French Grey panelling, original art, and a wet room with a drenching shower. Stephen, a product designer, has orchestrated the look, and furniture, rugs and fabrics chime contentedly with the architecture. Find top-notch coffee and tea on your tea tray, hand-pressed apple juice from the orchard, and exquisite vegetarian breakfasts delivered to you.

Rooms	1 suite for 2 with sitting room: £100–£110.
Meals	Pub 3 miles.
Closed	Rarely.

Stephen Morgan
Jericho,
Mells Down, Mells,
Frome, BA11 2RL
Tel   +44 (0)1373 813242
Email   mail@stayatjericho.co.uk
Web   www.stayatjericho.co.uk

Entry 407   Map 3

Somerset

Upper Crannel Farm Barn

Your views, across sheep and the lush Somerset Levels, reach to both Glastonbury and Wells; birds wing across a vast, silent sky. Phoebe has created a magical place: up you climb to the first floor of the barn, into a huge sitting room with a vast medieval painted fireplace. Each room is a work of art, with stacks of it on the walls – the kitchen is handsome and seductive, the bedroom is generous and richly clad. If you come with friends, there are extra rooms available. Breakfast will be left for you to cook when you want, you can walk across fields to climb Glastonbury Tor, and Wells is just five miles. This house is a treat, and Phoebe is too.

Minimum stay: 2 nights.

Rooms	1 double with sitting room & kitchen (extra bedrooms available): £120.
Meals	Pubs/restaurants 2.5 miles.
Closed	Rarely.

Phoebe Judah
Upper Crannel Farm Barn,
Glastonbury, BA6 9AD
Tel   +44 (0)1458 831758
Email   phoebe.judah@btinternet.com

Entry 408   Map 3

Coach House

Take a glass of wine to your private courtyard and absorb the peace; or picnic in the gardens. In the hamlet of Dulcote, a mile from Wells, is your own two-storey, two-bedroom coach house flooded with light, full of character and the latest mod cons. Downstairs, a black and white zebra theme; upstairs, white walls, crisp linen, high beams, a glimpse of Wells Cathedral and views that reach to the Mendips. Friendly Chumba the dog greets you and your (well-behaved) waggy friend. Karen leaves eggs from her hens and other goodies in your fridge so you can breakfast in your jim-jams. A delightful B&B for nature lovers and dog-walkers.

Minimum stay: 2 nights. Over 12s welcome.

Hillview Cottage

Catherine is a wonderful host: warm-spirited, cultured and humorous. She knows the area well, and is happy to show you around Wells Cathedral – she's an official guide. This is a comfy tea-and-cakes family home with rugs on wooden floors and antique quilts. Bedrooms have a French feel, the bathroom an armchair for chatting and there's a friendly sitting room with an open fire. The stunning vaulted breakfast room has huge beams, an old Welsh dresser with hand painted mugs, a cheerful red Aga, a wood-burner to sit by and glorious views; breakfasts are superb. Guests love it here; excellent value too.

Rooms	Annexe - 1 double, 1 twin sharing sitting room, sofabeds & kitchen (let to same party only): £95 per night for 1 bedroom plus £35 per extra person per night. Singles £90.
Meals	Pubs within 2 miles.
Closed	Rarely.

Rooms	1 twin/double, 1 twin sharing bath (let to same party only): £80–£90. Singles £50.
Meals	Pubs 5-minute walk.
Closed	Rarely.

	Karen Smallwood Coach House, Little Fountains, Dulcote, Wells, BA5 3NU
Tel	+44 (0)1749 678777
Mobile	+44 (0)7789 778880
Email	stay@littlefountains.co.uk
Web	www.littlefountains.co.uk

	Michael & Catherine Hay Hillview Cottage, Paradise Lane, Croscombe, Wells, BA5 3RN
Tel	+44 (0)1749 343526
Mobile	+44 (0)7801 666146
Email	cathyhay@yahoo.co.uk
Web	www.hillviewcottage.me.uk

Somerset

Stoberry House

Super swish B&B in this old coach house surrounded by 26 acres of parkland, but within walking distance of Wells; Frances has thought of everything and has oodles of local knowledge. Bedrooms are sumptuous and differently styled; two are in the main house, and there's one little love nest in a richly clad studio. Bathrooms are vamped up and spacious. There is a huge choice at breakfast: fresh fruit, porridge, boiled eggs with soldiers, prunes and berries, ham and salami, pancakes with grilled bacon, whatever you desire. Work it off with a stroll around the gorgeous gardens: the scents, sculptures and views are fantastic.

Minimum stay: 2 nights at weekends.

Rooms	1 double, 1 twin/double: £95–£155. Studio - 1 double with sitting room: £95–£155. Singles £65–£135.
Meals	Supplement for cooked breakfast. Pubs/restaurants 0.5 miles.
Closed	Rarely.

Frances Young
Stoberry House,
Stoberry Park,
Wells, BA5 3LD
Tel   +44 (0)1749 672906
Email   stay@stoberry-park.co.uk
Web   www.stoberry-park.co.uk

🚶 📖 🧴 📶 🚂 🍾 🍴

Entry 411   Map 3

Somerset

Beryl

A historical gem set in 13 acres of beautiful gardens and parkland. This stunning piece of gothic architecture, brimming with fine antiques, offers a wealth of luxury, warmth and welcome. Arrive for tea and cake and feel instantly relaxed in Holly and Mary-Ellen's cherished family home. Each unique bedroom has a talking point – an extravagantly draped four-poster, an original bath clad in mahogany reached by a tiny staircase. Wake to the aroma of locally sourced bacon – Aga-cooked breakfasts are a feast. The rose-filled garden is yours to enjoy; in warmer months dive into the refreshing outdoor pool while children have fun in the play area.

Chair lift to first floor. Byworth & Nowell jewellery boutique in the Coach House.

Rooms	6 doubles, 4 twin/doubles, 1 twin; 1 double with separate bathroom: £100–£160. 1 family room for 4: £140–£210. Singles £75–£95. Extra bed/sofabed available £30–£40 per person per night.
Meals	Pubs/restaurants within 1 mile. Kitchenette available.
Closed	Christmas.

Holly & Mary-Ellen Nowell
Beryl,
Hawkers Lane,
Wells, BA5 3JP
Tel   +44 (0)1749 678738
Email   stay@beryl-wells.co.uk
Web   www.beryl-wells.co.uk

🚶 🐾 🐈 📖 🧴 📶 🚂

Entry 412   Map 3

Somerset

Harptree Court

A gorgeous Georgian house that has been in Charles' family for generations. Inside all is elegant and grand, but this is very much a family home; there's a welcoming log fire in the hall and Charles and Linda are charming and relaxed. The interior gleams with flowers, art and polished wood, and the dining room looks onto the beautiful garden; warm, sunny bedrooms have delicate fabrics, china pieces and antiques, and bathrooms sparkle. An excellent breakfast of garden fruits, local honey and sausages sets you up for a walk in the grounds: acres of parkland with ponds, an ancient bridge, carpets of spring flowers. A peaceful delight.

Rooms	3 doubles, 1 twin/double: £130. Singles £80.
Meals	Pub 300 yds.
Closed	December/January.

Linda & Charles Hill
Harptree Court,
East Harptree, Bristol, BS40 6AA

Tel	+44 (0)1761 221729
Mobile	+44 (0)7970 165576
Email	bandb@harptreecourt.co.uk
Web	www.harptreecourt.co.uk

Entry 413   Map 3

Somerset

Burrington Farm

High in the Mendips, Ros and Barry's 15th-century longhouse is blissfully rural, yet Bristol, Bath and Wells are close. Their wonderful house glows: rugs and flagstones, books, burnished beams, paintings and fine old furniture. Guests have a cosy sitting room and bedrooms are charming; you'll need to be nimble to negotiate ancient steps and stairs. For those who prefer a bit more privacy there's a lovely family room in a separate green oak barn – stunningly converted and with views over the enchanting garden. Wake for a locally sourced breakfast round a big table. A friendly, relaxed and special place.

Rooms	1 double; 1 double, 1 twin sharing bath (let to same party only): £85–£120. Barn - 1 family room for 4: £100–£120. Singles £65.
Meals	Pub 10-minute walk.
Closed	Christmas.

Barry & Ros Smith
Burrington Farm,
Burrington, BS40 7AD

Tel	+44 (0)1761 462127
Mobile	+44 (0)7825 237144
Email	unwind@burringtonfarm.co.uk
Web	www.unwindatburringtonfarm.co.uk

Entry 414   Map 3

Somerset

Stonebridge

A country house with scrumptious food, a friendly black labrador and croquet on the lawn. Liz and Richard give you scones and tea, and your own independent wing of their listed house. You have two pretty bedrooms (one up, one down) with country furniture and super bathrooms. In winter, a wood-burner keeps your little sitting room cosy; in summer, laze in a sea of flowers. You feast on local eggs and homemade bread and jams for breakfast; Liz cooks memorable dinners too with home-grown veg. Just off the village road, it's close to Bristol airport, Wells and the M5, so the perfect pit-stop if you're on your way to Devon or Cornwall.

Children over 2 welcome.

Rooms	1 double, 1 twin/double: £75–£90. Singles £60–£65.
Meals	Dinner, 2-3 courses, £22.50–£27.50. Pub 2 miles.
Closed	Christmas.

Richard & Liz Annesley
Stonebridge,
Wolvershill Road,
Banwell, BS29 6DR
Tel   +44 (0)1934 822549
Email   liz.annesley@talktalk.net
Web   www.stonebridgebandb.co.uk

Entry 415   Map 3

Somerset

Church House

All is tickety boo in this Georgian rectory with views over seaside homes and the Bristol Channel. Terry and Tracey look after you impeccably and give you homemade cake in the conservatory overlooking the neat garden. You'll sleep peacefully in light and airy bedrooms all named after islands in the channel; swish bathrooms have underfloor heating to keep you toasty warm. Take breakfast in the dining room at a mahogany table: home-baked bread, homemade jams and marmalade, eggs from down the hill and local bacon. Walk it off on the coastal path, cycle along quiet lanes, or head for Weston and old-fashioned seaside fun.

Rooms	4 doubles, 1 twin: £85–£99. Singles from £70.
Meals	Pubs 400 yds.
Closed	Rarely.

Terry & Tracey Gill
Church House,
27 Kewstoke Road, Kewstoke,
Weston-super-Mare, BS22 9YD
Tel   +44 (0)1934 633185
Email   churchhouse@kewstoke.net
Web   www.churchhousekewstoke.co.uk

Entry 416   Map 2

Somerset

Taggart House

Past the church, up through the pretty village, to Andrew and Rachel's relaxed eco-friendly house. Through your own doorway, find smart bedrooms with tip-top linen, TV, a basket of books, French windows onto patios – perfect for an evening glass of wine – and sleek bathrooms with thick white towels. Wake for bacon and sausages from the Potting Shed Farm Shop, eggy bread, local jams. Walton Brook runs through the garden, a visiting pair of ducks can be spotted on the pond, and you can walk through ancient woodland to join the coastal path to Clevedon. Close to Portishead and only 25 minutes from Bristol. A leafy retreat.

Rooms	1 double, 1 twin/double (extra bed available, suitable for a child of 12 or under): £85–£95.
Meals	Pubs/restaurants within 2 miles.
Closed	Rarely.

Andrew & Rachel Francis
Taggart House,
Walton Street,
Clevedon, BS21 7AP
Tel   +44 (0)1275 316970
Email   rachel@taggarthouse.co.uk
Web   www.taggarthouse.co.uk

Entry 417   Map 3

Staffordshire

Manor House Farm

A working rare-breed farm in an area of great beauty, a Jacobean farmhouse with oodles of history. Behind mullioned windows is a glorious interior crammed with curios and family pieces, panelled walls and wonky floors… hurl a log on the fire and watch it roar. Three rooms have four-posters; one bathroom flaunts rich red antique fabrics. Chris and Margaret are passionate hosts who serve perfect breakfasts (eggs from their own hens, sausages and bacon from their pigs and home-grown tomatoes) and give you the run of a garden resplendent with plants, vistas, tennis, croquet, two springer spaniels and one purring cat. Heaven.

Minimum stay: 2 nights at weekends during high season.

Rooms	1 double, 2 four-posters: £68–£80. 1 family room for 4: £80–£100.
Meals	Pub/restaurant 1.5 miles.
Closed	Christmas.

Chris & Margaret Ball
Manor House Farm,
Prestwood, Denstone,
Uttoxeter, ST14 5DD
Tel   +44 (0)1889 590415
Mobile   +44 (0)7976 767629
Email   cmball@manorhousefarm.co.uk
Web   www.manorhousefarm.co.uk

Entry 418   Map 8

Suffolk

Pavilion House

A conservation village surrounded by chalk grassland — famous for its flora, fauna and butterflies; marked walks are straight from this 16-year-old red-brick house. Friendly Gretta teaches cooking and you are in for a treat: homemade cake, enormous breakfasts with her own bread and jams, proper dinners or simple suppers. Sleep peacefully in traditional, comfortable bedrooms (all downstairs) with crisp linen and TVs. There's a guest sitting room too: English comfort with an oriental feel, parquet floors, antiques, original drawings, a cosy log-burner. Wander the superb garden. Newmarket and Cambridge are close.

Rooms	1 double; 1 double, 1 twin/double, both with separate bath/shower: £85–£125. Singles £55–£60. Child bed available.
Meals	Lunch from £10. Dinner from £25. Supper from £15. BYO. Pub 1.5 miles.
Closed	Christmas.

Gretta & David Bredin
Pavilion House,
133 Station Road, Dullingham,
Newmarket, CB8 9UT

Tel	+44 (0)1638 508005
Mobile	+44 (0)7776 197709
Email	gretta@thereliablesauce.co.uk
Web	www.pavilionhousebandb.co.uk

Entry 419   Map 9

Suffolk

The Old Vicarage

Up the avenue of fine white horse chestnut trees to find just what you'd expect from an old vicarage: a Pembroke table in the flagstoned hall, a refectory table sporting copies of *The Field*, a piano guests can play, silver pheasants, winter log fires in the breakfast and drawing rooms and homemade cake on arrival. The house is magnificent, with huge rooms and passageways. Comfy beds are dressed in old-fashioned counterpanes; the twin has stunning far-reaching views. Weave your way through the branches of the huge copper beech to Jane's colourful garden; she grows her own vegetables, keeps hens, makes jams and cooks delicious breakfasts.

Children over 7 welcome.

Rooms	1 twin/double with separate bath (extra single room available, let to same party only), 1 twin with separate bath: £80–£90. Singles £50.
Meals	Packed lunch £6. Pub 1 mile.
Closed	Christmas.

Jane Sheppard
The Old Vicarage,
Great Thurlow,
Newmarket, CB9 7LE

Tel	+44 (0)1440 783209
Mobile	+44 (0)7887 717429
Email	s.j.sheppard@hotmail.co.uk
Web	www.thurlowvicarage.co.uk

Entry 420   Map 9

Suffolk

The Lucy Redman Garden and B&B

Off a country lane, through an estate village, hides this immaculate, thatched, 1930s house – a gem. Lucy and Dominic are full of life and fun. Lucy is an artistic garden designer so all glows with texture and colour, and the garden is a stunner. Family antiques blend with multi-cultural pieces, there are books, paintings and pets. Choose between the cosy, ochre-walled 'Indian' room upstairs and the 'Moroccan' down, with aqua walls and vibrant Mexican tiles. Wake to eggs from the hens, plum jams from the trees, and lovely homemade marmalade. Views swoop over garden, grazing horses and miles of Suffolk countryside. A happy place!

Rooms	1 double, 1 twin/double: £80-£90. Singles £70.
Meals	Pubs/restaurants 2 miles.
Closed	Rarely.

Lucy & Dominic Watts
The Lucy Redman Garden and B&B,
6 The Village, Rushbrooke,
Bury St Edmunds, IP30 0ER

Tel	+44 (0)1284 386250
Mobile	+44 (0)7503 633671
Email	lucyredman7@gmail.com
Web	www.lucyredman.co.uk

Entry 421   Map 10

Suffolk

The Old Manse Barn

A large, lush loft apartment in sleepy Suffolk; this uncluttered living space of blond wood, white walls and big windows has an urban feel yet overlooks glorious countryside. Secluded from the main house, in a timber-clad barn, all is fabulous and spacious: leather sofas, glass dining table, stainless steel kitchenette. Floor lights dance off the walls, surround-sound creates mood and you can watch the stars from your bed. Homemade granola, fruits, cold meats, cheeses and fresh pastries are popped in the fridge – bliss. There's peace for romance, solitude for work, a garden to sit in and lovely Sue to suggest the best pubs.

Rooms	Apartment - 1 double with kitchenette: £80-£90.
Meals	Pubs within walking distance.
Closed	Mid-January to end of February.

Sue & Ian Jones
The Old Manse Barn,
Chapel Road, Cockfield,
Bury St Edmunds, IP30 0HE

Tel	+44 (0)1284 828120
Mobile	+44 (0)7931 753996
Email	bookings@theoldmansebarn.co.uk
Web	www.theoldmansebarn.co.uk

Entry 422   Map 10

Suffolk

The Old Rectory Country House

In a hamlet of thatched cottages by the Church of St Lawrence sits a handsome rectory, quietly steeped in ancient history. Find elegant proportions, family antiques and owner Frank who asks only that you feel at home. The drawing room has an honesty bar and walking maps, the garden is a delight and you can use the pool. Feel spoiled in big smart bedrooms with pretty fabrics, smooth linen and lovely views; the Stables are charming with books, a garden suite and comfy sofas. Be lazy and have continental breakfast in your room, or rouse yourself for local sausages and bacon by a log fire in the magnificent dining room. A treat.

Check availability and book online through website.

Rooms	2 doubles, 1 twin/double, each with extra child's bed/cot: £75-£199. Stables - 3 doubles with extra single in 2, sharing sitting/dining room & kitchen (self-catering option available): £75-£199. Singles £65-£85 (Sun to Thurs only).
Meals	Meals £40 for guests booking the whole house only. Pub 1 mile.
Closed	Rarely.

	Frank Lawrenson
	The Old Rectory Country House, Great Waldingfield, Lavenham, Sudbury, CO10 0TL
Tel	+44 (0)1787 372428
Email	info@theoldrectorycountryhouse.co.uk
Web	www.theoldrectorycountryhouse.co.uk/rates.php

Entry 423   Map 10

Suffolk

The Pink Cottage

Beamed and brimming with rich colours, polished antiques, art and flowers. Tom and Fiona welcome you to their 17th-century cottage as friends, and everything is generously done. Bedrooms are in a separate wing; beds are topped with a pile of embroidered towels, a box of truffles tied with ribbon, a patchwork quilt; you'll find TVs and wine, books and an immaculate bathroom too. Breakfast is a passion and there's a huge choice – organic, garden-grown or local and all delicious: homemade jams, berries, eggs Benedict, wild mushroom omelette... out on the terrace when sunny. Three miles to medieval Lavenham; Constable country is a treat.

Minimum stay: 2 nights at weekends. Children over 6 welcome.

Rooms	1 double: £100-£125. 1 single sharing bath with double (let to same party only): £75-£100.
Meals	Pubs/restaurants 2-minute walk.
Closed	Rarely.

	Fiona Carville
	The Pink Cottage, Brent Eleigh Road, Monks Eleigh, Lavenham, Ipswich, IP7 7JG
Tel	+44 (0)1449 744211
Email	lavenhampink@gmail.com
Web	www.lavenhampink.com

Entry 424   Map 10

Suffolk

Copinger Hall

A stunning bay-windowed house which has been in the family since the 16th century, yet is anything but ancient in feel. At the end of a sweeping gravel drive, past the church which adjoins the garden, it is 'country smart', deeply comfortable and very much a home – complete with two noisily amiable dogs. Lisa is someone to whom throwing open the doors to guests brings immeasurable pleasure, a gifted and generous host. Breakfasts (superb breakfast menu!) are in the elegant dining room, and guests have the use of the drawing room, garden and tennis court. Head out for Aldeburgh, Lavenham and the music at Snape Maltings.

Rooms	1 double, 1 twin/double; 1 double with separate bath/shower: £100–£130. Singles £95.
Meals	Pub & restaurant within 1 mile.
Closed	Occasionally.

Lisa & Stephen Minoprio
Copinger Hall,
Brettenham Road, Buxhall,
Stowmarket, IP14 3DJ
Tel   +44 (0)1449 736000
Mobile +44 (0)7775 621715
Email   lisa@copingerhall.com

Suffolk

The Old Rectory

A handsome house surrounded by large gardens and sheep-dotted fields. Maggie's home is filled with beautiful things: old family china, prints, portraits, blue and white decorated lamps, polished wood – a piano you can play too. Bedrooms are peaceful and pretty; 'Rose' is reached up a few steps. Breakfast is well worth waking up for: granola, compote, homemade jams, home-buzzed honey, sausages and bacon from their own pigs; sourcing local food is a passion and Maggie loves to cook, so dinner will be equally good. Set off for Constable country, charming old wool town Lavenham, antiques in Long Melford, the coast... it's a fascinating spot.

Rooms	1 twin/double; 1 double with separate bathroom: £90–£100.
Meals	Dinner, 2-3 courses with wine, £20–£25. Pubs/restaurants 2 miles.
Closed	Rarely.

Maggie Lawrence
The Old Rectory,
Kettlebaston,
Ipswich, IP7 7QD
Tel   +44 (0)1449 740400
Email theoldrectorykettlebaston@gmail.com
Web   www.theoldrectorykettlebaston.co.uk

Suffolk

Holbecks House

Up the drive through parkland studded with ancient trees and step into the flagstoned hall of this 18th–century house. Find gracious rooms, soft colours, Persian rugs, antiques, hunting prints and books to browse. Perry is delightful and looks after you well; settle into big peaceful bedrooms with good beds, chocolates and long rural views. Just beyond the market town of Hadleigh, the house snoozes on a hill with acres of garden, orchard, croquet lawn, rose walk and pond. Explore Constable Country, visit the Munnings Art Museum in Dedham, Gainsborough's House in Sudbury and the cathedral city of Bury St Edmunds.

Minimum stay: 2 nights at weekends.

Rooms	1 double, 1 twin/double; 1 double with separate bath: £100–£145. Singles £85–£115.
Meals	Supper £20. BYO. Pubs/restaurants 0.5 miles.
Closed	Rarely.

Perry Coysh
Holbecks House,
Holbecks Lane, Hadleigh,
Ipswich, IP7 5PE

Tel	+44 (0)1473 823211
Mobile	+44 (0)7875 167771
Email	info@holbecks.com
Web	www.holbecks.com

Entry 427   Map 10

Suffolk

The Gables

A yellow ochre townhouse filled with original features, fireplaces and Farrow & Ball colours. Immaculate bedrooms have luxurious beds, TV, WiFi and a jar of homemade cookies or nutty chocolates, bathrooms have tip-top towels and scented lotions and there's a comfy guest sitting room on the first-floor landing. Breakfast on all things local, along with bowls of berries and Stuart's jams and muffins; on sunny days eat out in the walled garden. Hadleigh is a pretty, old Suffolk wool town in the heart of Constable country, there's a thriving cookery school down the road, the river Brett to walk along... ask Stuart, he knows Suffolk well.

Rooms	3 doubles, 1 twin: £95. Singles £75.
Meals	Pubs/restaurants 2-minute walk.
Closed	Rarely.

Stuart Service
The Gables,
108-110 High Street,
Hadleigh, Ipswich, IP7 5EL

Tel	+44 (0)1473 828126
Email	stuart@thegableshadleigh.co.uk
Web	www.thegableshadleigh.co.uk

Entry 428   Map 10

Suffolk

Poplar Farm House

Only a few miles from Ipswich but down a green lane, this rambling farmhouse has a pretty, whitewashed porch and higgledy-piggledy roof. All light, elegant and spacious with wonderful flowers, art, sumptuous soft furnishings (made by Sally) and quirky sculptures; expect comfy beds, laundered linen and smart bathrooms. Sally is relaxed and friendly and will give you eggs from her handsome hens, homemade bread, veg from the garden on an artistically laid table. Play tennis, swim, steam in the sauna or book one of Sally's arts and crafts courses, then wander in the woods beyond with beautiful dogs Shale and Rune. Great value.

Rooms	2 doubles, 1 twin sharing 2 bath/shower rooms: £70. Yurt - 1 double: £70. Singles £45.
Meals	Dinner, 3 courses, £15–£25. Packed lunch £7. Pub 1 mile.
Closed	Rarely.

Sally Sparrow
Poplar Farm House,
Poplar Lane, Sproughton,
Ipswich, IP8 3HL

Tel	+44 (0)1473 601211
Mobile	+44 (0)7950 767226
Email	sparrowsally@aol.com
Web	www.poplarfarmhousesuffolkbb.eu

Entry 429   Map 10

Suffolk

Church House

A short hop from riverside Woodbridge and musical Snape Maltings, between a conservation churchyard and a history-rich field, is something different and unusual: a customised house of gentle colours and textures, home to an architect and a designer. From the hand-carved, oak porch to the lovely wildlife garden, there's a feeling of warmth and delight. Under the eaves: two jewel-bright and comfortable bedrooms full of books and fresh flowers. In the kitchen: a big farmhouse table laid for beautiful breakfasts. And, a short walk away, an excellent village pub.

Minimum stay: 2 nights at weekends. Children over 6 welcome.

Rooms	1 twin/double; 1 twin/double with separate bath/shower: £80–£85. Singles £65–£70.
Meals	Pub 1 mile.
Closed	Rarely.

Sally & Richard Pirkis
Church House,
Clopton,
Woodbridge, IP13 6QB

Tel	+44 (0)1473 735350
Email	sallypirkis@gmail.com
Web	www.churchhousebandbsuffolk.co.uk

Entry 430   Map 10

Suffolk

Melton Hall

There's more than a touch of theatre to this beautiful listed house. The dining room is opulent red; the drawing room, with its delicately carved mantelpiece and comfortable sofas, has French windows overlooking the terrace. There's a four-poster in one bedroom, an antique French bed in another and masses of flowers and books. The grounds include a formal rose garden, orchid and wildflower meadow and a walled vegetable garden. Plenty to do and see nearby: river walks, shopping in pretty Woodbridge, the Heritage coast and the Saxon burial site Sutton Hoo. Return for a candle-lit dinner, and coffee in the drawing room afterwards.

Rooms	1 double; 1 double sharing bath with 1 single: £110-£135. 1 single: £65-£70.
Meals	Dinner, 1-3 courses, £19-£38. BYO. Pubs/restaurants nearby.
Closed	Rarely.

Lucinda de la Rue
Melton Hall,
Woodbridge, IP12 1PF

Tel	+44 (0)1394 388138
Mobile	+44 (0)7775 797075
Email	cindy@meltonhall.co.uk
Web	www.meltonhall.co.uk

Entry 431   Map 10

Suffolk

The Old Rectory

Step in to a generous flagstoned hall and a smiling welcome from Christopher. Archways lead down to the library (cosy with maps, books and open fire) and an elegant staircase leads to spacious bedrooms, one with delightful bow windows and a view of the sea. There are colourful rugs and art, pelmets and antiques, heaps of interesting books. Breakfast is good: full English or a continental spread, with eggs from the hens and homemade jams. Outside: acres of woodland, meadows, croquet lawn and veg garden (walled and wonderful). Walks galore on the Deben Peninsula, music at Snape Maltings… Suffolk at its best and peace reigns supreme.

Whole house available for weekly & weekend lets, please enquire with owner for price.

Rooms	2 doubles, 1 twin: £90-£120. Singles £70-£100. Extra bed/sofabed available £30 per person per night.
Meals	Dinner, 2-3 courses, £20-£30. Pub 5-minute walk.
Closed	Occasionally.

Christopher Langley
The Old Rectory,
Alderton,
Woodbridge, IP12 3DE

Tel	+44 (0)1394 410003
Email	clangley2015@hotmail.com
Web	www.oldrectoryaldertonbandb.co.uk

Entry 432   Map 10

Suffolk

Willow Tree Cottage

Seductively near RSPB Minsmere, medieval castles and the glorious Heritage coast. The evening sun pours into the back of this contemporary cottage with butter yellow walls; you are on the edge of the village but all is quiet with an orchard behind and a bird-filled garden for tea and cake. No sitting room, but easy chairs in your pretty bedroom face views. Caroline is a good cook and breakfast is delicious (try her kedgeree and homemade jams). Snape Maltings for music, Southwold for the famous pier, Aldeburgh with its shingle beach, boats, fun shops and good places to eat – all are close by. Holly the labrador adds to the charm.

Minimum stay: 2 nights at weekends.

Rooms	1 double: £70-£75.
	Singles £50-£55.
Meals	Pub/restaurant 1.5 miles.
Closed	Rarely.

Caroline Youngson
Willow Tree Cottage,
3 Belvedere Close, Kelsale,
Saxmundham, IP17 2RS

Tel	+44 (0)1728 602161
Mobile	+44 (0)7747 624139
Email	cy@willowtreecottage.me.uk
Web	www.willowtreecottage.me.uk

Entry 433   Map 10

Suffolk

Trustans Barn

Ancient oak beams have been carefully kept in this smart Suffolk barn conversion. It's a family affair here: friendly sisters Sally and Rosie give you contemporary bedrooms with artistic touches, king-sized beds, sleek bathrooms and drench showers. Breakfast is served at two scrubbed pine tables in the airy slate-floored breakfast room; a big blackboard lists tasty choices – everything from home-laid eggs and local sausages to home-grown tomatoes and muesli. Masses to do nearby: Snape Maltings music, wonderful old churches, summer festivals, the Heritage Coast… A great place for a peaceful holiday with a group of friends.

Minimum stay: 2 nights in high season.

Rooms	5 doubles, 1 twin/double: £95-£120.
Meals	Pubs less than a mile away.
Closed	Christmas.

Sally Prime
Trustans Barn,
Westleton Road, Darsham,
Saxmundham, IP17 3BP

Tel	+44 (0)1728 668684
Email	sallyandrosie@trustansbarn.co.uk
Web	www.trustansbarn.co.uk

Entry 434   Map 10

Suffolk

Oak Tree Farm

A magnificent ancient oak tree stands guard over this 300-year old Georgian-fronted farmhouse. John and Julian love all things Art Nouveau/Art Deco and their home is filled with pieces from those periods, including china with masses of different patterns; fine books galore too, and peaceful bedrooms with smart white linen. Breakfast is a moveable feast: in the conservatory in summer, or by the fire in the dining room in winter; the bird feeders get moved too so you're kept amused while you tuck in! You can wander the five-acre garden and meadows, pretty Yoxford village has antique shops to browse, and Snape Maltings is a hop.

Minimum stay: 2 nights at weekends. Children over 5 welcome.

Rooms	3 twin/doubles: £80.
	Singles £60.
Meals	Pubs/restaurants 5-minute walk.
Closed	Rarely.

Julian Lock & John McMinn
Oak Tree Farm,
Little Street, Yoxford,
Saxmundham, IP17 3JN

Tel	+44 (0)1728 668651
Mobile	+44 (0)7969 459261
Email	bookings@oaktreefarmyoxford.co.uk
Web	www.oaktreefarmyoxford.co.uk

Entry 435   Map 10

Suffolk

Church Farmhouse

This Elizabethan farmhouse is by the ancient thatched church in a little hamlet close to Southwold. Minsmere RSPB bird sanctuary, Snape Maltings and the coast are nearby for lovely days out. Sarah, characterful, well-travelled and entertaining, is also an excellent cook, so breakfast will be a treat with bowls of fruit, Suffolk bacon and free-range eggs; occasional candle-lit dinners are worth staying in for, too. Bedrooms have supremely comfy beds well-dressed in pure cotton. Although there is no sitting room, you can enjoy tea and cake and linger in the garden, there are flowers in every room and books galore.

Minimum stay: 2 nights at weekends. Over 12s welcome.

Rooms	1 double, 1 twin/double; 1 double
	with separate bath: £95-£110.
	Singles £65-£80.
Meals	Dinner £28.
	Pubs/restaurants within 4 miles.
Closed	Christmas.

Sarah Lentaigne
Church Farmhouse,
Uggeshall, Southwold, NR34 8BD

Tel	+44 (0)1502 578532
Mobile	+44 (0)7748 801418
Email	sarahlentaigne@btinternet.com
Web	www.churchfarmhousesuffolk.co.uk

Entry 436   Map 10

Suffolk

Valley Farm

Soaps and sweeties in baskets, walking and cycle route maps on tap, DVDs to borrow: some of the personal touches you'll find at this delightfully unpretentious B&B. The soft brick farmhouse in a lovely corner of Suffolk sits in over two acres of landscaped garden, with a play area for children, a field for kite flying, and an indoor solar-heated pool (shared with self-catering guests but can be booked just for you). The two carpeted bedrooms are friendly and comfortable; each has a spotless shower room. Jackie and Andrew have a passion for real food so breakfast is a spread of local produce, home-grown tomatoes and jams from their own soft fruits.

Minimum stay: 2 nights at weekends.

Rooms	1 double: £80–£100.
	1 family room for 3–4: £80–£120.
	Singles £80–£100.
Meals	Pub 0.4 miles.
Closed	Rarely.

Jackie Circus
Valley Farm,
Bungay Road, Holton,
Halesworth, IP19 8LY
Tel   +44 (0)1986 874521
Email   mail@valleyfarmholton.co.uk
Web   www.valleyfarmholton.co.uk

Entry 437   Map 10

Suffolk

Bulls Hall

Half a mile from the village of Occold – a B&B of character and peace. The house is 16th-century and listed, the lovely grounds – lawns, meadow, summerhouse and ponds – teem with wildlife. Warm, friendly Angela welcomes you to a cosy, traditional, unspoiled home: low doorways, a big inglenook, a deep new mattress on a vintage iron bed, books, guides, games and delightfully uneven brick floors. There's a long parquet'd double off the dining room, a staircase to a lofty family suite, and a beautiful breakfast to wake up to: Suffolk black bacon, homemade jams, eggs from the hens. Visit the Broads, stroll to the pub.

Minimum stay: 2 nights on bank holidays.

Rooms	1 double: £70–£80.
	1 suite for 4 with separate bath:
	£100–£140.
	Singles £50.
Meals	Pub/restaurant 0.5 miles.
Closed	Rarely.

Angela Hall
Bulls Hall,
Bulls Hall Road,
Occold, Eye, IP23 7PH
Tel   +44 (0)1379 678683
Email   angela.hall53@gmail.com

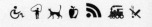

Entry 438   Map 10

Suffolk

Camomile Cottage

Aly and Tim's 16th-century longhouse is a feast of old beams, kilims, antiques and art. They give you homemade cake on arrival; relax in the garden or the guest lounge, kick off your shoes and enjoy a glass of wine by the log fire. Beamed bedrooms have period furnishings, goose down duvets, luxury linen, flowers and handmade chocolates; bathrooms have Molton Brown toiletries. Aly will also bring you tea in bed! Breakfast is in the garden room: cornbread toast, eggs from the hens, croissants and all sorts of cooked choices. Eye is an attractive old market town; Southwold, Bury St Edmunds and Snape Maltings are all close.

Minimum stay: 2 nights at weekends.

Rooms	2 doubles: £99-£110.
	Singles £85.
Meals	Pubs/restaurants 0.5 miles.
Closed	Rarely.

Aly Kahane
Camomile Cottage,
Brome Avenue,
Eye, IP23 7HW

Tel	+44 (0)1379 873528
Email	aly@camomilecottage.co.uk
Web	www.camomilecottage.co.uk

Entry 439   Map 10

Surrey

Swallow Barn

A converted squash court, coach house and stables, once belonging to next-door's manor, have become a home of old-fashioned charm. Full of family memories, and run very well by Joan, this B&B is excellently placed for Windsor, Wisley, Brooklands and Hampton Court; close to both airports too. Lovely trees in the garden, fields and woods beyond, a paddock and a swimming pool... total tranquillity, and you can walk to the pub. None of the bedrooms is huge but the beds are firm, the garden views are pretty and the downstairs double has its own sitting room. Breakfasts are both generous and scrumptious.

Children over 8 welcome.

Rooms	1 double with sitting room; 1 twin
	with separate shower: £90-£100.
	Apple Store - 1 twin: £90-£100.
	Singles £55.
Meals	Pub/restaurant 0.75 miles.
Closed	Rarely.

Joan Carey
Swallow Barn,
Milford Green, Chobham,
Woking, GU24 8AU

Tel	+44 (0)1276 856030
Mobile	+44 (0)7768 972904
Email	info@swallow-barn.co.uk
Web	www.swallow-barn.co.uk

Entry 440   Map 4

Surrey

Broadway Barn

If you love art, gardening and good food, you'll love Mindi and her brilliant conversion of a pretty brick Regency barn on Ripley High Street. You sleep in comfortable bedrooms styled with creativity: a painting from a Parisian laundrette, ceramic lamps with bird motifs, leather chests as tables. You relax in a long, light, mirrored conservatory with glazed terrace doors, and are free to wander around the newly planted walled garden. You breakfast deliciously on local eggs and home-baked treats... Minutes from Guildford and Wisley's RHS garden, the village has a Michelin-starred restaurant, cafés and pubs.

Rooms	4 doubles: £99.
	Singles £95.
Meals	Restaurant next door.
Closed	Rarely.

Mindi McLean
Broadway Barn,
High Street, Ripley,
Woking, GU23 6AQ
Tel +44 (0)1483 223200
Email mindi@broadwaybarn.com
Web www.broadwaybarn.com

Entry 441 Map 4

Surrey

South Lodge

The beautiful Surrey Hills surround this smart home overlooking the village green. Paul and Joanna's house gets the sun all day and has a country chic feel. They look after you well, and give you tea and cake on arrival, three cosy, pretty bedrooms in the eaves and locally sourced and homemade treats at breakfast. Joanna's catering business is run from the house so there are always people coming and going – this is a fun place to stay with a lovely friendly feel. Hop next door for a tasty supper at The Grumpy Mole (popular so you need to book). Near Dorking, and handy for Gatwick, too – it's a 15-minute drive.

Rooms	2 doubles; 1 twin with separate
	bath: £100–£115.
	Singles £95.
Meals	Evening meal with wine from £35.
	Pub next door.
Closed	Christmas.

Joanna Rowlands
South Lodge,
Brockham Green, Brockham,
Betchworth, RH3 7JS
Tel +44 (0)1737 843883
Email bookings@brockhambandb.com
Web www.brockhambandb.com

Entry 442 Map 4

Blackbrook House

Arriving at this elegant Victorian home surrounded by immaculate lawn, woodland, paddocks and a swing hanging from a huge conifer, you immediately want to explore. Emma and Rae are easy-going, and want you to unwind and feel at home. Bedrooms are spacious and smart with floral fabrics, deep pocket sprung mattresses and good linen; bathrooms are tip-top. Breakfast is a delicious spread: free-range eggs from next door, local bacon and sausages, freshly squeezed apple juice from the orchard. Admire the rose garden, enjoy a game of tennis, head out into the Surrey Hills. Return to a snug sitting room with TV and lots of books. Bliss.

The Dovecote at Greenaway

An enchanting cottage in an idyllic corner of Chiddingfold. People return time and again — for the house (1545), the garden blooming with flowers, vegetables, hens and dovecote, the glowing interiors, and Sheila and John. The sitting room is inviting with rich colours, flowers, beams and a roaring log fire; the turning oak staircase leads to bedrooms that are cosy and sumptuous at the same time, and bathrooms with deep roll top tubs and a pretty armchair. Breakfast is a spread with homemade bread and home-grown tomatoes. Gorgeous countryside, walks on the Greensand Way... who would guess London and the airports were so close?

Rooms	1 double: £90-£100.
	1 suite for 2: £95-£115.
	Singles from £60.
Meals	Pub 0.5 miles.
Closed	Christmas & New Year.

Rooms	1 double; 1 double, 1 twin sharing
	bath: £100-£125.
	Singles £100.
Meals	Pubs 300 yds.
Closed	Rarely.

	Emma & Rae Burdon
	Blackbrook House,
	Blackbrook, Dorking, RH5 4DS
Tel	+44 (0)1306 888898
Mobile	+44 (0)7880 723512
Email	blackbrookbb@btinternet.com
Web	www.surreybandb.co.uk

	Sheila & John Marsh
	The Dovecote at Greenaway,
	Pickhurst Road,
	Chiddingfold, GU8 4TS
Tel	+44 (0)1428 682920
Email	info@bedandbreakfastchiddingfold.co.uk
Web	www.bedandbreakfastchiddingfold.co.uk

Surrey

Colliers Farm

Acres of grounds and a restored 17th-century farmhouse with all the trimmings will make you want to stay longer. Step into a hallway with a welcoming wood-burner; Marina rustles up tea and cake (delicious brownies!) on flowery china – served outside with the roses and roaming hens in summer. Pastel walls blend with soaring beams, stained glass and vases of flowers. Luxurious bedrooms come with TVs, DVDs, iPod docks and tip-top bathrooms; one is downstairs, all have comfy armchairs. Breakfast in the elegant dining room is a local spread with homemade compotes, bread and marmalade. Trips to Goodwood, Guildford and Chichester are easy.

Rooms	2 doubles, 1 twin: £110–£160. Singles from £75.
Meals	Pubs/restaurants 0.25 miles.
Closed	Rarely.

Marina Shellard
Colliers Farm,
Midhurst Road, Fernhurst,
Haslemere, GU27 3EX
Tel   +44 (0)1428 652265
Email   info@colliersfarm.co.uk
Web   www.colliersfarm.co.uk

Entry 445   Map 4

Sussex

Lordington House

Croquet on the lawn in summer, big log fires and woolly jumpers in winter, brilliant food all year round. On a sunny slope of the Ems Valley, life ticks by peacefully as it has always done... The house is vast and impressive, a lime avenue links the much-loved garden with the AONB beyond and friendly guard dog Shep looks on. The 17th-century staircase is a glory, the décor is engagingly old-fashioned: Edwardian beds with firm mattresses and floral covers, carpeted Sixties-style bathrooms, toile wallpaper on wardrobe doors. A privilege to stay in a house of this age and character!

Children over 5 welcome. Pets by arrangement.

Rooms	1 double; 1 twin/double with separate bath/shower; 1 double sharing bath/shower with single: £100–£130. 1 single: £50–£65.
Meals	Packed lunch from £6. Pub 1 mile.
Closed	Rarely.

Mr & Mrs Hamilton
Lordington House,
Lordington,
Chichester, PO18 9DX
Tel   +44 (0)1243 375862
Email   hamiltonjanda@btinternet.com

Entry 446   Map 4

Sussex

Crows Hall Farm

The Renwicks are tremendous hosts. Their wonderful flagstone-halled farmhouse in the South Downs National Park is great for walking and cycling and close to Goodwood. Amanda's style is simple and cottagey, but never twee. She's gone for moss green walls, open brickwork and a classically dressed, big handmade bed in the main room; the second room has fantastic views of the walled garden and beyond. In between, the beamed bathroom is fab and fun, with flamingos, freestanding bath and shower (all yours, or shared with your own party). Breakfasts are local, flexible feasts on the terrace or in the quirky rustic kitchen. Marvellous!

Rooms are reached by their own staircase with private access.

Rooms	2 doubles sharing separate bathroom (let to same party only): £110–£150.
Meals	Pubs 2.5 miles.
Closed	Rarely.

Amanda Renwick
Crows Hall Farm,
Chilgrove Road, Lavant,
Chichester, PO18 9HP
Tel   +44 (0)1243 527855
Email   amanda@crowshall.com

Entry 447   Map 4

Sussex

Seabeach House

Sitting sleepily behind its white gate this pretty stone cottage is surrounded by the Sussex Downs National Park. Throughout Francesca's friendly home her love of folk art, rich oils, antiques and hand-painted pieces adds zest. Comfy cottagey bedrooms are on the ground floor; wake to local sausages and eggs, garden tomatoes, homemade jams with croissants and brioche. Francesca loves cooking, and dinner, with home-grown veg, is good too. Explore garden and fields, admire wide views from a pretty terrace and chat to Popeye the dog. There's art, theatre and sailing in Chichester, the castle in Arundel, and events galore at Goodwood.

Rooms	Annexe: 1 double, 1 twin sharing bath (let to same party only): £85–£150. Singles £75.
Meals	Dinner, 3 courses, £25. BYO. Pub 1 mile.
Closed	Rarely.

Francesca Emmet
Seabeach House,
Selhurst Park, Halnaker,
Chichester, PO18 0LX
Tel   +44 (0)1243 537944
Email   francescaemmet@hotmail.co.uk
Web   www.bandbatseabeachhouse.co.uk

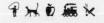

Entry 448   Map 4

Sussex

The Old Manor House

Wild flowers in jugs, old wooden floors and beams, pretty cottagey curtains: Judy's manor house near Chichester has bags of character and she is friendly and kind. Originally constructed round a big central fireplace, the rooms are all refreshingly simple allowing features to shine. Sunny bedrooms up steep stairs have seagrass flooring, limed furniture, gentle colours and warm bathrooms. Enjoy delicious breakfasts by the wood-burner in the dining room: fresh fruit smoothies and an organic full English. Great for horse racing, castle visiting, sailing, theatre and festivals; fantastic walks on the South Downs, too. Lovely.

Rooms	2 doubles: £95.
Meals	Pub/restaurant 500 yds.
Closed	Christmas.

Judy Wolstenholme
The Old Manor House,
Westergate Street, Westergate,
Chichester, PO20 3QZ
Tel +44 (0)1243 544489
Email judy@veryoldmanorhouse.com
Web www.veryoldmanorhouse.com

Entry 449   Map 4

Sussex

Stream Cottage

One of Sussex's prettiest villages, an endearing 1587 thatched cottage, the cheeriest hosts and a breakfast menu including blueberry pancakes, smoked salmon, homemade plum compote and, for the very hungry, 'The Famous Amberley Monty'! Through a private door and up a narrow staircase find your own sweet sitting room with comfy sofa and chair, lots of books and a charming bedroom with plenty of space and dual aspect low windows overlooking the garden. Your sparkling bathroom is downstairs (robes are provided) with big bottles of Cowshed potions and a sleek bath for resting weary limbs. Arundel and the South Downs await.

Rooms	1 double with separate bath & living room: £100. Singles £80. 10% discount for stays of 3 or more nights.
Meals	Pubs in village.
Closed	Christmas & occasionally.

Mike & Janet Wright
Stream Cottage,
The Square, Amberley,
Arundel, BN18 9SR
Tel +44 (0)1798 831266
Email janet@streamcottage.co.uk
Web www.streamcottage.co.uk

Entry 450   Map 4

Riverhill Lodge

Views and more views over the South Downs National Park from this handsome red-brick house with early Georgian origins. A sunny, airy sitting room with open fire and elegant cream and pink sofas looks onto the well-planted garden, and you breakfast on homemade bread, eggs from local hens and smoked bacon in the cosy terracotta-coloured dining room. Peaceful bedrooms are in pale, neutral colours, with fresh fabrics and deep mattresses; bathrooms are sleekly up-to-date and as warm as toast, with the thickest towels. Walk from the house for miles. There are good pubs nearby and the friendly Leavers provide masses of info.

Rooms	1 double, 1 twin/double: £100–£150.
	Singles £70–£75.
Meals	Pub 0.75 miles.
Closed	Christmas & occasionally Easter.

Christopher & Jenny Leaver
Riverhill Lodge,
Riverhill, Fittleworth, Petworth,
Pulborough, RH20 1JY
Tel   +44 (0)1798 343872
Email   bookings@riverhilllodge.co.uk
Web   www.riverhilllodge.co.uk

Entry 451   Map 4

Weston House

Come for Goodwood races and seasonal festivals galore – summer, music and literary. Return to comfortable bedrooms with armchairs, Portmeirion china and spotless en suite bathrooms; the sunny room at the back looks out over pretty garden, fields and the South Downs beyond (you're on the main road but it's surprisingly quiet). Cherry gives you breakfast at a long polished table by the fire in the lovely beamed dining room, or out on the stone terrace if it's summery. You're close to the theatre and sailing in Chichester and the castle in Arundel, Petworth is teeming with antique shops, and you can walk to the pub for a good supper.

Rooms	2 twin/doubles: £80–£90.
Meals	Pubs/restaurants 2-minute walk.
Closed	Christmas & New Year.

Cherry Corben
Weston House,
Tillington,
Petworth, GU28 0RA
Tel   +44 (0)1798 344556
Email   westonhousebookings@btinternet.com
Web   www.westonhousetillington.co.uk

Entry 452   Map 4

Sussex

The Hyde Granary

A 1,000-acre estate, where roe deer roam and the odd buzzard circles above. The granary stands at the end of a one-mile drive, alongside a coach house and clock tower, in the shadow of the big house. Airy interiors are just the ticket: timber frames, exposed walls, beams in the dining room and a drying room for walkers. Bedrooms are uncluttered and have a country feel: one has a claw-foot bath, the other is in the eaves. Margot, a homeopath, can realign your back after a long journey, and does super breakfasts. There's a small garden for sundowners in summer, you can walk to the village and Gatwick is close.

Rooms	1 double; 1 double with separate bath/shower: £90. Singles £65. Extra bed/sofabed available £15–£30 per person per night.
Meals	Pub 1.7 miles.
Closed	Christmas & New Year.

	Margot Barton
	The Hyde Granary,
	The Hyde, London Road, Handcross,
	Haywards Heath, RH17 6EZ
Tel	+44 (0)1444 401930
Email	margot@thehydegranary.com
Web	www.thehydegranary.com

Entry 453   Map 4

Sussex

The Jointure Studios

A thriving village with an arty heritage. In the centre is your apartment above a lovely big gallery/hall — with piano and wood-burning stove. Find a happy mix of antique and new, a quiet comfy bedroom with leafy views and a cosy sitting room with a kitchen area. Shirley leaves you homemade cakes and breakfast things, and each morning brings over a tray of fruits, croissants, local artisan bread and eggs for you to cook how you wish. The Ditchling Museum of Art + Craft is inspiring, South Downs National Park is your stomping ground, Brighton and Glyndebourne are close. Return and rustle up supper, or stroll down the road to a good pub.

Minimum stay: 2 nights at weekends.

Rooms	1 twin/double (apartment with sitting room and kitchen): £120. Stays of 2 nights or more £110. Singles £100.
Meals	Pubs/restaurants 1-minute walk.
Closed	Rarely.

	Shirley Crowther
	The Jointure Studios,
	11 South Street,
	Ditchling, BN6 8UQ
Tel	+44 (0)1273 841244
Email	gallery@jointurestudios.co.uk
Web	www.jointurestudiosbandb.co.uk

Entry 454   Map 4

Sussex

Blue Door Barns

Four charming flint barns hug a candle-lit courtyard... come with friends and family. You can choose to self-cater, or have breakfast arranged for you in Bryony and Emma's drawing room in the main house. Food is scrumptious, original and organic. Each space has been stylishly restored and has all the trimmings for a relaxed, pampering stay; two have kitchens and living rooms; all are decorated in warm whites, with splashes of colour and vintage pieces. Alfresco heaven with a rustic table under a rose-covered pergola, and a twinkling outdoor fireplace in the evenings. Wonderful picnics can be booked for Glyndebourne – only minutes away.

Rooms	The Sailor's House - 1 double: £110-£130. The Nook - 1 double: £130-£150. Little Lodge - 1 double, 1 sofabed: £195-£215 (prices for 2 £150-£170). The Lodge - 1 double, 1 twin: £215-£235 (prices for 2 £170-£190, not suitable for babies or toddlers).
Meals	Pub 2 miles.
Closed	Rarely.

	Bryony & Emma Blue Door Barns, 2 Cobbe Place, Beddingham, Lewes, BN8 6JY
Tel	+44 (0)1273 858893
Email	contact@bluedoorbarns.com
Web	www.bluedoorbarns.com

Entry 455   Map 4

Sussex

Netherwood Lodge

The scent of fresh flowers and a smattering of chintz over calm uncluttered interiors will please you. Engaging Margaret is a mine of local knowledge and offers you peaceful, cosy, ground-floor bedrooms beautifully dressed with wool carpets, designer interlined curtains, luxurious bed linens and gloriously comfortable beds. Enjoy an award-winning breakfast overlooking the garden (it's stunning); all is homemade or locally sourced. Then set off to discover this beautiful corner of East Sussex – ideal for walking, visiting National Trust houses and gardens and, of course, Glyndebourne.

Rooms	1 twin; 1 double with separate bath: £100-£125. Singles from £80.
Meals	Pub/restaurant 0.75 miles.
Closed	Rarely.

	Margaret Clarke Netherwood Lodge, Muddles Green, Chiddingly, Lewes, BN8 6HS
Tel	+44 (0)1825 872512
Email	netherwoodlodge@hotmail.com
Web	www.netherwoodlodge.co.uk

Entry 456   Map 5

Ocklynge Manor

On top of a peaceful hill, a short stroll from Eastbourne, find tip-top B&B in an 18th-century house with an interesting history – ask Wendy! Now it is her home, and you will be treated to home-baked bread, delicious tea time cakes and scrummy jams – on fine days you can take it outside. Creamy carpeted, bright and sunny bedrooms, all with views over the lovely walled garden, create a mood of relaxed indulgence and are full of thoughtful touches: dressing gowns, DVDs, your own fridge. Breakfasts are superb: this is a very spoiling, nurturing place.

Please see owners' website for availability.

Rooms	1 twin; 1 double with separate shower: £100–£110. 1 suite for 3: £110–£120. Singles from £50.
Meals	Pub 5-minute walk.
Closed	Rarely.

	Wendy Dugdill
	Ocklynge Manor,
	Mill Road, Eastbourne, BN21 2PG
Tel	+44 (0)1323 734121
Mobile	+44 (0)7979 627172
Email	ocklyngemanor@hotmail.com
Web	www.ocklyngemanor.co.uk/ availability_22.html

Entry 457   Map 5

The Flint Barns

An extraordinarily beautiful setting in the South Downs with views all the way to the sea, a pioneering English vineyard (discover the story and take a tour) – an unusual place to stay in huge style with a homely feel thanks to cheery Ade. More poshtel than hostel, find chunky doors, reclaimed oak, bedrooms with luxurious mattresses and shower rooms worthy of Babington House. A fabulous sitting room has plenty of seating for all, wood-burner and books; breakfast (and dinner if you want it) is at long tables in the lofty dining room: lovingly cooked and local. Spill out into the courtyard for summer barbecues, walk straight onto the South Downs Way.

Minimum stay: 2 nights.

Rooms	3 doubles: £110. 1 family room for 3: £140–£180. 1 bunk room for 2, 1 bunk room for 5 (dorm room with 5 singles), 1 bunk room for 4, 3 bunk rooms for 8 (en suite plus extra shower rooms): £80–£280.
Meals	Dinner, 2 courses, £20. Pubs 2-3 miles.
Closed	During picking & pruning season: mid-Jan to mid-Feb; end of Sept to end of Oct.

	Adrian Lamb
	The Flint Barns,
	Rathfinny Wine Estate, Alfriston,
	Polegate, BN26 5TU
Tel	+44 (0)1323 874030
Email	flintbarns@rathfinnyestate.com
Web	www.flintbarns.com

Entry 458   Map 5

Sussex

Globe Place

A listed 17th-century house beside the church in a tiny village, ten minutes from Glyndebourne. Alison — once chef to the Beatles — is a great cook and can provide you with a delicious and generous hamper, and tables and chairs too. Willie is a former rackets champion who gives tennis coaching; there's a court in the large, pretty garden, and a pool. Relax by the inglenook fire in the drawing room after a walk on the Cuckoo Trail or the South Downs, then settle down to a great supper — local fish, maybe, with home-grown vegetables. An easy-going, fun and informal household.

Over 12s welcome.

Rooms	2 doubles, 1 twin, each with separate bathroom: £90–£110. 2 singles sharing bathroom (let to same party only): £55. Cottage - 1 twin/double with sitting room: £90–£110.
Meals	Dinner £30. BYO wine. Hamper £35. Pub 10-minute drive.
Closed	Christmas.

	Alison & Willie Boone Globe Place, Hellingly, BN27 4EY
Tel	+44 (0)1323 844276
Mobile	+44 (0)7870 957608
Email	stay@globeplace.co.uk
Web	www.globeplace.co.uk

Entry 459   Map 5

Sussex

Old Whyly

Breakfast in a light-filled, chinoiserie dining room — there's an effortless elegance to this manor house, once home to one of King Charles's Cavaliers. Bedrooms are atmospheric, one in French style. The treats continue outside with a beautiful flower garden annually replenished with 5,000 tulips, a lake and orchard, a swimming pool and a tennis court — fabulous. Dine under the pergola in summer: food is a passion and Sarah's menus are adventurous with a modern slant. Glyndebourne is close so make a party of it and take a divine 'pink' hamper, with blankets or a table and chairs included. Sheer bliss.

Rooms	2 twin/doubles; 1 double with separate shower, 1 twin/double with separate bath: £98–£145. Singles by arrangement.
Meals	Dinner, 3 courses, £35. Hampers £38. Pub/restaurant 0.5 miles.
Closed	Rarely.

	Sarah Burgoyne Old Whyly, London Road, East Hoathly, BN8 6EL
Tel	+44 (0)1825 840216
Email	stay@oldwhyly.co.uk
Web	www.oldwhyly.co.uk

Entry 460   Map 5

Sussex

Thimbles

Enter the characterful hallway of this higgledy-piggledy house and fall under the spell of its charm. Imagine family antiques, pictures, plates, just-picked flowers and duvets as soft as a cloud: a timeless elegance, a fresh country style. Feast your eyes on the garden, six gentle acres that rise to fantastic views... a hammock, 89 varieties of roses, humming honey bees, a lake with an island (for barbecues!), a long lazy swing. Breakfasts and suppers are a dream: eggs from the hens, bacon from the pigs, jams from a jewel of a kitchen garden. Vicki, her family and Lottie the Irish terrier are the icing on the cake.

Rooms	1 suite for 2: £90.
	1 single sharing bathroom with family (extra bed available): £65.
	Extra bed/sofabed available £30 per person per night.
Meals	Dinner, 1-3 courses, £12.50-£21.50. Lunch £12.50. Pub 1 mile.
Closed	Rarely.

	Vicki Wood
	Thimbles,
	New Pond Hill, Cross in Hand,
	Heathfield, TN21 0NB
Tel	+44 (0)1435 860745
Mobile	+44 (0)7960 588447
Email	vicki.simonwood@btinternet.com
Web	www.thimblesbedandbreakfast.co.uk

Entry 461   Map 5

Sussex

Longbourn

Through the gates and down the drive to a big Victorian house in 12 lovingly nurtured acres. Longbourn is a smallholding with conservation flocks of sheep, pigs and fowl, and a farm shop on site – hence the exceptional breakfasts! (Fresh croissants too.) As for the house, it is large, light, immaculate and a perfect showcase for a fascinating collection of military lithographs. Big bedrooms, one opening to veranda and garden, have deep carpets and elegant wallpapers; the guests' drawing room is equally impressive. Roland and Jane, she an ex-costume designer, are completely charming and love to share their home.

Minimum stay: 2 nights in high season.

Rooms	1 double; 1 double with separate bath: £105-£155.
	Singles £85-£125.
Meals	Pubs/restaurants within 5 miles.
Closed	Rarely.

	Jane Horton
	Longbourn,
	Burwash Road, Broad Oak,
	Heathfield, TN21 8XG
Tel	+44 (0)1435 882070
Email	jane@longbourn1895.co.uk
Web	www.longbourn1895.co.uk

Entry 462   Map 5

Sussex

Luckhurst Place

Charlotte's house has a country feel with an artistic mix of furniture, fabrics and market treasures. Find masses of books, art, a wood-burner and rich burgundy colours in the open-plan space downstairs, while your bedroom upstairs is deeply comfy with a feather-topped big bed, and a reading room where you can make hot drinks. Tuck in to breakfast with glorious views, out on the decking when sunny: eggs from the hens, local sausages, pancakes and bacon. The rose-filled gardens are very pretty and there's a courtyard for afternoon tea; Sissinghurst and Great Dixter are nearby. Charlotte is relaxed and interesting – you'll feel very much at home.

Minimum stay: 2 nights.

Rooms	1 double with separate bath: £90–£100. Extra bed/sofabed available £30–£40 per person per night.
Meals	Pubs/restaurants 1 mile.
Closed	Rarely.

Charlotte Hammick
Luckhurst Place,
East Street,
Mayfield, TN20 6RJ
Tel   +44 (0)1435 874862
Email   charlotte.hammick@gmail.com

Entry 463   Map 5

Sussex

Rosebank

Come from London by train – it's an easy walk to your private retreat. This oak framed upper floor annexe has been designed with thought and contemporary style; a big airy space with huge sofa, TV, well-dressed bed; perfect for couples who like to come and go as they please. Kate leaves a generous continental breakfast to have when you fancy: home or local apple juice, croissants, fruit, organic yogurt… take it out onto the terrace when sunny. Plenty of literary and garden interest nearby so head out for Bateman's, Charleston House, Sissinghurst, Great Dixter and more. A simple bistro supper is a hop, good pubs further afield.

Minimum stay: 2 nights at weekends.

Rooms	Annexe - 1 double: £85–£100. Singles £75.
Meals	Continental breakfast. Pubs/restaurants 5-minute walk.
Closed	Rarely.

Kate Withnall
Rosebank,
Ladyfield, High Street,
Etchingham, TN19 7AG
Mobile   +44 (0)7866 524018
Email   rosebank@ladyfield.net
Web   www.rosebankbandb.com

Entry 464   Map 5

Sussex

King John's Lodge

Deep in the High Weald, down a maze of country lanes, is an enchanting 1650s house in eight acres of heaven: Jill's pride and joy. Inside: oak beams, stone fireplaces, big sofas, and a Jacobean dining room with leaded glass windows, fine setting for a perfect English breakfast. Wing chairs, floral fabrics, dressers with china bowls: the country-house feel extends to the comfortable, carpeted bedrooms. Discover Sissinghurst, Great Dixter, Rye… return to sweeping lawns, wild gardens, ancient apple trees, a woodland walk (spot Titania and Oberon) and a delightful nursery and tea room run by Jill's son.

Minimum stay: 2 nights at weekends & in high season.

Rooms	2 doubles, 1 twin: £95–£105. 1 family room for 3: £130–£150. Singles from £65.
Meals	Dinner, 3 courses, £30 (minimum 4). Pubs/restaurants 2.5 miles.
Closed	Rarely.

Jill Cunningham
King John's Lodge,
Sheepstreet Lane,
Etchingham, TN19 7AZ
Tel +44 (0)1580 819232
Email kingjohnslodge@aol.com
Web www.kingjohnslodge.com

Entry 465 Map 5

Sussex

Pelham Hall

A 14th-century hall house with a unique touch. Matthew and Chris have worked a stunning refurbishment here with antiques, gorgeous fabrics and hip style. Delightful bedrooms are filled with personality; the ground floor bedroom has French windows overlooking the charming garden; inventively designed bathrooms have plush robes and lotions. Breakfast by the wood-burner, or on the rooftop terrace in summer (glorious views across the Weald); tuck into homemade granola, compote, croissants, delicious cooked choices. Set out for Rudyard Kipling's Bateman's, garden gems Sissinghurst and Great Dixter; adorable Carlito the dog welcomes you home.

Minimum stay: 2 nights at weekends. Children over 11 welcome.

Rooms	1 double with private sitting room, 2 twin/doubles: £100–£135. Singles £100–£120.
Meals	Pubs/restaurants 8 miles.
Closed	Rarely.

Matthew Fox
Pelham Hall,
High Street, Burwash,
Etchingham, TN19 7ES
Tel +44 (0)1435 882335
Email bookings@pelhamhall.co.uk
Web www.pelhamhall.co.uk

Entry 466 Map 5

Sussex

The Cloudesley

One mile from the sea, a remarkable house full of beautiful things. Shahriar – photographer, holistic therapist, Chelsea gold-medal winner – has created an artistic bolthole: books, African masks, an honesty bar, chic bedrooms and two sitting rooms that double as art galleries. You are looked after with great kindness. Shahriar has a couple of treatment rooms where, in cahoots with local therapists, he offers massage, shiatsu and reiki. You breakfast on exotic fruits, Armagnac omelettes, or the full cooked works; in summer on a bamboo terrace. Don't miss Derek Jarman's cottage at Dungeness or St Clement's for great food.

Minimum stay: 2 nights at weekends. Children over 6 welcome. Whole house available.

Rooms	3 doubles, 2 twin/doubles: £80–£140. Extra bed £25.
Meals	Pubs/restaurants 5-minute drive.
Closed	Rarely.

Shahriar Mazandi
The Cloudesley,
7 Cloudesley Road,
St Leonards-on-Sea, TN37 6JN
Mobile   +44 (0)7507 000148
Email   s.mazandi@gmail.com
Web   www.thecloudesley.co.uk

🐦 📶 🚂 🍾 ✗

Entry 467   Map 5

Sussex

Swan House

Effortless style drifts through the beamed rooms of this boutiquey B&B in a 1490s bakery, from a roaring inglenook fireplace to an honesty bar in a mock bookcase – all run by relaxed creative hosts Brendan and Lionel. Bedrooms hold surprises: Elizabethan frescoes, an old pulley for bags of flour, doors with trompe-l'œil, seashell mosaics and handmade soaps. Step out into lively Old Hastings, wander down to see fishing boats tucked in for the night or find an antiques bargain. Seagulls herald the new day: pick a morning paper; breakfast like kings on organic croissants and local kippers (dinners also on request). Unique.

Minimum stay: 2 nights at weekends.

Rooms	3 doubles: £120–£150. 1 suite for 4: £115–£145.
Meals	Restaurants 2-minute walk.
Closed	Christmas.

Brendan McDonagh
Swan House,
1 Hill Street,
Hastings, TN34 3HU
Tel   +44 (0)1424 430014
Email   res@swanhousehastings.co.uk
Web   www.swanhousehastings.co.uk

🚶 🐕 📖 📶 🚂 🍾 ✗

Entry 468   Map 5

Warwickshire

The Old Manor House

An attractive 16th-century manor house with peaceful landscaped gardens sweeping down to the river Stour. The beamed double has oak furniture and a big bathroom; the fresh twin rooms (one in a private wing) are simply lovely. There is a large and elegant drawing and dining room for visitors to share, with antiques, contemporary art and an open fire. Jane prepares first-class breakfasts, and in warm weather you can have tea on the terrace: enjoy the pots of tulips in spring, old scented roses in summer, the meadow land beyond. A comfortable, lived-in family house with Stratford and the theatre close by. Guests love it here.

Children over 7 welcome.

Rooms	1 double, 2 twin/doubles, each with separate bath: £90–£110. Singles £50–£65.
Meals	Supper £20. Dinner, 3 courses, from £25. Restaurants nearby.
Closed	Rarely.

Jane Pusey
The Old Manor House,
Halford,
Shipston-on-Stour, CV36 5BT
Tel   +44 (0)1789 740264
Mobile +44 (0)7786 467916
Email   info@oldmanor-halford.fsnet.co.uk
Web   www.oldmanor-halford.co.uk

Entry 469   Map 8

Warwickshire

Stamford Hall

Soft hills and lines of poplars bring you to the high, pretty red-brick Georgian house with a smart hornbeam hedge. James, whose art decorates the walls, and Alice look after you impeccably but without fuss. You have a generous sitting room overlooking the garden, with gleaming furniture, early estate and garden etchings, and pastel blue sofas. Peaceful bedrooms are on the second floor and both have charm: soft wool tartan rugs on comfy beds, calming colours, attractive fabrics, restful outlooks. Wake to delicious breakfast and Alice's full English; walk it off in open countryside or head for Stratford.

Rooms	1 double, 1 twin: £85. Singles £60.
Meals	Pub 1 mile.
Closed	Christmas & occasionally.

James & Alice Kerr
Stamford Hall,
Fosse Way, Ettington,
Stratford-upon-Avon, CV37 7PA
Tel   +44 (0)1789 740239
Email   stamfordhall@gmail.com
Web   www.stamfordhall.co.uk

Entry 470   Map 8

Warwickshire

Grove Farm

Down quiet lanes to the house that Charlie was born in – her young family are the third generation to live here. Bright bedrooms up in the eaves have oak beams, gingham armchairs and comfy beds; small bathrooms, recently revamped. Hop down for homelaid eggs, homemade bread, sausages, bacon and black pudding from down the road – outside when the sun shines, or by the fire in the dining room. Children will love it: dogs, rabbits, hens all happy to have a pat, a swing, log cabin, dens and Flappy the cockerel too. Roses and gangs of cheerful hollyhocks dot the gardens, you can roam the woodland and owls hoot you to sleep. Charming.

Rooms	1 double: £80.
	1 family room for 4: £100–£160.
	Singles £50.
Meals	Pubs/restaurants 1.5 miles.
Closed	Rarely.

Charlie Coldicott
Grove Farm,
Stratford Road, Ettington,
Stratford-upon-Avon, CV37 7NX
Mobile   +44 (0)7774 776682
Email   grovefarmbb@btconnect.com

Entry 471   Map 8

Warwickshire

Cross o' th' Hill Farm

Stratford is a 12-minute walk by footpath across a field, and from the veranda you can see the church where Shakespeare is buried. The farm predates medieval Stratford with later additions to the house in 1860, though it has an earlier Georgian feel. All is chic, spacious and full of light with deco chandeliers, floor to ceiling sash windows, large uncluttered bedrooms and contemporary bathrooms. Wake to bird song, play the baby grand piano, enjoy croquet on the lawn and picnic in the gardens and orchards. Decima grew up here; she and David are charming hosts and passionate about art and architecture.

Minimum stay: 2 nights at weekends.

Rooms	2 doubles; 1 double with separate
	bath/shower: £96.
	Singles from £68.
Meals	Pubs/restaurants 15-minute walk.
Closed	6 December to 10 March.

Decima Noble
Cross o' th' Hill Farm,
Clifford Lane,
Stratford-upon-Avon, CV37 8HP
Tel   +44 (0)1789 204738
Mobile   +44 (0)7973 971067
Email   decimanoble@hotmail.com
Web   www.cross-o-th-hill-farm.com

Entry 472   Map 8

Warwickshire

Sequoia House

A riverside stroll along the old tramway path brings you to the centre of Stratford. Step into the handsome hallway of this impeccable Victorian house to find high ceilings, deep bays, generous landings and a homely sitting room. The Evanses downsized from the hotel they used to run here, and are happy to treat just a few guests: trouser presses (yes!) and piles of towels mingle with fine old furniture in immaculate bedrooms; two have Swan Theatre views. Hotel touches, a lovely warm welcome, Jean's cake on arrival and homemade preserves at breakfast. Park off road – or leave the car at home.

Rooms	4 doubles: £125. Singles £85.
Meals	Pub/restaurant 100 yds.
Closed	Christmas & New Year.

Jean & Philip Evans
Sequoia House,
51 Shipston Road,
Stratford-upon-Avon, CV37 7LN

Tel	+44 (0)1789 268852
Mobile	+44 (0)7833 727914
Email	info@sequoia-house.co.uk
Web	www.sequoia-house.co.uk

Entry 473   Map 8

Warwickshire

Salford Farm House

Beautiful within, handsome without. Thanks to subtle colours, oak beams and lovely old pieces, Jane has achieved a seductive combination of comfort and style. A flagstoned hallway and an old rocking horse, ticking clocks, beeswax, fresh flowers: this house is well-loved. Jane was a ballet dancer, Richard has green fingers and runs a fruit farm and farm shop nearby – you may expect meat and game from the Ragley Estate and delicious fruits in season. Bedrooms have a soft, warm elegance and flat-screen TVs, bathrooms are spotless and welcoming, views are to garden or fields. Wholly delightful.

Rooms	2 twin/doubles: £95. Singles £70.
Meals	Dinner £28. Restaurant 2.5 miles.
Closed	Rarely.

Jane & Richard Beach
Salford Farm House,
Salford Priors,
Evesham, WR11 8XN

Tel	+44 (0)1386 870000
Email	salfordfarmhouse@aol.com
Web	www.salfordfarmhouse.co.uk

Entry 474   Map 8

Warwickshire

Warwickshire

Austons Down

A fine modern country house with splendid views of the rural Vale of Arden. Your hosts are generous and chatty and look after you well. Their comfortable and relaxed family home has an elegant, light-filled sitting room complete with antiques, fabulous marquetry and open fire; bedrooms are fresh and traditional, bathrooms immaculate. Breakfast on homemade bread, compotes, a continental spread or full English. Admire Jacob sheep on the farm, relax in the terraced gardens. Plenty to visit nearby too: Warwick Castle, Stratford, National Trust properties, classic car museums… and the Monarch's Way is on the doorstep.

Shrewley Pools Farm

A charming, eccentric home and fabulous for families, with space to play and animals to see: sheep, bantams and pigs. A fragrant, romantic garden with a blossoming orchard and a fascinating house (1640), all low ceilings, aged floors and steep stairs. Timbered passages lead to large, pretty, sunny bedrooms (all with electric blankets) with leaded windows and polished wooden floors and a family room with everything needed for a baby. In a farmhouse dining room Cathy serves sausages, bacon, and eggs from the farm, can do gluten-free breakfasts and is happy to do teas for children. Buy a day ticket and fish in the lake.

Rooms	1 double, 2 twin/doubles: £90–£160. Singles £60–£140. Extra bed/sofabed available £15–£25 per person per night.
Meals	Supper from £15. Dinner £25–£50. Pubs/restaurants 1 mile.
Closed	Rarely.

Rooms	1 twin: £65. 1 family room for 4 (cot available): £110. Singles £55–£65. Dinner, B&B £65–£83 per person. Extra bed/sofabed available £20–£30 per person per night.
Meals	Packed lunch £5. Child's high tea £5. Pub/restaurant 1.5 miles.
Closed	Christmas.

	Lucy Horner
	Austons Down,
	Saddlebow Lane,
	Claverdon, CV35 8PQ
Tel	+44 (0)1926 842068
Mobile	+44 (0)7767 657352
Email	lmh@austonsdown.com
Web	www.austonsdown.com

	Cathy Dodd
	Shrewley Pools Farm,
	Five Ways Road, Haseley,
	Warwick, CV35 7HB
Tel	+44 (0)1926 484315
Mobile	+44 (0)7818 280681
Email	cathydodd@hotmail.co.uk
Web	www.shrewleypoolsfarm.co.uk

Marston House

A generous feel pervades this lovely family home; Kim's big friendly kitchen is the hub of the house. She and John are easy-going and kind and there's no standing on ceremony. Feel welcomed with tea on arrival, delicious breakfasts, oodles of interesting facts about what to do in the area. The house, with solar electricity, is big and sunny; old rugs cover parquet floors, soft sofas tumble with cushions, sash windows look onto the smart garden packed with birds and borders. Bedrooms are roomy, traditional and supremely comfortable. A special, peaceful place with a big heart, great walks from the door and Silverstone a short hop.

Rooms	1 twin/double with separate bath, 1 twin/double with separate shower: £95–£110. Singles £80.
Meals	Supper, 3 courses from £30. Dinner £35 (min. 4). Pub 5-minute walk.
Closed	Rarely.

Kim & John Mahon
Marston House,
Byfield Road, Priors Marston,
Southam, CV47 7RP
Tel   +44 (0)1327 260297
Mobile +44 (0)7813 831028
Email kim@mahonand.co.uk
Web   www.ivabestbandb.co.uk

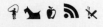

Entry 477   Map 8

Park Farm House

Fronted by a circular drive, the warm red-brick farmhouse is listed and old – it dates from 1655. Linda is friendly and welcoming, a genuine B&B pro, giving you an immaculate guest sitting room filled with pretty family pieces. The bedrooms sport comfortable mattresses, mahogany or brass beds, blankets on request, bathrobes, flowers and magazines; bathrooms are traditional but spotless. A haven of rest from the motorway (morning hum only) this is in the heart of a working farm yet hugely convenient for Birmingham, Warwick, Stratford and Coventry. You may get their own beef at dinner and the vegetables are home-grown.

Rooms	1 double, 1 twin: £79–£82. Singles from £48.
Meals	Dinner, 3 courses, from £25. Supper £19. Pub/restaurant 1.5 miles.
Closed	Rarely.

Linda Grindal
Park Farm House,
Spring Road,
Barnacle, Shilton,
Coventry, CV7 9LG
Tel   +44 (0)2476 612628
Web   www.parkfarmguesthouse.co.uk

Entry 478   Map 8

Wiltshire

Brook House

The minute you pull up in the drive you know you're in for a treat. Henry Lamb lived in this Georgian house, Evelyn Waugh came to visit, now it's the home of delightful Kate who gives you free-range sausages and homemade bread at breakfast. You'll love her farmhouse kitchen with its long cheerful table, the guest sitting room with its open log fire, and the beautiful, luxurious bedrooms, one with a balcony for the view. Gaze on with a glass of wine: the garden with its gorgeous planting and river running through, the visiting ducks, resident hens, the water meadows beyond. The village is charming, Salisbury is close.

Pets by arrangement.

Rooms	1 double, 1 twin/double: £90–£98. Singles £75.
Meals	Pub 3-minute walk.
Closed	Rarely.

Kate Seal
Brook House,
Homington Road, Coombe Bissett,
Salisbury, SP5 4LR
Tel   +44 (0)1722 718242
Mobile   +44 (0)7595 509937
Email   info@brookhousesalisbury.com
Web   www.brookhousesalisbury.com

Entry 479   Map 3

Wiltshire

The Garden Cottage

You'll love the Woodford Valley and this thatched cottage at the edge of the village. It has long views, stacks of character and traditionally decorated rooms: a ground floor twin with roll top bathroom and two cosy doubles upstairs that share a bathroom. Fabrics are flowered, headboards upholstered, mattresses top quality. Or choose to snuggle up by the wood-burner in the charming shepherd's hut and sleep out under the stars. Breakfast in the handsome kitchen, or pretty garden, on good things local and homemade – like Annie's soda bread. Sit out by the roses, honeysuckle and the ancient mulberry; head off to Avebury and Stonehenge.

Cash or cheque accepted. Arrivals before 4pm.

Rooms	2 doubles sharing bathroom (let to same party only); 1 twin with separate bathroom: £90. 1 shepherd's hut for 2 with shower, sink and loo: £90.
Meals	Pub 0.5 miles.
Closed	Occasionally.

Annie Arkwright
The Garden Cottage,
Upper Woodford,
Salisbury, SP4 6PA
Tel   +44 (0)1722 782447
Email   annie747@btinternet.com

Entry 480   Map 3

Wiltshire

The Mill House

In a tranquil village next to the river is a house surrounded by water meadows and wilderness garden. Roses ramble, marsh orchids bloom and butterflies shimmer. This 12-acre labour of love is the creation of ever-charming Diana and her son Michael. Their home, the time-worn 18th-century miller's house, is packed with country clutter – porcelain, foxes' brushes, ancestral photographs above the fire – while bedrooms are quaint, flowery and old-fashioned with firm comfy beds. Breakfasts are served at small tables in the pretty dining room. Diana has lived here for many many years, and has been doing B&B for at least 30 of them!

Children over 6 welcome.

Rooms	3 doubles, 1 family room for 4; 1 twin with separate bath: £100–£140. Singles from £70.
Meals	Pub 5-minute walk.
Closed	Rarely.

Diana Gifford Mead & Michael Mertens
The Mill House,
Berwick St James,
Salisbury, SP3 4TS
Tel +44 (0)1722 790331
Web www.millhouse.org.uk

🔊 ✕

Entry 481   Map 3

Wiltshire

Dowtys

A beautifully converted Victorian dairy farm with fabulous views over the Nadder valley. Peaceful, private, stylish bedrooms, one on the ground floor, have original beams, antiques and supremely comfy Vi-Spring beds; bathrooms are perfect. The sunny guest sitting room has a contemporary feel too, with its wood-burner and sliding doors to the well-tended garden. Enjoy a delicious breakfast in the old milking parlour, now the dining room, or on the terrace, sit beneath the espaliered limes in the lovely garden, dip into the National Trust woods. Footpaths start from the gate and your charming hosts will help you with all your plans.

Rooms	1 double with sitting room; 1 twin with separate bath/shower: £78–£95. 1 double with separate bath/shower (with 2nd triple bedroom only available as a family suite sharing bathroom): £78–£95. Singles from £60.
Meals	Packed lunch from £7. Pub 0.25 miles.
Closed	Rarely.

Di & Willi Verdon-Smith
Dowtys,
Dowtys Lane, Dinton,
Salisbury, SP3 5ES
Tel +44 (0)1722 716886
Email dowtys.bb@gmail.com
Web www.dowtysbedandbreakfast.co.uk

🐟 🐴 🔊 🚂 ✕

Entry 482   Map 3

Wiltshire

The Duck Yard

Independence with your own terrace, entrance and sitting room. Peace too, at the end of the lane; find a charming and colourful cottage garden, a summerhouse and free-ranging ducks and hens. Harriet makes wedding cakes, looks after guests well and cheerfully rustles up fine meals at short notice; breakfasts feature delicious homemade bread. Your carpeted bedroom and aquamarine bathroom are tucked under the eaves; below is the sitting room, cosy with wood-burner, books and old squashy sofas, leading to a sunny terrace. Good for walkers: maps are supplied and you may even borrow a dog.

Rooms	1 twin/double with sitting room: £70–£80. Singles £55.
Meals	Dinner, 3 courses, £25. Packed lunch £7. Pub 2 miles.
Closed	Christmas & New Year.

Harriet & Peter Combes
The Duck Yard,
Sandhills Road, Dinton,
Salisbury, SP3 5ER
Tel   +44 (0)1722 716495
Mobile +44 (0)7729 777436
Email harriet.combes@googlemail.com

Entry 483   Map 3

Wiltshire

Deverill End

Colourful gardens surround this comfortable house, and fantastic views of the Wiltshire downs and Wylye valley, fields of horses and tall steeple stretch as far as the eye can see. Sim and Joy are well-travelled and friendly; their sunny sitting room, warmed by a wood-burner, is full of books, art and African treasures. Comfortable bedrooms are all downstairs: soft colours, posies of flowers, little shower rooms. In the kitchen or dining room is where you feast on eggs and fruits from the garden, homemade jams and home-grown tomatoes in season – they used to grow 300 acres of them in Africa! Bath and Salisbury are an easy hop.

Children over 10 welcome.

Rooms	2 doubles, 1 twin: £75. Singles £60–£75.
Meals	Pub 5-minute walk.
Closed	Rarely.

Joy Greathead
Deverill End,
Deverill Road, Sutton Veny,
Warminster, BA12 7BY
Tel   +44 (0)1985 840356
Email deverillend@gmail.com
Web   www.deverillend.co.uk

Entry 484   Map 3

Wiltshire

Oaklands

A comfortable townhouse, a south-facing garden, two dear dogs and a lovely old Silver Cross pram sitting under the stairs. It was the first house in Warminster to have a bathroom; these have multiplied since and the interiors have had a makeover – no wonder this delightful, spacious 1880s house has been in the family forever. Andrew and Carolyn, relaxed and charming, serve delicious breakfasts in the lovely, light-suffused conservatory at the drawing room end. Bedrooms, desirable and welcoming, overlook churchyard, lawns and trees; find soft colours, cosy bathrooms, family antiques. Restaurants are a stroll.

Rooms	1 double; 1 double, 1 twin/double sharing bath (let to same party only): £70–£85. Singles from £55.
Meals	Pub/restaurant 0.5 miles.
Closed	Christmas & rarely.

Carolyn & Andrew Lewis
Oaklands,
88 Boreham Road,
Warminster, BA12 9JW

Tel	+44 (0)1985 215532
Mobile	+44 (0)7702 587533
Email	apl1944@yahoo.co.uk
Web	www.stayatoaklands.co.uk

Entry 485   Map 3

Wiltshire

Westcourt Farm

A medieval, Grade II* cruck truss hall house... beautifully restored by Rozzie and Jonny and snoozing amid wildflower meadows, hedgerows, ponds and geese. Delightful people, they love to cook and can spoil you rotten. Rooms are well decorated, crisp yet traditional, the country furniture is charming and the architecture fascinating. Bedrooms have comfortable beds and fine linen, bathrooms are spot-on; there's a lovely light drawing room and a barn for meetings and parties too. Encircled by footpaths and fields, Westcourt is the oldest house in a perfect village, two minutes from a rather good pub.

Rooms	1 double, 1 twin: £85. Singles £50.
Meals	Pub/restaurant in village.
Closed	Rarely.

Jonny & Rozzie Buxton
Westcourt Farm,
Shalbourne,
Marlborough, SN8 3QE

Tel	+44 (0)1672 871399
Email	rozzieb@btinternet.com
Web	www.westcourtfarm.com

Entry 486   Map 3

Wiltshire

Rushall Manor

A gorgeous country house – and Caroline is a treat of a host. The dining room shines with glass, antiques and family portraits; a particularly impressive admiral gazes benignly down as you tuck into breakfast: local eggs and sausages, and jams from the orchard. The harmonious sitting room has comfy sofas, books and games; pretty bedrooms have perfect mattresses and linen (and, from one, fantastic views up to Salisbury Plain); bathrooms come with cast-iron baths, scented soaps and lashings of hot water. Stonehenge and Salisbury are nearby, walks are good, and Caroline holds the village fête in her delightful garden.

Rooms	1 twin; 1 double, 1 twin, both with separate bath: £65–£100. Singles £65.
Meals	Dinner £30. Pubs 1 mile.
Closed	Rarely.

	Caroline Larken
	Rushall Manor,
	Rushall,
	Pewsey, SN9 6EG
Tel	+44 (0)1980 630301
Email	bandb@rushallmanor.com
Web	www.rushallmanor.com

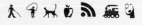

Wiltshire

Honeypot Cottage

Honeypot sits in the middle of a terrace of pretty slate-topped cottages overlooking the Kennet & Avon canal. Nicola has created three floors of artistic, easy living. Bedrooms (up steep stairs) are chic and sunny, the top-floor one with a balcony for stargazing, both with garden posies and views of swans gliding by. The shared bathroom is made for lingering in: music, candles, scented things. Breakfast (homemade bread and jams) is in the gorgeous Aga kitchen, or out in the summerhouse with wonderful views over Pewsey Vale. Nicola is friendly and relaxed and you can have the whole house to yourself if you want – a romantic treat.

Over 17s welcome.

Rooms	2 doubles sharing bath: £100. 1 single (in separate garden studio): £65–£110. First night £100, additional nights £90 per night.
Meals	Pub/café within 1.5 miles.
Closed	Rarely.

	Nicola Sidey
	Honeypot Cottage,
	Honeystreet,
	Pewsey, SN9 5PU
Tel	+44 (0)1672 851692
Email	info@honeystreet.biz
Web	www.honeystreet.biz

Wiltshire

The Limes

Through the electric gates, past the gravelled car park and the pretty, box-edged front garden and you arrive at the middle part of a 1620 house divided into three. The beams, stone mullions and leaded windows are charming, and Ellodie is an exceptional hostess. Immaculate, comfortable bedrooms have pretty curtains and fresh flowers, smart bathrooms have good soaps and thick towels, logs glow in the grate, and breakfasts promise delicious Wiltshire bacon, prunes soaked in orange juice and organic bread. You are on the main road leading out of Melksham – catch the bus to Bath from right outside the door.

Rooms	2 twin/doubles: £88-£95. 1 single: £60-£65.
Meals	Pub 1.5 miles.
Closed	Rarely.

Ellodie van der Wulp
The Limes,
Shurnhold House, Shurnhold,
Melksham, SN12 8DG
Tel   +44 (0)1225 790627
Mobile   +44 (0)7983 205719
Email   eevanderwulp@gmail.com

Entry 489   Map 3

Wiltshire

Bridges Court

You're in the heart of the village with its small shop, friendly pub and the Melvilles' lovely 18th-century farmhouse. They haven't lived here long but it's so homely you'd never tell. Dogs wander, horses whinny, there's a beautiful garden with a Kiftsgate rose and a swimming pool for sunny days. On the second floor, off a corridor filled with paintings, are three florally inspired bedrooms: comfortable, bright and spacious with views to the village green. Breakfast leisurely on all things local at the long table in a dining room filled with silver and china. And there's a pleasant guests' sitting room to relax in.

Rooms	1 double, 1 twin; 1 double with separate bath: £90. Singles £65. Discount for 3 nights or more, excluding Badminton w/e.
Meals	Pub in village.
Closed	Rarely.

Fiona Melville
Bridges Court,
Luckington, SN14 6NT
Tel   +44 (0)1666 840215
Mobile   +44 (0)7711 816839
Email   fionamelville2003@yahoo.co.uk
Web   www.bridgescourt.co.uk

Entry 490   Map 3

Wiltshire

Manor Farm

Farmyard heaven in the Cotswolds. A 17th-century manor farmhouse in 550 arable acres; horses in the paddock, dozing dogs in the yard, tumbling blooms outside the door and a perfectly tended village, with duck pond, a short walk. Beautiful bedrooms are softly lit, with muted colours, plump goose down pillows and the crispest linen. Breakfast in front of the fire is a banquet of delights, tea among the roses is a treat, thanks to charming, welcoming Victoria; she will arrange a table for dinner at the pub too. This is the postcard England of dreams, with Castle Combe, Lacock, grand walking and gardens to visit.

Over 12s welcome.

Rooms	2 doubles (1 with shower & bath, 1 with shower); 1 twin with separate bath: £90-£100. Singles £50.
Meals	Pub 1 mile.
Closed	Rarely.

Victoria Lippiatt-Onslow
Manor Farm,
Alderton, Chippenham, SN14 6NL

Tel	+44 (0)1666 840271
Mobile	+44 (0)7721 415824
Email	victoria.lippiatt@btinternet.com
Web	www.themanorfarm.co.uk

Entry 491   Map 3

Wiltshire

Manor Farm

The road through the sleepy Wiltshire village brings you to a charming Queen Anne house with a *petit château* feel, enfolded by a beautiful walled garden with wildflower meadow, hens and ducks, orchard and groomed lawns. Inside is as lovely. The eclectically furnished drawing room, shared among guests, has a real fire and a lived-in, family feel. Bedrooms are comfortable and elegant with Queen Anne panelling, feather pillows on comfortable beds, good art and garden views. Wake for scrumptious, all-organic breakfasts, served in the dining room or kitchen. Clare is an artist and runs a gallery and courses in the studio.

Children over 4 welcome. Pets welcome by arrangement.

Rooms	2 doubles, 1 twin: £100. 1 single: £65.
Meals	Pub 3-minute walk.
Closed	Christmas & New Year.

Clare Inskip
Manor Farm,
Little Somerford, Malmesbury,
Chippenham, SN15 5JW

Tel	+44 (0)1666 822140
Mobile	+44 (0)7970 892344
Email	clareinskip@gmail.com

Entry 492   Map 3

Wiltshire

Dauntsey Park House

Be awed by history here. Parts of the house – like the grand dining room where you breakfast – date from Elizabethan times; the stunning summer drawing room is Edwardian. Both rooms are yours to use. Emma and her Italian husband have four young children and a flair for matching new with old: a striking glass chandelier sets off the sturdy oak table beneath; a turbine keeps the house in hot water. Up a wide staircase, two wallpapered bedrooms with views to the river are huge and comfortable with a self-indulgent feel (one has a thunderbox loo!). St James the Great church with its 14th-century doom board is in the garden. Lovely.

Rooms	1 double, 1 twin: £120. Singles £90.
Meals	Pubs/restaurants in village.
Closed	1 November to 1 March.

Emma Amati
Dauntsey Park House,
Dauntsey,
Chippenham, SN15 4HT
Tel   +44 (0)1249 721777
Email   enquiries@dauntseyparkhouse.co.uk
Web   www.dauntseyparkhouse.co.uk

Entry 493   Map 3

Wiltshire

Duchy Rag House

Fable has it that King Charles owed his tailor a lot of money so Duchy of Lancaster land was given in payment for the debt… and the house got its name. It's a home with character: antiques, vases of lilies, portraits, a damask sofa by a wood-burner; best boutique rooms have sumptuous beds, robes, TV, WiFi and a tea tray with rather good home-baked flapjacks. Tuck into Wootton Bassett bangers and bacon with homemade bread in the morning; if you need to scoot early Richard and Karen can send you off with a 'breakfast to go' filled roll. Terraces with pots of agapanthus are perfect for a sundowner after a day in the Cotswolds.

Rooms	1 double; 1 double, 1 twin sharing bathroom (let to same party only): £60–£95. As a family suite (1 double, 1 twin sharing bath): £150.
Meals	Pubs/restaurants 1 mile.
Closed	Christmas.

Karen & Richard Alcock
Duchy Rag House,
Leigh,
Swindon, SN6 6RQ
Tel   +44 (0)1666 861136
Email   rickalcock@live.com
Web   www.duchyraghouse.co.uk

Entry 494   Map 3

Wiltshire

Bullocks Horn Cottage

Up a country lane is this hidden-away house which the delightful Legges have turned into a haven of peace. Liz loves fabrics and flowers and mixes them with flair, Colin has painted a mural for the conservatory, bright with plants and wicker sofa. Super bedrooms, both twins, have lovely views; the sitting room has a log fire, fine antiques, big comfy sofas, and the garden is so special it's appeared in magazines. Home-grown organic veg and herbs and local seasonal food make an appearance at dinner which, on balmy nights, you may eat under the arbour, covered in climbing roses and jasmine.

Children over 10 welcome.

Rooms	1 twin; 1 twin/double with separate shower: £95. Singles £62.50.
Meals	Dinner £25-£30. BYO. Pub 1.5 miles.
Closed	Christmas.

Colin & Liz Legge
Bullocks Horn Cottage,
Charlton,
Malmesbury, SN16 9DZ
Tel   +44 (0)1666 577600
Email   bullockshorn@clara.co.uk
Web   www.bullockshorn.co.uk

Entry 495   Map 3

Wiltshire

Carriers Farm

The stylishly converted dairies behind the main house are surrounded by acres of peaceful, organic pasture. Old milk churns act as planters, and you step in to delightful bedrooms 'Hare', 'Pheasant' or 'Fox'. Find restful whites with oak floors, pretty pine pieces, feather pillows and tip-top linen. Wake for delicious breakfast choices served in the sunny garden room: smoked salmon and cream cheese, homemade breads and jams, local ham and sausages, eggs from the hens. Fiona is friendly and helpful, and it's a treat to stay. Westonbirt Arboretum and Highgrove are close, and you can walk over the fields to supper at the pub.

Rooms	3 doubles: £85-£110. Singles £68.
Meals	Pubs within walking distance.
Closed	Rarely.

Fiona Butterfield
Carriers Farm,
Luckington Road, Sherston,
Malmesbury, SN16 0QA
Tel   +44 (0)1666 841445
Email   carriersfarm@btinternet.com
Web   www.carriersfarm.co.uk

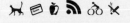

Entry 496   Map 3

Wiltshire

The Angel

Walk straight into the lively tearooms to be greeted by Tara and a counter groaning with homemade cakes. A lovely place to flop in fashionable armchairs, and sip a cup of tea or an Angel special cinnamon latte. Smartly done, from top to toe, find French-chic bedrooms (upstairs) with a tuck box filled with healthy nibbles, well-dressed big beds, gift bottles set on top of thick white towels. Owners Paul and Caroline's village smallholding provides bacon and sausages from rare breed pigs and eggs from the hens – delicious breakfasts and lunches are served in the tearooms. Head off into the pretty Cotswolds – the Arboretum and High Grove are close.

Rooms	3 doubles, 1 twin: £90–£120.
Meals	Pub 100 yds.
Closed	Rarely.

Tara Punter
The Angel,
High Street, Sherston,
Malmesbury, SN16 0LH
Tel   +44 (0)1666 840039
Email   tara@sherstonangel.co.uk
Web   www.sherstonangel.co.uk

Entry 497   Map 3

Worcestershire

South House Alpacas

If it's the good life you're after then look no further. This handsome Georgian house looks out over not only a beautiful walled garden complete with ancient mulberry tree but rows of neat vegetables, trellised vines and an orchard with a growing herd of alpacas. Guests stay on the first floor of the old coach house and the softly carpeted, beamed rooms are light and spacious with wooden furniture and gorgeous beds; shower with organic soap whilst gazing out on your Andean neighbours! Your charming hosts are passionate about their animals and their little slice of England – this is the most civilised self-sufficiency project imaginable.

Rooms	2 doubles: £110–£120.
Meals	Supper £15.
	Dinner, 2–3 courses, £25–£35.
	Pub 1 mile.
Closed	Rarely.

Amanda Dartnell
South House Alpacas,
Main Street, South Littleton,
Evesham, WR11 8TJ
Tel   +44 (0)1386 830848
Email   amandadartnell@icloud.com
Web   www.southhouse.co.uk

Entry 498   Map 8

Worcestershire

The Birches

Thoughtful Katharine is attentive; Edward puts you at ease humming a jolly tune. Come and go as you please from this self-contained annexe, spotless and contemporary. French windows lead to a pretty terrace, then to a charming garden opening to fields and views of the Malverns. Though the house is easily accessible, the tranquillity is sublime; plenty of spots to sit and ponder the view back to the timber-framed house. Hens pottering on the lawn lay eggs for breakfast, served – in your room – with local bacon and sausages, and bread from Ledbury's baker. Wander further for abundant leafy walks and lovely Regency Malvern.

Rooms	Annexe - 1 double: £80. Singles £60.
Meals	Pub/restaurant 0.3 miles.
Closed	Rarely.

Katharine Litchfield
The Birches,
Birts Street, Birtsmorton,
Malvern, WR13 6AW
Tel   +44 (0)1684 833821
Mobile   +44 (0)7875 458441
Email   katharine-thebirches@hotmail.co.uk
Web   www.the-birchesbedandbreakfast.co.uk

Entry 499   Map 8

Worcestershire

Old Country Farm & The Lighthouse

Ella's passion for this tranquil place – and conservation of its wildlife – is infectious. She's keen on home-grown and local food too so breakfast is delicious. Dating from the 1400s, the farm is a delightful rambling medley: russet stone and colour-washed brick, huge convivial round table by the Aga, rugs on polished floors. The sitting room has wood-burner, piano and books, and you sleep soundly in pretty, cottagey bedrooms: lovely linen, garden flowers. In winter you stay in The Lighthouse, down the lane: an inspired green-oak retreat with soaring beams, snug library, comfy downstairs bedrooms and roses in the garden. Magical.

Rooms	1 double; 1 double with separate bath; 1 double with separate shower: £65–£90. Singles £35–£55.
Meals	Pubs/restaurants 3 miles.
Closed	Rarely.

Ella Grace Quincy
Old Country Farm & The Lighthouse,
Mathon,
Malvern, WR13 5PS
Tel   +44 (0)1886 880867
Email   ella@oldcountryhouse.co.uk
Web   www.oldcountryhouse.co.uk

Entry 500   Map 8

Worcestershire

Huntlands Farm

Deep in the rural shires Lucy and Stephen run delightful B&B on a working farm (sheep, cattle, pigs). They've lovingly coaxed this 15th-century house back to life: huge rooms, two with four-posters, are deeply comfortable with patterned rugs on wide floorboards, reclaimed wardrobes and views over the orchard or farm. You get roll top tubs to wallow in, fluffy towels and local soaps. Breakfast in the convivial dining room on eggs from the hens, sausages from the pigs and homemade preserves. There's dinner too, roasts and stews or traditional Caribbean fare. The Malvern showground is nearby.

Minimum stay: 2 nights. Children over 10 welcome.

Rooms	2 doubles, 1 twin/double: £80–£100. 1 suite for 2: £95–£100. 1 family room for 4 with sofabed & separate bathroom (price for 2 adults & 2 children under 10): £70–£85.
Meals	Dinner, 3 courses, £24.50. Pubs/restaurants 0.5 miles.
Closed	Rarely.

Lucy Brodie
Huntlands Farm,
Gaines Road, Whitbourne,
Worcester, WR6 5RD

Tel	+44 (0)1886 821955
Mobile	+44 (0)7828 286360
Email	lucy@huntlandsfarm.co.uk
Web	www.huntlandsfarm.co.uk

Entry 501   Map 8

Yorkshire

Broomhead

High in the ancient county of Hallamshire, amid curlews and skylarks and 6,000 acres of National Park, is the renovated stable block of Broomhead Hall. This warm, light, contemporary conversion is home to a lovely young family, passionate about the land and their responsibility for it. After a day of trout fishing or picnicking beside Ewden Beck, bliss to come home to cosy soothing bedrooms with beds heaped with pillows and breathtaking views. A fire-warmed snug rammed with books, a huge oil painting of the grouse moor up high, eggs from their hens and home-baked bread at breakfast: it's fabulous.

Rooms	2 twin/doubles: £100. Singles £80.
Meals	Packed lunch £8. Pub/restaurant 2.5 miles.
Closed	Rarely.

Catherine Rimington Wilson
Broomhead,
Bolsterstone,
Sheffield, S36 4ZA

Tel	+44 (0)1142 882161
Mobile	+44 (0)7706 483346
Email	catherine_heaton@yahoo.co.uk
Web	www.broomheadestate.co.uk

Entry 502   Map 12

Yorkshire

Sunnybank

A Victorian gentleman's residence just a short walk up the hill from the centre of bustling *Last of the Summer Wine* Holmfirth, still with its working Picturedrome cinema (touring bands too), arts and folk festivals, restaurants and shops. Attentive hosts look after you when the Whites are away. Peaceful bedrooms have a mix of contemporary, Art Nouveau and Art Deco pieces, caramel cream velvets and silks, spoiling bathrooms and lovely valley or garden views. A full choice Yorkshire breakfast will set you up for a lazy stroll round the charming gardens, or a brisk yomp through rural bliss.

Minimum stay: 2 nights at weekends. Over 12s welcome.

Rooms	2 doubles, 1 twin/double (extra single bed): £68–£115. Singles £58–£105.
Meals	Afternoon tea, with sandwiches, on request. Packed lunch £12. Pubs/restaurants 500 yds.
Closed	Rarely.

Mike & Sue Ardley
Sunnybank,
78 Upperthong Lane,
Holmfirth, HD9 3BQ
Tel   +44 (0)1484 684065
Email   info@sunnybankguesthouse.co.uk
Web   www.sunnybankguesthouse.co.uk

Entry 503   Map 12

Yorkshire

Thurst House Farm

This solid Pennine farmhouse, its stone mullion windows denoting 17th-century origins, is English to the core. Your warm, gracious hosts give guests a cosy and carpeted sitting room with an open fire in winter; bedrooms are equally generous, with inviting brass beds, lovely antique linen and fresh flowers. Outside: clucking hens, two friendly sheep and a hammock in a garden with beautiful views. Tuck into homemade bread, marmalade and jams at breakfast, and good traditional English dinners, too – just the thing for walkers who've trekked the Calderdale or the Pennine Way.

Children over 8 welcome.

Rooms	1 double, 1 family room for 4: £80. Singles by arrangement.
Meals	Dinner, 4 courses, £25. BYO. Packed lunch £5. Restaurants within 0.5 miles.
Closed	Christmas & New Year.

David & Judith Marriott
Thurst House Farm,
Soyland, Ripponden,
Sowerby Bridge, HX6 4NN
Tel   +44 (0)1422 822820
Mobile   +44 (0)7759 619043
Email   judith@thursthousefarm.co.uk
Web   www.thursthousefarm.co.uk

Entry 504   Map 12

Yorkshire

Ponden House

Bump your way up the farm track to Brenda's sturdy house, high on the Pennine Way. The spring water makes wonderful tea, the ginger scones are delicious and the house hums with interest and artistic touches. Comfy sofas are jollied up with throws, there are homespun rugs and hangings, paintings, plants and a piano. Feed the hens, plonk your boots by the Aga, chat with your lovely hostess as she turns out fab home cooking; food is a passion. Bedrooms are exuberant, comfortable and cosy, it's great for walkers and there's a hot tub under the stars (bookable by groups in advance). Good value with a relaxed, homely feel.

Rooms	2 doubles; 1 twin with separate bath (occasionally sharing bathroom with family): £80–£85. Singles £50.
Meals	Dinner, 3 courses, £18. BYO. Packed lunch £6. Pub/restaurant 1 mile.
Closed	Rarely.

Brenda Taylor
Ponden House,
Stanbury,
Haworth, BD22 0HR
Tel   +44 (0)1535 644154
Email brenda.taylor@pondenhouse.co.uk
Web   www.pondenhouse.co.uk

Entry 505   Map 12

Yorkshire

Ponden Hall

A house brimming with atmosphere and said to be the inspiration for *Wuthering Heights*. Julie's knowledge of its history is impressive and she offers tours of her fascinating home. Arrive for tea and home-baked cake and soak up the mullion windows, huge flagstones, period pieces and original paintings. Bedrooms have just the right balance of luxury and individuality: an amazing box bed, rocking horse, raftered ceilings – and log stoves in two. A full Yorkshire breakfast is served in the magnificent main hall. Walk the Pennine Way, hop on a steam train at Keighley; Haworth is close too – for all things Brontë and independent shops.

Rooms	2 doubles: £85–£175. 1 family room for 4: £145.
Meals	Pubs/restaurants 10-minute walk.
Closed	24–30 December.

Julie Akhurst
Ponden Hall,
Ponden Lane, Stanbury, Haworth, Keighley, BD22 0HR
Tel   +44 (0)1535 648608
Email stay@ponden.force9.co.uk
Web   www.ponden-hall.co.uk

Entry 506   Map 12

Yorkshire

Lane House

Pam and art restorer Richard are chatty and friendly – love having guests, and happy to advise on trips. Their converted barn has an artistic vibe throughout. The big, attractive open-plan living space has a galleried landing above; airy bedrooms have soaring beams, striking light fittings, colourful throws. Pam likes to cook: tuck in to eggs from the hens, homemade granola, breads and jams; delicious, perhaps Lebanese or Moroccan, dishes for dinner too. The 50 acres are yours to wander: farmland, woods, a beck – and the four-mile Heritage Trail to Bentham. The neighbour's house is a work in progress – and mind the bumpy lane when you go!

Minimum stay: 2 nights at weekends.

Rooms	2 doubles: £85–£95.
	Singles £60.
	Dinner, B&B £60 per person.
	Extra bed/sofabed available £20 per person per night.
Meals	Dinner £15. BYO.
	Pubs/restaurants 0.5 miles.
Closed	Christmas.

	Pam Zahler
	Lane House,
	Fowgill, High Bentham,
	Lancaster, LA2 7AH
Tel	+44 (0)15242 61998
Email	pamzahler@hotmail.com
Web	www.lanehouseandcottage.co.uk

Entry 507   Map 12

Yorkshire

Ellerbeck House

Walk from the door of this beautifully restored country house, or head west to the Lakes, east to the Dales, north to Scotland. Period rooms display exquisite antiques and Harriet's artistic touch: sofas and curtains in dark pink and cream, Persian rugs on shiny oak floors, marble fireplaces, stained glass in the stairwell, huge sash windows overlooking the lawn. One window holds the breakfast table – full Cumbrian, at flexible times. Outside, a courtyard for sitting out with the birds and the breeze. It's all so pretty, as is this bucolic – yet accessible – spot near Kirkby Lonsdale, Settle, and Kendal of Mint Cake fame.

Rooms	1 double: £90.
	Singles £45–£55.
Meals	Pubs/restaurants 2 miles.
Closed	Rarely.

	Harriet Sharp
	Ellerbeck House,
	Westhouse, Ingleton,
	Carnforth, LA6 3NH
Tel	+44 (0)15242 41872
Email	harrietnsharp@gmail.com
Web	www.ellerbeckhouse.co.uk

Entry 508   Map 12

Yorkshire

Low Mill

Off the village green this handsome historic mill in the Dales keeps many of its original features. The huge beamed guest sitting room has a roaring fire, and the old waterwheel is working! Friendly relaxed Neil and Jane have restored their home, then filled it with interesting art, quirky sculpture, flowers and vintage gems. Bedrooms have tip-top linen and luxurious throws; bathrooms are fabulous. Eat well at separate tables on all things local and home-grown: bacon, pancakes, homemade bread; and for dinner, perhaps Yorkshire ham or herby lamb. The pretty riverside garden is perfect for chilling with a glass of wine.

Children over 11 welcome.

Rooms	2 doubles: £105–£170.
	1 suite for 2: £90–£160
	Singles £78–£170.
Meals	Dinner, 2-3 courses, £20–£25.
	Pubs 5-minute drive.
Closed	Rarely.

	Neil McNair
	Low Mill,
	Bainbridge,
	Leyburn, DL8 3EF
Tel	+44 (0)1969 650553
Email	lowmillguesthouse@gmail.com
Web	www.lowmillguesthouse.co.uk

Yorkshire

Stow House

Past ancient stone walls and fields of lambs you reach sleepy Aysgarth and this dignified rectory. Step inside to find – Shoreditch pizzazz! Sarah and Phil have swapped the world of London advertising for a dream house in the Dales; she does cocktails, he does breakfasts and their take on Victoriana is inspiring. Floors, banisters and sash windows have been restored, stairs carpeted in plush red, sofas covered in zinging velvet. Bathrooms are wow, bedrooms are soothing and the paper mâché hare's head above the bar says it all. A stroll down the hill are the Aysgarth Falls, beloved of Ruskin, Wordsworth and Turner.

Minimum stay: 2 nights at weekends.

Rooms	6 doubles, 1 family room for 3:
	£110–£175.
	Extra bed/sofabed available
	£10–£20 per person per night.
Meals	Pubs/restaurants 5-minute walk.
Closed	January & occasionally.

	Sarah & Phil Bucknall
	Stow House,
	Aysgarth,
	Leyburn, DL8 3SR
Tel	+44 (0)1969 663635
Email	info@stowhouse.co.uk
Web	www.stowhouse.co.uk

Yorkshire

The Grange

Through glorious Dales to the pretty village green, where you have a wing of this attractive, old stone house to yourselves. Step into an airy space with original oak beams, comfy sofa, Persian rug and books. Antique and contemporary pieces blend, the bed is clad in pure cotton, the simple shower room has fluffy towels, and there's a kitchen area for rustling up snacks. Your hosts are delightful: Sam has his cabinet making business in the outbuildings; Georgina (professional cook) brings over locally sourced breakfasts and hearty suppers: eggs from the hens, homemade marmalade, smoked salmon… lasagne, crumbles. A friendly place.

Minimum stay: 2 nights at weekends.

Rooms	1 double with sitting & kitchen area: £80. Singles £70. Dinner, B&B £110 per person.
Meals	Dinner, 2-3 courses, £30-£40. Light supper £15. Restaurant 75 yds.
Closed	Rarely.

Georgina Anderson
The Grange,
East Witton, Leyburn, DL8 4SL
Mobile +44 (0)7957 144467
Email georgina@thegrangebedand breakfast.co.uk
Web www.thegrangebedandbreakfast.co.uk

Entry 511   Map 12

Yorkshire

Manor House

It's the handsomest house in the village. Annie – warm, intelligent, fun – invites you in to spacious interiors elegantly painted, artfully cluttered. Tall shuttered windows and a big open fire, candles in sconces and heaps of flowers, wool carpets and charming fabrics: a genuinely relaxing family home. Bedrooms are a treat, one with green views on two sides and a bathroom with a French country feel; fittings are vintage but spotless. Breakfast is good too with eggs from the hens and local chipolatas and bacon. Stride the Dales, discover Georgian Richmond, a hop away; return to a delicious simple supper, with veg from the garden.

Rooms	1 double; 1 twin/double with separate bath: £95. Singles £80.
Meals	Supper, 2 courses, £25. BYO. Pubs 1 mile.
Closed	Christmas.

Annabel Burchnall
Manor House,
Middle Street,
Gayles,
Richmond, DL11 7JF
Tel +44 (0)1833 621578
Email annieburchnall@hotmail.com

Entry 512   Map 12

Yorkshire

Lovesome Hill Farm

Who could resist home-reared lamb followed by apple crumble cake? This is a working farm and the Pearsons the warmest people imaginable; even in lambing season mayhem they greet you with delicious homemade biscuits and Yorkshire tea. Their farmhouse is cosy with chequered tablecloths, comfy bedrooms (four in the old granary, one in the cottage) with garden and hill views, and a Victorian-style sitting room. Wake to award-winning breakfasts: their own bacon and sausages, home-laid eggs and homemade bread and jams. Easy access to A167 and brilliantly placed for walking the Moors and Dales; come for lambing breaks too, hop in the hot tub afterwards!

Rooms	1 double, 1 twin: £80–£90. 1 family room for 4: £110. 1 single: £42–£50. Gate Cottage - 1 double: £80–£90.
Meals	Dinner, 2 courses, £18–£25. BYO. Packed lunch £5. Pub 4 miles.
Closed	Rarely.

	John & Mary Pearson Lovesome Hill Farm, Lovesome Hill, Northallerton, DL6 2PB
Tel	+44 (0)1609 772311
Email	lovesomehillfarm@btinternet.com
Web	www.lovesomehillfarm.co.uk

Entry 513   Map 12

Yorkshire

Low Sutton

Judi and Steve care tremendously for their guests, and are passionate about Yorkshire. Their smallholding is a gem of sustainability and peace. Wood fires in the vast dining/sitting room and cosy snug burn fuel from their own copse; insulation and underfloor heating keep the homely rooms comfy; one of the sparkling bathrooms is solar-heated; undyed wool yarn is produced from the Ryeland sheep. There are dogs, chickens and six acres to explore; your horse is welcome too. Judi is a keen cook: expect good Aga dinners with veg from the garden, local produce and homemade jams for breakfast. Castles, markets, gardens – all in easy reach.

Rooms	2 doubles: £85. Singles £50.
Meals	Packed lunch £5. Dinner £25. Pub/restaurant 1.5 miles.
Closed	Rarely.

	Judi Smith Low Sutton, Masham, Ripon, HG4 4PB
Tel	+44 (0)1765 688565
Mobile	+44 (0)7821 600521
Email	info@lowsutton.co.uk
Web	www.lowsutton.co.uk

Entry 514   Map 12

Yorkshire

Firs Farm

The landscape is rural and rolling, the lanes are narrow and quiet, and Healey is pretty-as-a-picture: mellow York stone, smart gardens and immaculate paintwork on every house. Richard and Sarah, relaxed and genial, offer homemade cakes and coffee when you arrive and the cosy feel of their home makes you feel instantly at ease. Enjoy a sitting room with an open fire and fabulous fabrics, fresh and cottagey bedrooms with spotted upholstered windows seats, and vases of flowers in every corner. There are great views from the lovely walled garden, acres to roam, wonderful walking, and tip-top towns to visit all around.

Children over 10 welcome.

Rooms	1 double; 1 twin/double with separate bath/shower: £75–£90. Singles £65.
Meals	Packed lunch £7. Pubs/restaurants 1 mile.
Closed	Christmas & New Year.

	Richard & Sarah Townsend
	Firs Farm,
	Healey,
	Ripon, HG4 4LH
Tel	+44 (0)1765 688910
Email	sarah@firsfarmbandb.co.uk
Web	www.firsfarmbandb.co.uk

Entry 515   Map 12

Yorkshire

Laverton Hall

The hall is a beauty, even on a dull day, and the village is a dream. Half an hour from Harrogate find space, beauty, history (it's 400 years old), three walled gardens and comfort in great measure: beloved antiques, a rocking horse in the hall, feather pillows, thick white towels, and sumptuous breakfasts followed by delightful Rachel's Cordon Bleu dinner – delicious rack of lamb a favourite. The sunny guest sitting room is elegant and charming, the cream and white twin and the snug little single have long views to the river. The area is rich with abbeys and great houses, and then there are the glorious Dales to be explored.

Rooms	1 twin/double: £95. 1 single: £60.
Meals	Supper, 3 courses, £30. Pubs/restaurants 2 miles.
Closed	Christmas.

	Rachel Wilson
	Laverton Hall,
	Laverton, Ripon, HG4 3SX
Tel	+44 (0)1765 650274
Mobile	+44 (0)7711 086385
Email	rachel.k.wilson@hotmail.co.uk
Web	www.lavertonhall.co.uk

Entry 516   Map 12

Yorkshire

Mallard Grange

Perfect farmhouse B&B. Hens, cats, sheepdogs wander the garden, an ancient apple tree leans against the wall, guests unwind and feel part of the family. Enter the rambling, deep-shuttered 16th-century farmhouse, cosy with well-loved family pieces, and feel at peace with the world. Breakfast is generous – homemade muffins, poached pears with cinnamon, a sizzling full Monty. A winding steep stair leads to big, friendly bedrooms, two cheerful others await in the converted 18th-century smithy, and Maggie's enthusiasm for this glorious area is as genuine as her love of doing B&B. It's a gem!

Over 12s welcome.

Rooms	2 twin/doubles: £85–£110. Old Blacksmith's Shop & Carthouse - 2 twin/doubles on ground floor: £85–£110. Singles £80.
Meals	Pubs/restaurants 10-minute drive.
Closed	Christmas & New Year.

	Maggie Johnson Mallard Grange, Aldfield, Ripon, HG4 3BE
Tel	+44 (0)1765 620242
Mobile	+44 (0)7720 295918
Email	maggie@mallardgrange.co.uk
Web	www.mallardgrange.co.uk

Entry 517   Map 12

Yorkshire

Lawrence House

In an immaculate estate village, a classically elegant house run with faultless precision by John and Harriet – former wine importer and interior decorator. The house is listed and Georgian, the garden is formal, flagged and herbaceous, the position – by the back gate to Fountains Abbey and Studley Royal – is glorious. Enjoy linen sofas, books, heirlooms and log fire in the drawing room just for guests, and the promise of a very good dinner. Bedrooms and bathrooms are in a private wing, light, well-proportioned, full of special touches, with the largest at the front.

Rooms	1 twin/double, 1 twin: £120. Singles £80.
Meals	Dinner £30. Pub/restaurant 1 mile.
Closed	Christmas & New Year.

	John & Harriet Highley Lawrence House, Studley Roger, Ripon, HG4 3AY
Tel	+44 (0)1765 600947
Email	john@lawrence-house.co.uk
Web	www.lawrence-house.co.uk

Entry 518   Map 12

Yorkshire

Cold Cotes

Sue and Mark give you relaxation and a dollop of contemporary chic in their 1890s farmhouse on the edge of the Yorkshire Dales. There's a snug with a wood-burner and a sitting room with squashy sofas, open fire and books. Bedrooms have sitting areas and roomy bathrooms; those in the barn are just as comfortable. Outside find a series of dazzling 'zones' with a stone-flagged terrace, miniature geraniums, euphorbias and pots of blue agapanthus. In front is a red bed made up of oriental poppies, dahlias, tulips and penstemon, then stone steps down to a formal garden, filled with birdsong, for quiet contemplation. A peaceful place to stay.

Rooms	2 doubles, 1 twin/double: £85.
	3 suites for 2: £99–£110.
Meals	Grazing platters £9.95; desserts £4.95.
	Pub/restaurant 2.5 miles.
Closed	Rarely.

Sue Bailey
Cold Cotes,
Felliscliffe,
Harrogate, HG3 2LW

Tel	+44 (0)1423 770937
Mobile	+44 (0)7970 713334
Email	info@coldcotes.com
Web	www.coldcotes.com

Entry 519   Map 12

Yorkshire

No 1 Harrogate

In a quiet corner in the heart of town, this handsome Victorian house is a treat — and Rachel is as elegant and eclectic as her home. The airy rooms are full of original art, antiques and fascinating finds from around the world; the sitting room is inviting with white linen sofas, fabulous wood fireplace, books and flowers in jugs. You snooze in cosily luxurious bedrooms — comfy beds, pretty fabrics, a colourful kilim — and Rachel serves a delicious breakfast with fantastic fresh fruit salad, hearty eggs, smoked salmon, excellent coffee. Harrogate keeps you busy: Georgian architecture, amazing Turkish baths, quirky shops, cafés galore.

Whole house self-catering option available. Station 10 minutes away.

Rooms	2 doubles; 1 twin sharing bathroom
	with single: £65–£80.
	1 single: £35–£45.
Meals	Continental breakfast.
	Pubs/restaurants 5-minute walk.
Closed	Rarely.

Rachel Grimmer
No 1 Harrogate,
1 Cambridge Terrace,
Harrogate, HG1 1PN

Mobile	+44 (0)7932 621261
Email	mail@rachelgrimmer.com
Web	www.no1harrogate.com

Entry 520   Map 12

Yorkshire

Cundall Lodge Farm

Ancient chestnuts, crunchy drive, sheep grazing, hens free-ranging. This four-square Georgian farmhouse could be straight out of Central Casting. Smart, traditional rooms have damask sofas, comfy armchairs, bright wallpapers and views to Sutton Bank's White Horse or the river Swale – and tea and oven-fresh cakes welcome you. Spotless bedrooms are inviting: pretty fabrics, antiques, flowers, Roberts radios. This is a working farm and the breakfast table groans with eggs from the hens, homemade jams and local bacon. The garden and river walks guarantee peace, and David and Caroline are generous and delightful.

Over 14s welcome.

Rooms	2 doubles, 1 twin/double: £80–£95.
Meals	Packed lunch £7.
	Pubs/restaurants 2 miles.
Closed	Christmas & January.

Caroline Barker
Cundall Lodge Farm,
Cundall, York, YO61 2RN

Tel	+44 (0)1423 360203
Mobile	+44 (0)7773 494260
Email	enquiries@cundall-lodgefarm.co.uk
Web	www.cundall-lodgefarm.co.uk

Entry 521   Map 12

Yorkshire

Carlton House

Quietly tucked into a corner of the sedate green, a short stride from the pub, lies a stylishly renovated 18th-century farmhouse. The old wash house, tractor shed and stable have become airy, chic, characterful rooms with beams and fabulous bathrooms. In summer, pull up a chair in a pretty yard with hanging baskets or find a tranquil spot in the charmingly secret garden. The dining room with open fire is a delight, so linger over a breakfast of delicious local produce, then set off for market towns, dales and moors. There's a big-hearted family feel here – Denise's oat and raisin crunchies and soda bread are to die for! Lovely.

Rooms	Outbuildings - 2 doubles,
	1 twin/double: £68–£85.
	Singles £55.
Meals	Pub/restaurant 2-minute walk.
Closed	Rarely.

Denise & David Mason
Carlton House,
Sandhutton,
Thirsk, YO7 4RW

Tel	+44 (0)1845 587381
Email	info@carltonbarns.co.uk
Web	www.carltonbarns.co.uk

Entry 522   Map 12

Yorkshire

The Old Rectory

Once the residence of the Bishops of Whitby this elegant rectory has a comfortable lived-in air. Both Turner and Ruskin stayed here and probably enjoyed as much good conversation and comfort as you will. Bedrooms are pretty, traditional and with grand views; the drawing room is classic country house with a fine Venetian window and enticing window-seat, gleaming antiques and flowers. The graceful, deep pink dining room looks over a large garden of ancient redwood and walnut trees. Caroline and Tim are charming, breakfasts are generous; wander at will to find an orchard, tennis court and croquet lawn.

Children over 3 welcome.

Rooms	1 double with separate bath & dressing room, 1 twin/double with separate bath & shower: £70–£74. Singles from £45.
Meals	Pub/restaurant opposite.
Closed	Rarely.

Tim & Caroline O'Connor–Fenton
The Old Rectory,
South Kilvington, Thirsk, YO7 2NL

Tel	+44 (0)1845 526153
Mobile	+44 (0)7981 329764
Email	ocfenton@talktalk.net
Web	www.oldrectorythirsk.co.uk

Entry 523 Map 12

Yorkshire

Shallowdale House

Phillip and Anton have a true affection for their guests so you will be treated royally. Sumptuous bedrooms dazzle in yellows, blues and limes, acres of curtains frame wide views over the Howardian Hills, bathrooms are immaculate. You breakfast on the absolute best: fresh fruit compotes, dry-cured bacon, homemade bread. Admire the amazing garden, then walk off in any direction straight from the house. Return to a cosily elegant drawing room with a fire in winter, and an enticing library. Dinner is a real treat – coffee and chocolates before you crawl up to bed? Bliss.

Minimum stay: 2 nights at weekends. Over 12s welcome.

Rooms	2 twin/doubles; 1 double with separate bath/shower: £115–£150. Singles £95–£120.
Meals	Dinner, 4 courses, £39.50. Pub 0.5 miles.
Closed	Christmas & New Year.

Anton van der Horst & Phillip Gill
Shallowdale House,
West End,
Ampleforth, YO62 4DY

Tel	+44 (0)1439 788325
Email	stay@shallowdalehouse.co.uk
Web	www.shallowdalehouse.co.uk

Entry 524 Map 12

Yorkshire

Corner Farm

Tea and home-baked cakes on arrival: you get a lovely welcome here! This peaceful farmhouse is so well insulated it's snug and warm even on the coldest day. With York so close and stunning estates nearby, this is a cosy nest from which to explore the area – or just the village pub. Bathrooms are swish and bedrooms are light, fresh and comfortable: cast-iron beds, fine sheets, cute satin cushions. Much-loved Dexters graze on six acres – Tim and Sharon are aiming for self-sufficiency – and apples from the orchard are pressed for your breakfast, flexibly served and with lots of choice, including home-laid eggs.

Rooms	1 double, 1 twin: £80–£95.
	Singles £55–£65.
Meals	Packed lunch £4. Pub 100 yds.
Closed	Rarely.

Sharon Stevens
Corner Farm,
Low Catton, York, YO41 1EA
Tel   +44 (0)1759 373911
Mobile   +44 (0)7711 440796
Email   cornerfarmyork@gmail.com
Web   www.cornerfarmyork.co.uk

Entry 525   Map 13

Yorkshire

The Mount House

A dollop of stylish fun in the rolling Howardian Hills (an AONB), Nick and Kathryn's redesigned village house is light, airy and filled with gorgeous things – good antiques, heaps of photographs, splashy modern art and flowers. The ground-floor twin with white cast-iron beds has its own cosy book-filled sitting room; the sunny upstairs double has views across roof tops to open countryside. Continental breakfasts are a treat, in the garden if it's fine, and Kathryn – an excellent cook – will spoil you at supper too if you wish. Discover Castle Howard, Nunnington Hall, old market towns and great walking on the doorstep; only 20 minutes from York too.

Minimum stay: 2 nights at weekends & in high season.

Rooms	1 double, 1 twin with sitting room;
	1 double with separate bath: £90–£140.
	Singles £75–£100.
Meals	Continental breakfast.
	Dinner, 3-4 courses, £30–£40. BYO.
	Pub/restaurant 200 yds.
Closed	Rarely.

Kathryn Hill
The Mount House,
Terrington, York, YO60 6QB
Tel   +44 (0)1653 648206
Mobile   +44 (0)7780 536937
Email   mount.house@clayfox.co.uk
Web   www.howardianhillsbandb.co.uk

Entry 526   Map 13

Yorkshire

Hunters Hill

The moors lie behind this elegant farmhouse, and it's just yards from the National Park. Farmland, woods and great views... the position is marvellous and you can walk from the door. The house is full of light and flowers; bedrooms are pretty but not overly grand, and look onto valley or church. The lovely lived-in drawing room displays comfortable old sofas, paintings and fine furniture; rich colours, hunting prints and candles at dinner create a warm and cosy feel. The family has poured affection and life into this interesting house and the result is a home that's charming and remarkably easy to relax in... Wonderful.

Rooms	1 double; 1 twin/double with separate bathroom: £90-£110. Singles £55.
Meals	Dinner, 3 courses, £35. Pub/restaurant 10-minute walk.
Closed	Rarely.

Jane Otter
Hunters Hill,
Sinnington,
York, YO62 6SF
Tel   +44 (0)1751 431196
Email   ejaneotter@gmail.com

Entry 527   Map 13

Yorkshire

Helmsley Garden Cottage & Railway Carriage

Your own stone cottage with hydrangeas at the door – perfect! Tucked behind Louise's house and antique shop, it looks on to a sunny patch of garden and is filled with gorgeous furniture, old beams and warm charm. The dining room is cosy with comfy armchairs, tea-making things and homemade treats; there's a little table for tasty meals too – Louise brings it all to you. Upstairs find your pretty bedroom under the eaves. Or you can choose to stay in the amazing vintage carriage under an apple tree – children love it! A short walk to cafes and Helmsley Castle; return, settle with a book on an elegant antique sofa and feel completely at home.

Please see owners' website for availability calendar. Self-catering option in Railway Carriage.

Rooms	1 double with private dining & sitting rooms: £140. Carriage - 1 double with sitting area, 1 bunk room: £140. Singles £120. Extra bed/sofabed and cot available free of charge.
Meals	Dinner from £10 per person. Extra breakfasts £10 per person. Pubs/restaurants 1-minute walk.
Closed	Rarely.

Louise Craig
Helmsley Garden Cottage &
Railway Carriage,
1 Bondgate, Helmsley,
York, YO62 5BW
Tel   +44 (0)1439 771864
Email   louise.craig@aol.co.uk
Web   www.helmsley-gardencottage.co.uk/

Entry 528   Map 13

Yorkshire

No 54

No. 54 is in the middle of a peaceful row of attractive terraced houses a few minutes walk from the centre of town. Step inside to find a great mix of antique, vintage and quirky pieces, flagged floors, rugs and open wood fires. The inviting, supremely comfortable bedrooms are in a single-storey extension overlooking a secluded courtyard full of shrubs, climbers and pretty flowers; bathrooms are sparkling. Lizzie is warm and friendly and her home baking and breakfasts are delicious. The walking is good too, and on sunny days the back doors are thrown open onto the patio and garden – lovely! This is a happy welcoming place.

Children over 11 welcome.

Rooms	2 doubles, 1 twin: £50–£100. Singles £70–£85.
Meals	Restaurants 10-minute walk.
Closed	Christmas & New Year.

Lizzie Would
No 54,
Bondgate,
Helmsley, YO62 5EZ
Tel   +44 (0)1439 771533
Email lizzie.would@no54.co.uk
Web   www.no54.co.uk

Entry 529   Map 13

Yorkshire

Brickfields Farm

Down a long peaceful track, but a stone's throw from bustling Kirkbymoorside, is this walker's paradise. Friendly Janet sends you off to the North Yorks Moors with maps and information, and a tasty breakfast, served at separate tables in the conservatory overlooking guinea fowl and sheep. Bedrooms, one in the house and others in the barn or converted cow shed, are lovely: a French vintage four-poster, antiques, heavy curtains, sprung mattresses, flowers, a hidden fridge. All have stunning views over the fields. Bathrooms have big open showers, thick towels and plenty of lotions. Come to be pampered.

Rooms	1 twin: £100–£130. Barn - 4 suites for 2: £100–£130. Cow Shed - 1 four-poster suite for 2, 1 suite for 2: £100–£130.
Meals	Pub/restaurant 1 mile.
Closed	Rarely.

Sheila Trousdale Ward & Neil Ward
Brickfields Farm,
Kirkby Mills,
Kirkbymoorside, YO62 6NS
Tel   +44 (0)1751 433074
Email bookings@brickfieldsfarm.co.uk
Web   www.brickfieldsfarm.co.uk

Entry 530   Map 13

Yorkshire

Habton House Farm

Mellow stone, smart painted windows and a warm relaxed greeting from Lucy and James: a good start! You breakfast well here too, on home-produced sausages, bacon, eggs and jams, all delicious, at a big table in an elegant dining room. There are two cosy sitting rooms with wood fires to choose from, and the smartly done bedrooms have a pleasing medley of modern and vintage pieces, views of hill and river and immaculate bathrooms. Visit the pigs, fish for brown trout in the river, hire a bike; further afield are the North Yorks Moors and the coast. A tasty supper at the local pub is an added bonus.

Children over 8 welcome.

Rooms	3 doubles, 1 twin/double: £85–£110. Singles £60–£90.
Meals	Pub 0.5 miles.
Closed	20 December to 14 February.

Lucy Haxton
Habton House Farm,
Little Habton, Malton, YO17 6UA
Tel   +44 (0)1653 669707
Mobile   +44 (0)7876 433351
Email   habtonhouse@gmail.com
Web   www.habtonhouse.co.uk

Entry 531   Map 13

Yorkshire

Low Farm

The first thing you see is the amazing view – it's a jaw-dropper! This handsome old farmhouse in the heart of the North Yorks Moors National Park will relax you from the moment you step in – a warm home where Linda welcomes with tea and homemade cake. Fresh comfortable bedrooms have far-reaching views and immaculate en suite bathrooms. In the morning, feast on freshly squeezed juice and homemade jam, Whitby kippers or the full works, all sourced locally; the polished table in the cosy dining room is set with pretty china and flowers. Castle Howard is a hop, the walks are fabulous and you can stroll to the village bistro.

Rooms	1 double, 1 twin: £90–£110. Singles £90–£110.
Meals	Packed lunch available. Pub 0.25 miles.
Closed	Rarely.

Linda & Andrew Dagg
Low Farm,
Rosedale Abbey,
Pickering, YO18 8SE
Tel   +44 (0)1751 417003
Email   adagg@moorsweb.co.uk
Web   www.lowfarmrosedale.co.uk

Entry 532   Map 13

Flamborough Rigg Cottage

Even in the North Yorks Moors it's rare to find a spot so remote – rarer still to find such luxury in an 1820s farmhouse set in fields of lambs. Philip and Caroline know how to delight guests with brilliant bathrooms, crisp linen, delicious meals from home-grown produce. They've melded modern touches with handsome antiques, like contemporary art around a grandfather clock in the vaulted dining room – it works. Both light bedrooms have French windows to an orchard garden and views over hills that cry out for walking. Dogs are welcome, Whitby coast is ten miles, and there's supper and company to round off the day.

Union Place

A listed Adam Georgian townhouse – elegance epitomised. Lofty well-proportioned rooms with polished floors and cornices and fireplaces intact are delightfully dotted with sophisticated, quirky *objets*: bead-and-embroidery lampshades and chandeliers, bone china, a small mirrored Indian ceramic child's dress – and your urbane host Richard's accomplished paintings. Bedrooms, one painted duck egg blue, one green with floral wallpaper, are beautiful, with lots of lace and fine linen; the claw-foot roll top in the shared bathroom cuts a dash. Breakfast is unbeatable… then it's off to explore the North Yorkshire Moors. Superb.

Rooms	2 doubles: £85-£95. Singles £65.
Meals	Supper platter £15. Pub 2 miles.
Closed	Rarely.

Rooms	2 doubles sharing bath: £70-£75.
Meals	Pubs/restaurants within walking distance.
Closed	Christmas.

Philip & Caroline Jackson
Flamborough Rigg Cottage,
Middlehead Road,
Stape, Pickering, YO18 8HR
Tel   +44 (0)1751 475263
Email   enquiries@flamboroughriggcottage.co.uk
Web   www.flamboroughriggcottage.co.uk

Richard & Jane Pottas
Union Place,
9 Upgang Lane,
Whitby, YO21 3DT
Tel   +44 (0)1947 605501
Email   pottas1@btinternet.com
Web   www.unionplacewhitby.co.uk

Yorkshire

20 St Hilda's Terrace

Little back lanes, an old gate, a secret walled garden and a large bay-windowed Georgian house. You're bang in the heart of Whitby yet the feel is very peaceful with light and airy rooms, fresh flowers, botanical fabrics, elegant antiques and original art. Your pretty bedroom is reached up a graceful staircase; find high ceilings, a plump bed, antique furniture and views through sash windows. Your breakfast is continental and you can have it in the drawing room, the garden on fine days, or in bed if you're feeling lazy. Stroll to the beach for wild walks, romp on the Yorkshire Moors, explore the shops in town – returning will be a pleasure.

Rooms	1 double with separate bath/shower: £80.
Meals	Continental breakfast. Pubs/restaurants 0.3 miles.
Closed	Rarely.

Pip Baines
20 St Hilda's Terrace,
Whitby, YO21 3AE
Tel   +44 (0)1947 602435
Email   marylouisa@talktalk.net

Yorkshire

Thorpe Hall

Arrive and listen: nothing, bar the wind in the trees and the odd seagull. The eye gathers glimmering sea and mighty headland, the final edge of the moors… are there still smugglers? This old listed house smells of polish and flowers, the drawing room breathes history. Angelique is a delight and has furnished it all, including TV-free bedrooms (one downstairs), with an eclectic mix of old and new; wonky walls and creaky floors add to the atmospheric feel. She's hung contemporary art on ancient walls and made a veg patch with young Phoebe. David helps out with simple breakfast when he's not globetrotting. The very opposite of stuffy.

Rooms	3 doubles, 1 twin; 3 doubles sharing separate bath & shower rooms: £70-£90. Singles £70-£80. Extra bed/sofabed available £15 per person per night.
Meals	Pub within 0.25 miles.
Closed	Usually Christmas & January.

Angelique Russell
Thorpe Hall,
Middlewood Lane, Fylingthorpe,
Whitby, YO22 4TT
Tel   +44 (0)1947 880667
Email   thorpehall@gmail.com
Web   www.thorpe-hall.co.uk

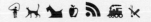

Yorkshire

Dale Farm

Huge skies as you drive along the open road to Dale Farm... the sea is just over the brow. Nifty inside too: bedrooms and bathrooms sparkle in whites and beach blues; mattresses are luxurious and handmade (the double is snugly in the attic); lots of books in the sitting room. Paul is a keen cook so breakfast is a varied feast: home-grown tomatoes, salmon from a local smokehouse, full English and more; hearty suppers too! Peaceful woodland surrounds you; the logs fuel the biomass boiler and fires. Ramble and find Paul's metal sculptures and a fire-pit in the woods, croquet on the lawn, a beach down the road with a café... lovely.

Rooms	1 double, 1 twin; 1 triple with separate bathroom: £90. 3 cabins for 2 (bathroom & wc in house, 50yds; short breaks at £60 per night): £350 per week. Singles £70. Extra bed/sofabed available £20 per person per night.
Meals	Dinner, 3 courses, from £15. Pubs/restaurants 2 miles.
Closed	Rarely.

	Elizabeth Halliday
	Dale Farm,
	Bartindale Road,
	Hunmanby, Filey, YO14 0JD
Tel	+44 (0)1723 890175
Mobile	+44 (0)7751 674706
Email	elizabethhalliday1@gmail.com
Web	www.dalefarmholidays.co.uk

Entry 537   Map 13

Yorkshire

The Wold Cottage

Drive through mature trees, and a proper entrance with signs, to a listed Georgian manor house in 300 glorious acres; tea awaits in the guest sitting room. The graceful dining room has heartlifting views across the landscaped gardens, and there are many original features: fan-lights, high ceilings, broad staircases. Bedrooms are sumptuous, traditional, with lots of thoughtful extras: chocolates, biscuits, monogrammed waffle robes. You are warmed by straw bale heating, and the food is local and delicious. An award-winning breakfast sets you up for a day of discovery: visit RSPB Bempton Cliffs, and the Wolds that have inspired David Hockney.

Minimum stay: 2 nights at weekends & in high season.

Rooms	2 doubles, 2 twins: £100-£130. Barn - 1 double: £100-£130. Barn - 1 family room for 4: £100-£160. Singles £60-£75.
Meals	Supper £28. Wine from £15.
Closed	Rarely.

	Derek & Katrina Gray
	The Wold Cottage,
	Wold Newton, Driffield, YO25 3HL
Tel	+44 (0)1262 470696
Mobile	+44 (0)7811 203336
Email	katrina@woldcottage.com
Web	www.woldcottage.com

Entry 538   Map 13

Village Farm

Tucked behind houses and shops, this was once the village farm with land stretching to the coast. Now the one-storey buildings overlooking a courtyard are large bedrooms in gorgeous colours with luxurious touches. Chrysta, who moved from London, is living her dream and looks after you well: baths are deep, beds crisply comfortable, heating is underfoot. Delicious breakfasts are served at wooden tables in a cheerful light room with a contemporary feel; dinner is candlelit and locally sourced. Stride the cliffs, watch birds at Flamborough Head or make for Spurn Point – remote and lovely.

Dowthorpe Hall

Caroline is lovely, cooking is her passion and she trawls the county for the best; fish and seafood from Hornsea, Dexter beef, game from the local shoot; her fruits and veg are home-grown. All is served in a sumptuous Georgian dining room by flickering candlelight, after which you retire to a comfortable drawing room; this is a marvellously elegant, and happy, house. Sleep peacefully on a luxurious mattress, wake to the aroma of bacon, sausages, eggs and home-baked bread. There are acres of gorgeous garden to roam – orchards, pathways, potager and pond – and a trio of historic houses to visit.

Rooms	1 double, 1 twin/double: £80. 1 family room for 4: £80-£95. Singles £60.
Meals	Dinner, 2-3 courses, £18-£22. Pubs/restaurants within 20 yds.
Closed	Rarely.

Rooms	1 twin/double; 1 double with separate bathroom: £90-£110. Singles £70.
Meals	Dinner £25. Pubs 0.25-5 miles.
Closed	Rarely.

Chrysta Newman
Village Farm,
Back Street, Skipsea,
Driffield, YO25 8SW
Tel   +44 (0)1262 468479
Email info@villagefarmskipsea.co.uk
Web   www.villagefarmskipsea.co.uk

John & Caroline Holtby
Dowthorpe Hall,
Skirlaugh, Hull, HU11 5AE
Tel   +44 (0)1964 562235
Email john.holtby@farming.co.uk
Web   www.dowthorpehall.com

Channel Islands

Guernsey

Seabreeze

Maggie's house – the most southern on Guernsey – comes with enormous sea views: Herm and Sark glistening in the water under a vast sky, framed by a pretty front garden. The breakfast terrace is hard to beat. Find sofas in the conservatory, entertaining stories from Maggie and Francis, fabulous walks, a beach for picnics. The house started life as HQ for French pilots in WWI; these days warm, rustic interiors make for a great island base. It's not grand, just very welcoming with rooms that hit the spot: bathrobes, super showers, fresh flowers. Use the bikes (or hire locally) then spin up the lane to a top island restaurant. Brilliant.

Self-catering available in studio.

Rooms	2 twin/doubles: £75-£110. 1 studio for 2 with kitchenette: £125. Singles £55-£75.
Meals	Pubs/restaurants 500 yds & 0.5 miles.
Closed	14 December - 1 March.

Maggie Talbot-Cull
Seabreeze,
La Moye Lane, Route de Jerbourg,
St Martin, GY4 6BN

Tel	+44 (0)1481 237929
Email	seabreeze-guernsey@mail.com
Web	www.guernseybandb.com

Entry 541   Map 4

Scotland

Aberdeenshire

Castle of Park

A long leafy drive, rose gardens, laburnum walk, a secret tunnel through rhododendrons... a splendid setting for a peaceful retreat. Rebecca loves to entertain and has brought an ancient castle back to life. Find all the trimmings you'd expect from this slice of history: Great Hall, drawing, snooker and morning rooms, wood stoves and open fires, rich colours and furnishings, art and intriguing antiques. Bedrooms have delicious comfort and tea trays; steep stairs lead to the Tudor Room on the second floor. There are surprises in every corner – a swimming elephant table, twin golden unicorns, a cheetah rug... Wonderful!

Pets by arrangement.

Rooms	1 double, 1 four-poster: £110.
	1 suite for 2: £140.
	Singles £100.
	Dinner, B&B £90-£130 per person.
Meals	Pubs/restaurants 5 miles.
Closed	Rarely.

Becky Wilson
Castle of Park,
Cornhill,
Banff, AB45 2AX
Tel   +44 (0)1466 751595
Email   enquiries@castleofpark.co.uk
Web   www.castleofpark.co.uk

Entry 542   Map 19

Aberdeenshire

Lynturk Home Farm

The stunning drawing room, with pier-glass mirror, baby grand and enveloping sofas, is reason enough to come; the food, served in a candlelit, deep-sage dining room, is delicious, with produce from the farm. You're treated as friends here and your hosts are delightful. It's peaceful, too, on the Aberdeenshire Castle Trail. The handsome farmhouse has been in the family since 1762 and you can roam the surrounding, rolling, 300 acres. Inside: flowers, polished furniture, Persian rugs, family portraits and supremely comfortable bedrooms. "A blissful haven," says a guest.

Rooms	1 double, 2 twin/doubles: £100.
	Singles £60.
Meals	Dinner, 4 courses, £30.
	Pub 1 mile.
Closed	Rarely.

John & Veronica Evans-Freke
Lynturk Home Farm,
Alford, AB33 8HU
Tel   +44 (0)1975 562504
Mobile +44 (0)7773 389793
Email   lynturk@hotmail.com

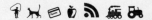

Entry 543   Map 19

Angus

Newtonmill House

The house and grounds are in perfect order; the owners are warm, charming and discreet. This is a little-known part of Scotland, with glens and gardens to discover; fishing villages, golf courses and deserted beaches, too. Return to a cup of tea in the sitting room or summerhouse, a wander in the lovely walled garden, and a marvellous supper of local produce; Rose grows interesting varieties of potato and her hens' eggs make a great hollandaise! Upstairs are crisp sheets, soft blankets, feather pillows, flowers, homemade fruit cake and warm sparkling bathrooms with thick towels. Let this home envelop you in its warm embrace.

Dogs by arrangement.

Rooms	1 twin; 1 double with separate bath: £100-£120. Singles from £70.
Meals	Dinner, £30-£38. BYO. Packed lunch £10. Pub 3 miles.
Closed	Christmas.

	Rose & Stephen Rickman Newtonmill House, Brechin, DD9 7PZ
Tel	+44 (0)1356 622533
Mobile	+44 (0)7793 169482
Email	rrickman@srickman.co.uk
Web	www.newtonmillhouse.co.uk

Entry 544   Map 19

Argyll & Bute

Achanduin Cottage

Sara's restoration of this old crofthouse is just right. The feel is restful, comfortable, understated. Everything's well chosen: rustic and reclaimed pieces, interesting art, colourful rugs. The bright east suite has its own sitting room with wood-burner; the west room has a fine mahogany bed, old farmhouse desk and a grand roll top bath in its bookish bathroom. All this set back in yachty Ardfern, sitting pretty on its Highland Loch... Perfect for Highland lovers – Donald's an outdoors guide – for lovers of art, good food and conversation – Sara's an inspired cook; both have a keen sense of place and sustainability.

Rooms	1 double: £75. 1 suite for 2: £90.
Meals	Pub 200 yds.
Closed	Rarely.

	Sara Wallace Achanduin Cottage, Ardfern, Lochgilphead, PA31 8QN
Tel	+44 (0)1852 500708
Email	sara@achanduincottage.co.uk
Web	www.achanduincottage.com

Entry 545   Map 14

Argyll & Bute

Melfort House

A truly seductive combination of a wild landscape of ancient woods and hidden glens with rivers that tumble to a blue sea and a big, beautiful house with views straight down the loch. The whole place glows with polished antiques, oak floors, exquisite fabrics, prints and paintings. And Yvonne and Matthew are brilliant at looking after you – whether you're super-active, or not – their fabulous Scottish food's a treat. Bedrooms have soft plaids, superb views and handmade chocolates; bathrooms have huge towels and locally made soaps. Sally forth with boots or bikes, return to a dram by the log fire. Don't book too short a stay!

Rooms	2 twin/doubles, 1 suite for 2: £95-£125. Singles from £70. Sofabed £15.
Meals	Dinner, 3 courses, from £32. Packed lunch £10. Pub/restaurant 400 yds.
Closed	Rarely.

	Yvonne & Matthew Anderson Melfort House, Kilmelford, Oban, PA34 4XD
Tel	+44 (0)1852 200326
Mobile	+44 (0)7795 438106
Email	relax@melforthouse.co.uk
Web	www.melforthouse.co.uk

Argyll & Bute

Glenmore

A pleasingly idiosyncratic traditional country house with no need to stand on ceremony. Built in the 1800s but with 1930s additions setting the style, find solid oak doors and floors, red-pine panelling, Art Deco pieces and a unique carved staircase. Alasdair's family has been here for 150 years and many family antiques remain. One of the huge doubles can be arranged as a suite to include a single room and a sofabed; bath and basins are chunky 30s style with chrome plumbing. From the organic garden and the house there are magnificent views of Loch Melfort with its bobbing boats; you're free to come and go as you please.

Rooms	1 double with separate bath/shower: £85-£100. 1 family room for 5: £95-£170. Singles £50-£65.
Meals	Pub 0.5 miles, restaurant 1.5 miles.
Closed	Christmas & New Year.

	Melissa & Alasdair Oatts Glenmore, Kilmelford, Oban, PA34 4XA
Tel	+44 (0)1852 200314
Mobile	+44 (0)7786 340468
Email	oatts@glenmore22.tsnet.co.uk
Web	www.glenmorecountryhouse.co.uk

Argyll & Bute

Greystones

A baronial mansion built for the owner of a diamond mine. He clearly liked a good view – a five-mile sweep across Oban bay lands on the Isle of Mull. Inside, bright white interiors soak up the light, while coolly uncluttered bedrooms have chic bathrooms and well-dressed beds. One has a turret with armchairs looking out to sea, another has a vast walk-in shower, three have the view. You breakfast downstairs on honey-drenched porridge while watching boats come and go on the water. There's a sitting room with smart sofas, a list of local restaurants, a library of DVDs. Castles and gardens wait, as do ferries to far-flung islands.

Minimum stay: 2 nights in bigger rooms.

Rooms	4 doubles: £120–£150.
	1 suite for 2: £165.
Meals	Pubs/restaurants 5-minute walk.
Closed	Rarely.

Mark & Suzanne McPhillips
Greystones,
13 Dalriach Road,
Oban, PA34 5EQ

Tel	+44 (0)1631 358653
Email	stay@greystonesoban.co.uk
Web	www.greystonesoban.co.uk

Entry 548   Map 17

Argyll & Bute

Ardtorna

Come for perfect comfort and uninterrupted views of loch and mountain. These thoughtful, professional hosts are happy to share their new, open-plan, eco-friendly house where contemporary Scandinavian and Art Deco styles are cleverly blended with homely warmth. Sink into a bedroom with a wall of glass for those views; each has a wet room or spa bath with Molton Brown treats. Flowers and jauntily coloured coffee pots decorate the oak table in the stunning dining room, and food is home-baked and delicious. Argyll brims with historic sites and walks; return to watch the sun go down over the Morvern hills. Fabulous.

Rooms	4 twin/doubles: £99–£200.
	Singles £99.
Meals	Pub/restaurant 3 miles.
Closed	Rarely.

Karen O'Byrne
Ardtorna,
Mill Farm, Barcaldine,
Oban, PA37 1SE

Tel	+44 (0)1631 720125
Mobile	+44 (0)7867 785524
Email	info@ardtorna.co.uk
Web	www.ardtorna.co.uk

Entry 549   Map 17

Argyll & Bute

Callachally House

By the small fishing river at the mouth of the Glen, settled into its own wooded grounds, is a big Scottish farmhouse (once a drovers' inn) where on a still summer night you hear the lapping of the sea. A fine, traditional, cultured place, it's been in Ian's family since time began and overflows with colour and character. Bedrooms share bathrooms and each is a gem: old polished floors topped with bright rugs, chalky blue walls hung with paintings; you might hear sheepdogs barking at night. Wake to a fine breakfast (Ian loves to cook), head off down winding roads with views of islands and mountains, return to sprawling armchairs by the log fire.

Rooms	3 doubles sharing 2 bathrooms (adjoining twin available): £50-£75. Pets welcome, £10 per stay. Singles available, £50 per night.
Meals	Restaurants 2 miles away.
Closed	December-March.

Ian Mazur
Callachally House,
Glenforsa, Aros,
Isle of Mull, PA72 6JN

Mobile	+44 (0)7887 950126
Email	jasmazur@gmail.com
Web	www.largeholidayhousemull.co.uk

Entry 550   Map 17

Argyll & Bute

Meall Mo Chridhe

Caring owners, exquisite food and a welcome sight amid the savage beauty of Britain's most westerly village. The warm ochre walls of this listed Georgian manse peep through wooded gardens across the Sound to Mull. Rooms are beautiful – French antiques, a wood stove, roll top baths – but it's the food that draws most to this far-flung spot. What David magics from his 45-acre smallholding (a bit of everything that grows, grunts, bleats or quacks) Stella transforms into feasts. Dine on spiced mackerel, minted lamb, hazelnut meringue; and duck eggs at breakfast. A gem buried in spectacular, wild walking country.

Rooms	3 doubles: £103-£204. Singles £51.50-£102.
Meals	Dinner from £37. Pub 0.25 miles.
Closed	Rarely.

Stella & David Cash
Meall Mo Chridhe,
Kilchoan, Acharacle, PH36 4LH

Tel	+44 (0)1972 510238
Mobile	+44 (0)7730 100639
Email	enquiries@westcoastscotland.co.uk
Web	www.westcoastscotland.co.uk

Entry 551   Map 17

Ayrshire

Alton Albany Farm

Discover Ayrshire... pine forests, hills and wild beauty. Alasdair and Andrea (sculptor/garden photographer) are generous hosts who love having you to stay – your visit starts with tea, coffee and cake. There's an arty vibe with their work on display; the dining room brims with garden books and games; large bedrooms have cosy lamps and more books. Big breakfasts by a log fire are a treat, perhaps with haggis, garden fruit, homemade bread. Rich in wildlife and orchids the garden has a rambling charm, the salmon-filled river Stinchar runs past and dogs are welcome – resident Clover and Daisy are friendly. Great fish restaurant nearby.

Rooms	1 double; 1 double, 1 twin sharing bath (let to same party only): £80–£85. Special group rates for 6 friends or family. Singles £50.
Meals	Pubs/restaurants 7-minute walk.
Closed	Rarely.

Andrea & Alasdair Currie
Alton Albany Farm,
Barr, Girvan, KA26 0TL

Tel	+44 (0)1465 861148
Mobile	+44 (0)7881 908764
Email	alasdair@gardenexposures.co.uk
Web	www.altonalbanyfarmbandb.wordpress.com

Dumfries & Galloway

Chlenry Farmhouse

Handsome in its glen; a traditional family farmhouse full of old-fashioned comfort with charming, well-travelled owners and friendly dogs. In peaceful bedrooms with leafy views, solid antiques jostle with photos, flowers, bowls of fruit, and magazines on country matters. There are capacious bath tubs, robes – and suppers for walkers: the Southern Upland Way passes nearby. Breakfasts are properly fortifying and evening meals can be simple or elaborate, often with game or fresh salmon. Convenient for ferries to Belfast and Larne; Galloway gardens and golf courses are close too – return to a snug sitting room with an open fire.

Rooms	1 double, 1 twin sharing bath; 1 twin/double with separate bath: £90. Singles £50.
Meals	Supper £20. Dinner, 4 courses, £40. Packed lunch £6. Pub 1.5 miles.
Closed	Christmas, New Year, February & occasionally.

David & Ginny Wolsley Brinton
Chlenry Farmhouse,
Castle Kennedy, Stranraer, DG9 8SL

Tel	+44 (0)1776 705316
Mobile	+44 (0)7704 205003
Email	wolseleybrinton@aol.com
Web	www.chlenryfarmhouse.com

Dumfries & Galloway

Chipperkyle

This beautiful Scottish-Georgian family home has not a hint of formality, and the sociable Dicksons put you at your ease. Your sitting and dining rooms connect through a large arch; find gloriously comfy sofas, family pictures, rugs on wooden floors, masses of books and a constant log fire. Upstairs: good linen, striped walls, armchairs and windows with views – this wonderful house just gets better and better. There are 200 acres, dogs, cats, donkeys and hens – children can collect the eggs and go on tractor rides. The countryside is magnificent, beaches fabulous and this is a classified dark sky area. A house full of flowers and warmth.

Minimum stay: 2 nights at weekends & in high season.

Rooms	1 double (cot available); 1 twin with separate bath/shower: £110. Discounts for children.
Meals	Occasional dinner from £20 (available for groups). Pub 3 miles.
Closed	Rarely.

Willie Dickson
Chipperkyle,
Kirkpatrick Durham,
Castle Douglas, DG7 3EY
Tel   +44 (0)1556 650223
Mobile +44 (0)7917 610008
Email   willie@chipperkyle.co.uk
Web   www.chipperkyle.co.uk

Entry 554   Map 11

Dumfries & Galloway

The House on the Shore

Impossible not to be wowed by this incredible shoreline setting with views across the Solway Firth. The 1,250-acre estate has been in Jamie's family for generations; he and Sheri are excellent hosts and love their dower house with its rich and varied woodland and wildlife, formal gardens and stupendous views. Grand but with a family feel, this is old country house style at its best with rugs on polished floors, paintings, open fires and fresh flowers. The farm produces its own meat, an enormous walled kitchen garden is being restored, and a peach tree fruits abundantly; you'll eat well. Very special.

Rooms	1 double, 1 twin: £90–£100. Singles £65–£80.
Meals	Dinner, 3 courses, £25. BYO. Pub/restaurant 2 miles.
Closed	Rarely.

Jamie & Sheri Blackett
The House on the Shore,
Arbigland, Kirkbean,
Dumfries, DG2 8BQ
Tel   +44 (0)1387 880717
Email   sheri@arbigland.com
Web   www.arbiglandestate.co.uk

Entry 555   Map 11

Dumfries & Galloway

The Waterside Rooms

Prepare to be given a thorough looking after! Generous spirited Nic and Julie gave up their day jobs, travelled around Europe in a camper van and ended up here, dipping their toes in the Solway Firth. Birdwatchers will swoon, burnt out city folk will find balm, independence seekers will adore their own entrance to a neat-as-a-pin suite: peaceful colours soothe in a comfy sitting room, well-dressed bedroom and sparkling shower room; your own fridge too. Breakfast on a feast of local produce and homemade breads and preserves in the colourful main house, sit in the pretty garden with its watery views, walk, cycle, sail. Blissful.

Rooms	1 suite for 2 with sitting room: £95. Extra bed/sofabed available £12 per person per night.
Meals	Pub/restaurant 3 miles.
Closed	Rarely.

Nic & Julie Pearse
The Waterside Rooms,
Dornock Brow House, Dornock,
Eastriggs, Annan, DG12 6SX
Tel   +44 (0)1461 40232
Email   enquiries@thewatersiderooms.co.uk
Web   www.thewatersiderooms.co.uk

Entry 556   Map 11

Dumfries & Galloway

Holmhill Country House

Among the rolling hills of Dumfries and Galloway, by the banks of the Nith, is a hidden gem of a Georgian country house. It was a favourite of philosopher Thomas Carlyle, who had his own pipe-smoking spot in the marvellously colourful garden. There are seven acres to explore, utter tranquillity, stunning views of the Keir Hills and excellent fishing. Rosie and Stewart love sharing their family home with guests, and can treat you to breakfast, and possibly dinner, by the fire in the graceful dining room. Masses of space everywhere, each room deftly combining rustic virtue with modern savoir-faire.

Pets by arrangement.

Rooms	2 twin/doubles: £105. Singles £75.
Meals	Dinner, 3 courses, £30. Pubs/restaurants 0.5 miles.
Closed	Christmas & New Year.

Rosie Lee
Holmhill Country House,
Thornhill, DG3 4AB
Tel   +44 (0)1848 332239
Email   booking@holmhill.co.uk
Web   www.holmhill.co.uk

Entry 557   Map 15

Dumfries & Galloway

Three Glens

Getting here is just part of the adventure – up a steep track to an environmentally friendly build with 360 degree views. Emerging from the stone dyke that breaks the hill, the house is surrounded by sheep and a rolling landscape. Greg will welcome you in, make you feel at home and feed you well: a full Scottish breakfast, a sumptuous dinner, and everything (just about) sourced from the farm. Head off on stunning walks, visit castles – or simply stay put and relax. Sheep horns for hooks, a biomass wood-burner, a wall of windows that swish open; luxurious en suite bedrooms await downstairs. Stop, unwind and feel your heart soar.

Dogs welcome but not in the house.

Rooms	2 doubles, 2 twins: £200. Dinner, B&B £135 p.p.
Meals	Dinner, 3 courses with wine, £35. Pubs/restaurants 5-minute walk.
Closed	Rarely.

	Neil & Mary Gourlay
	Three Glens,
	Moniaive, Thornhill, DG3 4EG
Tel	+44 (0)1848 200589
Mobile	+44 (0)7974 757654
Email	info@3glens.com
Web	www.3glens.com

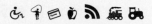

Dumfries & Galloway

Rammerscales

A family home at the heart of a working farm. Malcolm grew up here and he and Francesca love sharing their historic home with its colourful history. The feel throughout is of slightly faded grandeur: a huge long library with old rugs and masses of books, a drawing room with sporting art, comfy sofas and roaring log fire, and upstairs two simply done big bedrooms. Eat breakfast at a table made from the quarterdeck of HMS Bellerophon, a battleship that fought at Trafalgar: local eggs, sausages and jams, and bacon from their own pigs. You'll find golf courses, and lochside and woodland walks; join the Annandale Way from the door.

Rooms	1 twin; 1 twin/double with separate bath: £88. Singles £54.
Meals	Dinner £30. Inn 2 miles.
Closed	Occasionally.

	Francesca Leslie
	Rammerscales,
	Hightae,
	Lockerbie, DG11 1LD
Tel	+44 (0)1387 810229
Email	Contact@rammerscales.com
Web	www.rammerscales.com

Dumfries & Galloway

White Hill

Fresh air, huge gardens and stacks of Scottish charm. The aged paint exterior is forgotten once you're inside this treasure-trove of history and heritage. The Bell-Irvings are natural hosts; twenty generations of their family have lived here and worn the floorboards dancing. Throw logs on the fire, ramble round the azalea'd gardens or explore the woods, fish the river, and dine opulently under the gaze of portraits of their 'rellies'. Breakfast is a delightfully hearty affair. A very special chance to share a real ancestral home in the Scottish borders with a kind, funny, lovely couple (and their very friendly springer spaniel).

Dumfries & Galloway

Byreburnfoot House

Tucked away up a gravelled drive overlooking the banks of the salmon-rich Esk, this pretty Victorian forester's house combines traditional charm with modern comforts. Find an elegant and rural decor, with airy rooms, wooden floors and antique pieces — grandfather clock, writing desk, chandeliers. Beds are big, the linen is trimmed and views are sublime. Warm hosts Bill and Lorraine are keenly green-fingered: their 1.5 acres of orchards, flower-fringed lawns and organic kitchen garden are productive — and their cooking is delicious! Bill is happy to arrange salmon and trout fishing. Stay a few days and become part of it all.

Rooms	2 twins: £98. Singles £54.	Rooms	2 doubles; 1 twin/double with separate bath: £100–£110. Singles £70. Dinner, B&B £85 per person.
Meals	Dinner £30. Pubs/restaurants 4 miles.	Meals	Dinner, 3 courses, £30. Packed lunch from £7.50. Pub/restaurant 5 miles.
Closed	Rarely.	Closed	Rarely.

	Robin & Janet Bell-Irving White Hill, Ecclefechan, Lockerbie, DG11 1AL		**Bill & Loraine Frew** Byreburnfoot House, Canonbie, DG14 0XB
Tel	+44 (0)1576 510206	Tel	+44 (0)1387 371209
Email	johnbi@talktalk.net	Mobile	+44 (0)7764 194901
Web	www.aboutscotland.com/south/whitehill.html	Email	enquiries@byreburnfoot.co.uk
		Web	www.byreburnfoot.co.uk

Entry 560   Map 15

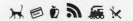

Entry 561   Map 15

Edinburgh

2 Cambridge Street
(The Dynamite Club)

A mischievous humour, tinged with historical and cultural references, alerts you to the specialness of this place, a ground-floor B&B in the lee of Edinburgh Castle, in the heart of theatre land. Find fin-de-siècle Scotland, with darkly striking colours on walls, antiques aplenty, and a captivating attention to detail. There are interactive art installations that sing and play, a line of old theatre seats up on the wall, photos and 'objets' serving startling and original purposes. Erlend and Hélène are delightful and free-spirited; Erlend, a quietly spoken (but don't be fooled) Shetlander, serves a breakfast to remember.

Rooms	2 doubles: £95–£140.
	Singles £90–£110.
Meals	Pubs/restaurants 1-minute walk.
Closed	Christmas.

Erlend & Hélène Clouston
2 Cambridge Street
(The Dynamite Club),
Edinburgh, EH1 2DY
Tel   +44 (0)131 478 0005
Email   erlendc@blueyonder.co.uk
Web   www.wwwonderful.net

Entry 562   Map 15

Edinburgh

14 Hart Street

The brightly lit Georgian house has a smart front of polished brass and glossy paint. The warm raspberry hall is lined with art, and the graceful dining room is just as inviting: decanters on the sideboard, period furniture, glowing lamps, and a welcoming home-baked something. Fresh bright bedrooms are elegant and comfortable with whisky and wine on a tray and smart, sparkling bathrooms. Wake for breakfast at a beautifully polished table, with plenty of coffee, newspapers and chat; James and Angela are easy to talk to and love having guests to stay. Perfect for a peaceful city break, and Princes Street is a five-minute walk.

Rooms	2 doubles, 1 twin/double: £90–£120.
Meals	Restaurants 10-minute walk.
Closed	Rarely.

James & Angela Wilson
14 Hart Street,
Edinburgh, EH1 3RN
Tel   +44 (0)131 557 6826
Mobile   +44 (0)7795 203414
Email   hartst.edin@virgin.net
Web   www.14hartst.com

Entry 563   Map 15

Edinburgh

Edinburgh

10 London Street

A Roman X marks this special spot: a beautiful Georgian terraced house in Edinburgh's world heritage New Town, home to descendants of Scots author John Gibson Lockhart. Step into a family home of period elegance and charming informality: accept a dram by the fire in the sash-windowed drawing room (with baby grand piano), relax at the dining table over a leisurely continental breakfast. Sleep undisturbed in 'Beauregard', with its lovely views and paintings; or 'Gibson' with its off-courtyard privacy and self-catering option. The best of Edinburgh is a stroll away, the new tram service from the airport is an easy glide into town.

Geraldsplace

Elegant Georgian New Town... so splendid and handsome it's a World Heritage Site. Welcoming, enthusiastic, charming Gerald runs a B&B on one of its finest streets. His patio basement apartment is full of character, comfort and colour. Bedrooms have cosiness, warmth, fine fabrics, excellent art... and special extras: DVDs and a book swop shelf, a laptop with fast broadband, a tea tray, a decanter of single malt whisky; bathrooms are newly done. Breakfast is a feast and mostly organic. There's a private garden opposite, an incredibly convenient location and, of course, Gerald, your brilliantly well-informed, up-to-the-minute host.

Minimum stay: 3 nights.

Rooms	2 doubles (1 with self-catering option): £160.
Meals	Continental breakfast. Pub/restaurant 500 yds.
Closed	Rarely.

Rooms	2 twin/doubles: £89-£129. Additional supplement during festivals: £69-£99.
Meals	Restaurants within 3-minute walk.
Closed	Rarely.

Pippa Lockhart
10 London Street,
Edinburgh, EH3 6NA
Tel   +44 (0)131 556 0737
Email   pippalockhart@gmail.com
Web   www.londonstreetaccommodation.co.uk

Gerald Della-Porta
Geraldsplace,
21b Abercromby Place,
Edinburgh, EH3 6QE
Tel   +44 (0)131 558 7017
Mobile   +44 (0)7766 016840
Email   gerald11@geraldsplace.com
Web   www.geraldsplace.com

Entry 564   Map 15

Entry 565   Map 15

Edinburgh

11 Belford Place

Guests love Sue's modern townhouse, quietly tucked away in a private road above the Water of Leith yet a short distance from the city. From the wooden-floored entrance a picture-lined staircase winds upward. Handsome bedrooms display china cups and floral spreads; dazzling bathrooms have Molton Brown goodies. Wake for Stornoway black pudding, kedgeree, homemade jams and delicious ginger compote at the gleaming table. Owls sometimes hoot in the pretty sloping garden, there's an outside luggage store, parking is free and art galleries and Murrayfield Stadium are nearby.

Minimum stay: 2 nights in August. Over 12s welcome.

Rooms	2 twin/doubles: £70–£120.
Meals	Restaurants 10-minute walk.
Closed	Christmas.

	Susan Kinross
	11 Belford Place,
	Edinburgh, EH4 3DH
Tel	+44 (0)131 332 9704
Mobile	+44 (0)7712 836399
Email	suekinross@blueyonder.co.uk

Edinburgh

12 Belford Terrace

Leafy trees, a secluded garden, a stone wall and, beyond, a quiet riverside stroll. On the doorstep of the Modern Art and Dean galleries with Edinburgh's theatres and restaurants just a 15-minute walk, this Victorian end terrace, beside Leith Water, oozes an easy-going elegance, helped by Carolyn's laid-back but competent manner. Garden level bedrooms have their own entrance and are big and creamy with stripy fabrics, antiques, sofas and huge windows. (The single has a Boys Own charm.) Carolyn spoils with crisp linen, books and biscuits and a delicious, full-works breakfast. After a day in town, relax on the sunny terrace.

Rooms	1 double, 1 twin/double: £70–£110. 1 single with separate shower: £40–£55.
Meals	Pub/restaurants within 10-minute walk.
Closed	Christmas.

	Carolyn Crabbie
	12 Belford Terrace,
	Edinburgh, EH4 3DQ
Tel	+44 (0)131 332 2413
Email	carolyncrabbie@blueyonder.co.uk

Edinburgh

Millers64

Who could fail to relax here after a busy day? The bedrooms are comfortable and contemporary, the hosts are knowledgeable and friendly, and the breakfasts are stupendous (jam and marmalade courtesy of Louise and Shona's mum), served gourmet style at the big table. This elegant terraced villa is reached via Leith Walk, a wide busy thoroughfare that gets you to Edinburgh's hub in 20 minutes on foot; Leith's waterfront is an easy half mile. Victorian stained glass and cornices mix with a serene eastern theme (note the stylish pewter sinks from Thailand) and the quietest room is at the back.

Minimum stay: 3 nights in high season. Over 12s welcome.

Rooms	1 double: £110–£140.
	1 suite for 2: £120–£160.
	Singles from £80.
Meals	Pubs/restaurants 0.5 miles.
Closed	25 July to 2 August.

Louise Clelland
Millers64,
64 Pilrig Street,
Edinburgh, EH6 5AS

Tel	+44 (0)131 454 3666
Email	louise@millers64.com
Web	www.millers64.com

Entry 568   Map 15

Edinburgh

Wallace's Arthouse Scotland

The apartment door swings open to a world of white walls, smooth floors, modern art, acoustic jazz, and smiling Wallace with a glass of wine – well worth the three-storey climb up this old Assembly Rooms building. Your host – New York fashion designer and arts enthusiast, Glasgow-born, not shy – has created a bright, minimalist space sprinkled with humour and casual sophistication. Bedrooms capture light and exude his inimitable style; the kitchen's narrow bar is perfect for a light breakfast. Leith is Edinburgh's earthy side with its docks and noisy street life, but fine restaurants abound and the centre is close. Memorable.

Rooms	2 doubles: £120.
	Singles £95.
Meals	Pubs/restaurants 10 yds.
Closed	Christmas Eve & Christmas Day.

Wallace Shaw
Wallace's Arthouse Scotland,
41-4 Constitution Street,
Edinburgh, EH6 7BG

Tel	+44 (0)131 538 3320
Mobile	+44 (0)7941 343714
Email	cawallaceshaw@mac.com
Web	www.wallacesarthousescotland.com

Entry 569   Map 15

Edinburgh

Two Hillside Crescent

Leave your worries behind as you enter this exquisitely restored Georgian townhouse. All is peaceful, spacious and light, with an upbeat contemporary feel. Bedrooms are on the first and second floors: imagine sleek modern furniture, big beds, superb mattresses, clouds of goose down, crisp linen, and immaculate bathrooms with organic toiletries and lashings of hot water. Over a superb breakfast your charming hosts will help you get the most out of your stay. Calton Hill is across the road for the best views of the city, and you're a stroll from the start of the Royal Mile. Wonderful.

Rooms	5 twin/doubles: £125-£165. Singles from £95.
Meals	Pubs/restaurants across the road.
Closed	Rarely.

Elaine Adams
Two Hillside Crescent,
Edinburgh, EH7 5DY
Tel   +44 (0)131 556 4871
Email   info@twohillsidecrescent.com
Web   www.twohillsidecrescent.com

East Lothian

Glebe House

A treasure of a home – and host! A perfect Georgian family house with all the well-proportioned elegance you'd expect, it is resplendent with original features – fireplaces, arched glass, long windows – that have appeared more than once in interiors magazines. Bedrooms are light and airy with pretty fabrics and lovely linen. The beach is a stone's throw away, views are leafy-green, golfers have over 21 courses to choose from. There's also a fascinating sea bird centre close by – and you are 30 minutes from Edinburgh: regular trains bring you to the foot of the castle.

Rooms	1 double, 1 four-poster; 1 twin with separate bath: £120-£130. Singles by arrangement.
Meals	Restaurants 2-minute walk.
Closed	Christmas & New Year.

Gwen & Jake Scott
Glebe House,
Law Road, North Berwick, EH39 4PL
Tel   +44 (0)1620 892608
Mobile +44 (0)7973 965814
Email   gwenscott@glebehouse-nb.co.uk
Web   www.glebehouse-nb.co.uk

Fife

Myres Castle

The impressive drive curves round to Myres – bronze hippos bask in the loch amongst the gunnera, Highland cattle graze contentedly. Visited by Mary Queen of Scots and Sir Walter Scott, this yellow ochre slice of history is dreamy – and surprisingly cosy. Bedrooms are luxurious with a chaise longue, canopied beds and even a canopied bath! 'Rose' has a radiator with a cupboard for your PJs; climb the turret stairs to 'Tower' – watch the sun go down, soak in the bath at one end of the room, slip under tartan covers and count the stars. You have the freedom to wander, and there are lots of places to sit and breathe in the garden. Magical.

Over 12s welcome.

Rooms	3 doubles, 2 twin/doubles: £150–£220.
Meals	Pub/restaurants 2.5 miles.
Closed	Rarely.

Henry & Amanda Barge
Myres Castle,
Auchtermuchty,
Cupar, KY14 7EW
Tel +44 (0)1337 828350
Email enquiries@myrescastle.co.uk
Web www.myrescastle.co.uk

Entry 572   Map 15

Fife

Greenlaw House

With superb views towards the Lomond Hills, Debbie's bright, warm converted farm steading will please you the moment you step in. There's a interesting blend of antiques and fascinating modern art throughout. The oak-floored sitting room has Afghan rugs, sofas by a log-burner, books, a grand piano; catch the summer sun on the decked area. Bedrooms have posies of garden flowers and views over the beautiful stone-walled garden; the upstairs one is more lived-in. Debbie loves to cook: smoked salmon, homemade granola and jams, porridge with cream. Falkland Palace, hunting haunt of the Stuart kings, is close, and the walks are wonderful.

Rooms	1 double; 1 double, 1 twin sharing a bath (let to same party only): £80–£90. Singles £50.
Meals	Dinner £25–£30. Restaurants 15-minute drive.
Closed	Christmas & New Year.

Debbie Butler
Greenlaw House,
Braeside, Collessie,
Cupar, KY15 7UX
Tel +44 (0)1337 810413
Email butlerjackson@googlemail.com
Web www.greenlawhouse.com

Entry 573   Map 15

Fife

Kinkell

An avenue of beech trees patrolled by guinea fowl, Hebridean sheep and Highland cows leads to the house. If the sea views and salty smack of St Andrews Bay air don't get you, step inside and have your senses tickled. Your hosts are wonderful and offer you a glass of something on arrival; the elegant drawing room has two open fires, rosy sofas, a grand piano – gorgeous. Bedrooms and bathrooms are immaculate and sunny. Sandy and Frippy are great cooks and make full use of local produce. Gaze on the sea from the garden, head down to the beach, walk the wild coast. A friendly, comfortable family home.

Online booking available.

Rooms	3 twin/doubles: £100. Singles £60.
Meals	Dinner £30. Restaurants 2 miles.
Closed	Rarely.

Sandy & Frippy Fyfe
Kinkell,
St Andrews, KY16 8PN

Tel	+44 (0)1334 472003
Mobile	+44 (0)7836 746043
Email	fyfe@kinkell.com
Web	www.kinkell.com

Entry 574   Map 16+19

Glasgow

64 Partickhill Road

Be greeted by three free-range hens and Gertie the terrier on arrival at this relaxed family home. It's the bustling West End but the road is peaceful and there's a lovely big garden. Caroline and Hugh are lovers of the arts: the house is full of pictures, vintage finds and books. There are wood floors, rugs, a fire in the comfy sitting room and your bedroom is bright and spacious. Tuck into a delicious breakfast, in the conservatory, of good croissants, organic bacon and sausages, homemade bread and jams. Easy for the underground, trendy cafés and delis, museums, theatres and the university. A city treat.

Rooms	1 double (extra twin available): £80–£90.
Meals	Packed lunch available. Pubs/restaurant 0.25 miles.
Closed	Occasionally.

Caroline Anderson
64 Partickhill Road,
Glasgow, G11 5NB

Tel	+44 (0)141 339 1946
Mobile	+44 (0)7962 144509
Email	carolineanderson64@gmail.com

Entry 575   Map 15

Highland

The Grange

A Victorian townhouse with its toes in the country: the mountain hovers above, the loch shimmers below and the garden slopes steeply to great banks of rhododendrons. Bedrooms, the one in the turret with a sumptuous bathroom, are large, luscious, warm and inviting: crushed velvet, beautiful blankets, immaculate linen – all ooze panache. Expect decanters of sherry, innovative décor, a Louis XV bed and a superb suite with contemporary touches. Elegant breakfasts are served at mahogany tables with linen napkins; Joan's warm vivacity and love of B&B means guests keep coming back. And just a 10-minute walk into town.

Rooms	2 doubles: £130–£140.
	1 suite for 2: £130–£145.
Meals	Restaurants 12-minute walk.
Closed	Mid-November to March.

Joan & John Campbell
The Grange,
Grange Road,
Fort William, PH33 6JF
Tel   +44 (0)1397 705516
Email   info@thegrange-scotland.co.uk
Web   www.thegrange-scotland.co.uk

Entry 576   Map 17

Highland

Arisaig House

Imposing Arisaig – a 19th-century industrialist's highland fantasy – sits in a walkers' paradise; the views to Skye are to die for. In former days it was a hotel; now Sarah, who has known Arisaig all her life, revels in returning house and gardens to their former glory. The sitting room is bright with Sanderson sofas, portraits and paintings and a huge open fire, and bedrooms are spacious and charming, with comfortable furniture and updated bathrooms. Lovely generous Sarah, passionate Slow Food member, serves breakfasts, high teas and dinners at the long oak table: don't miss the Stornoway black pudding!

Rooms	4 twin/doubles, 6 suites for 2:
	£145–£165.
	Singles £85.
Meals	Dinner, 3 courses, from £25.
	Pub/restaurant 3 miles.
Closed	Rarely

Sarah Winnington-Ingram
Arisaig House,
Arisaig, PH39 4NR
Tel   +44 (0)1687 450730
Email   sarahwi@arisaighouse.co.uk
Web   www.arisaighouse.co.uk

Entry 577   Map 17

Highland

The Berry

Drive through miles of spectacular landscape then bask in the final approach down a winding single-track road to Allt-Na-Subh – just five houses overlooking the loch. Joan, who is friendly and kind, prepares delicious meals in her Rayburn-warmed kitchen – the hub of this character-filled house. Inside is fresh and light with stylish bedrooms – one up, one down; the sitting room has a log fire and stunning views. Eat fish straight from the boats, pop over to Skye, stride the hills and spot golden eagles, red deer and otters. The perfect place for naturalists and artists, or those seeking solace. A hidden gem.

Minimum stay: 2 nights.

Rooms	1 double with separate shower; 1 double sharing bath with owner: £80. Singles from £45.
Meals	Dinner, 3 courses with wine, £30. Packed lunch £10. Pub 3 miles.
Closed	Rarely.

	Joan Ashburner The Berry, Allt-Na-Subh, Dornie, Kyle of Lochalsh, IV40 8DZ
Tel	+44 (0)1599 588259

Highland

Aurora

The perfect spot for walkers and climbers (single-track roads, lochs, rivers and mountains) and the perfect B&B for groups: three smart, uncluttered bedrooms have flexible sleeping arrangements and spick and span shower rooms. The guest sitting room is light and airy with binoculars, books to borrow, maps and a small fridge for your wine – stay put for glorious sunsets and views to Harris. Breakfast time is generously bendy; good seasonal food is important here and you eat round a big table. There's a drying room and bike storage, but those wanting to relax will love it here too.

Over 12s welcome.

Rooms	2 doubles: £78–£88. 1 triple: £120–£132. Singles £68–£78.
Meals	Packed lunch £6. Pub/restaurant within 0.5 miles.
Closed	November–March.

	Ann Barton Aurora, Shieldaig, Torridon, IV54 8XN
Tel	+44 (0)1520 755246
Email	info@aurora-bedandbreakfast.co.uk
Web	www.aurora-bedandbreakfast.co.uk

Highland

The Peatcutter's Croft

Some say there's more beauty in a mile on the west coast than in the rest of the world put together – vast skies, soaring mountains, shimmering water, barely a soul in sight. Pauline and Seori left London to give their family the freedom to roam. Now they have a colourful cast of companions: sheep, hens, ducks, rabbits – all live here. In the adjoining byre: country simplicity, a Norwegian wood-burner, colour, texture and style. Sea eagles patrol the skies, porpoises bask in the loch, red deer come to eat the garden. This, coupled with Pauline's home cooking, makes it very hard to leave. Dogs and children are very welcome.

Rooms	1 apartment for 2 with mezzanine for 2 children: £70. Singles from £45. £100 for family of 4.
Meals	Dinner, 3 courses, £30. BYO. Pub/restaurant 30 miles.
Closed	Christmas.

Seori & Pauline Burnett
The Peatcutter's Croft,
Croft 12, Badrallach, Dundonnell,
Garve, Ullapool, IV23 2QP
Tel   +44 (0)1854 633797
Email   info@peatcutterscroft.com
Web   www.peatcutterscroft.com

Entry 580   Map 17

Highland

The Old Ferryman's House

This former ferryman's house is small, homely and lived-in, just yards from the river Spey with its spectacular mountain views. Explore the countryside or relax in the garden with a tray of tea and homemade treats; plants tumble from whisky barrels and pots and you can spot woodpeckers. The sitting room is cosy with a wood-burning stove and brimming with books and magazines (no TV). Generous Elizabeth, a keen traveller who lived in the Sudan, cooks delicious, imaginative meals: herbs and veg from the garden, eggs from her hens, heathery honeycomb, homemade bread and jams. An unmatched spot for explorers, and very good value.

Rooms	1 double, 1 twin/double sharing 1 bath and 2 wcs with single: £75. 1 single: £37.50.
Meals	Dinner, 3 courses, £25. BYO. Packed lunch £7.50.
Closed	Occasionally in winter.

Elizabeth Matthews
The Old Ferryman's House,
Boat of Garten, PH24 3BY
Tel   +44 (0)1479 831370

Entry 581   Map 18

Highland

Craigiewood

The best of both worlds: Highland remoteness (red kites, wild goats) and Inverness just four miles away. The landscape surrounding this elegant cottage exudes a sense of ancient mystery… woodpeckers, deer, glorious roses all round. Araminta is a delightful host and her home has a lovely family feel; bedrooms are old-fashioned and cosy; the drawing room is snug with stove and books. Gavin almost built the house single-handed, planting a glorious garden here, and many throughout Scotland – his special touch remains. Meander up through rowan trees to a view point, sit and enjoy the peace. Inverewe, Attadale and Cawdor – all on the doorstep.

Rooms	2 twins: £80–£90.
	Singles £40–£50.
Meals	Pub 2 miles.
Closed	Christmas & New Year.

Araminta Dallmeyer
Craigiewood,
North Kessock, Inverness, IV1 3XG

Tel	+44 (0)1463 731628
Mobile	+44 (0)7831 733699
Email	2minty@craigiewood.co.uk
Web	www.craigiewood.co.uk

Entry 582   Map 18

Highland

Knockbain House

This is a well-loved farm, its environmental credentials supreme, and David and Denise are warm and interesting. A beautiful setting, too: landscaped gardens, a 700-acre farm (cows, lambs, barley) and rolling countryside stretching to Cromarty Firth. A grandfather clock ticks away time to relax: by floor-to-ceiling windows and a wood-burner in the antiques-filled sitting room; over a breakfast of local and home-grown produce; with a drink on the pond-side terrace; in bedrooms with fresh bathrooms and stunning views. David can advise on great walks, and has made maps of the farm's footpaths. Revel in the glorious unspoilt nature.

Babes in arms & children over 10 welcome.

Rooms	1 double, 1 twin: £70–£95.
	Singles £40–£45.
Meals	Dinner from £25.
	Pubs/restaurants 1 mile.
Closed	Christmas & New Year.

David & Denise Lockett
Knockbain House,
Dingwall, IV15 9TJ

Tel	+44 (0)1349 862476
Mobile	+44 (0)7736 629838
Email	davidlockett@avnet.co.uk
Web	www.knockbainhouse.co.uk

Entry 583   Map 18

Highland

Wemyss House

The peace is palpable, the setting overlooking the Cromarty Firth is stunning. Take an early morning stroll and spot buzzards, pheasants, rabbits and roe deer. The deceptively spacious house with sweeping maple floors is flooded with light and fabulous views, big bedrooms are warmly decorated with Highland rugs and tweeds, there's Christine's grand piano in the living room, Stuart's handcrafted furniture at every turn, and a sweet dog called Bella. Aga breakfasts include homemade bread, preserves and eggs from happy hens. Dinners are delicious; Christine and Stuart are wonderful hosts.

Rooms	2 doubles, 1 twin/double: £115–£120.
Meals	Dinner, 3 courses, £38.
	Restaurants 15-minute drive.
Closed	Rarely.

Christine Asher & Stuart Clifford
Wemyss House,
Bayfield, Tain, IV19 1QW
Tel   +44 (0)1862 851212
Mobile +44 (0)7759 484709
Email   stay@wemysshouse.com
Web   www.wemysshouse.com

Entry 584   Map 18

Highland

St Callan's Manse

Fun, laughter and conversation flow in this warm and happy home. You share it with prints, paintings, antiques, sofas, amazing memorabilia, two dogs, four ducks, 10 hens and 1,200 teddy bears of every size and origin. Snug bedrooms have pretty fabrics, old armoires, flower-patterned sheets and tartan blankets; your sleep will be sound. Caroline cooks majestic breakfasts and dinners; Robert, a fund of knowledgeable anecdotes, can arrange just about anything. Their Highland hospitality knows no bounds! All this in incomparable surroundings: 60 acres of land plus glens, forests, buzzards, deer and the odd golden eagle. A gem.

Dogs by arrangement.

Rooms	1 double, 1 double, each with
	separate bath: £90.
	Singles £65.
Meals	Dinner, 2–4 courses, £20–£35. BYO.
	Pub/restaurant in village 1.5 miles.
Closed	March & occasionally.

Robert & Caroline Mills
St Callan's Manse,
Rogart, IV28 3XE
Tel   +44 (0)1408 641363
Email caroline@rogartsnuff.me.uk
Web   www.spanglefish.com/
          stcallansmanse

Entry 585   Map 21

Isle of Skye

The Cottage Stein

John and Fiona are warm and welcoming – you'll feel at home straight away. They've renovated their 200-year-old crofter's cottage with love and contemporary style, the views from bedrooms and guest sitting room are astonishing and a short walk takes you to the edge of the loch. Wake to breakfast in the cosy dining room – continental and cooked options, including full Scottish and lighter and sweeter choices, are all served with John's delicious homemade bread. Heaps to do nearby: boat trips, art galleries, Dunvegan Castle and great walks. Supper is easy: it's a stroll to Skye's oldest inn and a seafood restaurant – both right on the water.

Minimum stay: 2 nights in high season. Over 12s welcome.

Rooms	1 double, 1 twin/double: £95–£110. Singles £70–£85.
Meals	Pubs/restaurants 1-minute walk.
Closed	Rarely.

John & Fiona Middleton
The Cottage Stein,
Stein, Waternish, IV55 8GA

Tel	+44 (0)1470 592734
Mobile	+44 (0)7742 193901
Email	stay@thecottagestein.co.uk
Web	www.thecottagestein.co.uk

Entry 586   Map 17

Lanarkshire

The Lint Mill

Rolling hills, fields of sheep and a babbling stream surround this perfectly peaceful converted mill. Deborah and Colin escaped city life to create a smallholding full of flowers, beehives, vegetables, funky sheep, pigs, chickens with fancy houses and horses with a dressage paddock. The light, roomy wing has a separate entrance and private garden, a spiral staircase, its own sitting room and a big wood-burner. Unwind, walk in the countryside, enjoy the fruits (and scones) of their labour, get creative in their artists' studio or pop to excitement in Edinburgh or Glasgow. Foodies will be treated to all manner of local delights.

See website for availability calendar.

Rooms	1 double with sitting room & conservatory: £90–£105. Singles £50. Extra bed/sofabed available £40 per person per night.
Meals	Dinner, 2-4 courses, £20–£30. Supper £10. Platter for 2, £15. Restaurants 2 miles.
Closed	Rarely.

Colin & Deborah Richardson-Webb
The Lint Mill,
Carnwath, Lanark, ML11 8LY

Tel	+44 (0)1555 840042
Mobile	+44 (0)7966 164742
Email	info@thelintmill.co.uk
Web	www.thelintmill.co.uk

Entry 587   Map 15

Lanarkshire

Cormiston Farm

Wend your way through the soft hills of the Clyde Valley to a Georgian farmhouse in 26 acres of farmland and mature garden. Richard's a keen cook and produce from the walled garden – including delicious eggs from the quails – takes centre stage. Wonderful to retire to quiet, spacious rooms with bucolic views, stunning beds and rich fabrics; characterful Art Deco bathrooms, too. Tuck nippers up in bunks, then slip back for a snifter in front of the log fire in the sitting room. It's home from home, and licensed, too! There's untamed landscape to explore – and the children will love the friendly alpacas.

Rooms	2 doubles, each with separate bath: £86–£108. Singles £65–£81. Extra bunk room available.
Meals	Dinner, 4 courses, £25–£30. Supper, 2 courses, £20. Pub 2 miles.
Closed	Rarely.

	Richard Philipps Cormiston Farm, Cormiston Road, Biggar, ML12 6NS
Tel	+44 (0)1899 221507
Email	info@cormistonfarm.com
Web	www.cormistonfarm.com

Moray

Westfield House

Sweep up the drive to the grand home of an illustrious family: Macleans have lived here since 1862, and there are 500 peaceful acres of farmland. Inside: polished furniture and burnished antiques, a tartan-carpeted hall, an oak stair hung with ancestral oils. Veronica cooks sublimely; dinner is served at a long candelabra'd table, with vegetables from the vegetable garden. A winter fire crackles in the guest sitting room, old-fashioned bedrooms are inviting (plump pillows, fine linen, books, lovely views), the peace is deep. The coast is close and the walking is splendid; a historic house in a perfect setting and Veronica is charming.

Rooms	1 twin; 1 twin with separate bath & shower: £100. 1 single with separate bath: £50–£55. Extra bed/sofabed available £20 per person per night.
Meals	Supper, 2 courses, £20. Dinner, 3 courses, £25. Pub 3 miles.
Closed	Rarely.

	Veronica Maclean Westfield House, Elgin, IV30 8XL
Tel	+44 (0)1343 547308
Email	veronica.maclean@yahoo.co.uk
Web	www.westfieldhouseelgin.co.uk

Perth & Kinross

Beinn Bhracaigh

Excellent views stretch out from this Victorian villa. All the bedrooms are in relaxing creams, with duck-egg blues in throws and subtly patterned cushions propped like toast in a toast rack; TVs and fine Scottish soaps complete the Perthshire picture. Friendly hosts give you a continental breakfast in your room or a full Scottish and good coffee at separate tables in the dining room. Great fun and conviviality can be had in the evening when guests take over the honesty bar with its many wines and more than 50 whiskies. Amble to Pitlochry Theatre; discover an area rich with castles, fishing, white water rafting and walks.

Minimum stay: 2 nights at weekends. Children over 8 welcome.

Rooms	8 doubles, 3 twin/doubles: £69–£102. 1 suite for 2: £89–£129. Singles from £49.
Meals	14 pubs/restaurants within 10-minute walk.
Closed	Rarely.

James & Kirsty Watts
Beinn Bhracaigh,
14 Higher Oakfield,
Pitlochry, PH16 5HT
Tel   +44 (0)1796 470355
Email   info@beinnbhracaigh.com
Web   www.beinnbhracaigh.com

Entry 590   Map 15+18

Perth & Kinross

Cuil an Duin

Rhododendrons form a brilliant guard of honour to escort you to the front door, and you arrive to tea and scones in the drawing room. Admire mountain views, head off into woodland, roam the gardens, chat to the horses – the 20 acres are stunning. Inside is just as good: elegant rooms, Persian rugs, modern art, flowers, a gleaming Bechstein; sunny bedrooms are luxuriously comforting. Happy hens foraging in the fields lay your breakfast eggs, artisan shops provide the trimmings. Sally and David are charming, Jack Russell Teddy and Chloe the cat stay behind the kitchen door until given the all clear, and there are outdoor pursuits galore.

Minimum stay: 2 nights. Over 12s welcome.

Rooms	1 double, 1 twin/double; 1 double with separate bath: £115–£145. Singles £100–£130.
Meals	Pubs/restaurant 1.5 miles.
Closed	Rarely.

Sally Keay & David Royce
Cuil an Duin,
Ballinluig,
Pitlochry, PH9 0NN
Tel   +44 (0)1796 482807
Email   enquiries@cuil-an-duin.com
Web   www.cuil-an-duin.com

Entry 591   Map 15+18

Perth & Kinross

Essendy House

Down a tree-lined drive blazing with colour, Tess and John's charming country house is surrounded by lochs, castles and serenity. Inside is cosy and comfortable with warm fires, flowers, porcelain, Italianate murals and an unusual collection of family artefacts. Traditionally furnished bedrooms have antiques, good linen, garden views and silk or floral touches. Enjoy hearty breakfasts and suppers in the huge dining room or family kitchen; the terrace is heaven in summer. There's lots to do: visit cathedral and theatre, walk in Macbeth's Birnam Wood, play golf, ski, fish and admire the swooping ospreys.

Perth & Kinross

Mackeanston House

They grow their own organic fruit and vegetables in the walled garden, make their own preserves, bake their own bread. Likeable and energetic – Fiona a wine buff and talented cook, Colin a tri-lingual guide – your hosts are hospitable people whose 1690 farmhouse combines informality and luxury in peaceful, central Scotland. Light-filled bedrooms have pretty fabrics, fine antiques, TVs and homemade cake. Roomy bathrooms have robes and a radio; one has a double shower (with a seat if you wish it). Dine by the log fire in the dining room, or in the conservatory with views to Stirling Castle.

Rooms	1 double, 1 twin: £110.
	Singles £55.
	Dinner, B&B £80 per person.
Meals	Packed lunch £5.
	Supper, 2 courses, £25.
	Pub/restaurant 2 miles.
Closed	Christmas & New Year;
	February/March.

Rooms	1 double, 1 twin/double: £90-£104.
	Singles £65-£67.
	Dinner, B&B £79-£85 per person.
	Extra bed/sofabed available £25 per
	person per night.
Meals	Dinner, 3 courses, £33; 4 courses, £36.
	Pub 1 mile.
Closed	Rarely.

	John Monteith
	Essendy House,
	Blairgowrie, PH10 6QY
Tel	+44 (0)1250 884260
Mobile	+44 (0)7841 121538
Email	johnmonteith@hotmail.com
Web	www.essendy.org

	Fiona & Colin Graham
	Mackeanston House,
	Doune, Stirling, FK16 6AX
Tel	+44 (0)1786 850213
Mobile	+44 (0)7921 143018
Email	info@mackeanstonhouse.co.uk
Web	www.mackeanstonhouse.co.uk

Entry 592   Map 15+18

Entry 593   Map 15

Perth & Kinross

Old Kippenross

What a setting! Old Kippenross rests in 150 peaceful acres of gorgeous park and woodland overlooking the river Allan — spot red squirrels and deer, herons, dippers and otters. The 15th-century house has a Georgian addition and an air of elegance and great courtesy, with its rustic white-vaulted basement, and dining and sitting rooms strewn with soft sofas and Persian rugs. Sash-windowed bedrooms are deeply comfortable, warm bathrooms are stuffed with towels. Susan and Patrick (an expert on birds of prey) are welcoming, the food is good and there's a croquet lawn in the walled garden.

Children over 10 welcome. Dogs by arrangement only.

Rooms	1 double, 1 twin/double (adjoining single room, let to same party only): £108–£112. Singles £69–£71.
Meals	Dinner £30. BYO. Pub 1.5 miles.
Closed	Rarely.

Susan & Patrick Stirling–Aird
Old Kippenross,
Kippenross,
Dunblane, FK15 0LQ
Tel   +44 (0)1786 824048
Email   kippenross@hotmail.com
Web   www.oldkippenross.co.uk

Entry 594   Map 15

Scottish Borders

Fauhope House

Near to Melrose Abbey and the glorious St Cuthbert's Way, this solid 1890s house is immersed in bucolic bliss. Views soar to the Eildon Hills through wide windows with squashy seats; all is luxurious, elegant, fire-lit and serene with an eclectic mix of art. Bedrooms are warm with deeply coloured walls, pale tartan blankets and soft velvet and linen; bathrooms are modern and pristine. Breakfast is served with smiles at a flower-laden table and overlooking those purple hills. A short walk through the blooming garden and over a footbridge takes you to the interesting town of Melrose, with shops, restaurants and its own theatre.

Rooms	3 twin/doubles: £100–£140. Singles from £60.
Meals	Pub/restaurant 0.5 miles.
Closed	Rarely.

Ian & Sheila Robson
Fauhope House,
Gattonside, Melrose, TD6 9LU
Tel   +44 (0)1896 823184
Mobile +44 (0)7816 346768
Email   info@fauhopehouse.com
Web   www.fauhopehouse.com

Entry 595   Map 15

Scottish Borders

Whitehouse Country House

A proud avenue of trees leads to Angela and Roger's handsome 19th-century country house in the heart of the Scottish Borders. They have been welcoming guests for over 20 years providing comfort, relaxation and great hospitality. Enjoy log fires and deep armchairs in the elegant dining and drawing rooms, traditional bedrooms with the most comfortable beds and glorious views from every room. Angela's cooking is heavenly and she uses wild salmon, game and the finest in-season local produce. Explore historic Border towns, cycle the Tweed Cycle Way, walk St Cuthbert's Way – your hosts know the area well and are happy to advise.

Pets by arrangement.

Rooms	1 double, 2 twins: £120-£140. Singles £80-£90. Dinner, B&B £109-£119 per person. Extra bed/sofabed available £25-£35 per person per night.
Meals	Dinner £22-£29. Supper tray £10. Packed lunch £7. Pub 3 miles.
Closed	Rarely.

Angela & Roger Tyrer
Whitehouse Country House,
St Boswells, Melrose, TD6 0ED

Tel	+44 (0)1573 460343
Mobile	+44 (0)7877 800582
Email	stay@whitehousecountryhouse.com
Web	www.whitehousecountryhouse.com

Entry 596   Map 16

Scottish Borders

Singdean

Remote, high up and rugged. You have your own entrance to a smart-and-soulful suite in this glorious Border cottage. You'll be toasty warm and comfortable: find an enormous double bed, delicious linen, exposed stonework, reclaimed wood cladding and thick fabrics. Take a deep breath out, light the candles, scent the bath… romantics will be thrilled to bits. Fresh, ski-style breakfasts are brought to you, packed lunches can be sorted and if you don't want to budge, have supper with friendly Christa and Del. They'll even drop you at the pub and pick you up. Walks are awe-inspiring but Hawick has cashmere!

Rooms	1 suite for 2: £135-£148.
Meals	Packed lunch & supper included by prior arrangement (voluntary contribution to the Landscaping Fund). Pub 6 miles.
Closed	Rarely.

Christa & Del Dobson
Singdean,
Newcastleton, TD9 0SP

Tel	+44 (0)1450 860622
Email	info@alppine.co.uk
Web	www.alppine.co.uk/

Entry 597   Map 16

Duchray Castle

Warm friendly Frances has thought of everything: a furnished terrace by the round tower, logs ablaze in the Great Hall, sofas, books, magazines, DVDs, and Arran Aromatics by the bath. Deep in the Trossachs National Park, at the end of the long forest track, you arrive in the clearing and there is the castle – simple, beautiful and steeped in five centuries of history. Inside all is deliciously cosy. Bedrooms are relaxing (the grandest with a log-burner), bathrooms are sleek, there are spiral stone stairs, sweeping wood floors, gilded mirrors, and breakfasts of the finest local produce. Stay a long weekend – or more.

Minimum stay: 2 nights.

Rooms	2 doubles, 1 twin, 1 four-poster: £105–£185. Singles £75–£105.
Meals	Pubs/restaurants 2.5 miles.
Closed	Rarely.

Frances Bigwood
Duchray Castle,
Duchray Road,
Aberfoyle, FK8 3XL
Tel   +44 (0)1877 389333
Email   frances@duchraycastle.com
Web   www.duchraycastle.com

Entry 598   Map 14

Cardross

Dodge the lazy sheep on the long drive to arrive (eventually!) at a sweep of gravel and lovely old Cardross in a gorgeous setting. Bang on the enormous ancient door and either Archie or Nicola (plus labradors and lively Jack Russells) will usher you in. And what a delight it is; come here for a blast of Scottish history! Traditional big bedrooms have airiness, long views, antiques, wooden shutters, towelling robes and good linen; one bathroom has a cast-iron period bath. The drawing room is vast, the house is filled with warm character, the Orr Ewings can tell you all the history.

Over 14s welcome.

Rooms	1 twin; 1 twin with separate bath: £110–£120. Singles £70–£75.
Meals	Occasional dinner £35. Pubs/restaurants 3–6 miles.
Closed	Christmas & New Year.

Sir Archie & Lady Orr Ewing
Cardross,
Port of Menteith,
Kippen, FK8 3JY
Tel   +44 (0)1877 385223
Email   enquiries@cardrossestate.com
Web   www.cardrossestate.com

Entry 599   Map 15

Stirling

Powis House

A sprawling 18th-century mansion with the volcanic Ochil Hills as a stunning backdrop and a colourful entrance hall of antlers and stuffed animals. Country style bedrooms invite with polished old floors, tartan throws, garden views and original bathrooms. You have a huge dining room with warming wood-burner, a guest lounge on the first floor, a sunny stone-flagged patio with places to sit and acres of estate with a woodland walk to explore. Colin and Jane are caring and interesting; Colin is a keen cook and has ghost stories galore to share. Historical Stirling is close: castle, university, festival and more.

Rooms	2 doubles, 1 twin: £90–£100. Singles £65.
Meals	Dinner, 4 courses with coffee, £25. Pub/restaurant 3 miles.
Closed	Rarely.

Jane & Colin Kilgour
Powis House,
Stirling, FK9 5PS
Tel   +44 (0)1786 460231
Email   info@powishouse.co.uk
Web   www.powishouse.co.uk

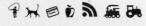

Entry 600   Map 15

Stirling

Quarter

This stately 1750s house commands views across Stirling's lush countryside and comes complete with crunching gravel drive, original ceiling dome and open fires. It was owned by the same family for generations until the Macleans took over its high ceilings, cornicing features and sash windows. Pad your way upstairs to two comfortable bedrooms and bathrooms, brightened with a pretty floral touch. Breakfast is a grand affair at a long polished table in the dining room (the free-range hens providing the eggs). You are cocooned in extensive grounds, yet have easy access to Stirling, Edinburgh, Perth and Glasgow.

Dogs welcome by arrangement.

Rooms	1 twin/double, 1 twin: £110. Singles £65.
Meals	Pub/restaurant 4 miles.
Closed	Rarely.

Pippa Maclean
Quarter,
Denny, FK6 6QZ
Tel   +44 (0)1324 825817
Email   quarterstirling@hotmail.co.uk
Web   www.quarterstirling.com

Entry 601   Map 15

Pairc an t-Srath

Richard and Lena's lovely home overlooks the beach at Borve – another absurdly beautiful Harris view. Inside, smart simplicity abounds: wooden floors, white walls, a peat fire, colourful art. Airy bedrooms fit the mood perfectly: trim carpets, chunky wood beds, Harris tweed throws, excellent shower rooms (there's a bathroom, too, if you want a soak). Richard crofts, Lena cooks, perhaps homemade soup, venison casserole, wet chocolate cake with raspberries. Views from the dining room tumble down hill, so expect to linger over breakfast. You'll spot otters in the loch, while the standing stones at Callanish are unmissable.

Kinloch

Never a dull moment here in Wegg's house and you're encouraged to feel at home. All is friendly and full of interest with gorgeous food, good company and a happy dog. The house, built in the 70s, is comfy with books, photos, easy chairs and art. Bedrooms (one downstairs) are fresh and sunny; views across the loch are enormous and sunrises spectacular. Breakfasts and dinners are wonderfully sociable occasions and Wegg loves cooking: homemade bread, eggs from his hens, barbecued freshly caught trout. Wander the woodland garden and machair, fish the loch, spot the birds… return to relax by the log fire. A special place.

Minimum stay: 2 nights at weekends.

Rooms	2 doubles, 1 twin: £104–£108.
	1 single: £52–£54.
Meals	Dinner, 3 courses, £37.
	Restaurant 3 miles, pub 7 miles.
Closed	Rarely.

Rooms	1 twin/double; 1 twin/double with
	separate bath: £98.
	1 single with separate bath: £49.
Meals	Dinner £25. Packed lunch £5–£8.
	Restaurant 5 miles.
Closed	Rarely.

	Lena & Richard MacLennan
	Pairc an t-Srath,
	Borve, Isle of Harris, HS3 3HT
Tel	+44 (0)1859 550386
Email	info@paircant-srath.co.uk
Web	www.paircant-srath.co.uk

	Wegg Kimbell
	Kinloch,
	Grogarry, Isle of South Uist, HS8 5RR
Tel	+44 (0)1870 620316
Email	wegg@kinlochuist.com
Web	www.kinlochuist.com

Wales

Carmarthenshire

Mount Pleasant Farm

Wake to circling red kites with a breathtaking backdrop of the Black Mountain. Every room has wonderful views, and Sue and Nick are warm and delightful hosts. Food is a passion here and you'll enjoy homemade bread and jams, deep yellow eggs, organic veg and local lamb and pork; vegetarians are spoiled too – Sue is a brilliant cook. After dinner there's snooker, a log fire, a cosy sofa; then a seriously comfy bed in a room with a lovely country-house feel. There are excellent walks in the valley, fly fishing on the Towy, Llyn y Fan Fach in Brecon Beacons National Park; Aberglasney and the Botanic Gardens are nearby too.

Over 12s welcome. 1.5 hours from Pembroke Dock.

Rooms	1 twin/double; 1 twin/double, 1 twin sharing bath (let to same party only): £70-£75.
Meals	Dinner, 3 courses with wine, £20. Pub/restaurant 3 miles.
Closed	Christmas.

Sue & Nick Thompson
Mount Pleasant Farm,
Llanwrda, SA19 8AN
Tel   +44 (0)1550 777537
Email   nick@rivarevival.co.uk

Entry 604   Map 7

Carmarthenshire

Sarnau Mansion

Listed and Georgian, this handsome house has 16 acres of grounds complete with pond, well-tended walled garden and woodland with nesting red kites. Bedrooms are calm and traditionally furnished with heritage colours, art poster prints and green views; big bathrooms have plenty of hot water. The oak-floored sitting room with leather Chesterfields has French windows leading onto the rhododendron lawn, the guest dining room has separate tables, and there's home cooking from Cynthia. A peaceful place from which to explore beaches, castles and more – 15 minutes from the National Botanic Garden of Wales.

Children over 5 welcome.

Rooms	2 doubles, 1 twin; 1 double with separate bath: £80-£90. Singles £45-£55.
Meals	Dinner, 3 courses, around £25. BYO. Pub 1 mile.
Closed	Rarely.

Cynthia & David Fernihough
Sarnau Mansion,
Llysonnen Road, Bancyfelin,
Carmarthen, SA33 5DZ
Tel   +44 (0)1267 211404
Email   d.fernihough@btinternet.com
Web   www.sarnaumansion.co.uk

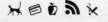

Entry 605   Map 6

Carmarthenshire

The Glynhir Estate

This fine old house on a Huguenot estate stands on the western edge of the Black Mountain. Outside: a waterfall, a two-acre kitchen garden, a brigade of chickens, and peacocks that patrol the grounds with panache. Inside, the house has spurned the urge to take itself too seriously and remains decidedly lived in. Find William Morris wallpaper in the dining room, lemon trees in the conservatory and old cabinets stuffed with interesting things in the sitting room. Country-house bedrooms fit the mood perfectly: smart and comfortable with excellent bathrooms. You can ride, walk, fish or visit Aberglasney – just ask Katy.

Rooms	5 doubles: £85–£104.
	1 family room for 4 (suitable for 2 adults and 1-2 children under 12): £104–£122.
	Singles £55.
Meals	Dinner from £19.50.
	Pubs/restaurants 2 miles.
Closed	November–March.

Katy Jenkins
The Glynhir Estate,
Glynhir Road, Llandybie,
Ammanford, SA18 2TD
Tel   +44 (0)1269 850438
Mobile   +44 (0)7810 864458
Email   enquiries@theglynhirestate.com
Web   www.theglynhirestate.com

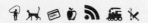

Entry 606   Map 7

Ceredigion

Broniwan

The Jacobs began farming organically here in the 70s and concentrate now on their kitchen garden – meals celebrate their success. Their cosy ivy-clad home is quietly, colourfully stylish, with books, watercolours and good local art; the attractive guest bedroom has a traditional Welsh bedspread and views to the Preseli Hills. There are acres to roam and the meadow garden's pond brims with life. Carole is passionate about history and literature and can advise on days out: try the Museum of Quilts in Lampeter, or Aberglasney, an hour's drive. Do linger; this is such a rich spot.

Minimum stay: 2 nights.

Rooms	1 double: £80–£90.
	Singles £45.
Meals	Dinner £25–£30. BYO.
	Restaurants 7-8 miles.
Closed	Rarely.

Carole & Allen Jacobs
Broniwan,
Rhydlewis,
Llandysul, SA44 5PF
Tel   +44 (0)1239 851261
Email   broniwan@btinternet.com
Web   www.broniwan.weebly.com

Entry 607   Map 6

Ceredigion

Ffynnon Fendigaid

Arrive through rolling countryside – birdsong and breeze the only sound; within moments you will be sprawled on a leather sofa admiring modern art and wondering how a little bit of Milan arrived here along with Huw and homemade cake. A place to come and pootle, with no rush; you can stay all day to stroll the fern-fringed paths through the acres of wild garden to a lake and a grand bench, or opt for hearty walking. Your bed is big, the colours are soft, the bathrooms are spotless and the food is local – try all the Welsh cheeses. Wide beaches are close by, red kites and buzzards soar above you. Pulchritudinous.

Rooms	2 doubles: £75-£80.
	Singles £47-£50.
Meals	Dinner, 2-3 courses, £20-£22.
	Pub 1 mile.
Closed	Rarely.

Huw Davies
Ffynnon Fendigaid,
Rhydlewis, Llandysul, SA44 5SR

Tel	+44 (0)1239 851361
Mobile	+44 (0)7974 135262
Email	ffynnonf@btinternet.com
Web	www.ffynnonf.co.uk

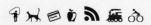

Entry 608   Map 6

Conwy

St Curigs Church

Blessed are those who enter, especially mountain lovers of a gregarious nature. This converted church is a proper family home so be prepared to fit in with all and sundry: Welsh harp may echo in the domed mosaic ceiling, there are marble pillars and stained glass and breakfast is taken at a large table beneath the pine-vaulted apse. Bedrooms are country cosy and in one four-poster a stone pulpit watches over you while underfloor heating keeps it all warm. The views to Snowdon are glorious, walks galore lead from the door and after tackling the sensational Glyders you can soak in the hot tub. Ecclesiastical bohemia at its best.

Rooms	2 twins, 2 four-posters: £70-£75.
	1 bunk room for 4: £20 per person
	including breakfast.
	Extra rooms available.
Meals	Pub 300 yds.
Closed	Rarely.

Alice Douglas
St Curigs Church,
Capel Curig,
Betws-y-Coed, LL24 0EL

Tel	+44 (0)1690 720469
Email	alice@alicedouglas.com
Web	www.stcurigschurch.com

Entry 609   Map 7

Conwy

Pengwern Country House (Snowdonia)

The steeply wooded Conwy valley snakes down to this stone and slate property set back from the road in Snowdonia National Park, and the walks are wonderful. Inside has an upbeat traditional feel: a large sitting room with tall bay windows and pictures by the Betws-y-Coed artists who once lived here. Settle with a book by the wood-burner; Gwawr and Ian are naturally friendly and treat guests as friends. Bedrooms have rough plastered walls, colourful fabrics and super bathrooms; one comes with a double-ended roll top tub and views of Lledr Valley. Breakfast on fruits, herb rösti, soda bread – superb.

Minimum stay: 2 nights.

Rooms	1 double, 1 twin/double, 1 four-poster: £72-£84. Singles from £62.
Meals	Packed lunch £5.50. Pubs/restaurants within 1.5 miles.
Closed	Christmas & New Year.

	Gwawr & Ian Mowatt
	Pengwern Country House,
	Allt Dinas, Betws-y-Coed, LL24 0HF
Tel	+44 (0)1690 710480
Email	gwawr.pengwern@btopenworld.com
Web	www.snowdoniaaccommodation.co.uk

Entry 610   Map 7

Denbighshire

Plas Efenechtyd Cottage

Efenechtyd means 'place of the monks' but there's nothing spartan about Dave and Marilyn's handsome brick farmhouse. Breakfasts of local sausages, eggs from their hens, salmon fishcakes with mushrooms and homemade bread are served at a polished table in the dining room with exotic wall hangings from Vietnam and Laos. Light bedrooms have an uncluttered feel, excellent mattresses and good linen; bathrooms are warm as toast. In the pretty cottage garden: a summerhouse and Marilyn's beehive. Motor to Ruthin, with its windy streets and interesting shops, or strike out for Offa's Dyke with a packed lunch; this is stunning countryside.

Rooms	2 doubles, 1 twin: £75. Singles £50.
Meals	Packed lunch £6. Pub 1.6 miles.
Closed	Rarely.

	Dave Jones & Marilyn Jeffery
	Plas Efenechtyd Cottage,
	Efenechtyd, Ruthin, LL15 2LP
Tel	+44 (0)1824 704008
Mobile	+44 (0)7540 501009
Email	info@plas-efenechtyd-cottage.co.uk
Web	www.plas-efenechtyd-cottage.co.uk

Entry 611   Map 7

Flintshire

Plas Penucha

Swing back in time with polished parquet, tidy beams, a huge Elizabethan panelled lounge with books, leather sofas and open fire — a cosy spot for Nest's dogs and for tea in winter. Plas Penucha — 'the big house on the highest point in the parish' — has been in the family for 500 years. Airy, old-fashioned bedrooms have long views across the garden to Offa's Dyke and one has a shower in the corner. The L-shaped dining room has a genuine Arts & Crafts interior; outside, rhododendrons and a rock garden flourish. There are views to the Clwydian Range and beyond is St Asaph, with the smallest medieval cathedral in the country.

Rooms	1 double, 1 twin: £76. Singles £38.
Meals	Dinner £19. Packed lunch £5. Pub/restaurant 2-3 miles.
Closed	Rarely.

Nest Price
Plas Penucha,
Pen y Cefn Road,
Caerwys, Mold, CH7 5BH
Tel   +44 (0)1352 720210
Email nest@plaspenucha.co.uk
Web   www.plaspenucha.co.uk

Entry 612   Map 7

Flintshire

Gladstone's Library

If this glorious, unusual, historic and stunning place fails you as a retreat, then look deep within yourself. You have 250,000 books, silence, space, convivial company if you need it, Clwyd Theatr Cymru and Chester but 15 minutes away. Eucharist is held every weekday, delicious local food is there for you in the bistro, an open fire and sofas in the Gladstone room. The staff are lovely, the mood sheer old-fashioned decency. It is a Roberts radio, rather than TV, place. Bedrooms are warm, simple and unpretentious. Come for as long as you need to recover from this mad world. It will, for all adults, feel like a privilege.

Reception 8.30am–5pm. Check in from 2pm, check out 10am; you can use facilities and library once you have checked out. If arriving after 5pm please let us know in advance.

Rooms	14 doubles, 3 twins: £85-£90. 7 singles: £70.
Meals	Restaurant on site. Breakfast 8am–9am, Mon–Fri; 8.30am–9.30am, Sat & Sun. Lunch 12 noon–2pm. Dinner 6.45pm–7.15pm.
Closed	Christmas & New Year.

Gladstone's Library,
Church Lane, Hawarden,
Deeside, CH5 3DF
Tel   +44 (0)1244 532350
Email enquiries@gladlib.org
Web   www.gladstoneslibrary.org

Entry 613   Map 7

Gwynedd

Y Goeden Eirin

A little gem tucked between the sea and the mountains, an education in Welsh culture, and a great place to explore wild Snowdonia, the Llyn peninsula and the dramatic Yr Eifl mountain. Inside presents a cosy picture: Welsh-language and English books share the shelves, paintings by contemporary Welsh artists enliven the walls, an arty 70s décor mingles with sturdy Welsh oak in the bedrooms – the one in the house the best – and all bathrooms are super. Wonderful food is served alongside the Bechstein in the beamed dining room – the welcoming, thoughtful Eluned and John have created an unusually delightful space.

Rooms	1 double, 2 twin/doubles (Sea & Mountain Rooms, shower only): £80–£90. Singles £60–£70. Dinner, B&B £88–£118 per person.
Meals	Dinner, 4 courses, £28. Wine from £14. Packed lunch £12. Pub/restaurant 0.75 miles.
Closed	Christmas, New Year & occasionally.

John & Eluned Rowlands
Y Goeden Eirin,
Dolydd, Caernarfon, LL54 7EF
Tel   +44 (0)1286 830942
Mobile   +44 (0)7708 491234
Email   john_rowlands@tiscali.co.uk
Web   www.ygoedeneirin.co.uk

Entry 614   Map 6

Gwynedd

The Slate Shed at Graig Wen

Sarah and conservationist John spent months travelling in a camper looking for their own special place and found this lovely old Welsh slate cutting mill… captivated by acres of wild woods and stunning views. You'll feel at ease as soon as you step into their eclectic modern home with its reclaimed slate and wood, cosy wood-burners, books, games, snug bedrooms (one downstairs) and superb bathrooms. Breakfast communally on local eggs and sausages, honey from the mountainside, homemade bread and granola. Hike or bike the Mawddach Trail, climb Cadair Idris, wonder at the views… and John's chocolate brownies.

Minimum stay: 2 nights at weekends & in high season. Children over 10 welcome.

Rooms	4 doubles, 1 twin/double: £75–£130. Singles £65.
Meals	Packed lunch £6.50. Pub 5 miles.
Closed	Rarely.

Sarah Heyworth
The Slate Shed at Graig Wen,
Arthog, LL39 1YP
Tel   +44 (0)1341 250482
Email   hello@graigwen.co.uk
Web   www.slateshed.co.uk

Entry 615   Map 7

Gwynedd

The Old Rectory on the lake

Hike to Cadair Idris – the scenery is breathtaking. Return to a hot tub under the stars, and champagne to toast your good fortune. This lakeside B&B in southern Snowdonia is utterly spoiling and Ricky has become a chef of reputation. Slow-roast lamb shank, fillet of local salmon, a trio of Welsh ices; the menus change each day. Spacious bedrooms (one is downstairs) have ever-changing views, bathrooms are sumptuous and you wake to the smell of Welsh bacon: breakfasts are to die for. Binoculars for the birds, a wonderful welcome for you, candlelit dining… it's bliss.

Minimum stay: 2 nights at weekends, 3 on bank holidays.

Rooms	4 doubles: £120.
	Singles £70.
Meals	Dinner, 4 courses, £30 (not Weds).
	Pub 4 miles.
Closed	January.

	Ricky Francis
	The Old Rectory on the lake,
	Talyllyn, LL36 9AJ
Tel	+44 (0)1654 782225
Email	enquiries@rectoryonthelake.co.uk
Web	www.rectoryonthelake.co.uk

Entry 616   Map 7

Monmouthshire

Myrtle Cottage

Boldly tackle the steep road up for a slice of heaven in Llandogo. You're in the heart of Ed and Tori's home, and along with little Elsie, George, Alicia and Amelia, they make terrific hosts. The sunny bedroom has French windows leading to the garden, and lovely wide views across the Wye Valley. Tori bakes fabulous breads, cakes and waffles and breakfasts in the family kitchen are scrumptious. Hike up and down the river, visit the pub at Brockweir, drop in for a beer at Ed's brewery – we recommend Humpty's Fuddle! On the first Saturday of the month you can enjoy a delicious stone-baked pizza at the brewery too.

Please note, the bendy road up the hill and the driveway farm track are steep, and may not be suitable for all vehicles, especially in winter!

Rooms	1 double sharing bath with family
	(extra bed for children available):
	£70. Singles £50.
Meals	Monthly pizza evenings at Brewery.
	Picnics & lunches £7.50–£25.
	Pubs/restaurants 3 miles.
Closed	Rarely.

	Edward & Tori Biggs
	Myrtle Cottage,
	Llandogo,
	Monmouth, NP25 4TP
Mobile	+44 (0)7824 663550
Email	shop@meadowfarm.org.uk

Entry 617   Map 7

Monmouthshire

Upper Red House

Head down the lane into deepest Monmouthshire and the meadows, orchards and woodland of Teona's organic farm. There are six ponds and miles of bushy hedges; bees, ponies, peafowl and wild flowers flourish. The 17th-century house, restored from dereliction, has lovely views, flagstones and oak, limewashed walls and a magical feel. Up steep stairs are rustic bedrooms with beams, lots of books, no TV; the attic rooms get the best views of all. Bathrooms are simple, one has a huge old roll top tub. After a good vegetarian breakfast at the long kitchen table take a farm tour, explore Offa's Dyke or the Wye Valley – and enjoy the silence.

Children over 8 welcome.

Rooms	2 doubles: £80-£95. 2 singles sharing bath with 1 double (let to same party only): £35-£45.
Meals	Vegetarian packed lunch £6. Pubs/restaurants 3.5 miles.
Closed	Rarely.

Teona Dorrien-Smith
Upper Red House,
Llanfihangel-Ystern-Llewern,
Monmouth, NP25 5HL
Tel   +44 (0)1600 780501
Email   upperredhouse@mac.com
Web   www.upperredhouse.co.uk

Entry 618   Map 7

Monmouthshire

Penpergwm Lodge

On the edge of the Brecon Beacons, a large and lovely Edwardian house. Breakfast round the mahogany table, relax by the fire in the sitting room with books to read and piano to play. The Boyles have been here for years and pour much of their energy into three beautiful acres of parterre and potager, orchard and flowers. Bedrooms are gloriously traditional – ancestral portraits, embroidered bed covers, big windows, good chintz – with garden views; bathrooms are a skip across the landing. A pool and tennis for the sporty, two summerhouses for the dreamy, a good pub you can walk to. Splendid, old-fashioned B&B.

Rooms	2 twins, each with separate bath: £75. Singles £45.
Meals	Pub 250 yds.
Closed	Rarely.

Catriona Boyle
Penpergwm Lodge,
Penpergwm,
Abergavenny, NP7 9AS
Tel   +44 (0)1873 840208
Email   boyle@penpergwm.co.uk
Web   www.penplants.com/#

Entry 619   Map 7

Pembrokeshire

Pembrokeshire Farm B&B

Down a beautiful lane flanked by moss-covered walls, two miles from Narberth, is an old fortified longhouse in 25 rolling acres – pristine, peaceful and cosy. Here live three dogs, three donkeys, cats, hens and friendly hosts Rayner and Carol. There's a real fire and books aplenty, equine paintings and fantastic art, and big gorgeous gardens with croquet, a lake and a boat to mess about in. The décor is traditional, the bed linen immaculate, the bathrooms are spanking new and the views to the Preseli Hills gorgeous. Narbeth's restaurants are good but Carol's cooking is fabulous.

Pembrokeshire

Knowles Farm

The Cleddau estuary winds its way around this organic farm – its lush grasses feed the cows that produce milk for the renowned Rachel's yogurt. Your hosts love the land, are committed to its conservation and let you come and go as you please; picnic in the garden, wander the bluebell woods, discover a pond; dogs like it too. You have your own entrance to old-fashioned, lived-in pretty bedrooms with comfy beds, simple bathrooms, glorious views and an eclectic selection of books to browse. Breakfast and supper are fully organic or very local: delicious! If Gini is busy with the farm there are terrific riverside pubs that serve dinner.

Rooms	1 double; 1 double with separate bath: £90–£100. Singles £80–£90.
Meals	Dinner, 3 courses, from £30. Pubs/restaurants 2 miles.
Closed	Rarely.

Rooms	2 doubles; 1 twin with separate bath: £75–£90. Singles £50.
Meals	Supper from £12. Dinner, 4 courses, £22, (not in school holidays). Packed lunch £6. Pub 1.5 miles, restaurant 3 miles.
Closed	Rarely.

	Rayner & Carol Peett Pembrokeshire Farm B&B, Caermaenau Fawr, Clynderwen, SA66 7HB
Tel	+44 (0)1834 860338
Mobile	+44 (0)7796 615332
Email	info@pembrokeshirefarmbandb.co.uk
Web	www.pembrokeshirefarmbandb.co.uk

	Virginia Lort Phillips Knowles Farm, Lawrenny, SA68 0PX
Tel	+44 (0)1834 891221
Email	ginilp@lawrenny.org.uk
Web	www.lawrenny.org.uk

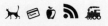

Pembrokeshire

Cresselly House

Imagine staying at the Georgian mansion of an old country friend – that's what it's like to stay at Cresselly. Step into a sunny square hall with a sweeping stair and the ancestors on the walls. Beeswax and lavender scent the air, cosy bedrooms are as grandly traditional as can be, new bathrooms sparkle and views swoop over the park. For breakfast or dinner (if requested) you can seat yourself at the fine Georgian mahogany dining table, gleaming from many decades of polishing. The walking and riding are glorious, and there's impressive stabling for your horse: this is the heartland of the South Pembrokeshire Hunt.

Rooms	3 doubles, 1 twin: £110-£150. Singles £95.
Meals	Dinner, 2 courses, £25-£55. Pub 1 mile.
Closed	Rarely.

Hugh Harrison-Allen
Cresselly House,
Cresselly,
Kilgetty, SA68 0SP
Tel   +44 (0)1646 651992
Email   info@cresselly.com
Web   www.cresselly.com

Entry 622   Map 6

Pembrokeshire

Awelon

Wonderful views of Manorbier beach from this whitewashed family house. Katherine's home has a relaxed, natural feel with Scandinavian furniture, wide French windows and plenty of books and games. She gives you cosy bedrooms with Welsh blankets, white linen and sparkling shower rooms; tea trays too with homemade cake. Breakfast is at a polished round table looking over the Pembrokeshire Coast Path: homemade muesli, award-winning bacon, vegetarian choices... most locally sourced and all delicious. Enjoy an evening drink on the terrace with the beautiful garden beyond – then it's only a stroll to the popular village pub for supper.

Rooms	1 double; 1 twin with separate bath/shower: £70-£85. Singles £40-£60.
Meals	Pubs/restaurants 5-minute walk.
Closed	Christmas.

Katherine Henderson Bowen
Awelon,
Pembroke Road,
Manorbier, Tenby, SA70 7SX
Tel   +44 (0)1834 871587
Email   katherine@manorbierbedandbreakfast.co.uk
Web   www.manorbierbedandbreakfast.co.uk

Entry 623   Map 6

Pembrokeshire

Hayston

Calm, friendly dogs greet you in the courtyard of this attractive Pembrokeshire farmhouse surrounded by pretty bantams and barns. Nicky and Johnny's home is a relaxed place; rooms have a comfortable, faded grandeur and the garden has lovely spots to sit. Have breakfast in the deep-red beamed dining room with books, flowers and a big log fire, or out on the terrace in the morning sun. Up a wide staircase to a cottagey bedroom with a garden view; sometimes you can stay in the sunny coach house (up stone steps) if it's not let to self-catering guests. Castles, surfing championships, stunning beaches and brilliant coastal walks are all on the doorstep.

Pets by prior arrangement.

Rooms	1 twin/double with separate bath: £90. Singles £70.
Meals	Pubs/restaurants 3 miles. Simple suppers available if without transport.
Closed	Christmas.

Nicola Rogers
Hayston,
Merrion,
Pembroke, SA71 5EA
Tel   +44 (0)1646 661462
Email haystonhouse@btinternet.com
Web   www.haystonfarmhouse.co.uk

Entry 624   Map 6

Pembrokeshire

Penfro

This is fun – idiosyncratic and a tad theatrical, rather than conventional and uniformly stylish. The Lappins' home is an impressive Georgian affair, formerly a ballet school. Judith is warm and friendly; her taste – she's also a WW1 expert – is eclectic verging on the wacky and she minds that guests are comfortable and well-fed. You eat communally at the scrubbed table in the flagged Aga kitchen: tasty dinners, homemade jams and good coffee at breakfast. The garden is big and beautiful so enjoy its conversational terrace. And discuss which of the three very characterful bedrooms will suit you best, plumbing and all!

Minimum stay: 2 nights at weekends in summer and on bank holidays.

Rooms	1 double; 1 double, 1 twin, both with separate bath: £75-£95. Singles £60-£85. Extra bed/sofabed available £10-£15 per person per night.
Meals	Dinner, 3 courses, £20. Packed lunch from £8. Owners can cater for gluten free diets at no extra cost. Pub 250 yds.
Closed	Rarely.

Judith Lappin
Penfro,
111 Main Street,
Pembroke, SA71 4DB
Tel   +44 (0)1646 682753
Mobile +44 (0)7763 856181
Email info@penfro.co.uk
Web   www.penfro.co.uk

Entry 625   Map 6

Pembrokeshire

Pentower

Curl up with a cat and watch the ferries – or sometimes a porpoise – coasting to Ireland; French windows open onto the terrace and a glorious vista. Mary and Tony are warm and interesting hosts; their turreted 1898 house has an easy-going atmosphere, quarry tiled floors, decorative fireplaces and an impressive staircase. Spotless bedrooms are light and airy, with large showers; the Tower Room has the views. Wake for a very good full English (or Welsh) breakfast in the tiled dining/sitting room – tuck in while admiring the panoramic view over a bay full of boats. Fishguard is a short stroll, and the stunning coastal path is nearby.

Pembrokeshire

Cefn-y-Dre Country House

Geoff and Gaye want your stay to go without a hitch, and they're proud of the rich history of their house. Solid, handsome and 500 years old, Cefn-y-Dre is on the fringe of the Pembrokeshire Coast National Park with views to the Preseli Hills. The sitting room is set aside for guests, notable for its striking red chairs used during Prince Charles' investiture in 1969 – quite a talking point! Geoff is a great cook who takes pleasure in using local produce and home-grown veg from the large garden; not so long ago he trained at Ballymaloe. St David's, with its ancient cathedral, is nearby, as are some of Britain's finest beaches.

Rooms	1 double, 1 twin/double: £85-£90. Singles £55.
Meals	Packed lunch £5. Pubs/restaurants 500 yds.
Closed	Occasionally.

Rooms	1 double, 1 twin/double; 1 double with separate bath/shower: £89-£109. Singles £70-£79.
Meals	Dinner, 3 courses, £26.50. Pubs/restaurants 2 miles.
Closed	Rarely.

Tony Jacobs & Mary Geraldine Casey
Pentower,
Tower Hill,
Fishguard, SA65 9LA
Tel   +44 (0)1348 874462
Email   sales@pentower.co.uk
Web   www.pentower.co.uk

Gaye Williams & Geoff Stickler
Cefn-y-Dre Country House,
Fishguard, SA65 9QS
Tel   +44 (0)1348 875663
Email   welcome@cefnydre.co.uk
Web   www.cefnydre.co.uk

Entry 626   Map 6

Entry 627   Map 6

Powys

The Farm

Lose yourself in the wildlife, from a warm-hearted Welsh Marches B&B. There are just five sheep remaining now (all pets!) and your hosts have hearts of gold. Find fresh flowers on the Welsh dresser, a big dining table with a lovely garden view, breakfasts locally sourced and marmalades, jams and bread homemade. (And special diets easily catered for.) Overlooking the garden – yours to enjoy – are big bedrooms with TVs, clock-radios, tea and coffee making facilities and WiFi; one is on the ground floor in an extension, ideal for the less sprightly. Montgomery and Bishop's Castle, lovely little towns, are a must-see.

Rooms	1 double, 2 twin/doubles: £85–£95. Stays of 2 nights or more £80. Singles £50.
Meals	Dinner from £25. Pubs/restaurants 2 miles.
Closed	Rarely.

Sandra & Alan Jones
The Farm,
Snead,
Montgomery, SY15 6EB
Tel +44 (0)1588 620281
Email asj.farmsnead@btconnect.com
Web www.thefarmsnead.co.uk

Powys

The Old Vicarage

Come for vast skies, forested hills and quilted fields that stretch for miles. This Victorian vicarage is a super base: smart, welcoming, full of comforts. You get a log fire in a cosy sitting room, a small restaurant with long country views and fancy bedrooms that spoil you all the way. Chef Tim has quite a pedigree, the food is delicious, local suppliers are noted on menus, and much is grown in the garden, where chickens run free. Resist laziness and take to the hills for glorious walking and cycling: the Kerry Ridgeway is on your doorstep as is Powis Castle.

Rooms	2 doubles, 1 twin/double: £95–£120. 1 suite for 4: £150. Singles £70.
Meals	Dinner, 3 courses, £30. Packed lunch & picnics available. Pub 3 miles.
Closed	Christmas & New Year.

Tim & Helen Withers
The Old Vicarage,
Dolfor, Newtown, SY16 4BN
Tel +44 (0)1686 629051
Mobile +44 (0)7753 760054
Email tim@theoldvicaragedolfor.co.uk
Web www.theoldvicaragedolfor.co.uk

Powys

The Old Vicarage

A wide hall, deep window sills and expanses of glass have created a light and appealing home. On the edge of the hamlet, this Arts and Crafts house has spectacular views. Pat serves afternoon tea when you arrive, and breakfast is in a snug spot by the wood-burner. Bedrooms are traditional, big and blessed with homemade biscuits, tea trays and flowers; both have views across gardens, woodland and paddocks – there are acres to explore. The veg patch provides for dinner and you can enjoy a sunset drink in the walled garden. Walks are wonderful – Offa's Dyke footpath is close by – and Hay-on-Wye is a 30-minute drive.

Rooms	1 double; 1 twin with separate bath: £90-£105. Singles £55-£65.
Meals	Dinner, 3 course set menu, £28. BYO. Please inform us of any special dietary requirements. Packed lunches available by request. Pub 3 miles.
Closed	Rarely.

Patricia Birch
The Old Vicarage,
Evancoyd, Presteigne, LD8 2PA
Tel   +44 (0)1547 560951
Mobile   +44 (0)7903 859012
Email   pat.birch38@gmail.com
Web   www.oldvicaragebandb-welshborder.co.uk

Entry 630   Map 7

Powys

Rhedyn

Come here if you need to remember how to relax. Such an unassuming, little place, but with real character and soul: great comfort too. Find exposed walls in the bedrooms, funky lighting, pocket sprung mattresses, lovely books to read, and calm colours; bathrooms are modern and delightfully quirky. But the real stars of this show are Muiread and Ciaran: warm, enthusiastic and engaging, with a passion for good local food and a desire for more self sufficiency – pigs and bees are planned next. This is a totally tranquil place, with agreeable walks through the Irfon valley, and bog snorkelling too!

Rooms	3 doubles: £95. Singles £85. Dinner, B&B £75 per person.
Meals	Dinner, 3 courses, £28. Packed lunch £7.50. Pub/restaurant 1 mile.
Closed	Rarely.

Muiread & Ciaran O'Connell
Rhedyn,
Cilmery,
Builth Wells, LD2 3LH
Tel   +44 (0)1982 551944
Email   info@rhedynguesthouse.co.uk
Web   www.rhedynguesthouse.co.uk

Entry 631   Map 7

Powys

Hafod Y Garreg

A unique opportunity to stay in the oldest house in Wales – a fascinating, 1402 cruck-framed hall house, built for Henry IV as a hunting lodge. Informal Annie and John have filled it with a charming mix of Venetian mirrors, Indian rugs, pewter plates, rich fabrics and oak pieces. Dine by candlelight in the romantic dining room – all sorts of delicious dishes; tuck into a big breakfast in the sweet conservatory. Bedrooms are luxuriously comfortable with embroidered linen, quirky lamps, nifty bathrooms. Reach this relaxed retreat by a bumpy track up across gated fields crowded with chickens, cats… a peaceful, special place.

Rooms	2 doubles: £92. Singles from £80.
Meals	Dinner, 3 courses, £27. BYO. Pubs/restaurants 2.5 miles.
Closed	Christmas.

Annie & John McKay
Hafod Y Garreg,
Erwood,
Builth Wells, LD2 3TQ
Tel   +44 (0)1982 560400
Email   john-annie@hafod-y.wanadoo.co.uk
Web   www.hafodygarreg.co.uk

Entry 632   Map 7

Powys

Pottery Cottage

Balm for urban souls searching for a retreat… This gorgeous old potter's shed, once worked in by Adam Dworski, is now a village hideaway sprinkled with beautiful objects and books. Nothing could be lovelier than sitting up in the wide bed, clouded over by Hungarian goose down and contemplating the pretty garden laid out at your feet. Hungry? Put an idle hand out for Emma's breakfast basket which bustles with local apple juice, bread and pastries, organic yogurt, fruit, Hay Deli granola. Make your own proper coffee, choose when to come and go. Stride the hills, find great pubs, return to a soak in a big tub with a glass of wine. Bliss.

Rooms	1 double with extra mattress & cot available: £75-£85.
Meals	Pub in village & pubs/restaurants 1 mile.
Closed	Rarely.

Emma Balch
Pottery Cottage,
Clyro, Hereford, HR3 5SB
Tel   +44 (0)1497 822931
Mobile   +44 (0)7879 373431
Email   doblemdesign@gmail.com
Web   www.potterycottageclyro.com

Entry 633   Map 7

Powys

The Old Store House

Unbend here with agreeable books, chattering birds, and Peter, who asks only that you feel at home. Downstairs are a range-warmed kitchen, a sunny conservatory overlooking garden, chickens, ducks and canal, and a charmingly ramshackle sitting room with a wood-burner, sofas and a piano – no babbling TV. Bedrooms are large, light and spotless, with more books, soft goose down, armchairs and bathrooms with views. Breakfast, without haste, on scrambled eggs, local bacon and sausages, blistering coffee. Bliss – but as far from tickety boo as possible. Walk into the hills from the back door.

Children over 6 welcome.

Rooms	3 doubles, 1 twin: £80. Singles £40.
Meals	Packed lunch £4. Pub/restaurant 0.75 miles.
Closed	Rarely.

	Peter Evans
	The Old Store House,
	Llanfrynach,
	Brecon, LD3 7LJ
Tel	+44 (0)1874 665499
Email	oldstorehouse@btconnect.com
Web	www.theoldstorehouse.co.uk

Entry 634   Map 7

Powys

Ty'r Chanter

Warmth, colour, children and activity: this house is huge fun. Tiggy welcomes you like family; help collect eggs, feed the lambs, drop your shoes by the fire. The farmhouse and barn are stylishly relaxed; deep sofas, tartan throws, heaps of books, long convivial table; views to the Brecon Beacons and Black Mountains are inspiring. Bedrooms are soft, simple sanctuaries with Jo Malone bathroom treats. The children's room zings with murals, toys, kids' sitting room, sandpit – it's child heaven. Walk, fish, canoe, book-browse in Hay or stroll the estate. Homemade cakes and whisky to help yourself to: fine hospitality and Tiggy is wonderful.

Rooms	3 doubles: £95. 1 twin (children's room with separate bath/shower): £20 per child. Singles £55.
Meals	Packed lunch £8. Pub 1 mile.
Closed	Christmas.

	Tiggy Pettifer
	Ty'r Chanter,
	Gliffaes, Crickhowell, NP8 1RL
Tel	+44 (0)1874 731144
Mobile	+44 (0)7802 387004
Email	tiggy@tyrchanter.com
Web	www.tyrchanter.com

Entry 635   Map 7

Swansea

Blas Gwyr

Llangennith was once a well-kept secret — now walkers, riders, surfers and beach bunnies of all ages flock. Close to the bustling bay is an extended 1700s cottage with a youthful facelift. All is simple but stylish: bedrooms (two overlooking the road) are modern and matching; bathrooms and wet rooms come with warm floors and fluffy towels. Everything from the bedspread to the breakfast is local: make sure you try the laverbread. After a day at sea, fling wet gear in the drying room and linger over a coffee in the courtyard, or walk to the pub for a sun-kissed pint. Laid-back bliss.

Rooms	1 double, 1 double with sofabed, 1 twin/double, 1 suite for 2-4: £115-£125. Children from £15.
Meals	Packed lunch available. Dinner £27.50-£30 (selected weekends). Pub 150 yds.
Closed	Rarely.

Dafydd James
Blas Gwyr,
Plenty Farm, Llangennith, SA3 1HU
Tel   +44 (0)1792 386472
Mobile   +44 (0)7974 981156
Email   info@blasgwyr.co.uk
Web   www.blasgwyr.co.uk

Entry 636   Map 2

Wrexham

Worthenbury Manor

Welcome to one half of a big country house on the border of Wales and Shropshire. Congenial, generous Ian and Elizabeth look after you wonderfully well. The guest sitting room is warmed by a log fire in winter; the dining room has listed Jacobean panelling. Choose between two comfortable bedrooms, one decorated in Georgian style, one in Jacobean, both with rich drapes, chandeliers, fresh coffee and antique four-posters. Wake refreshed for a beautifully cooked breakfast: local and home-grown produce, home-baked bread and Ian's impressive marmalades; dinner too is a treat. Visit Erddig, Chirk Castle, Powis…

Reductions on longer stays; enquire with owners.

Rooms	1 four-poster; 1 four-poster with separate bath: £80-£100. Singles £50-£65. Dinner, B&B £70-£80 per person. Extra bed/sofabed available £20-£30 per person per night.
Meals	Dinner, 3 courses, £30. Supper, 2 courses, £20. BYO. Pub/restaurant 5 miles.
Closed	24-28 December.

Elizabeth & Ian Taylor
Worthenbury Manor,
Worthenbury, LL13 0AW
Tel   +44 (0)1948 770342
Email   enquiries@worthenburymanor.co.uk
Web   www.worthenburymanor.co.uk

Entry 637   Map 7

Photo: www.istock.photo.com (lazertech)

Quick reference indices

Wheelchair-accessible

At least one bedroom and bathroom accessible for wheelchair users. Phone for details.

England

Channel Islands

Scotland

Wales

Children of all ages welcome

These owners have told us that they welcome children of all ages. Please note cots and highchairs may not necessarily be available.

England

Credit cards accepted
These owners have told us
that they accept credit cards,
most commonly Visa and
MasterCard.

Quick reference indices

Scotland

Wales

Vegetarian meals
These owners provide
vegetarian meals on request.

England

Quick reference indices

Quick reference indices

Pets welcome
Please let the owner know if
you want to bring pets.

Sawday's Garden Lovers collection
www.sawdays.co.uk/collections/garden-lovers

Photo: Rock Farm House, Kent

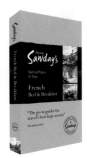

Alastair Sawday has been publishing books for over 21 years, finding Special Places to Stay in Britain and abroad. All our properties are inspected by us and are chosen for their charm and individuality, and with 12 titles to choose from there are plenty of places to explore. You can buy any of our books at a reader discount of 25%* on the RRP.

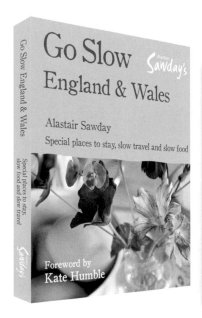
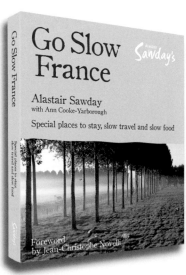

List of titles:	RRP	Discount price
British Bed & Breakfast	£15.99	£11.99
British Hotels and Inns	£15.99	£11.99
Pubs & Inns of England & Wales	£15.99	£11.99
Dog-friendly Breaks in Britain	£14.99	£11.24
French Bed & Breakfast	£15.99	£11.99
French Châteaux & Hotels	£15.99	£11.99
Italy	£15.99	£11.99
Portugal	£12.99	£9.74
Spain	£15.99	£11.99
Go Slow England & Wales	£19.99	£14.99
Go Slow France	£19.99	£14.99

*postage and packaging is added to each order

How to order:

You can order online at: www.sawdays.co.uk/bookshop/
or call: **+44(0)117 204 7810**

Sawday's Garden Lovers collection
www.sawdays.co.uk/collections/garden-lovers

Photo: Great Chalfield Manor, Wiltshire

Alastair
Sawday's

'More than a bed
for the night…'

Britain
France
Ireland
Italy
Portugal
Spain

www.sawdays.co.uk

Self-Catering | B&B | Hotel | Pub | Treehouses, Cabins, Yurts & More

Photo: Nonsuch House, entry 102

Sawday's Garden Lovers collection
www.sawdays.co.uk/collections/garden-lovers

Photo: Tregoose, Cornwall

Jo...

TIME AWAY IS F...
SPEND IN THE WRO...
BACK IN 1994, W...

Twenty years on, we're st...
on a crusade to stamp o...
and help our guests fin...

If you have one, w...
to take the pl...

LIBRARY
PALO ALTO CITY

www.cityofpaloalto.org/library

ALASTAIR & TOBY SAWDAY

"Trustworthy, friendly and helpful – with a reputation
for offering wonderful places and discerning visitors."
JULIA NAISMITH, HOLLYTREE COTTAGE

"Sawday's. Is there any other?"
SONIA HODGSON, HORRY MILL

WHY BECOME A MEMBER?

Becoming a part of our 'family' of Special Places is like being awarded a Michelin star. Our stamp of approval will tell guests that you offer a truly special experience and you will benefit from our experience, reputation and support.

A CURATED COLLECTION

Our site presents a relatively small and careful selection of Special Places which helps us to stand out like a brilliantly shining beacon.

INSPECT AND RE-INSPECT

Our inspectors have an eagle-eye for the special, but absolutely no check-lists. They visit every member, see every bedroom and bathroom and, on the lucky days, eat the food.

QUALITY, NOT QUANTITY

We don't pretend (or want) to be in the same business as the sites that handle zillions of bookings a day. Using our name ensures that you attract the right kind of guests for you.

VARIETY

From country-house hotels to city pads and funky fincas to blissful B&Bs, we genuinely delight in the individuality of our Special Places.

LOYALTY

Nearly half of our members have been with us for five years or more. We must be doing something right!

The friendly crew

GET IN TOUCH WITH OUR MEMBERSHIP TEAM...

+44 (0)117 204 7810

members@sawdays.co.uk

...OR APPLY ONLINE

sawdays.co.uk/joinus

Kent

Eggpie B&B at Pond Cottage

Afternoon tea and cake is offered on arrival – in the sunken garden in summer. Hard to believe that this stunning house in the middle of Eggpie Lane is just minutes from the A21. It started life in 1580 as a gamekeeper's cottage; now it is listed and loved, by delightful hosts Graham and Mandy. Settle in amongst low beams, standing timbers, ancient slabs, and a charming medley of armchairs and sofas around the inglenook. Three lovely bedrooms are decorated in keeping with the country cottage feel, and an inspired Kentish breakfast is served in the oldest part of the house. Visit Chartwell, Knole, Hever, Penshurst Place.

Minimum stay: 2 nights during busy periods.

Rooms	2 doubles; 1 double sharing bath (let to same party only): £90–£150. Singles £90–£135.
Meals	Restaurant 1 mile.
Closed	Rarely.

	Amanda Webb
	Eggpie B&B at Pond Cottage,
	Eggpie Lane, Weald,
	Sevenoaks, TN14 6NP
Mobile	+44 (0)7768 820281
Email	enquiries@eggpiebandb.com
Web	www.eggpiebandb.com

Entry 253   Map 5

Kent

Charcott Farmhouse

The 1750s farmhouse is rustic and family orientated, and if you don't come expecting an immaculate environment you will enjoy it here. In the old bake house there's a small sitting room with original beams and bread oven, TV and WiFi; relax in here on cooler days, with cats and a dog to keep you company. On sunny days tea is served in the garden. Bedrooms are pretty and comfy with blankets and eiderdowns, oriental rugs and antique furniture. Nicholas – a tad eccentric for some – is half French and cooks amazing breakfasts on the Aga, while Ginny's great grandfather (Arnold Hills) founded West Ham football team. Come and go as you please.

Rooms	2 twins; 1 twin with separate bath: £75–£90. Price varies according to season. Singles from £55.
Meals	Pub 5-minute walk.
Closed	Rarely.

	Nicholas & Ginny Morris
	Charcott Farmhouse,
	Charcott, Leigh,
	Tonbridge, TN11 8LG
Tel	+44 (0)1892 870024
Mobile	+44 (0)7734 009292
Email	charcottfarmhouse@btinternet.com
Web	www.charcottfarmhouse.com

Entry 254   Map 5